T0302125

Ignorance and Uncertainty

Born out of a belief that economic insights should not require much mathematical sophistication, this book proposes novel and parsimonious methods to incorporate ignorance and uncertainty into economic modeling, without complex mathematics. Economics has made great strides over the past several decades in modeling agents' decisions when they are incompletely informed, but many economists believe that there are aspects of these models which are less than satisfactory. Among the concerns are that ignorance is not captured well in most models, that agents' presumed cognitive ability is implausible, and that derived optimal behavior is, sometimes, driven by the fine details of the model rather than the underlying economics. Compte and Postlewaite lay out a tractable way to address these concerns, and to incorporate plausible limitations on agents' sophistication. A central aspect of the proposed methodology is to restrict the strategies that are assumed to be available to agents.

Olivier Compte is a Professor at the Paris School of Economics and Ecole des Ponts ParisTech.

Andrew Postlewaite is the Harry P. Kamen Professor of Economics and a Professor of Finance at the University of Pennsylvania.

Econometric Society Monograph Series

Editors:

Andrea Prat, Columbia University
Stéphane Bonhomme, University of Chicago

The Econometric Society is an international society for the advancement of economic theory in relation to statistics and mathematics. The Econometric Society Monograph series is designed to promote the publication of original research contributions of high quality in mathematical economics and theoretical and applied econometrics.

Books in the Series

I. Molchanov & F. Molinari, *Random Sets in Econometrics*, 2018
B. Honore, A. Pakes, M. Piazzesi, & L. Samuelson (eds.), *Advances in Economics and Econometrics: Eleventh World Congress, Vols. I & II*, 2017
S. Maurer, *On the Shoulders of Giants: Colleagues Remember Suzanne Scotchmer's Contributions to Economics*, 2017
C. P. Chambers & F. Echenique, *Revealed Preference Theory*, 2016
J.-F. Mertens, S. Sorins, & S. Samir *Repeated Games*, 2015
C. Hsiao, *Analysis of Panel Data: Third Edition*, 2014
C. Cameron & P. Trivedi, *Regression Analysis of Count Data, 2nd Ed.*, 2013
A. Harvey, *Dynamic Models for Volatility and Heavy Tails, with Applications to Financial and Economic Time Series*, 2013
D. Acemoglu, M. Areilano, & E. Dekel (eds.), *Advances in Economics and Econometrics: Theory and Applications, Tenth World Congress, Vols. I, II, & III*, 2013
M. Fleurbaey and F. Maniquet, *A Theory of Fairness and Social Justice*, 2011
R. Vohra, *Mechanism Design: A Linear Programming Approach*, 2011
K. Samphantharak & R. Townsend, *Households as Corporate Firms: An Analysis of Household Finance Using Integrated Household Surveys and Corporate Financial Accounting*, 2009
I. Gilboa, *Theory of Decision under Uncertainty*, 2009
F. Vega-Redondo *Complex Networks*, 2007
R. Blundell, W. Newey, & T. Persson, *Advances in Economics and Econometrics: Theory and Applications, Ninth World Congress, Vols. I, II, & III*, 2006
J. Roemer, *Democracy, Education, and Equality*, 2006
C. Blackorby, W. Bossert, & D. Donaldson, *Population Issues in Social Choice Theory, Welfare Economics and Ethics*, 2005
R. Koenker, *Quantile Regression*, 2005
C. Hsiao, *Analysis of Panel Data: Second Edition*, 2003
M. Dewatripont, L. P. Hausen, & S. J. Turnovsky (eds.), *Advances in Economics and Econometrics:Theory and Applications, Eighth World Congress, Vols. I, II, & III*, 2003
E. Ghysels, N. Swanson, & M. Watson (eds.), *Essays in Econometrics: Collected Papers of Clive W. J. Granger, Vols. I & II*, 2001.
S. Strøm (ed.), *Econometrics and Economic Theory in the 20th Century: The Ragnar Frisch Centennial Symposium*, 1999.
A. C. Cameron & P. K. Trivedi, *Regression Analysis of Count-Data*, 1998.
D. Jacobs, E. Kalai, & M. Kamien (eds.), *Frontiers of Research in Economic Theory: The Nancy L. Schwartz Memorial Lectures*, 1998.
D. M. Kreps & K.F. Wallis (eds.), *Advances in Economics and Econometrics: Theory and Applications, Seventh World Congress, Vols. I, II, & III*, 1997
R. Guesnerie, *A Contribution to the Pure Theory of Taxation*, 1995

Continued on page following the index

Ignorance and Uncertainty

Olivier Compte
Paris School of Economics

Andrew Postlewaite
University of Pennsylvania

CAMBRIDGE
UNIVERSITY PRESS

CAMBRIDGE
UNIVERSITY PRESS

University Printing House, Cambridge CB2 8BS, United Kingdom

One Liberty Plaza, 20th Floor, New York, NY 10006, USA

477 Williamstown Road, Port Melbourne, VIC 3207, Australia

314-321, 3rd Floor, Plot 3, Splendor Forum, Jasola District Centre, New Delhi - 110025, India

79 Anson Road, #06-04/06, Singapore 079906

Cambridge University Press is part of the University of Cambridge.

It furthers the University's mission by disseminating knowledge in the pursuit of education, learning and research at the highest international levels of excellence.

www.cambridge.org
Information on this title: www.cambridge.org/9781108422024
DOI: 10.1017/9781108379991

First published 2019

A catalogue record for this publication is available from the British Library

Library of Congress Cataloging in Publication data
Names: Compte, Olivier, author. | Postlewaite, Andrew, author.
Title: Ignorance and uncertainty / Olivier Compte, Paris School of Economics, Andrew Postlewaite, University of Pennsylvania.
Description: Cambridge, United Kingdom ; New York, NY : Cambridge University Press, 2018. | Series: Econometric society monograph series |
Includes bibliographical references and index.
Identifiers: LCCN 2018015100 | ISBN 9781108422024 (hardback)
Subjects: LCSH: Economics–Mathematical models. |
Decision making–Mathematical models. | Game theory–Mathematical models.
Classification: LCC HB135 .C63164 2018 | DDC 330.01/5195–dc23
LC record available at https://lccn.loc.gov/2018015100

ISBN 978-1-108-42202-4 Hardback
ISBN 978-1-108-43449-2 Paperback

To Kevin and Justin
To Delphine, for her patience …
and her impatience

Contents

Preface

This book grew out of attempts to explain what we do outside our profession – economics – and from the belief that many of our insights do not, or should not, require much mathematical sophistication. Attempts to explain the winner's curse in simple words and to model it as a simple selection bias was a point of departure: in competitive auctions, bidders who are more optimistic about the value of an object are more likely to win the auction (this is the selection bias), and winners are thus likely to be disappointed when they subsequently learn their value of the object. A formal statement of this logic should not require knowing differential equations.

In the pursuit of simpler models, we introduce *direct strategy restrictions* on agents' behavior. That is, rather than assuming that an individual tries to learn how much to bid when his value for a painting is $1,100 and how much to bid should his value be $1,200, we examine individuals trying to figure out what fraction of their valuation they should bid, whatever that value is. Mathematically the simplification is that we are trying to determine the value of a scalar, a fraction, rather than a huge number of scalars, one for each possible value of the painting that the individual might have.

From a pragmatic perspective, much of our effort boils down to investigating models in which a single dimension of behavior is endogenized at a time.

This book also grew out of discomfort with the predictions of some of our models, a rising gap between economic intuition and the output of models, the feeling that conclusions sometimes reflect the prodigious cognitive capabilities with which we endow the agents in our models, rather than true economic forces, and that the level of sophistication often draws attention to less relevant mathematical details at the expense of economic intuition. Part II illustrates our discomfort as simply as possible in the hope that it can be read without prior knowledge of the models discussed.

Last, this book critiques the near universal way that our discipline models ignorance and information: we mostly abandon the central tenet that an agent's ignorance be modeled as a probability distribution over states. We focus instead on what agents can plausibly perceive, without making *a priori* recommendations on the mathematical form that these perceptions should take, and on what agents can plausibly make of these perceptions.

Modeling the unknown seems to be a contradiction in terms. How can one describe the unknown without providing overly detailed contours to it? A central step in understanding how this is achieved in economic models is in realizing that a model contains two perspectives: that of the agent whose behavior we try to understand or characterize, and that of the analyst who acts as an omniscient outsider, making precise the economic environment and what is unknown to the agent.

For some problems, the two perspectives may coincide. When a die is thrown, both the analyst and the agent may be ignorant of the face that will show up, and it seems fine to assume that each face has a one-in-six chance, and that the agent understands this as well.

Most economic situations fall short of such easily quantifiable ignorance. Typically, neither the analyst nor the agent knows the chances of each outcome, nor even all possible outcomes. For the sake of modeling, the analyst generally posits a specific set of outcomes, and specific chances of those outcomes. This mathematical object, a probability distribution, is a modeling convenience for the analyst. Yet, behavior is then analyzed as though agents could exploit the precise specification, as if they were as omniscient as the analyst who sets out the model.

A central contribution of this book is to give direct strategy restrictions a prominent role. These restrictions may not only lead to more parsimonious models, and models that are less subject to the criticism expressed above – the dependence of predictions on less relevant aspects of the model. They may also constitute an effective way to disentangle the analyst's and the agent's perspectives by limiting the ability of agents to exploit parameters that the analyst introduced for her convenience, and which were not meant to be known by the agent, or at least not intended to significantly drive the agents' decisions.

Last but not least, asking that one define the range of available strategies prompts the analyst to think about what constitutes a reasonable range, taking into consideration the agent's thinking or limitations. In this way, sophistication or bounded rationality considerations can be introduced into an otherwise standard model. Defining the range of available strategies also highlights something omitted from standard models: information lies not only in what one observes and perceives, but also in what one makes of one's perceptions.

Comments and Warnings.

1. *Ignorance and Uncertainty.* The book is about modeling, and the title highlights one of the main challenges in constructing a model: how does one reconcile the analyst's need to define the economic environment in detail and yet keep agents ignorant of many aspects of the environment that, for the sake of mathematical modeling, the analyst has made artificially precise? How can one reconcile the analyst's need to quantify the uncertainty that agents face

through the definition of exact probability distributions, and yet avoid making agents too knowledgeable of the details of the model itself? The book proposes that one may keep agents somewhat ignorant of the model's fine details by limiting their ability to exploit these details.

2. *Credits.* Modeling ignorance is central to our discipline and many of the issues we discuss have been mentioned by others. We don't suggest that we are the first to address them. We sometimes cite papers that can be identified as seminal for an issue, but we do not cite all the papers that are related to our discussion. The same comment applies to the many applied topics covered in this book: we build on decades of modeling efforts, and do not provide an extensive discussion of the literature on each of the topics covered.

3. *Audience.* We wrote this book in the hope that it can reach multiple audiences, including people with only a knowledge of basic economics (though some understanding of the objectives of modeling will help). For this reason, the more technical discussions, or the discussions that assume some knowledge of the literature have often been relegated to the comments sections of each chapter, or to footnotes.

The book is intended to be a complement to a textbook, not a substitute, with the hope that it will help readers better understand economic modeling and its foundations, that it will suggest an alternate path, or at least trigger a critical appraisal of the literature we discuss.

4. *Warning.* While this book is a critique of the standard way to model ignorance – the Bayesian methodology – we do not advocate discontinuing that line of research. Rather, we view the book as highlighting difficulties in interpreting the results obtained from standard models and in applying them to real problems. Our view is that the book provides a guide for questioning or reevaluating the plausibility of the predictions obtained in such models, and that it provides one (of possible many) alternatives to the standard methodology to address the difficulties that we identify.

5. *Organization.* Part I is meant to provide an easy access to the main issues in constructing a model, in particular the link between the set of strategies available to the agents, and the agent's knowledge about the structure of the model implicit in his ability to optimize among these strategies. Chapter 1 describes this link in an environment with no uncertainty. Chapters 2 and 3 explain the challenges of modeling an uncertain environment. Chapter 4 motivates direct strategy restrictions while Chapter 5 analyzes some implications of our modeling approach.

Part II discusses important issues addressed by the discipline (information aggregation, mechanism design, surplus extraction, folk theorems, comparative statics) in light of our central concern – the possibility that models provide agents too many instruments, and that insights are sometimes driven by this richness.

Part III discusses a number of standard applications, suggesting various ways to improve the balance between a sufficiently rich environment and a reasonably rich set of instruments.

Apart from Part I, most chapters are self-contained, and can be read independently of each other, although the reader may benefit from reading Chapters 12 to 14 sequentially.

6. *Acknowledgments.* The authors wish to thank Vincent Crawford, Itzhak Gilboa, Ron Spiegler, Vincent Crawford and especially Larry Samuelson, for detailed and useful comments on a preliminary version of the book. We have benefited from discussions with Andrew Caplin, Guillaume Fréchette, Harold Cole, Dirk Krueger, Dan Levin, Laurent Mathevet, Paul Milgrom and Jean Tirole; from extensive correspondence and/or exchanges with Alessandra Casella, Paul Klemperer and Michael Woodford; and, lastly, from encouragement from Jeff Ely. Olivier Compte thanks Philippe Jehiel for more than two decades of invaluable interactions, and Diego Aranega for agreeing to be distracted from his usual targets. Andy Postlewaite would like to thank David Schmeidler for decades of discussions. We also thank Joonbae Lee for proofreading and assistance on figures, and Alecia McKenzie for numerous editorial improvements.

7. The cartoons which appear at the beginning of Chapters 6–10 have been used with permission from Diego Aranega.

Introduction

1. This book has three goals: methodological, critical, pragmatic. It questions the way economic models deal with ignorance and uncertainty, and proposes alternative modeling strategies. It questions some of the main insights of the literature, and observes that they are sometimes a result of special features of our models. Last, it questions the high degree of mathematical technicality embodied in many standard economic analyses and suggests how one might reduce it.

These goals are linked. One element of the connection stems from how ignorance is typically modeled, via the *Bayesian methodology*, which consists of making precise what is not known: if you don't know the number of balls in an urn, define the range of plausible numbers and a probability distribution over them. This allows the analyst to artificially quantify the unknown but it embodies significant technical sophistication, often foregoing plausibility and parsimony.

A second element lies in the exercise of modeling itself, which attempts to combine two often conflicting perspectives, that of the analyst, who takes an omniscient perspective, describing in detail an artificial economic environment to be analyzed, and that of the agent, not meant to be omniscient, who is nevertheless assumed to know or behave as if he knew the details of the model.

A third element rests on how perceptions are handled in standard models. Typically, perceptions are modeled as a probability distribution over consequences and come with the recipe that defines how to use them, namely through expected utility maximization. In practice, a perception is akin to an ingredient in search of a recipe. A perception is useless if one does not know how to use it. A perception may sometimes be misleading, and better discarded. Information has to do both with what one perceives, and with one's ability to use and benefit from what one perceives.

2. This book is more generally about modeling. As emphasized in many economics and game theory textbooks, models are meant to illuminate some aspects of an economic problem or strategic situation, to shape intuition, or to help us detect when intuition is flawed. In this quest, the analyst inevitably

1

makes simplifications and approximations, and focuses on the ingredients that seem most relevant while omitting those that seem of second-order importance and would only distract us.

Simple models have a virtue. However, eventually, we are interested in a simple model only to the extent that we believe that it captures an essential aspect of behavior present in real-world problems. A challenge is that in the process of simplifying the environment, some irrelevant details may become salient, or acquire undue importance. We may think that a simple model of auction should consider agents whose values are either high or low, say 100 or 10. If we analyze such a model, behavior will eventually be driven by the particular values 100 and 10, and the hoped-for simplification may become the seed for complex behavior driven by the analyst's particular choice of values (100 and 10).

A seemingly easy fix to such a concern would be to define a richer environment in which values can take any value from 10 to 100. Yet, the fix is often an illusion. Other, less obvious details such as the value of the upper limit 100 may acquire undue importance, and without care, we may make predictions that hinge on agents behaving as though they could determine, among other things, that having a value close to 100 also means likely having the highest value for the object.

This book is about understanding why and when some details of models have undeserved importance (Part I and Part II), and about suggesting means to avoid this (Part III).

3. In short, a modeling exercise consists of finding an appropriate balance between a possibly rich economic environment – yet simple enough to be handled mathematically – and a set of instruments (or strategies) with which we endow the agents, thereby enabling them to adjust to that environment. When the balance is off, for example when an agent is endowed with a set of instruments that gives him implausible powers of discernment, some irrelevant details of the environment description can take on unwarranted importance because agents end up behaving as if they were knowledgeable of special aspects of the environment that were introduced solely as simplifying modeling devices. When this happens, a model's predictions can be driven by the inner structure of the model rather than reflecting true economic forces, or they can fail to account for relevant forces (Part II).

How can an analyst restore the balance between the economic environment considered and the instruments or strategies provided to each agent to exploit it?

The usual path consists of further enriching the environment. As suggested in our auction example, if it is too easy for agents to exploit the structure of the basic model, one might decrease their knowledge about their environment. The Bayesian methodology accomplishes this by introducing further uncertainty, defining a more complex model in which parameters of the basic model are realizations of a random variable.

Often, however, enriching the environment comes at the expense of parsimony, with no guarantee, as our auction example suggests, that the balance is restored. Also, in standard models, a richer environment often implies a richer set of instruments as well: rather than choosing a bid when one's value is 10 and a bid when one's value is 100, in the enriched environment, the potential buyer may in principle choose a bid for each value realization between 10 and 100.

This book suggests an alternative. It advocates direct restrictions on the set of instruments with which agents are endowed. We do not necessarily argue against enriching the environment, but rather against simultaneously enriching the set of instruments available to the agent. In Part III, we provide several standard economic environments and suggest plausible strategy restrictions. The models considered are possibly quite rich, in the sense that the economic environment (what the agent cares about, what the agent perceives) takes values in a continuum. *Despite the richness*, they are strategically simple.

In summary, analysts typically prefer simple models. What makes a model complex is not the profusion of data assumed to be available to the agent, but the degree to which agents are able to process the data: what is the range of possible behaviors allowed? A model may be descriptively rich, yet strategically simple. Part III considers models that are rich enough to avoid triviality, and yet simple strategically, with a single dimension of behavior examined at a time.

4. *Ignorance and uncertainty.* Our work has been driven by pragmatism, and the desire to convey economic intuition as simply as possible. We believe the exercise also contributes to the debate on how to model ignorance and uncertainty.

There has been a huge effort to extend economic models to worlds in which agents face uncertainty or ignore some aspects of the situations that they face. The work of Savage (1954) is the culmination of this effort, leading to a representation of decision making under uncertainty in which agents make choices as if they had a utility function over consequences and a personal probability distribution (or belief) over consequences, and used that belief to maximize expected utility.

This way of thinking about ignorance remains today at the heart of the economist's toolbox. We refer to this as the *Bayesian methodology*: for any aspect of a problem where the analyst thinks the agent lacks complete knowledge, define the possible realizations of that aspect and a probability distribution over them.

Another challenge has been to *incorporate* the methodology into economic models. In itself, the methodology places no restrictions on what agents believe. Beliefs mirror what agents choose. An agent may choose to bet all his fortune on a horse named Daisy, thereby reflecting his belief that Daisy is a sure win. However, if one wants to study horse races in which there is some uncertainty about the winner, a model that assumes that an agent could have arbitrary beliefs such as the above one seems too flexible.

In practice, analysts typically impose discipline on how beliefs are incorporated into models. Discipline can be imposed by assuming that the agent's belief bears some relationship with the actual "chance" that this particular horse wins, however questionable defining this "chance" objectively might be. More generally, it is achieved by assuming a *consistency* condition on beliefs, taking the form of a possibly stochastic relationship between signals (capturing perceptions) and states (capturing elements or aspects of the environment).[1]

For example, suppose we wish to model how an agent reacts to hunger, where hunger is used as a proxy for the level of depletion of the reserves in the agent's body. As an analyst, one may posit a stochastic relationship (or probability distribution) between hunger levels and the level of reserves. Then, to any hunger perception, the analyst (and the agent if he knows the model) may associate a belief – a probability distribution over reserve levels.

5. There are two well-known difficulties with the approach described above. First, it often gives rise to an *overly precise* representation of what the agent is supposed to be ignorant about. Probabilistic beliefs are an instrument invented by analysts to structure, analyze and describe the behavior of agents. Yet, by and large, as a *positive* description of behavior, beliefs remain a somewhat implausible construct. Not because agents would *not* form beliefs; agents undoubtedly have some elements of likelihood in mind when making a decision. But whatever form agents' beliefs actually take, they are surely more casual than what the Bayesian methodology assumes.

Second, when the consistency route mentioned above is adopted, the approach potentially gives rise to an *overly accurate* representation of what the agent knows.[2] To illustrate with an extreme example, one might be ignorant of whether the square root of 73,057 is above or below 281.56, or unable to say whether it is above or below 281.56 within 5 seconds.[3] Since there is an objective answer to that question (281.56 is larger than the square root of 73,057), the consistency route that assumes there is a stochastic relationship

---

[1] In games, incorporating the Bayesian methodology has been done by assuming a consistency condition among beliefs held by different players (Harsanyi). Myerson (2004, page 1824) justifies this consistency condition as follows: "If we can assume any arbitrary characteristics for the individuals in our model, then why could we not explain the surprising behavior even more simply by assuming that each individual has a payoff function that is maximized by this behavior? Thus, to avoid such trivialization of the economic problem, applied theorists have generally limited themselves to models that satisfy Harsanyi's consistency assumption."

[2] Or, more generally, driven too much by the distribution chosen by the analyst, an assumption made for lack of a better model, for her convenience only.

[3] This example can be seen as a variation of one provided in Lipman (1999), which we shall discuss in Chapter 21. See also Chapter 5. The example is extreme because, to the analyst, there is no underlying uncertainty about the correct answer.

between the correct answer and the agent's perception necessarily restricts beliefs to the correct answer, in spite of the fact that the agent might only have a vague impression about whether one number exceeds the other.

More generally, even in problems where the analyst assumes some uncertainty over the underlying state, the consistency route does not simply provide a mechanism to translate signals or perceptions into a precise belief; it also provides a perfect guide to using these perceptions, as though that information was always immediately available to the agent – the agent just needs to maximize expected utility given the belief associated with the perception.

In practice, I can have erroneous perceptions that a particularly dangerous activity is safe, or that betting on Daisy is a sure win: perceptions are signals that one might use, and sometimes profitably ignore or take with caution. The conclusion that some perceptions should be ignored or taken with caution constitutes information, and this information may or may not be easily available to the agent, or easily quantified.

Said differently, a perception is like an ingredient without a recipe. To accompany your asparagus with a sauce mousseline, you may know that you need oil, butter, whipped cream, eggs and heat, but if you don't know how to combine those ingredients, you won't come close to a sauce mousseline, and if you don't keep track of temperature, you will end up with a greasy omelet.

This book is an attempt to address the idea that perceptions are one thing, learning to deal with them is another. It is an attempt to disentangle perceptions and information, to disentangle ingredients and recipes, and to disentangle the data the agent gets from the various ways he may use it. Accurate perceptions are valuable, as quality products may improve a meal. But information also stems from the ability to determine the profitable uses of perceptions.

6. This book argues that one cannot eschew drawing a precise connection between the specific conditions agents face and how they perceive them. As for the consistency route, this connection is defined by the analyst and represented as a joint distribution over specific conditions and perceptions. However, in light of the discussion above:

(i) we are agnostic about the mathematical form taken by perceptions, favoring, when possible, simpler mathematical objects having plausible interpretations;

(ii) we do not assume that agents know the distribution, but assume that by comparing experience from different strategies, they identify which performs best;

(iii) we avoid assumptions that facilitate agents' overly exploiting that distribution, and we do this by *limiting a priori* the strategies available to each agent. In this constrained world, "information" will embody not only the perceptions or the data that an agent gets, but also what she can make of them – for example, the set of possible recipes available (or made available) to her.

6   Ignorance and Uncertainty

In short, we do not propose a universal way to deal with ignorance and uncertainty. Different economic environments and different degrees of sophistication call for different ingredients and different recipes. Part III is like a cookbook. For each kind of dish, it proposes basic ingredients and a basic set of recipes, from which each agent finds the one most suited to her taste. We do not claim that there is a unique way to define the set of recipes. We aim for a basic cookbook, characterizing what seems to us essential aspects of a number of strategic phenomena. Other sets of recipes, possibly characterizing other ways by which agents comprehend their strategic environment, and possibly conforming better with experimental evidence, would shape results and intuitions differently. In the end, one must judge the various restrictions on the set of strategies allowed to the agent by their usefulness in shaping our thinking and understanding of strategic behavior, and their empirical support.

References

Lipman, B. L. (1999). Decision theory without logical omniscience: toward an axiomatic framework for bounded rationality. *The Review of Economic Studies*, 66 (2), 339–361.

Myerson, R. B. (2004). Comments on "Games with Incomplete Information Played by 'Bayesian' Players, I–III." *Management Science*, 50 (12), 1818–1824.

Savage, L. J. (1954). *The Foundations of Statistics*, New York: John Wiley and Sons, 1954.

PART I

Modeling Challenges

As analysts, we use formal models to describe the situations that agents face. In doing so, we take the perspective of an omniscient outsider who would have superior knowledge of the details of the interaction: we choose the strategies available to agents, as well as the payoff structure, that is, the payoffs that each agent gets as a function of the strategies played. Most often, we also wish to prevent agents from knowing with precision the payoff structure. To that end we introduce an *information structure*, which describes the uncertainty about the payoff structure, and the (possibly stochastic) process that generates what agents perceive or observe conditional on each possible payoff structure.

Although a model is an analyst's tool, not meant to be known with precision by the agents being described, the mere assumption that an agent can compare the performance of the strategies available to him grants him some implicit knowledge of the model, or *inside knowledge*. The objective of Part I is to explain the connection between optimization and inside knowledge, to explain how modeling choices have consequences on the degree to which agents can exploit the structure of the model itself.

Why is this important? By constructing a model that endows agents with overly precise knowledge of the model itself, we run the risk of deriving insights that hinge on that unrealistic assumption. Models need not be realistic, but we hope that the insights that we derive from them are not too strongly driven by unrealistic features of the model.

CHAPTER 1

Action Space

1. Economic theory studies decision problems and strategic interactions, with the objective of understanding and/or predicting the behavior of agents involved in these situations.

Modeling a decision problem or a strategic interaction begins by specifying a set of *actions*, which agents may choose from, and a *payoff structure*, which is a formal description of how actions translate into payoffs for each agent. There exists an extraordinarily vast array of decision problems or strategic situations because, in principle, there is no *a priori* limit on the space of possible actions available, nor limits on the possible mappings from actions to payoffs.

Analysts have considerable freedom in choosing the action space and the payoff structure when constructing models, and a great achievement of game theory has been to identify, within that vast array of situations, simple situations that provide insight into important real-world problems, and for which behavior can be described or characterized. One such example is the Prisoner's Dilemma.

2. The prisoner's dilemma is a two-player game in which each player has only two actions (i.e., a two-by-two game), confess (*C*) or not confess (*N*), with the property that confessing is a better option for each individual whatever choice the other makes, and where *both not confessing* is a better outcome than *both confessing*.

The following matrix describes payoffs that are consistent with the properties described above:[1]

	C	*N*
C	1,1	4,0
N	0,4	3,3

Given these payoffs, each player individually finds that confessing is a better strategy, because $1 > 0$ and $4 > 3$. Confessing is said to be a dominant

---

[1] The matrix indicates that if player 1 chooses *N* and player 2 chooses *C*, player 1 gets 0 and player 2 gets 4.

strategy. The prediction is that both confess despite *both not confessing* being a better joint outcome, thereby reflecting the conflict between private objectives (confessing is individually better) and social objectives (both not confessing is jointly better).

3. A virtue of the formal description above is that it can be used across disparate applications: beyond the dilemma that prisoners might face, there are many interactions that fit naturally in the two-by-two game above, with "not confessing" characterizing a *cooperative* strategy, and "confessing" characterizing a *selfish* strategy. These broadly defined labels (cooperative and selfish) may capture different behaviors depending on context. But this is precisely why the model is useful, making it easily applicable across a large variety of situations.

4. Another virtue is that the prediction holds not just for a single specification of the payoff parameters, but for a large range of values, as long as the dominance relations hold. In particular, the agents need not have precise knowledge of the parameters of the model for the prediction to hold.

We emphasize the latter point, as this is central to the critique of the literature that we address in this book. In writing down a payoff structure, we take an outsider's perspective, defining what each player gets as a function of the pair of actions played. In solving the game, we derive "optimal" choices for each player as though they knew the payoff structure. As analysts, we avoid complicating the model further; we avoid being precise about what each player actually knows about the payoff structure.[2]

The reason for doing so is parsimony. A model is meant to be an analyst's tool, a parsimonious way to represent reality, helping to explain economic insights which seem relevant. For the sake of parsimony, we generally solve the model as if the agents had precise knowledge of its parameters, hoping (without formally verifying) that the insights drawn from the model do not hinge on this questionable assumption. The prisoner's dilemma safely passes this test.

5. The restriction to two actions ("not confess," the cooperative strategy, and "confess," the selfish strategy) provides a parsimonious model of the conflict between private and social objectives. There are many contexts, however, in which one could imagine varying degrees of cooperative behavior, and where the restriction to two actions could be viewed as unrealistic. In an attempt to assess the strength of the forces away from "full" or efficient cooperation, one may want to enrich the model with multiple levels of cooperation.

But there is a tension: while the restriction to two actions enables the analyst to capture the basic strategic effect, further quantification of this effect

---

[2] Analysts sometimes take a different view, assuming that payoffs are precisely known, and known to be known, etc. We discuss this alternative view at the end of this chapter.

through a more "realistic" action space is subject to the criticism that the solution implicitly assumes that the agents of the model have substantial knowledge of the structure of the model. The next example illustrates that tension.

6. *A partnership game.* Consider a standard partnership problem in which each of two agents $i = 1, 2$ picks an effort level e_i where the effort level can be any non-negative real number. Agent i's gain from the pair (e_1, e_2) is defined as $g_i^\gamma(e_1, e_2)$, with:

$$g_i^\gamma(e_1, e_2) = \gamma \sqrt{e_1 e_2} - e_i^2.$$

An *equilibrium* outcome in this model is a pair of actions (e_1^*, e_2^*) from which neither player wants to deviate unilaterally.[3] The equilibrium effort levels satisfy $e_i^* = \frac{1}{4}\gamma$, while the socially efficient levels would satisfy $e_i^{**} = \frac{1}{2}\gamma$.[4] The model allows one to quantify the effect of both agents following private objectives, each ignoring the positive externality on the other and the higher welfare that would result from a marginal increase in effort.

Despite being possibly more realistic in terms of the strategy space, the model implicitly makes implausible cognitive assumptions: the equilibrium outcome relies on agents behaving as though they knew the details of the model (e.g., the functional forms associated with gain and cost functions for each player) or as if they had learned which effort level was optimal among all possible levels.

7. *Coming to play an equilibrium.* Models are typically silent about how players come to play according to the equilibrium strategies the analyst identifies. One natural hypothesis is that equilibrium is the outcome of a learning process, the stable point from which individual experiments with alternative strategies are unprofitable. In this view, the cognitive assumption is not that players know the parameters of the model, but that they have learned which of their available strategies is best.

There are at least two dimensions that make learning difficult: the number of alternatives to be compared, and changes in the environment. The plausibility of the implicit cognitive assumption may therefore differ a great deal across models. In the prisoner's dilemma, the agent need only compare two actions, and best responses are unaffected by changes in the underlying payoff structure as long as the dominance relations continue to hold. In the partnership game, the cognitive assumption is stronger: the agent must compare many effort

[3] See the note at the end of this chapter for some history and motivation.
[4] Formally, an equilibrium is a pair (e_i^*, e_j^*) such that, for each i, the gain $g_i^\gamma(e_i, e_j^*)$ is maximum at e_i^*. The social optimum is a pair (e_i^{**}, e_j^{**}) such that the total gain $g_i^\gamma(e_i, e_j) + g_j^\gamma(e_i, e_j)$ is maximum at (e_i^{**}, e_j^{**}).

levels, and changes in the underlying model parameters result in changes in best responses. This discussion relates to the well-known tradeoff between exploration and exploitation. In a changing environment, the sum of exploration and exploitation times is bounded, and finding the action best suited to the current environment is more difficult when the number of actions considered increases.

For the sake of parsimony, equilibrium analysis typically ignores these considerations. A prediction is obtained for each model specification, and as the specification varies (e.g., as γ varies), one predicts a different equilibrium outcome $(e^*(\gamma))$. In so doing, however, we run the risk of taking these predictions too seriously, forgetting that the relationship $e^*(\gamma)$ relies on agents quickly adjusting correctly and costlessly to variations in the payoff structure.

For example, in a changing environment (exhibiting somewhat persistent variations in γ), players might find it easier to track variations in γ by comparing only two effort levels, say $e_i \in \{1,4\}$, with the consequence that, in effect, the game actually played by agents is better described by a two-by-two game. Then, for example, when $\gamma = 6$, the game can be summarized by the matrix:

	$e_2 = 1$	$e_2 = 4$
$e_1 = 1$	5,5	11,-4
$e_1 = 4$	-4,11	8,8

and it has the structure of the prisoner's dilemma.

8. *Equilibrium as a shortcut.* Said differently, the payoff functions that we define are a modeling convenience, as is the static formulation that we adopt. These assumptions allow us to bypass the complex issues associated with learning and the possibility that the situations (hence the payoff functions) that agents face vary without their being precisely aware of these underlying variations. We solve for equilibrium as though agents knew γ precisely, and we obtain a prediction for each model specification (γ).

Thus, while the addition of strategies may make the model seem more realistic, this gives rise to predictions that are more finely tuned to the exact model specification assumed, ignoring the possibility that this addition actually diminishes agents' ability to tailor behavior to the underlying payoff structure.

In specifying payoff functions, we implicitly assume that there is a well-defined underlying payoff structure, and that this structure has some stability or permanence which enables some form of learning and some behavioral adjustment to that structure. With a richer underlying parameter space, however, the presumption that all parameters have permanence is less compelling.

9. The traditional answer to the concerns expressed above is that, if we think that agents do not know the structure of the model parameters, we should include in the model a description of what they are ignorant of and how that ignorance is accommodated. Modeling what agents ignore is a challenge that we will address. Let us simply observe for now that this traditional line of thought pushes the difficulty one step further. It produces models that lie in a richer parameter space (this richer parameter may be, for example, a distribution over possible realizations of γ), and strategies that also lie in a richer set, as we typically allow agents to condition behavior on whatever signal they get that might be correlated with γ.

10. Finally, we observe that the point we raise is not specific to games, but applies to decision problems as well. Setting aside questions of convergence to equilibrium, we make the simple observation that finding

$$a^*(s) = \arg\max_{a \in A} u(a, s)$$

is cognitively less demanding when A is a smaller set. Also, a richer action space comes with a richer parameter space (as all payoffs need to be specified), and the stability or permanence of these parameters over time becomes a strong assumption.

To summarize: Models typically endow agents with the ability to ascertain which action is best without questioning how this is achieved. One possibility is that the agent knows the structure of the model itself; another is that, having faced related situations in the past, he has come to know which alternative is best. Whichever one finds more convincing, the agent is assumed to behave as if he knew how to compare the alternatives available, or as if model parameters had enough permanence to make learning plausible.

One consequence is that there is a tension: one may add strategies to make the model descriptively more realistic, but this addition imposes a greater cognitive demand, or permanence of a larger number of model parameters, hence a possibly less realistic model.

Further Comments

Nash Equilibrium. The equilibrium concept used throughout the book is called a Nash equilibrium, named after John Nash (1950). An earlier version of this idea was formulated by Antoine Augustin Cournot (1838) in his analysis of competition between two firms. With two players for example, it defines a pair of actions (a_1^*, a_2^*) from which neither player finds it attractive to change his behavior unilaterally.

A common justification for equilibrium is that it is a plausible outcome of a learning process which would have converged. Once (a_1^*, a_2^*) is played, experience cannot provide a player with incentives to change his behavior. It is a stable outcome.

A second common justification is that players reach equilibrium play through introspection, rather than learning. This type of justification puts a heavy burden on the agents knowing in detail the structure of the game they are playing, and thinking about all the consequences of these details. For this reason, analysts following this path often start with the precautionary statement that the model is common knowledge among agents: each agent knows the model, knows that others know, etc.

Our view is that the learning interpretation is more plausible for many economic problems that employ Nash equilibria.

Exploration, exploitation and the "considered" set. The idea of the tradeoff between exploration and exploitation dates back to Thompson (1933), whose motivation came from clinical trials – when different treatments are available for a certain disease and one must decide which treatment to use on the next patient. In a seminal paper, Simon (1955) argued that a key aspect of decision making is the subset of actions that agents actually consider (out of those a priori available), and that this subset depends on the extent of exploration. In his view, exploration is driven by the speed with which aspirations decline or increase after a bad or good experience, with unmatched aspirations leading to exploration of new alternatives.

On the aim of modeling. Osborne (2002, page 2) writes: "Game-theoretic modeling starts with an idea related to some aspect of the interaction of decision-makers. We express this idea precisely in a model, incorporating features of the situation that appear to be relevant. This step is an art. We wish to put enough ingredients into the model to obtain nontrivial insights, but not so many that we are led into irrelevant complications; we wish to lay bare the underlying structure of the situation as opposed to describe its every detail."

References

Cournot, A. A. (1838). *Recherches sur les Principes Mathematiques de la Theorie des Richesses*, New York: L. Hachette.

Nash, J. (1950). Equilibrium points in n-person games. *Proceedings of the National Academy of Sciences*, 36(1), 48–49.

Osborne, M. J. (2002). *An Introduction to Game Theory*, Oxford: Oxford University Press.

Simon, H. (1955). A behavioral model of rational choice. *The Quarterly Journal of Economics*, 69(1), 99–118.

Thompson, W. R. (1933). On the likelihood that one unknown probability exceeds another in view of the evidence of two samples. *Bulletin of the American Mathematics Society*, 25, 285–294.

CHAPTER 2

Ignorance and Uncertainty

1. Most if not all situations involve an element of ignorance: about the consequence of our actions, about the preferences of others, about what others know, etc. In the previous chapter, we described two strategic situations in which players are modeled as though both agents knew all payoff parameters. Sometimes this is an innocuous assumption. To examine or illustrate the tension between private and social incentives, the primary issue is not the extent to which players know the payoff structure, and details concerning what each player knows or ignores can be legitimately set aside.

There are situations, however, where ignorance seems to play a central role: when a seller meets a buyer, the seller is typically ignorant of how much the buyer might be willing to pay for the object; when a firm bids on an oil field, it is typically ignorant of the exact quantity of oil that the field contains; when a firm launches a new product, it is ignorant of the degree to which price and quality affect demand; when we make a gift which we think thoughtful, we are ignorant of how well it will be appreciated, and when we make a public statement, we are ignorant of the degree to which it will generate approval or resentment.

2. To model what an agent is ignorant of, say a characteristic s that the agent cares about, we typically define the *set* S of possible characteristics and a *probability distribution* π over possible realizations of $s \in S$.

Ignorance about some relevant characteristic is thus modeled as uncertainty over that characteristic.

One interpretation of the state s is that it corresponds to one particular *situation* that the agent could be facing. Ignorance about the current situation is modeled as a random selection from the set of possible situations.

3. *Dice.* This modeling of ignorance fits well with throwing dice. A die is about to be thrown, and the agent is ignorant of which face will land up. Modeling that ignorance by saying that there are six possible states and a one-in-six chance to see any particular state makes perfectly good sense.

In real economic problems, however, there is a difficulty. Here, sometimes the die may have six faces, sometimes eight, and we don't get to see the number of faces. As analyst, we bypass this difficulty by applying the same modeling technique, enriching the state description so that it includes the realized number s *and* the number of faces $n \in \{6, 8\}$. The state thus becomes a pair (s, n). But while defining the probability $\pi(s = 5 \mid n)$ of seeing a five when there are n faces poses no difficulty, the probability $\pi(n)$ of facing an n–sided die is more difficult to interpret.

One interpretation is that there is a large population of dice that the agent may face, a fraction $\pi(6)$ of which has six faces, and the agent has an equal chance of facing any one of the dice in the population. In other words, to the agent, all dice look alike, and any die situation can be viewed as a (uniform) random draw from the set of all possible die situations.[1]

Most economic models fit this *generalized* die example. We give two illustrations.

4. *Buyer's valuation.* A buyer has a valuation s for an object, and the seller is ignorant of the valuation. Ignorance is modeled by defining a set S of possible valuations, say $S = \{6, 8\}$, and a probability distribution π over possible values.

The situation differs from the simple die example in that the buyer has a well-defined valuation s, which is not random. Where then does randomness come from?

Randomness captures the idea that the buyer might have been picked from a pool of potential buyers with differentiated characteristics: for a fraction $\pi(8)$ of buyers, the value is eight, for the others, the value is six. But from the seller's perspective, all buyers look alike.[2]

Thus, although a seller faces a specific buyer, we treat that current buyer as though he was drawn uniformly from the population of buyers. So, we do not model the *specific* interaction where the buyer has a specific valuation s, but rather the *generic or anonymized* situation where the buyer is picked randomly from a population of potential buyers.

In the example, six and eight are the possible *individual characteristics* of the buyers which one could face. The distribution π is a *characteristic of the population* of buyers.

When one thinks carefully, the move from individual characteristics to generic or population characteristics is already implicit in the simple die example. Think of a die that has *already* been thrown, showing a specific face, say $s = 5$, which the agent cannot see. Although the agent faces a specific "thrown die" having the characteristic 5, we model the agent as though he was facing a generic "thrown die," or a draw from a very large population of "thrown dice," or a die "to be thrown."

---

[1] Many economists would interpret π differently, suggesting that π is only meant to capture the uncertainty in the *agent's mind*, about the number of faces. We shall come back to this in Chapter 5 and the Miscellanea.

[2] We reiterate that π is often thought of representing the uncertainty in the *seller's mind* rather than an actual distribution over possible buyers.

Said differently, to model ignorance, we move from the description of an isolated situation to consider a random pick from a set of pooled situations.

5. *Oil fields.* Similarly, assume that we are interested in the quantity of oil in a particular oil field. We are ignorant of the actual quantity q. We model this ignorance by defining the set Q of values that q could take and a probability distribution over the possible quantities.

The example can be interpreted along the previous lines. Any given oil field is special. It has its own characteristics which make it different from any other oil field. However, possibly because oil field characteristics are hard to interpret, all oil fields are pooled into the same category. Given that (coarse) categorization, we can define the fraction $F(q_0)$ of oil fields with a quantity of oil q below q_0.

Now when we face a particular oil field, we treat it as though it was drawn uniformly from the population of oil fields. Given this assumption, one can interpret $F(q_0)$ as the probability that the quantity of oil in the current oil field is below q_0.

As in previous examples, elements of Q are the possible individual characteristics of the oil fields (which the bidder cares about), and F is a characteristic of the population of oil fields.

6. *Quantification.* Modeling ignorance reduces to defining a set of states S and a probability distribution π over states. Technically, the distribution π allows the analyst to *quantify* ignorance, and rank the various alternatives available to the agent: if one defines the utility $u(a,s)$ associated with each possible action $a \in A$ and state $s \in S$, then, given π, actions may be compared according to expected utility:

$$v(a,\pi) = \sum_{s \in S} \pi(s)u(a,s).$$

This in turn allows the analyst to generate a behavioral prediction. If two actions a^0 and a^1 are available to the agent, and if

$$v(a^0,\pi) > v(a^1,\pi)$$

then the analyst will predict that a^1 is not used. More generally, if A is the set of actions available, the analyst will predict that the agent chooses $a^* = \arg\max_a v(a,\pi)$.

7. *Who knows what?* We shall come back extensively to this issue in Chapter 5. We wish to think of π as a probability distribution defined by the analyst, which accurately reflects the agent's environment, as if a die selecting the situation faced by the agent was about to be thrown and the *analyst* knew the characteristics of that die. We do that because we eventually want to tie behavior to the agent's ultimate welfare, and the distribution π is what makes this possible.

The analyst then simply solves the model, assuming that the agent behaves *as if* he knew the model itself, hence here, *as if* the agent knew the probability distribution over states.

Whether the agent knows π or behaves as if he knew π, the prediction is the same but the interpretation is different. Assuming that the agent knows π is often questionable. In trying to model ignorance (the state s), we end up assuming that the agent knows quite precisely the structure of what he is ignorant about (i.e., the distribution π). That assumption seems reasonable if the agent comes upon a six-sided die which he understands to be unbiased: when he sees it, he can recognize that it has six faces, and that each face seems equally likely. When the agent meets a typical buyer however, it is less obvious that he would immediately picture the population of buyers to which that buyer belongs, even less so the characteristics of that population of buyers.

The assumption that the agent behaves *as if* he knew π is seemingly less problematic in that it only requires that the agent behaves as if he knew the ranking over the choices available to him, given the pool of problems that he faces (as characterized by π). For example, one may argue that *from experience*, having observed the valuations of a long sequence of buyers, the agent will eventually get a good idea of the population of buyers he typically faces; or that from experience, having observed the consequences of various attempts to extract surplus from these buyers, he will eventually learn which action to choose (i.e., what price to offer).

Still, even if this "based on experience" argument seems reasonable, it presumes some permanence in the process that generates these encounters (as discussed below). In addition, it may end up being a strong assumption when many alternatives are compared.

8. Learning from experience. Experience helps, but it helps to the extent that future situations bear some relationship with past situations. If one held the view that any new situation is entirely disconnected from past ones, there would be little scope for agents to learn how to adjust behavior over time, as past experience would always be irrelevant.

Now think of a possibly biased six-sided die. Imagine that after many throws of this die, one is told the proportion of occurrences of a given face, say five. Although the bias is unknown, the proportion of five's provides a good estimate of the chance that a five shows up in the next throw.

In this example, experience helps because one assumes that the *same* die is thrown repeatedly. Of course, this assumption could be weakened. One could assume that there are two dice, each having a possibly different bias, and one of the two is thrown. If in addition we assume that for each throw, the die thrown is selected according to a possibly stochastic but unchanging selection process, we get the same conclusion: the proportion of occurrences of a given face, say five, will give a good estimate of the chance that a five shows up. With persistence in the situation faced (here, the same selection process over two given dice), one may learn from experience.

9. *Real and hypothetical processes.* To sum up, we model ignorance by assuming a probability distribution π over the set of specific situations s that the agent might face. The distribution π characterizes the typical or representative situation that he confronts. Next we assume that the agent behaves as if he knew π, or as if π was persistent enough for the agent to learn the optimal behavior under π.

In this exercise, we treat π as if it had real content, as if π described the true process by which the actual situation faced by the agent is selected. However, neither the agent nor the analyst is in a position to identify the "true" process over the situations that the agent faces. In the hope of identifying or learning the "true" process, one may compile past data about the situations faced in the past, and construct an empirical probability distribution over states. The idea that any situation faced can be viewed as a random draw from the empirical distribution remains an assumption.

The general issue is that eventually learning from past data hinges on making *a priori* assumptions on the set of processes that may generate the data. In particular, one may never check from experience whether the "real" process belongs to that set. One may only learn the process that is most plausible among a set of *a priori* thought-to-be-plausible processes.

Think of possibly biased coins being tossed. To identify from experience which bias is most plausible, one must first hypothesize a set of plausible biases. If one starts from the idea that all coins have the same bias, and that only two biases are plausible (e.g., either the coin tosses have 60 percent chance of being tails, or 60 percent chance of being heads), a large number of coin tosses showing a large enough majority of tails will be strong evidence for the first hypothesis. Eventually, experience likely confirms one of the two hypotheses.

In principle, however, the set of possible hypotheses may be as large as the set of possible sequences of toss realizations. It is only by restricting (arbitrarily) the set of possible hypotheses, making assumptions on the characteristics of the population of coins being thrown, or on the process that selects coins, that one can make predictions over the next toss. In the above example, one could instead start from the idea that initially there are equal numbers of coins biased in favor of tails and heads, so that a large majority of tails makes subsequent tosses of heads more likely.

A data-generating process appears "true" insofar as we have put a priori constraints on plausible processes. Unfortunately, these constraints are often arbitrary. We use the distribution π as a shortcut to characterize a typical situation, but this distribution remains a somewhat artificial theoretical construct.

We illustrate these points, once again, with a more concrete example.

10. *Writing and editing.* A weekly magazine publishes short stories. The format is constrained: the story must fit an exact number of lines, within a special layout. The publisher's software is complex and cannot be shared with writers, so writers are asked to send stories using a simple word-processing software. The consequence is that there is no guarantee that the text sent

by authors fits exactly within the layout. The publisher may suppress words, modify the order of some words, or artificially create spaces within the text to ensure that it fits. To reduce editorial workload, writers are given a target length, taking the form of a number of lines in the simple software. Still, the text never fits perfectly, because the writing style (length of words used, number of dialogues and paragraphs) affects the final number of lines.

The publisher's problem consists of providing an appropriate target length τ to authors. Any target length τ for the text written in the writer's software generates another length L in the publisher's format. The editor cares about the ratio $s = L/\tau$, but this variable is not common to all text, as the writing style matters.

Based on experience, and to help him choose the appropriate target τ, the publisher may construct an empirical distribution $\pi(s)$. This may be sufficient to give the editor a rough idea of what to expect from future texts. However, the distribution π reflects a characteristic of the writing styles used by *previous* authors, and there is no particular reason to expect this distribution to remain the same or to change according to a regular pattern.

11. *Degrees of freedom.* The description above leaves two open questions: the precision with which situations are described, and the coarseness of categorization.

Consider again the oil field example. The agent might care about whether q is below or above some given threshold q_0. Then the relevant precision consists of defining only two states, depending on whether q is below or above q_0. Or he might care about the exact quantity, in which case the state coincides with the actual quantity q; or he might also care about the extraction cost γ as well, in which case the state consists of the pair (q, γ).

Concerning the coarseness of categorization, there are also many degrees of freedom. For example, one could focus on the oil fields that cross a given latitude, and restrict attention to those. In principle, there are arbitrarily many observable characteristics (e.g., geologic characteristics) which could be used to refine the categorization of oil fields being considered.

As in the previous chapter, there is a tension: the more details one includes in the description of the underlying state, the greater the cognitive demand. As one enriches the description of each possible situation, one also expands the set of parameters that characterizes a typical situation (π becomes a more complex object), and the hypothesis that there is parameter stability over many dimensions is less compelling.

> **To summarize**: Ignorance about a given situation is modeled as though the situation was generic, drawn from a given pool of situations according to a given distribution. As in the previous chapter, agents are then assumed to behave as if they knew the model – here, the distribution.
>
> One challenge is to give real content to this distribution. The empirical distribution is a good candidate. Any new situation is special,

possibly disconnected from any past situation encountered; yet one may define a broad category of situations (oil fields), pooling distinct situations into the same category, treating as noise within category differences, implicitly assuming uniform selection among situations within the same category. We homogenize *a priori* heterogenous situations, hypothesizing that what has been observed in the past will repeat itself. By doing so, however, we force regularities that may not exist. We create a pool with a somewhat arbitrary mean, an arbitrary representative situation, with other situations being viewed as noisy variations around that average situation. We ignore the fact that the whole pool itself may vary.

Behavioral predictions should thus be made with caution on two grounds: (i) they are based on a somewhat artificial theoretical construct; (ii) they are based on the presumption that agents evaluate alternatives as if they knew this artificial construct. That artificial construct may be a useful tool, but one hopes the predictions obtained do not rely too heavily on it.

Further Comments

"Un coup de dés jamais n'abolira le hasard." *Never will a throw of dice abolish chance,*[3] *which we freely interpret: whatever attempt to quantify the unknown, whatever probabilities you might consider applying to the cases you think possible, uncertainty will prevail.*

Frequencies and probabilities. Our interpretation of the distribution π as a representative situation, viewed as a random draw from a set of pooled situations, goes back to the origins of statistics, which attempted to derive stable frequencies of attributes (height, age of death) from a long series/class/group of observations (population).[4] *Using a terminology later introduced by Richard von Mises (1957), one may define a collective as a long sequence of observations (e.g., the colors of a large number of plants), and the probability of an attribute s (e.g., a specific color) as the frequency with which that attribute occurs in the collective considered. Probabilities are defined in relation to a given collective, but one does so only on the condition that enlargements of the collective would not affect the frequencies of the attributes.*[5]

---

[3] A poem by Stéphane Mallarmé, 1897 Cosmopolis.

[4] See, for example, Venn (1876), who also questions the possibility to obtain such stability in any natural environment different from games of chance. See Hacking (2006) for a more careful historical account.

[5] "We will say that a collective is a mass phenomenon, or a repetitive event, or, simply, a long sequence of observations for which there are sufficient reasons to believe that the relative frequency of the observed attribute would tend to a fixed limit if the observations were indefinitely continued." von Mises (1957, page 15).

Stability of frequencies is thus viewed as a critical assumption to define probabilities. Yet, except for properly or narrowly defined experiments, one does not expect the property to hold. One may try to define the collective "fruit" and the attribute "weight," but the composition of the basket matters, with no guarantee that enlargements of the collective will respect the initial composition. One may try to isolate lemons, but again, the type of seed, the terrain, the exposition to sun all matter, with no guarantee that enlargement of the collective of lemons will leave the weight distribution of lemons unaffected.[6]

This lack of stability is inescapable in most economic problems, and many analysts generally prefer to avoid using the terminology "probability" to refer to the frequency with which a piece of fruit weighs s, because that frequency lacks an objective basis. Analysts generally argue that when "probabilities" cannot be properly or objectively defined, π should be thought of as a subjective or personal probability, either located in the agent's mind, or meant to be an abstract representation consistent with the choices that he makes.[7]

We take a more pragmatic approach. We do not object to using π as if it had permanence, and calling it a probability distribution as if it were objective. What this chapter suggests is only that cautions be taken with respect to π, that it is an artificial construct derived from a hypothetical pooling or categorization of experiences that our individual may face, and that, in addition, it may not be persistent. The justification for its use is (i) that behavior must inevitably be broadly related to experience, and (ii) that π may be a sufficiently good approximation of the experiences that our individual has faced in the past and will face in the future.

On "experience-guided" choices. *Our perspective emphasizes both the pooling of various situations and the guidance that experience provides, captured by means of a distribution that we take to be objective, not a construction in the agent's mind. The idea of pooling various situations to guide choices is reminiscent of Case-Based Theory (Gilboa and Schmeidler (1995)), and their motivation is similar – to avoid reliance on "personal" distributions. There are differences however. First, there isn't an "objective" underlying distribution of cases π in that work. Second, agents assign personal weights on past experience as a function of the similarity they perceive between experiences, with the consequence that agents eventually behave as if they had a "personal" distribution of frequencies π′.*

References

Gilboa, I. & Schmeidler, D. (1995). Case-based decision theory. *The Quarterly Journal of Economics*, 110(3), 605–639.

---

[6] Similar examples related to population heights are discussed in Venn (1876).
[7] We shall come back to this discussion in Chapter 5 and the Miscellanea.

Hacking, I. (2006). *The Emergence of Probability: A Philosophical Study of Early Ideas about Probability, Induction and Statistical Inference*, 2nd edn, Cambridge: Cambridge University Press.

Venn, J. (1866). *The Logic of Chance: An Essay on the Foundations and Province of the Theory of Probability, with Special Reference to Its Application to Moral and Social Science*, London and Cambridge: Macmillan.

von Mises, R. (1957). *Probability Statistics and Truth*, 2nd revised edn, New York: Dover Publication Inc.

Observations, Perceptions and Strategies

1. A seller may not know a candidate buyer's valuation, yet his own valuation might provide some indication about that buyer's valuation. At the very least, knowing his own valuation will help when posting a price, avoiding posting one that would generate losses if accepted. An agent may not know the exact quantity of oil in an oil field up for auction, but he may receive an expert opinion about the quantity. While not perfectly accurate, it may help him make a forecast and choose an adequate bid. An individual may not know with precision the danger he faces when walking through an unknown neighborhood, yet a feeling of fear can guide him in making appropriate decisions.

In other words, agents are often *partially* ignorant of the situations they face: they know some aspects of these situations, or they may make observations or get perceptions that are relevant to these situations; such knowledge, observations, or perceptions may guide or influence their choices.

Modeling an agent's observations or perceptions is important not only because they can affect agents' behavior, but also because the extent to which agents react to those observations, or are influenced by these perceptions, is sometimes the main object of analysis. We wish to understand the extent to which a bidder shades his bid below his own valuation, the extent to which a seller increases a posted price above his valuation, the extent to which one trusts expert advice, or the extent to which one flees when experiencing fear.

2. Many things qualify as "observations" or "perceptions." We require only that they potentially *influence* behavior. If one categorizes choice problems into two groups (difficult problems and easy problems), then when one faces a particular problem, whether it is perceived as difficult or easy will be referred to as an observation. An observation may be any sensory perception such as fear, anxiety or feeling upset, or even a raw and subconscious perception to be processed. An observation may also be the opinion of an expert telling me about the quality of the product I consider buying. It may also be a rich set of geological data which I might use to form an opinion about the quantity of oil in an oil field.

Throughout the book, we often use the word "observation" as a generic term, yet sometimes "perception" would be more appropriate. Technically, one key aspect of observations or perceptions is that they are exogenous variables; they are *not* choice variables. They are reflections of the context in which the decision is taken. They are contextual variables. Eventually, decisions will be the result of contextual variables *and* choice variables.

The particular way in which contextual variables and choice variables jointly affect decisions will depend on applications. Sometimes, we will model agents who condition choices on observations, and sometimes we will think of the agent getting raw perceptions, and having imperfect control over how these perceptions are processed.

3. Perceptions or observations, and more generally, contextual variables, are important in that they may help the agent behave in ways that increase his welfare. One modeling challenge is making precise the relationship between what the agent perceives and what enhances his welfare.

Formally, we refer to $z \in Z$ as a possible observation/perception. Calling $s \in S$ the underlying state that characterizes what the agent cares about, we refer to the perception-state pair (z,s) as a *situation*, with the understanding that only the perception z (and not the state s) can influence the agent's decisions, and we define a probability distribution ω over possible situations.

This differs from the previous chapter in that we expand the notion of situation to explicitly include what the agent perceives or observes. Having expanded the definition of a situation, we proceed as before. We move from the description of an *isolated* situation (z,s) to consider a *generic* situation, as though it were chosen randomly from a set of pooled situations. A pair (z,s) describes one particular situation one may face. The distribution ω is a characteristic of the population of situations that one may face.

The distribution ω is a critical ingredient because it defines the (stochastic) relationship between what the agent perceives (z) and what affects his welfare (s).

4. *Dice again.* To understand the logic of defining a distribution over situations, consider a simple die example. Assume that after the die has been thrown, the agent is told whether the face is an odd or even number. A situation is a pair (z,s) where $z \in \{o,e\}$ describes what he is told and $s \in \{1,...,6\}$ describes the actual face. Assuming that the die is unbiased, and that the agent is told the truth, we can define the joint probability over situations (z,s), and summarize it as follows:

$\omega(z,s)$	1	2	3	4	5	6
o	1/6	0	1/6	0	1/6	0
e	0	1/6	0	1/6	0	1/6

This table, for example, indicates that the probability of $(o,2)$ is 0. It also indicates that the probability of $(e,2)$ is 1/6. Constructing ω thus poses no difficulty: the assumption that the die is unbiased and that the agent is told the truth is sufficient to pin down the distribution ω.

Furthermore, the table can be used to derive conditional probabilities. If one considers a bet where the agent is told that s is odd and where he wins whenever s is below or equal to 3, one can compute the conditional probability

$$\omega(s \leq 3 \mid o) = \frac{\sum_{s \leq 3} \omega(o,s)}{\sum_s \omega(o,s)} = \frac{1/6 + 1/6}{1/6 + 1/6 + 1/6} = 2/3$$

and conclude that the chance of winning is more favorable if he is told that s is odd than if he is told nothing.

5. *Dice continued.* The logic extends to more general examples. Consider dice having two characteristics: the number of faces n (either $n = 6$ or 8) and a color c (either $c = blue$ or red). The agent cares about the number of faces, because this affects the attractiveness of betting on whether a particular face, say five, shows up when the die is thrown: since a five is less likely with an eight-sided die, the gains from betting are less with an eight-sided die than a six-sided die. The agent, however, does not observe the number of faces. He only observes its color.

In general, the agent has no reason to suspect that the color could be useful. However, if he knows or if he learns that compared to blue dice, red dice are more likely to have eight faces, then, even though he doesn't care about color per se, using color to decide on betting behavior could prove valuable.

This is modeled by assuming a particular distribution over the situations (c,n) that the agent faces. For example:

	$n = 6$	$n = 8$
$c = b$	1/4	1/4
$c = r$	1/6	1/3

The interpretation is as in the previous chapter. There is a large population of dice that the agent may face, a fraction $\omega(b,6) = 1/4$ of which is blue and has six faces. Any situation that the agent faces can be viewed as a (uniform) random draw from the set of all possible die situations. The consequence is that when the die is red, the agent has a greater chance of facing an eight-sided die. Moreover, the population characteristics, defined by ω, allow us to compute the chance that the agent faces an eight-sided die when the die is red, say:

$$\Pr(n = 8 \mid c = r) = \frac{1/3}{1/3 + 1/6} = \frac{2}{3}.$$

6. *Fear and danger.* Many economic models can be portrayed in ways that are akin to the generalized die example above. Think of an individual walking in an unknown neighborhood, possibly facing danger. The individual cares about whether there is danger or not, say $s = D, N$, but he typically does not learn the

state before it is too late to act. However, he may get early sensory perceptions that can guide his choice to retreat, to increase attention or to confidently continue on his way. To simplify, we summarize these perceptions as a binary signal $z \in \{f, n\}$ where f stands for *fear*, and n for *no fear*.

Ideally, one would like to experience fear (and flee) if and only if there is danger. However, one could experience fear when there is no danger, and, similarly, one could face imminent danger without experiencing fear. To describe a typical situation that one may face, we can define the distribution ω over possible situations (z, s), for example:

$z\backslash s$	D	N
f	0.1	0.06
n	0.01	0.83

As with the red die above – where the color was an indication that the die is not favorable – fear is an indication of danger. When one doesn't experience fear, the odds of danger are given by the conditional probability:

$$\omega(D \mid n) = \frac{\omega(n, D)}{\omega(n, D) + \omega(n, N)} = 0.01/0.84 = 1.2\%$$

while, when once experiences fear, the odds are

$$\omega(D \mid f) = \frac{\omega(f, D)}{\omega(f, D) + \omega(f, N)} = 0.1/0.16 = 62.5\%.$$

7. *Strategies and strategic variables.* Modeling ignorance reduces to defining a set of states S, a set of observations Z, and a probability distribution ω over $S \times Z$. The distribution ω allows the analyst to *quantify* the consequence of partial ignorance, rank the various strategies available to the agent, and make predictions about behavior.

A strategy is no longer an action, but a map that defines how the agent *reacts* to or is influenced by observations. Formally, define the utility $u(a, s)$ associated with each possible action $a \in A$ and state $s \in S$. A strategy σ is defined as a function that maps each observation z to an action $\sigma(z) \in A$. Then, given ω, the strategy σ may be evaluated according to the expected utility that it generates:

$$v(\sigma, \omega) = \sum_{(z,s)} \omega(z, s) u(\sigma(z), s).$$

This, in turn, allows the analyst to generate a behavioral prediction. If the two strategies σ^0 and σ^1 are available to the agent, and if

$$v(\sigma^0, \omega) > v(\sigma^1, \omega),$$

then the analyst will predict that σ^1 is not used.

Sometimes, it will be more appropriate to think of the influence of z as stochastic, rather than deterministic. In this case, we shall refer to $\sigma(a,z)$ as the probability that action a is taken when z is perceived or observed. Then, given ω, the strategy σ is evaluated as follows:

$$v(\sigma,\omega) = \sum_{(a,z,s)} \omega(z,s)\sigma(a,z)u(a,s).$$

Anticipating the next chapter, we emphasize that having defined a strategy does not imply that the agent can modify his behavior in ways that serves his interests. If an agent has a single strategy available (for example because his action derives mechanically from his observation), he has no control. Control comes from the assumption that multiple strategies are compared. For that reason, we will often parameterize the strategies available to the agent by a choice variable, or *a strategic variable*, say $\lambda \in \Lambda$, and define by

$$\Sigma = \{\sigma^{\lambda}, \lambda \in \Lambda\}$$

the set of strategies available to the agent. λ is a strategic variable, z is a contextual variable, and both variables jointly affect behavior ($\sigma^{\lambda}(z)$).

8. Our cautions in the previous chapter continue to apply. The first caution concerns the fact that the distribution ω is an artificial construct, based on properties of a typical situation, or the population of situations that one faces. Apart from special examples (such as the simple die example), there is no reason to think that the proportions or probabilities $\omega(z,s)$ are immutable. Assume ω reflects one's past experiences of walking in unknown neighborhoods. It is impossible to know whether future experiences of walking in unknown neighborhoods will follow a similar pattern. Whether one experiences fear could vary as a function of unrelated emotional stress. Whether one actually faces danger could depend on the type of clothes one is wearing when traveling in these neighborhoods, and changes in one's preference for fancy clothes could then lead to changes in the likelihood of danger.

The second caution concerns what the agent is assumed to know of ω.[1] The assumption that the agent knows ω is peculiar. In trying to limit the extent to which the agent knows the characteristics of what he cares about (the state s), we essentially assume the agent knows the (hypothetical) joint process (ω) that generates the pairs (z,s). The assumption that the agent behaves as if he knew ω is seemingly weaker, yet it may end up being a strong cognitive assumption when many strategies are compared.

---

[1] The distribution ω plays the same role as the distribution π in Chapter 2, and the same comments apply.

9. To illustrate, we return to the fear/danger example. Assume that once in the potentially dangerous neighborhood, the individual can either flee or stay, and that there is a cost c of fleeing and a cost C of staying when there is danger. In terms of strategies, the individual might stay whether he feels fear or not; flee the neighborhood whether he feels fear or not; or let fear guide his choice, by flying if and only if he feels fear. The latter strategy is best among those three strategies when:

$$\omega(D \mid n) < \frac{c}{C} < \omega(D \mid f). \tag{3.1}$$

Indeed, the first inequality ensures that fleeing is too costly when no fear is felt $(z = n)$, and the second inequality ensures that staying is too costly when fear is felt $(z = f)$.[2]

The inequalities (3.1) thus provide a general condition on relative costs and on conditional probabilities $\omega(D \mid z)$ that ensures that fear is a useful signal to the agent. As in the prisoner's dilemma examined in Chapter 1, this condition is satisfied for a wide range of model parameters (here, this would be the distribution ω). So, while the (behavioral) prediction is derived as though the agent knew the distribution ω, it does not rely on the agent knowing precisely ω. The assumption that the agent behaves as if he knew ω seems, here, reasonable.

10. So far we have described observations as binary signals: even or odd, blue or red, fear or no fear. In the same way that analysts have considerable freedom in choosing the action space, they also have considerable freedom in selecting the set Z of observations. In pursuit of more realistic models, one might define z as a level of chemical that produces a feeling of fear and make it a continuous variable, say $z \in [0,1]$. A situation then consists of a pair (z,s) where $z \in [0,1]$ and $s \in \{D,N\}$. And a typical situation is modeled as a draw from the set of all possible situations, assuming a particular joint distribution ω over $[0,1] \times \{D,N\}$. To fix ideas, assume that the conditional probability

$$\omega(D \mid z) \equiv \frac{\omega(z,D)}{\omega(z,D) + \omega(z,N)}$$

is continuous and increasing in z.

For any $\lambda \in [0,1]$, define σ^λ as the strategy in which the agent flees when his fear level gets too high, above the threshold λ. When $\lambda = 0$, the agent

---

[2] Conditional on event $z \in \{n,f\}$, staying yields a cost $C\,\omega(D \mid z)$, to be compared with the cost c of fleeing. Alternatively, one can express the total expected cost L associated with that strategy as:

$$L = \Pr(f)c + \Pr(n,D)C,$$

and check that when the inequalities (3.1) hold, the cost L is smaller than both c (the cost of fleeing all the time), and $C\Pr(D)$ (the cost of never fleeing).

flees always. When $\lambda = 1$, the agent never flees. If the agent can compare all strategies σ^λ, he optimally sets λ at a value λ^* such that:

$$\omega(D \mid \lambda^*) = \frac{c}{C}. \tag{3.2}$$

Indeed, when $z > \lambda$, the chance of danger is $\omega(D \mid z)$, and it exceeds c/C, justifying that one flees, while; when $z < \lambda$, the chance of danger is below c/C, justifying that one does not flee.[3]

The consequence is that as the cost of danger C increases relative to c (smaller c/C), the probability $\omega(D \mid \lambda^*)$ must decrease, hence the optimal threshold λ^* must decrease as well. In other words, when the stakes are high, the agent is more sensitive to fear, and Equation (3.2) allows quantification of the degree to which the strategic response λ^* varies as a function of model parameters (here, the cost ratio c/C and the distribution ω).

This is analogous to Chapter 1 where we compared the prisoner's dilemma and the continuous partnership game. In the binary signal model, the agent's strategy is unresponsive to small changes in c/C or ω – the agent flees when he feels fear.[4] In the continuous signal model, the agent's strategy is responsive, and the degree to which it is responsive is quantified.

Whether the agent's actual mental processing system undergoes such fine tuning is questionable. The model suggests a higher sensitivity to signals when the stakes are higher, and the model makes precise what higher stakes mean. At a qualitative level, the prediction seems reasonable.

Beyond the qualitative insight, the continuous model proposes a response tailored to ω, as though the agent could adjust behavior perfectly and instantaneously to ω, as well as to variations in ω. However, the ability of agents to adjust λ^* to changes in ω or c/C could be limited. If these variations go unnoticed, the simple binary model might be a more appropriate model.

11. *Shortcuts again.* Many models are shortcuts that abstract from learning issues. The distribution ω is a modeling convenience, a somewhat artificial theoretical construct to which we implicitly ascribe permanence, omitting the possibility that the distribution or "typical situation" could shift over time.

In real problems, there is no reason to expect such permanence as a general rule. Hence, part of the behavioral adjustment that agents undergo in practice must have something to do with adjusting to variations in the typical situation

---

[3] Alternatively, one may proceed as in Footnote 2, and compute the expected loss $L(\lambda)$ from using σ^λ: $L(\lambda) = c\Pr(z > \lambda) + C\Pr(z < \lambda, D)$. This expression generalizes that obtained in the binary model (interpreting the event $\{z > \lambda\}$ as the agent experiencing fear – i.e., $\{z > \lambda\} \equiv f$). The optimal strategy minimizes the loss $L(\lambda)$ at a value λ^* solving $c(\omega(\lambda^*, D) + \omega(\lambda^*, N)) = C\omega(\lambda^*, D)$, a condition equivalent to Equation (3.2).

[4] Technically, the binary signal model corresponds to a continuous-signal model in which the threshold λ is constrained to take only three values, $\lambda = 0$, $\lambda = 1$ or some given $\lambda_0 \in (0, 1)$: when $\lambda = 0$, the agent always flees; when $\lambda = 1$, the agent always stays; otherwise, he flees if and only if $z > \lambda_0$. This constraint impedes a smooth adjustment of λ.

faced. This behavioral adjustment is ignored. Models neglect the fact that behavior must be driven by attempts to track variations in the distribution ω. The analyst typically solves the model as though there were no such variations.

Said differently, behavior in models is driven by two parameters: the current observation z, which is meant to track variations in the underlying state s, and the distribution ω, which is meant to describe what a typical situation is. The model is solved as if ω were observable, as if changes in ω were tracked perfectly.

In solving models, the analyst may thus be subject to two types of bias: real behavior might be *more sensitive* to recent experience than predicted in models, with the agent actually behaving as if he were overestimating variations in the typical situation faced;[5] or, real behavior might be *less sensitive* to recent experience than predicted in models, with the agent behaving as if he were underestimating variations in the typical situation faced.

12. *Games.* So far, we have dealt with decision problems. Games are modeled analogously. With two players, $s = (s_1, s_2)$ is a state variable, for example characterizing each player's preference; and $z = (z_1, z_2)$ is a pair where z_i defines agent i's observation. The joint distribution ω over (z, s) defines a typical game situation, or typical pairwise interaction.

A strategy for player i is a function σ_i that maps observations into actions. A prediction of play is now a pair of strategies $\sigma^* = (\sigma_i^*, \sigma_j^*)$ that has the property that neither player wants to deviate unilaterally:

$$\sigma_i^* \in \arg\max_{\sigma_i} E_\omega u_i(\sigma_i(z_i), \sigma_j^*(z_j), s_i), \text{ for each } i \text{ and } j \neq i.$$

Obviously, the earlier cautions continue to apply. One can pool all past auction situations to artificially construct a typical auction situation: each player comes with a value s_i for the object, and pooling auction situations (s_1, s_2) generates a joint distribution over values. The distribution obtained through such pooling, however, doesn't necessarily carry over to future auctions.

13. In the examples we provided, the state variable s reflects the agents' preferences within the current situation, and ω defines the type of situations that the agents are facing. As for our generalized die example (which can have either six or eight faces), the notion of state can be enriched. For example, one could consider various types of situations, each characterized by a distribution ω_θ over situations (z, s), with $\theta \in \Theta$, and define a state as a pair

$$\bar{s} = (s, \theta)$$

---

[5] For example, one may take recent bad experiences (i.e., danger without fear) as variations in the typical situation one faces while these bad experiences were simply bad luck, that is, not signaling any adverse variation in the typical situation faced.

with the understanding that $u(a,\bar{s}) = u(a,s)$. One could also introduce a richer z to model the idea that agents might have imperfect perceptions of the typical situation θ.[6] This richer model can be used to capture the idea that there are variations in the type of situations that agents are facing ($\theta \in \Theta$), and that agents do not have precise knowledge of the type (θ) of situation they face.

While it is always possible to make a model more complex, what is gained in terms of realism may be illusory. Each time that we wish to qualify an assumption that seems too strong (say precise knowledge of ω), we are forced to be precise in exactly *how* we wish to depart from that assumption. Modeling the idea that agents have only a vague idea of some underlying parameter is difficult.

Eventually, the modeling exercise consists of setting aside the less relevant details (perceptions of ω for example), and focusing on what seems more relevant (z). We take as given that players behave as if they knew the distribution ω, because we think (or hope) that the assumption of this knowledge is not critical to the insights the model gives us.

> **To summarize**: In modeling partial ignorance, the analyst relies on defining a relationship between what the agent perceives (z) and what his welfare depends on (s). This is done as in the previous chapter, by defining a probability distribution (ω) over situations (z,s), as though the situation faced by the agent was generic, drawn from a given pool of situations characterized by ω.
>
> Defining ω is an essential step. A strategy may incorporate the influence of a perception (z), and the distribution ω then permits the analyst to quantify the welfare associated with each such strategy. As in the previous chapter, however, we should be cautious about behavioral predictions on two grounds: (i) they are based on a somewhat artificial theoretical construct; and (ii) they are based on the presumption that agents evaluate strategies as though they knew this artificial construct. This may be a strong assumption when many strategies are compared.

Further Comments

Choice and influence. *Strategies are often defined as mappings from obser-vations to actions. This might suggest a process by which decisions are made, where the agent makes a conscious choice based on what he observes. We prefer an interpretation in which a strategy characterizes the* influence *of "observations/perceptions/context" on behavior. This influence may be stochastic (incorporating some random unmodeled elements and suggesting some limits on control), and it can be either conscious or subconscious.*

---

[6] Formally, one could introduce an enriched observation as a pair $\bar{z} = (z, \omega_{\bar{\theta}})$ where $\omega_{\bar{\theta}}$ is meant to be a perception of the distribution from which (z,s) is drawn.

Subjective priors versus the analyst's perspective. Most game theory models start with an assumption that defines a stochastic relationship ω between "states" and "signals." We do not depart from this assumption, but our justification or interpretation of it differs from the classic justification.

Following Harsanyi, many analysts think of the distribution ω as a subjective prior (or personal probability distribution), commonly shared by agents (common priors) - who, then, optimize given ω, or act as though they did.[7]

To us, the stochastic relationship only defines the analyst's perspective. It characterizes in detail the pool of situations under consideration. The agent does not know ω, nor is he using personal conjectures about ω, for if he did, we would wish to include them in the description of what he perceives (z).[8] *The distribution ω may eventually shape his decisions, but only insofar as it shapes the evaluations of the strategies examined, and not because of some further mental processing involving ω.*

The standard perspective on knowledge. The tradition in standard models is that if an agent does not know something, one ought to define precisely what he believes about what he does not know. An agent may not know some underlying state (the number of faces of the die), but he can correctly identify everything he does not know (the die has either six or eight faces). There have been attempts to weaken this assumption by defining (precisely!) everything that he considers possible, and by allowing the true state to be outside what the agent considers possible.[9] *For example, even though the die either has six or eight faces from the analyst's perspective, the agent may think possible that the die has either six or ten faces, and be unaware that it could have eight faces.*[10]

---

[7] Harsanyi's Nobel lecture (page 142) summarizes the classic justifications: "I shall assume also that the two players will try to estimate these probabilities on the basis of their information about the nature of the relevant social forces, using only information available to both of them. In fact, they will try to estimate these probabilities as an outside observer would do, one restricted to information common to both players [...] Moreover, I shall assume that, unless he has information to the contrary, each player will act on the assumption that the other player will estimate these probabilities [...] much in the same way as he does. This is often called the common prior assumption [...] Alternatively, we may simply assume that both players will act on the assumption that both of them know the true numerical values of these probabilities so that the common priors assumption will follow as a corollary."

[8] In particular, we often avoid using the terminology "signal" to refer to z, because a signal suggests that some inferences are to be made based on some representation, say ω_0, of the process that generates z. But, we would then want to include ω_0 in the description of what the agent perceives.

[9] See Dekel, Lipman and Rustichini (1998). Also see Samuelson (2004) for a discussion of the literature on knowledge.

[10] More generally, the Bayesian methodology entails endowing agents with a precise probability distribution over what he thinks the underlying states are (i.e., a prior). Attempts to diminish the precision of the agents' thoughts about what they do not know are subject to the same objection. One may endow agents with a set of priors, rather than a single prior, but that set itself is typically precisely defined.

In contrast, our view is that (i) within an isolated situation (z,s), the perception z may conceivably be a sophisticated object (possibly akin to a probabilistic judgment), but it need not necessarily be so; (ii) the relationship (ω) between z and s is spelled out and provides the analyst's perspective regarding the set of situations that the agents face.[11] Importantly, the agent cannot access ω, and consequently he cannot treat the perception z as a signal from which inferences can be drawn, as a Bayesian or the analyst could. He is stuck with his perceptions. Since he compares alternatives and chooses those that perform better, his behavior is as if he had some knowledge of ω, but this knowledge cannot be made explicit (by him). See Chapter 5 for further discussion.

Heuristics and biases. *In response to the rational choice model, Simon (1955) proposed focusing on the process by which decisions are made. Much of the heuristics and biases literature follow this tradition.[12,13] Our approach shares with that tradition the idea that decision processes do not necessarily involve sophisticated probabilistic beliefs.*

The work on heuristics and biases sometimes emphasizes the biases that a given all-purpose heuristic generates, while also recognizing that heuristics may have good overall fitness value.[14] Our work falls in the latter tradition. We do not treat heuristics as exogenously given, and, for example, allow the agent to treat with caution whatever judgment his heuristic suggests: various strategies/heuristics (or caution levels) are compared, with the evaluation based on experienced welfare.

Heuristics, rule of thumbs and "rule rationality." *The terminology "heuristics" or "rules" is often used to describe how decisions are taken across many different situations. Formally, there is no difference between a strategy and a rule/heuristic. So, to the extent that agents can maximize performance over rules, the concept of "rule rationality" (i.e., maximization over rules) is not different from standard performance maximization across strategies. The concept becomes different when one introduces implementation costs. If a rule or strategy is more complex than another, there may exist a tradeoff between*

---

[11] This illustrates why we distinguish between an isolated situation (characterized by (z,s)) and the representative situation or set of pooled situations characterized by ω. To a subjectivist, the distribution ω is meant to be a representation of an isolated situation (possibly involving elaborate thinking about the class of situations to which the current one belongs).

[12] Tversky and Kahneman (1974) described general-purpose heuristics that people use to make intuitive judgments, and that provide various convincing sources of discrepancies between perceptions of likelihood and likelihoods.

[13] This is also true for the work on procedural rationality. Osborne and Rubinstein (1998) analyze procedures to evaluate and compare alternatives, showing how evaluations based on small samples may generate biases.

[14] See Gilovitch and Griffin (2002) for a review.

rules that are better fitted to the environment and others that are less costly to implement.[15,16]

There are formal links between what we propose and "rule rationality" in that a restriction to a given strategy set Σ can always be seen as an assumption on a cost structure: zero cost for strategies in Σ, and very large costs outside.[17] *However, we think that there are motives other than implementation costs that justify strategy restrictions, and we prefer to take Σ as a primitive, rather than try to endogenize it based on a hypothetical cost structure which may be hard to justify.*[18]

References

Aumann, R. (1997). Rationality and bounded rationality. *Games and Economic Behavior*, 21, 2–14.

Dekel, E., Lipman B. and Rustichini, A. (1998). Standard state-space models preclude unawareness. *Econometrica*, 66, 159–173.

Gilovich, T. and Griffin, D. (2002). Introduction – heuristics and biases: then and now. In T. Gilovich, D. Griffin and D. Kahneman, eds., *Heuristics and Biases: The Psychology of Intuitive Judgment*, Cambridge: Cambridge University Press, pp 1–18.

Harsanyi, J. (1997). Games with incomplete information. In T. Persson, ed., *Nobel Lectures, Economics 1991–1995*. Singapore: World Scientific Publishing Co, pp. 136–152.

Krussell, P. and Smith, A. (1996). Rules of thumb in macroeconomic equilibrium. A quantitative analysis. *Journal of Economic Dynamics and Control*, 20, 527–558.

Rosenthal, R. (1993). Rules of thumb in games. *Journal of Economic Behavior & Organization*, 22(1), 1–13.

Rubinstein, A. (1986). Finite automata play the repeated prisoner's dilemma. *Journal of Economic Theory*, 39, 83–96.

Samuelson, L. (2004). Modeling knowledge in economic analysis. *Journal of Economic Literature*, 42(2), 367–403.

Savage, L. J. (1953). *The Foundations of Statistics*. New York: Wiley.

Simon, H. (1955). A behavioral model of rational choice. *The Quarterly Journal of Economics*, 69(1), 99–118.

Sims, C. (2003). Implications of rational inattention. *Journal of Monetary Economics*, 50, 665–690.

Tversky, A. and Kahneman, D. (1974). Judgment under uncertainty: heuristics and biases. *Science*, 185(4157), 1124–1131.

---

[15] See Rubinstein (1986) for a simple application of this idea to repeated games. The strategies considered are deterministic automata, and complexity is measured by the number of states required to define the automaton. See also Aumann (1997) and Rosenthal (1993).

[16] The rational inattention literature (Sims (2003)) has close ties with "rule rationality." Each monitoring technology can be viewed as a strategic variable, to which the analyst attaches an informational cost (defined exogenously).

[17] In this spirit, Krussell and Smith (1996) examine a macroeconomic model in which the savings decision of the representative agent may either follow a rule of thumb (a constant fraction of revenues), or the fully optimal strategy, but at a larger cost.

[18] Consider for example a two-state automaton with stochastic transitions. One may think that implementation costs are small because there are only two states, or large because approximating it with a deterministic automaton requires many states.

CHAPTER 4

Strategies and Strategy Restrictions

1. We are interested in modeling agents who aim to do as well as possible, or, in other words, to behave in ways that truly serve their interests. Two remarks are in order. First, if an agent has no alternatives to compare, then there is not much to predict: theory has value only insofar as agents have alternatives to compare. Second, if an individual entertains bizarre ideas about the consequences of his actions, and if these bizarre ideas drive behavior and are never confronted with real consequences, then it is difficult to say that he truly serves his interests. And if we predict that an agent makes a bet because he thinks that the odds are always favorable to him, no matter what bet he makes, we provide an explanation of his behavior that is unlikely to be convincing.

Naturally, agents may sometimes be misled by their perceptions. They may misperceive what is in their best interest. We sometimes perceive danger that isn't there. Our modeling of observations or perceptions specifically allows for that: it makes precise the discrepancies between the underlying state (whether there is danger or not), and the agent's perception of danger (the level of fear).

Our interest however is not in pointing out discrepancies, but in explaining or predicting how an agent might cope with these discrepancies, assuming that on average, he acts in a way that (truly) serves his best interests (i.e., that enhances his actual expected welfare). In our continuous fear/danger example, the threshold above which an agent optimally flees summarizes how the agent copes with his misperceptions. When confronting danger is more costly, the threshold diminishes, making the agent more sensitive to fear. Analogously, when the brain tends to produce higher fear levels, the threshold rises to maintain the behavioral response (fleeing) at a reasonable level.

2. Economic models combine two ingredients. They simultaneously introduce misperceptions and ways to cope with them. Misperceptions are generally modeled through coarse or noisy observations (our parameter z). Coping with misperceptions is done through optimization across a number of alternative strategies – or instruments (our parameter λ), within a properly defined economic environment. *Optimization* is the tool that captures agents' concern for their welfare. The *economic environment* is what we previously called

37

the typical or representative situation that agents face, formalized as a (hypothetical) distribution ω over situations. That distribution quantifies the relationship between the agent's true interest (s) and his perception (z). In this way, the agent is confronted with the actual consequences of his actions.

3. The modeling challenge is to strike a balance between an agent's possible misperceptions and the instruments that we endow him with to cope with these misperceptions. Too few instruments may result in behavior that is mostly driven by the noisy perceptions we introduce, or by the limitations on alternatives. If one sees no other alternatives beyond staying home or jumping out of the window, one will find that staying home is best, not noticing that taking the stairs is an option. With too many instruments, behavior may be so finely tuned to the (hypothetical) typical situation faced that agents are able to undo misperceptions in unrealistic ways. We shall come back to this.

Formally, consider an agent whose preferences are characterized by a state s, and a utility function $u(a,s)$ over possible actions $a \in A$ and states $s \in S$. The best strategy for the agent consists of choosing for each state s the action that maximizes $u(a,s)$:

$$\overline{\sigma}(s) = \arg\max_{a \in A} u(a,s).$$

The strategy $\overline{\sigma}$ can be interpreted as a perfect response to the underlying state s. To model partial ignorance, we have introduced observations z and a distribution ω over situations (z,s). A strategy σ is then a function that maps observations into actions. Next we endow the agent with a set of strategies which we designate Σ. Given ω, we assume that he behaves according to the strategy σ^* that maximizes expected utility:

$$\sigma^* = \arg\max_{\sigma \in \Sigma} E_\omega u(\sigma(z),s).$$

We interpret a strategy as an *instrument*, and the set Σ as a set of instruments through which the agent parses the environment, and adjusts to it. In many applications, we will assume that the strategies are of a parameterized form:

$$\Sigma = \{\sigma^\lambda, \lambda \in \Lambda\},$$

with λ being interpreted as the choice or strategic variable.

4. Our primary objective in this chapter is to discuss the challenges and issues associated with modeling the strategy restriction Σ. Strategy restrictions are central to this book. We view strategy restrictions as a primitive in modeling ignorance. Noisy or coarse observations are, of course, a good candidate for generating restrictions, as they may prevent the agent from choosing the optimal strategy $\overline{\sigma}$ (obtained under perfect information). We shall argue that *other* classes of restrictions can be useful modeling devices as well.

5. We begin by exploring the restrictions that observations generate. To describe these restrictions, it is instructive to consider, state by state, the behavioral response that a strategy generates.

Given ω, a strategy σ defines, for each s, a behavioral response: the agent chooses $\sigma(z)$ with probability $\omega(z \mid s)$. We denote by $\rho = (\rho_s)_{s \in S}$ that behavioral response, where each ρ_s is a probability distribution over actions.[1] The strategy $\overline{\sigma}$ generates a perfect response to the underlying state. In general, a strategy σ will generate an imperfect response to the underlying state. A restriction Σ is equivalent to a restriction on the set of stochastic responses assumed to be available to the agent, say $\rho \in R$. We illustrate with several examples.

6. *Dice.* An agent is asked to bet on whether a six-sided die's face when rolled is less than or equal to 3. He wins 20 if $s \leq 3$ and loses 10 otherwise.

 (i) If the agent sees the face of the die before betting, he is not risking much. He can adjust his betting behavior to what he sees, and what he sees (the face) is all that matters to him. This corresponds to the strategy $\overline{\sigma}$.
 (ii) If he is only told whether the face is odd or even before betting, he can no longer perfectly adjust his bet to the actual face – he does not see it – but he can adjust his bet to what he is told, and, for example, decide to bet if and only if he is told that s is an odd number (the probability of winning is then $2/3$).
(iii) If told nothing, he simply decides whether to bet or not. If he bets, his chance of losing is $1/2$.

The difference between these three cases is the extent to which the agent can condition his behavior on the underlying state. At one extreme, the agent can precisely condition his behavior on the underlying state s, betting if and only if $s \leq 3$. At the other extreme, his behavior is independent of the underlying state. In between, some dependence is feasible, yet he must behave the same when $s = 1, 3$ or 5, and behave the same when $s = 2, 4, 6$.

Formally, in the latter case, what the agent observes (and does not observe) puts constraints on the set of feasible behavioral responses. This set is:

$$R = \{\rho, \rho_2 = \rho_4 = \rho_6 \text{ and } \rho_1 = \rho_3 = \rho_5\}.$$

7. Consider the danger/fear example discussed in the previous chapter. Ideally, the agent would like to flee if and only if there is imminent danger. But, what he "sees" is whether he experiences fear. He may flee when, and only when, he experiences fear, but there will be occasions when he flees even though there is no danger, and occasions when he stays even though there

---

[1] The probability distribution ρ_s specifies for each a the probability $\rho_s(a)$ of taking action a. For a given σ, $\sigma(a, z)$ is the probability that a is taken when z is observed, thus we have: $\rho_s(a) \equiv \sum_z \omega(z, s) \sigma(a, z)$.

is danger. Specifically, recall the data concerning the typical situation that he faces, summarized by the distribution ω:

$z\backslash s$	D	N
f	0.1	0.06
n	0.01	0.83

The strategy in which he flees when he fears danger generates a stochastic response, characterized by the probability ρ_s that he flees under s. If there is danger $(s = D)$, he flees with probability:

$$\rho_D = \omega(f \mid D) = \frac{\omega(f,D)}{\omega(n,D) + \omega(f,D)} = \frac{0.10}{0.11} = 90.9\%.$$

If there is no danger $(s = N)$, he flees with probability:

$$\rho_N = \omega(f \mid N) = \frac{\omega(f,N)}{\omega(f,N) + \omega(n,N)} = \frac{0.06}{0.89} = 6.7\%.$$

Thus, his response is not perfectly attuned to the underlying state. This is precisely what our modeling of observations was meant to produce: a noisy response to the underlying state.

The generalized fear/danger example can be understood in the same way. Each threshold strategy σ^λ in which the agent flees when the fear level z is above λ generates a stochastic response ρ^λ. Optimizing across all threshold strategies is equivalent to optimizing across a restricted family of stochastic responses, all bounded away from the perfect response $\overline{\rho} = (\overline{\rho}_D, \overline{\rho}_N) = (1,0)$.

8. *A simple investment problem.* Consider an agent choosing an investment level x. Assume the cost of investment is $c(x) = x^2/2$, and the revenue from investment is proportional to x, equal to sx. The profit G from investment is thus:

$$G(x,s) = sx - x^2/2.$$

To an agent who knows s, the optimal choice of investment coincides with s. So, if S is the set of possible values for s, the optimal investment function, which we denote $\overline{y}$, is:

$$\overline{y}(s) = s \text{ for all } s \in S.$$

To an agent who does not know s, however, the strategy $\overline{y}$ is not feasible: the agent cannot perfectly tailor actions to circumstances; he can condition behavior on whatever observation available, but s is not observed.

Assume now that the agent misperceives the return. For any s, his perception of s is a noisy estimate z:

$$z = \eta s$$

where $\eta > 0$ and s are random variables. To fix ideas, assume that $\log \eta$ is normally distributed with mean 0 and variance μ^2, and that s is uniformly distributed on $[0,1]$. This defines a joint distribution ω over situations (z,s). We denote by $\phi(z)$ the conditional expectation $\phi(z) \equiv E_\omega[s \mid z]$.

A strategy is a function that maps each possible z to an investment level $y(z)$. Among these functions, the optimal function is just the conditional expectation:[2]

$$y^*(z) = \phi(z).$$

The following graph plots the optimal investment function for $\mu = 0.2$.

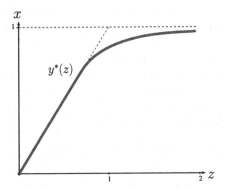

The distribution ω has the property that s is below 1 with certainty and the graph illustrates how the agent takes that "knowledge" into account. Any perception z much above 1 is properly discounted.

This effect can also be illustrated by considering stochastic response functions. For any strategy y, the stochastic response can be characterized by the probability $Q_s^y(x)$ that he invests less than x when the state is s. Below, we plot the optimal response function $Q_s^{y^*}(x)$ for two values of s, 0.5 and 1 (for $\mu = 0.2$ and for $\mu = 0$ – dotted function).

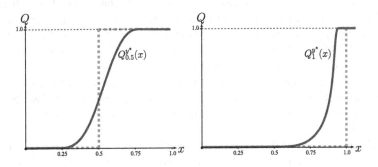

---

[2] This is because for any given z, the expected profit from investing x is $x\phi(z) - x^2/2$, so the optimal investment is $\phi(z)$.

When there is no noise ($\mu = 0$), the optimal response function is a step function (the agent invests exactly s when the state is s). With noise, response functions are stochastic: they deviate from the step function. The second graph also illustrates how the agent exploits the structure of the model: he never chooses an investment above 1, hence always underinvests when $s = 1$.

9. *Noisy observations preclude perfect responses. Yet what one observes is not all that matters. We must also define how observations are used, or what agents can make of them: limitations in processing or exploiting observations may also preclude perfect responses.* We describe several examples below.

a. An agent may be told that the rolled die was an even number. If the agent does not perceive that this information could be relevant to his potential gain from betting, then we could have assumed that he was told nothing in the first place.

In the fear/danger example, the fear level may be a continuous variable z. The agent, however, may not be able to finely condition his behavior on that fear level. If the fear level only triggers a behavioral response once it reaches a predetermined level λ_0, then, as far as the agent's behavior is concerned, his perception can be summarized by a binary signal, either $z > \lambda_0$, or $z < \lambda_0$.

In each of the above examples, observations and the limitations on the ability to use these observations jointly constrain the agent's behavioral response. In both cases, the limitation is amenable to modeling where observations are made coarser. We describe below an example in which limitations (on how observations can be used) are *not* equivalent to a coarsening of the observations.

b. Consider a more elaborate version of the fear/danger example with three underlying states (No danger, Danger, Huge danger), each ideally calling for a different behavioral response (stay, be attentive, flee). Assume that the behavioral response depends mechanically on the agent's state of mind (secure, stressed, alarmed), and that the link between the fear level z (e.g., directly generated by darkness and noise recognition) and the state of mind is mediated by some chemical present in the brain: the level λ of this chemical affects susceptibility to fear, and z and λ jointly produce a psychological response that depends on the product $y = \lambda z$. If $y < y_0$, the agent feels secure. If $y \in (y_0, y_1)$ he feels stressed. If $y > y_1$, he feels alarmed.

The agent is assumed to have no control over z, y_0 and y_1, but he has control over the level λ of the chemical. By increasing λ, he becomes more susceptible to the fear level z, and this increases the chance that he becomes attentive or that he flees.

The main point of this example is that the agent cannot selectively act on stress or on alarm. He has some control over these two psychological states, but they cannot be controlled independently. This example is not equivalent to one in which we would just appropriately modify the signals received and allow full control over actions given that signal.[3]

c. Some firms specialize in predicting the likelihood that an internet user clicks on an advertisement and subsequently purchases the product advertised. These two predictions (click and buy) are based on the user's recent and less recent internet activity. The set of possible activity profiles, even restricted to the last ten minutes, is huge, and there is an extraordinarily large number of ways to code that activity, and compile it to give these two predictions. Needless to say, which of these possible algorithms makes the *best* prediction (given the gains that the firm derives from clicks and from buys) is an impossible task.

Changes in algorithms are tested regularly. Of course, only a tiny fraction can ever be tested. In any case, whether a change is beneficial is difficult to evaluate, as gains could be a consequence of a temporary change in the typical situation faced.[4]

d. Consider another example: bidding in a first-price auction.[5] Each agent knows his value for the object for sale. This value is taken to be what he observes, say v. The question is how he should translate that value into a bid, b. In principle, any bid function

$$b = \sigma(v)$$

could qualify as a potential strategy. As in previous examples, the task of comparing all possible ways to deal with one's observations seems impossible. Figuring out what is a good shading factor is less ambitious but a more reasonable task. He would then consider a restricted number of strategies each characterized by a shading factor λ:

$$\sigma^\lambda(v) = \lambda v.$$

Although the agent might benefit from enlarging the set of strategies he compares, the analyst may want to restrict the analysis to the smaller set of strategies, because that restriction captures some cognitive limitation that agents face in identifying a strategy that performs well.

---

[3] To see why, assume that the agent always faces Danger. Whatever signal z the agent gets, the result should be the stressed state (and the "being attentive" response). When the distribution over z has a sufficiently large support, then for any λ, there is always a chance that he either erroneously remains secure (for low realizations of z) and or be erroneously alarmed (for high realizations of z). He may wish to choose a level λ to increase the chance of being attentive, but that will also increase the chance of being alarmed.

[4] A change in the parameter of an algorithm plays the same role as the change in the chemical level λ in previous example: it modifies predictions simultaneously across all ads.

[5] In a first-price auction, each agent bids, and the highest bidder wins and pays his bid.

10. Previous arguments appealed to realism to justify restrictions. Agents may not fully exploit their observations because they may not have full control over the choice of action. Alternatively it may be impossible to compare all possible ways to exploit observations. We want to emphasize a more philosophical justification. If agents were to fully exploit their observations, they could end up exploiting finely the structure of a model that was only meant to be a hypothetical/artificial description of their environment. There is then a risk that one falls prey to the von Neumann critique:[6]

"There is no sense in being precise when you don't even know what you are talking about."

The investment problem provides an illustration of that, with the investor finely exploiting the modeler's distributional assumptions. The investor probably has a vague idea that his estimate of revenues is subject to errors. Nevertheless, the prediction portrays a decision optimally tuned to the characteristics of his imperfect perception and the underlying state. The prediction is a function that is hard to describe in words, driven by *a priori* assumptions on the support of S, and vulnerable to the above critique. In addition, it predicts that the expected investment level remains the same regardless of the quality of the observations that one makes (e.g., regardless of the variance of the estimation error) – a prediction that one might want to question.

11. In the investment model, the agent behaves as though he knew all conditional expectations $\phi(z)$. This is cognitively demanding and can be weakened. There are two standard ways to do this. One consists of reducing the set of actions available, as in Chapter 1, and a second consists of reducing the number of signals. We first present these two restrictions and, after that, we introduce a less standard restriction that directly limits the set of investment functions $y(z)$ that the investor considers.

Case 1: Coarse action space. Assume that the agent has the choice between investing x_0 and not investing at all. Coarsening the action space amounts to restricting the set of strategies to a subset Y_1 of the set of functions compared by the agent:

$$Y_1 = \{y \in Y, y(z) \in \{0, x_0\}\}.$$

When ϕ is increasing, the optimal strategy is a threshold strategy, with investment taking place if and only if z is sufficiently large, that is, above some threshold $\underline{z}$.[7] We represent below this restriction by plotting several possible threshold strategies, setting $x_0 = 1$.

---

[6] This is a quote attributed to von Neumann.

[7] Not investing yields 0. Investing x_0 yields $\phi(z)x_0 - (x_0)^2/2$, hence investing is a better strategy whenever $\phi(z) > x_0/2$, that is, whenever $z > \phi^{-1}[x_0/2]$. So the optimal threshold is $\underline{z}^* = \phi^{-1}[x_0/2]$.

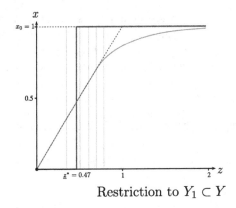

Restriction to $Y_1 \subset Y$

In our numerical example, the optimal threshold is $\underline{z}^* = 0.47$ and the optimal strategy is plotted in thick lines.

Case 2: Coarse signal space. Assume that the agent only perceives whether the signal is high or low (e.g., above or below z_0). This implies a restriction to a subset Y_2 of the set of functions, as the agent is constrained to choosing the same investment (e.g., x_L) for all signals $z \leq z_0$ and the same investment (e.g., x_H) for all signals $z > z_0$.

Graphically, we show below what the restriction implies, by plotting various possible strategies, setting $z_0 = 0.5$. We draw with thick lines the optimal strategy.

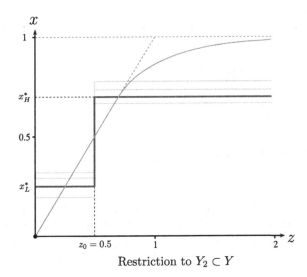

Restriction to $Y_2 \subset Y$

Case 3: Coarse mappings. A less common assumption consists of imposing direct restrictions on the investment functions considered. Define a (cautious) strategy y^λ as a proportional investment strategy that invests a fraction λ of z, and assume that the agent optimizes only among these cautious strategies:

$$Y_3 = \{y^\lambda, \lambda > 0\}.$$

Graphically, we represent below several of these cautious strategies.

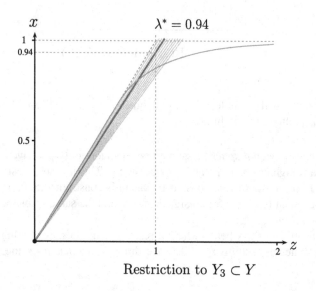

Restriction to $Y_3 \subset Y$

The thick line represents the optimal cautious strategy in our numerical example. The payoff associated with a cautious strategy y^λ is $\lambda Esz - Ez^2\lambda^2/2$, so the optimal shading level λ^* is

$$\lambda^* = \frac{Esz}{Ez^2} = \frac{Ez\phi(z)}{Ez^2}.$$

In the context of our illustration, one obtains:[8]

$$\lambda^* = E\eta/E\eta^2 \text{ and } Ey^{\lambda^*} = Es\frac{(E\eta)^2}{E\eta^2}.$$

12. *Discussion.*
a. Case 3 is generally thought to be an illegitimate restriction: the behavior generated cannot result from direct restrictions on the action space (the density over investments is everywhere positive), nor can it result from imperfect observability. To see this, observe that case 3 leads to noisy behavior

---

[8] For $\mu = 0.2$, the optimal shading factor is $\lambda^* = 0.94$.

even if there is no randomness in s (and just randomness in perception z); while in traditional models, there cannot be randomness in behavior without randomness in s.

b. For any given marginal distribution over s, imperfect observability implies that expected investment coincides with the expected value Es:

$$Ey_\omega^* = E_\omega \phi(z) = E_z E[s \mid z] = Es. \tag{4.1}$$

In contrast, our illustration shows that the agent becomes more cautious in expectation (because $(E\eta)^2 < E\eta^2$) when μ is positive.

c. Viewed as a restriction on the set of admissible investment functions, the restriction to linear functions does not seem less legitimate than the previous restrictions. All three cases amount to a weakening of the cognitive assumption made in the first model, in the sense that the agent no longer behaves as though he knew all conditional expectations $\phi(z)$. In case 1, he need only know the threshold $\underline{z}^*$ above which investing x^0 yields positive profits. In case 2, he behaves as if he knew $x_L^* \equiv E[\phi(z) \mid z < z_0]$ and $x_H^* \equiv E[\phi(z) \mid z > z_0]$. In case 3, he behaves as if he knew $\lambda^* = Ez\phi(z)/Ez^2$.

If one views agents as learning from experience, without prior knowledge of the model, case 3 is not more demanding than other models. It only requires learning one parameter, the optimal shading factor λ^*. In comparison, case 2 requires learning two parameters, x_L^* and x_H^*.

We note that the first two cases create discontinuities at arbitrary points, while the linear restriction maintains smoothness.

d. We noted earlier that each y generates for each s a noisy investment function that can be characterized by the function Q_s^y, where $Q_s^y(x)$ is the probability that the agent chooses an investment level below x when the state is s. The following graph plots the functions $Q_s^{y^\lambda}(x)$ for various values of λ and $s = 0.5$.

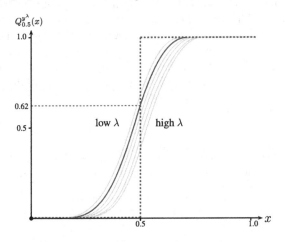

As in the basic model, each y^λ embodies some noise/mistakes in the choice of investment. A key difference is that the agent has a single instrument (λ) to correct for his mistakes: the agent may shift the distribution over investment, but cannot affect the general shape of his mistakes.

In contrast, in the basic model, an agent can easily adjust the shape of his mistakes to characteristics of the underlying distribution ω. In particular, if s is nonrandom, the agent will learn to ignore his signals, and choose the correct investment level s.

e. Case 3 can be interpreted as a model in which the agent is subject to exogenous trembles, akin to the trembles that have been proposed as a selection device to assess the robustness of equilibria to small behavioral perturbations (Selten 1975).[9]

To see this, assume s is nonrandom, and consider the following alternative model: whenever the agent targets investment x, he implements a noisy choice ηx; his objective is to find the optimal target x^*, taking into account the noise in his decision process.

His gain from targeting x is:

$$sxE\eta - E\eta^2 x^2/2.$$

Solving for the optimal target yields:

$$x^* = \frac{E\eta}{E\eta^2}s = \lambda^*s.$$

Determining the optimal target x^* in this model is thus formally equivalent to finding the optimal shading factor λ^* in the previous model. In other words, the noise term η can be viewed as a behavioral perturbation that *directly* limits the agent's ability to tailor his behavior to the underlying state (s), without needing to introduce noise in the underlying state.

f. Case 3 analyzes a particular restriction, linear functions of z. Alternative restrictions could be motivated as follows. In addition to his point estimate z, the agent comes with a precise but misspecified model (ω_0) of the underlying distribution over states and signals. Assume that he first uses this enriched perception (z, ω_0) to compute a subjective expectation $\phi_{\omega_0}(z) \equiv E_{\omega_0}[s \mid z]$. Then, being aware that his view may be incorrect, he attempts to treat it with caution by comparing (by experience) investment strategies of the form:[10,11]

$$y^\lambda(z, \omega_0) \equiv \lambda\phi_{\omega_0}(z).$$

[9] One difference is that we do not restrict attention to small trembles.
[10] In standard models, ω_0 would be considered a prior, and be the exclusive determinant of behavior. Here, the prior shapes the family of responses, without being the exclusive determinant of behavior.
[11] We may either assume that ω_0 does not change across situations, or assume that it varies, in which case we would redefine a situation as a triple (z, ω_0, s) and ω as a distribution over these situations.

More generally, an agent's perception may involve broad considerations of the type of situations to which the current one belongs. Whether these considerations take the form of a precise prior or not, our view is that they shape the family of responses that the agent considers, or at least justify the ones that we, as analysts, endow the agents with.

g. A possible complaint is that little guidance is offered regarding which direct restrictions are plausible. Our view is that knowing ω (or being able to fully exploit ω) is a strong assumption, and that there are many ways to weaken it. The plethora of possible restrictions is simply a reflection of the strength of the usual assumption, and of the numerous ways that a strong assumption can be weakened.

h. One prediction of the basic model (with unconstrained action space) is that the expected investment level coincides with Es, regardless of the assumption one makes about the quality or coarseness of the observations made (see Equation (4.1)).[12] This may appear to be a questionable conclusion which hinges on the agent finely exploiting the distribution ω. If one views ω as a modeler's descriptive tool to capture ignorance of the underlying state, one may find it desirable to limit the degree to which agents can exploit the model itself. Case 3 achieves this goal, and illustrates how one may arrive at a qualitatively different conclusion with investment being reduced when estimates are noisier.

We do not claim that direct strategy restrictions will necessarily lead to underinvestment. Through the choice of the noise structure and the strategy restrictions, one incorporates the underlying basis of mistakes, while simultaneously endowing agents with *some* ability to adjust to these mistakes through optimization. Whether this joint assumption leads to overinvestment or underinvestment depends on the nature of the restrictions.

i. There is a general concern that conclusions sometimes hinge too finely on agents knowing fine details of the model. Responses to this concern have been proposed in the literature, and we discuss them at length in the Miscellanea. Briefly, one response is to enrich the model, assuming multiple priors and a different objective function (maxmin or robust decision making). A second response is the traditional Bayesian route: if one objects to the agent knowing the model, one ought to put a probability distribution over the possible models that he might face, and describe the signal that he gets about which of these models applies. The path proposed provides a more parsimonious route.

To summarize: (a) It is not enough to describe what the agent observes or perceives to define the extent of ignorance. We also need to describe

---

[12] That is, whatever assumption one makes on Z and the conditional probability distributions $\{\omega(. \mid s)\}_s$.

how the agent can use the signals he gets. (b) Strategies are instruments to parse the environment. They allow the agent to adjust (to some extent) to both the current state and the typical situation faced. (c) Eventually, the objective is a balanced model in which agents have imperfect perceptions or cognitive constraints, and are also given some instruments/tools to overcome these imperfect perceptions. (d) We often model imperfect perceptions by introducing noise. However, as modelers, we cannot avoid being precise about the structure of the noise that we introduce. This is a constraint on modeling, but an undesirable constraint. It would be preferable to model vagueness directly. (e) If we are not careful about the set of instruments that we endow the agents with, agents' optimal behavior may depend unrealistically on this unavoidable precision. The role of strategy restrictions is to mitigate our inability to model vagueness directly. (f) Strategy restrictions may reflect the preconceptions that agents entertain about the environment, and the strategic variables are meant to reflect the agent's awareness that his preconceptions may not be correct, allowing him to take them with caution.

Further Comments

Exploration in a rich strategy space. *Many economic problems are cast as static problems that abstract from learning issues and the possibility that the environment might change over time. One can view Herbert Simon's 1955 seminal paper as a critique of the classic methodology: the process by which agents arrive at a strategy may be critical to understanding behavior. The institutions that survive are those equipped with heuristics that enable adjustment to a varying environment.*

A key feature of the adjustment mechanism that Herbert Simon considered is that not all strategies are simultaneously considered. Rather, attention is restricted to the subset of strategies explored, with the idea, for example, that the more slowly aspirations decline after bad experiences, the larger the set of strategies explored can become. Still, independent of the strength of experimentation, when the set of alternatives is arbitrarily rich, the search for new alternatives must be guided, plausibly by intuition. If one continues to try new but implausible and poorly performing strategies, one will soon realize that it is profitable to quickly adjust aspirations down to avoid these unnecessary trials. Simon does not elaborate on the determination of the basin over which search occurs. One may interpret our strategy restriction as a restriction on search, focused on intuitively plausible strategies.

Dealing with dynamics. *Note that while we always assume permanence of ω, the economic environment that it describes may embody variations, possibly with some partial persistence (as the "dynamic situations" examined* *in Chapter 12 to 14 will illustrate), and the questions raised by Simon (1955) could be formally addressed within the framework that we describe. For example, one could define a class of dynamic strategies that only differ from one another through the speed with which aspirations decline after bad experiences, and assess the "optimal" speed of decline given ω.[13] Of course, the conclusion would again rely on the permanence of this more sophisticated object ω, but it may provide intuition about the forces that affect the dynamics of aspiration levels.*

Finding the best strategies. Procedural rationality. Our work maintains the classic assumption that strategies are compared according to the "correct" criterion, and that the best strategy among those considered is selected. Yet, even if the environment does not change, finding better strategies may be difficult, not only because of the richness of the strategy space, but also because evaluations and comparisons of strategies must eventually depend on experience; and the procedures by which these experiences are stored, gathered, processed and used may lead to biased decisions, with no guarantee that in the end agents play a Nash equilibrium. In that respect we depart from the procedural rationality literature (Osborne and Rubinstein (1998)) that analyzes these biases. To be more precise, models in that literature may be viewed as learning models in which each agent uses an a priori determined procedure to adapt his behavior, and in which the analyst examines the rest point of that process in the long run.[14] This is in the spirit of the path set out by Simon (1955), but while Simon suggested that better heuristics would survive, this literature mostly considers exogenous procedures, without allowing the possibility of marginal adjustments (that would improve performance) as past experiences are processed, even if these exogenous procedures happen to perform very poorly within the class of problems to which they are applied. Agents use misspecified models and act as if they were not aware of the misspecification, even if this results in poor performance.

What restrictions? Any modeling enterprise comes with restrictions, and defining z and ω constitutes restrictions. We add direct strategy restrictions Σ as a way of limiting the degree to which agents exploit ω, which we take to

---

[13] Simon (1955, Footnote 7) alludes to a grand model of this sort in which heuristics would be compared and possibly selected on the basis of their overall performance.

[14] Formally, let Σ_i be the set of strategies available to i, and let $q_{-i} \in \Delta(\Sigma_{-i})$ describe the random behavior of players other than i. A procedure λ_i generates for each q_{-i} a random selection $Q_{i,\lambda_i}^{q-i} \in \Delta(\Sigma_i)$, whereby σ_i is selected with probability $Q_{i,\lambda_i}^{q-i}(\sigma_i)$. In the long run, a rest point of this process is a distribution q for which $q_i = Q_{i,\lambda_i}^{q-i}$ for all i. In many bounded rationality models, the choice procedure λ_i is set exogenously, or there are fixed rules that determine how past observations translate into choices. In contrast, our approach endogenizes λ_i, and allows for adjustments (within a given range) in this procedure λ_i that might improve the selection of σ_i given q_{-i} and λ_{-i}.

be unknown by the agent. Whether these restrictions concern z, ω or Σ, the challenge is in figuring which ones are more reasonable.

One may view the psychophysics literature[15] and recent advances in neuroeconomics as motivating a particular form of noise (i.e., an assumption on ω), or as establishing behavioral regularities that suggest a strategy restriction Σ that one might want to incorporate in a theoretical model. For example, Khaw et al. (2017) examine agents facing many simple lotteries, each involving a participation cost c and gains equal to either x or 0. They propose a model that uses results from psychophysics to motivate a particular noise structure to represent perceptions of x and c. In addition, their experimental data establishes a behavioral regularity ("scale invariance") : agents behave as if they perceived a noisy estimate of the ratio x/c, independently of the magnitudes of c and x. One might want to represent this scale invariance regularity as a restriction on strategies, and explore the consequences of that assumption in other contexts. The psychophysics literature also suggests that while agents may have some awareness of the magnitude of their errors in some dimensions, they may have difficulties appreciating that magnitude in other dimensions (Zhang et al. (2013)), or at least correcting for errors in these dimensions.[16]

While grounding restrictions in experimental work is clearly desirable, we also find useful the theoretical exercise of identifying plausible restrictions that yield results that accord with intuition. First, this may help structure experiments and/or empirical work.[17] Second, not all restrictions yield interesting insights, and some restrictions may yield insights that conflict with intuitions. In addition, at times, one may find that given the restrictions, there is no equilibrium in which players choose one of the admissible strategies. We do not view this lack of existence of an equilibrium as problematic. It often suggests a need to alter the model, either by modifying the strategy restriction, or by enriching the environment.

Restrictions and overfitting. *As economists, one of our objectives is to find a model of the environment that generates reliable predictions of variables that we care about (s), based on exogenous variables (z). In this endeavor, we find it helpful to use intuition to structure the data that we get (simplifying z), to directly limit the set of possible explanatory models that are considered, to penalize those that would be too complex, or to put restrictions on the set of admissible prediction functions.[18] In other words, while we are interested in the quality of the prediction $a(z, \lambda_m)$ that model λ_m provides, as measured by*

---

[15] See Glimcher (2011, pp 81-93) for a historical account of the psychophysics literature.
[16] One consequence of not restricting the strategy set is that agents are modeled as though they could always perfectly assess the quality of their perceptions (see Chapter 10). See also Chapter 19 where the shape the perception errors assumed plays a central role.
[17] By identifying restrictions that lead to intuitively plausible behavior, we give empirical economists tools with which they can organize data about actual choices.
[18] Tibshirani (1996)), for example, considers a subset of linear prediction functions of z for which the sum of all absolute weights put on each dimension of z is bounded by some given scalar.

some loss function $L(a, s)$, we have learned to restrict our search to a subclass of models $\lambda_m \in M$, or to consider a modified loss function that is meant to incorporate the fact that, although λ_m may work well on past data $\{(z_t, s_t)_t\}$, it may perform poorly on subsequent data.

The agents that we have been describing are in a position similar to that of economists. They have a different loss function, but they too face the risk of finding a strategy that works well on a particular subset of experiences (past experiences) and not well on new ones.

References

Glimcher, P. (2011). *Foundations of Neuroeconomic Analysis*, New York: Oxford University Press.

Khaw, M. W., Ziang, L. and Woodford, M. (2017). Risk aversion as a perceptual bias, CESifo working paper, University of Munich.

Tibshirani, R. (2011). Regression shrinkage and selection via the lasso: a retrospective. *Journal of the Royal Statistical Society*, Series B (Statistical Methodology), 73(3), 273–282.

Selten, R. (1975). A reexamination of the perfectness concept for equilibrium points in extensive games. *International Journal of Game Theory*, 4(1), 25–55.

Simon, H. (1955). A behavioral model of rational choice. *The Quarterly Journal of Economics*, 69(1), 99–118.

Zhang H., Daw, N. D. and Maloney, L. T. (2013). Testing whether humans have an accurate model of their own motor uncertainty in a Speeded Reaching Task. *PLoS Computational Biology*, 9(5), e1003080.

CHAPTER 5

Knowledge and Beliefs

1. We analyze agents who behave to maximize their self-interest. Of course, agents may not know what is in their best interest. One obstacle is that some relevant information may not be available to the agent. In the die example, betting would be easy if the winning face was observed. Similarly, in a first-price auction, bidding would be simple if one had access to others' bids.

A second obstacle is that an agent may misperceive his interests. In the danger/fear example, fear is a signal associated with danger. Sometimes the perception is correct, sometimes not. In the investment problem, the observation $z = \eta s$ may be interpreted as a perception of the return s. The degree to which the perception is correct depends on η.

The agent's pursuit of optimal outcomes must then be less ambitious: it cannot be exactly achieved in every instance. One hopes, however, that "on average," the agent behaves in a way that is consistent with this goal.

In Chapter 2, we gave content to what we mean by "on average." If an agent cannot hope for an optimal outcome in every situation, he may accomplish this in expectation over "typical situations" that he faces or experiences. *As analysts*, we represent these typical situations by a probability distribution over states.

There are two assumptions here. The first is that, as discussed in Chapters 2 and 3, the distribution itself is an artificial theoretical construct. The second assumption is that agents behave as if they knew that distribution. We emphasize "as if." What can be said about agents' *actual* knowledge?

2. Our basic assumption is that by comparing strategies, the agent settles on the strategy that performs best across the situations he faces. So, although the agent's behavior is the same as if he had known the model, he does not need to know the model, but only manage to evaluate the strategies available and adopt the best among those available.

Formally, consider a decision problem characterized by a set of states S, a probability distribution π over these states, and a set of possible actions A. The prediction is obtained by computing

$$a^* = \arg\max_a E_\pi u(a,s).$$

The prediction is computed *as if* the agent knew π. In standard models, π is taken to be the agent's belief over the underlying state, often meant to capture the uncertainty in the *agent's mind* over these states. In our model, π is simply a mathematical object that hopefully represents well the typical situation faced by the agent, and this allows us to calculate the performance of each strategy, hence identify the best performing among those available.[1]

Indeed, an agent need not even have in mind that there is a set of underlying states S, and, even less so, a probability distribution π over the underlying state. He may not even understand probabilities. The prediction may be correct simply because the agent has observed that on average one option is better than the others. The distribution π helps us *as analysts* to make precise these comparisons.

Knowledge of the optimal strategy stems from the ability to compare alternatives. Agents need to be able to do this much and not more.

3. *A more complex die problem.* Consider 74 throws of a six-sided die with the numbers one through six written on the faces. Define s as the sum of the throws. We consider bets in which the agent wins when the sum s exceeds 140 and loses otherwise. Call P the winning probability ($P = \Pr(s > 140)$), and ρ the ratio $P/(1-P)$.

The agent may decline to bet. Suppose that if he bets, he gets \$50 in the event that s exceeds 140, otherwise he loses \$10. When he bets, in expectation he gets $Pu(50) + (1-P)u(-10)$, and when he does not, he gets $u(0)$. So, betting is preferable when:[2]

$$\frac{u(0) - u(-10)}{u(50) - u(0)} > \rho.$$

In most cases, this comparison does not hinge on a precise assessment of ρ.

Let us now modify the choice problem. Assume that the agent has the option to increase or decrease the stakes of the bet by any factor α, possibly down to 0 (in which case he does not bet). The expected gain associated with α is:

$$Pu(\alpha 50) + (1-P)u(-\alpha 10)$$

and the optimal choice is a stake α^* that solves:

$$\frac{u'(-10\alpha^*)}{5u'(50\alpha^*)} = \rho. \tag{$*$}$$

---

[1] Our interpretation of π is consistent with the way applied or econometric work is done. There, the analyst uses real data to estimate or approximate the typical situation faced by agents.

[2] u is a concave, differentiable utility function.

Solving for the optimal α^* amounts to assuming that the agent behaves as if he knew with precision the probability P or equivalently, the ratio ρ.

4. The previous example illustrates that allowing the agent to choose optimally among many stake levels α is tantamount to endowing that agent with a precise idea of P. Although P is a well-defined scalar, one feels that the agent's betting decision (α) would be easier if he was provided with the actual value of P. We can solve the model as if P was known, but the fact that the agent might not know P with precision seems relevant to his decision.

5. *Perceptions and as-if beliefs.* In Chapter 3, we considered problems in which agents receive signals that guide their choices. We modeled these problems by assuming a set of states S, a set of perceptions Z, and a probability distribution ω over these situations (z, s).

With no constraints imposed on strategies beyond the fact that they are mappings from observations to actions, one can treat the optimization over strategies as a family of independent optimization problems, one for each observation z. Given perception z, the conditional distribution over states $\omega(\cdot \mid z)$ describes the uncertainty that the agent faces. His optimal choice is characterized for each z by:

$$\sigma^*(z) = \arg\max_a E_{\omega(\cdot|z)} u(a, s).$$

The solutions to these problems thus coincide with the ones which we would obtain if the agent knew each posterior probability distribution $\omega(\cdot \mid z)$. In standard models, a posterior $\omega(\cdot \mid z)$ is called a posterior belief, or Bayesian belief. As for the distribution π, the terminology "belief" suggests a perception in the agent's mind, while the posterior is just a convenient tool which enables the analyst to represent the agent's decision problem and calculate the performance of each alternative available. For clarity, we shall refer to these posteriors as *as-if beliefs*.

6. Agents need not necessarily know ω, nor the posteriors $\omega(\cdot \mid z)$; they need only determine what alternative is best. Of course, when the set of observations Z and the set of actions A both lie in very rich spaces, and when all functions from Z to A are compared, this implicitly assumes a great deal of knowledge. Not surprisingly, when agents are endowed with that many degrees of freedom in comparing strategies, (i.e., assumed to have sufficient ability to exploit the distribution ω), behavior becomes finely tailored to that distribution. In the investment problem where all investment functions are compared, agents act in the same way as when they know with precision each conditional expectation $E[s \mid z]$.

The analyst may wish to model agents as not needing to know ω, but the optimization that compares all strategies leads to behavior that is the same as if the agent did know a great deal about ω.

7. *Complex die problem continued.* Optimization across all stake levels leads us to portray agents who act as if they knew P with precision. Another way to see the strength of optimization is to introduce misperceptions in this problem. Assume that the agent gets noisy perceptions of ρ, say $\widehat{\rho}$ such that

$$\widehat{\rho} = \mu\rho$$

for some positive random variable μ. Casting this problem in our usual notation, ρ is the state that the agent cares about ($s \equiv \rho$), and $\widehat{\rho}$ is an observation ($z \equiv \widehat{\rho}$). A strategy is then a function that maps each $\widehat{\rho}$ into an investment $\alpha(\widehat{\rho})$. If there are no direct constraints imposed on strategies, the optimal strategy is:

$$\alpha^*(\widehat{\rho}) = \alpha^* \text{ for each } \widehat{\rho}.$$

Misperceptions have no effect because ρ is a well-defined object and there is no randomness in ρ. Even if our motivation for introducing misperceptions is to model an agent somewhat ignorant about ρ, optimization across all strategies has the same effect as informing him of ρ: at the optimum, he acts as if he had known ρ.

We introduce misperceptions to understand how they affect behavior, but the standard modeling strategy may endow the agent with the tools to perfectly correct these misperceptions.

8. A consequence of direct strategy restriction is that optimization may no longer perfectly correct misperceptions. We illustrate this below.

The equation ($*$) defines a best response to ρ. Denote it $\overline{\alpha}(\rho)$. Next consider the following family of strategies indexed by $\lambda \in [0, 1]$

$$\alpha^\lambda = \overline{\alpha}(\lambda\widehat{\rho}).$$

When $\lambda = 1$, the agent takes his perception at face value. When $\lambda \neq 1$, this is as though he applied a constant factor λ to his perception. If we endow the agent with the ability to optimize across possible values of λ, we effectively endow him with some ability to maximize welfare, but not fully. He is aware that his perception may be incorrect, but this is insufficient to fully undo the discrepancies between his perception and the actual value of ρ.

To see that this is likely to generate cautious behavior in general, observe that in events where he underestimates the probability of winning to the point where he does not invest, applying caution has no detrimental effect (he is not investing anyway). However, in events where he overestimates, caution is good.

9. *Belief-perceptions and as-if beliefs.* The analyst has a great deal of freedom in defining the nature of the agent's perceptions. In the previous example, the probability $\widehat{\rho}$ can be viewed as a *belief-perception* about the chance of winning, taking the form of a point estimate. But, this belief-perception could be a

more sophisticated object (e.g., a probability distribution β over the chances of winning, or more generally, a probability distribution over the underlying state s). We do not argue that it would be desirable to do so; we only illustrate the distinction that we make between belief-perceptions and as-if beliefs.

Whatever assumption one makes about the nature of the agent's belief-perception β and about the mental representations or inferential processes that generate them, our approach requires that one defines the joint distribution ω over pairs (β, s). A strategy, then, maps belief-perceptions into actions, and to predict the behavior of an agent facing no direct strategy constraints, we would solve:

$$\sigma^* = \arg\max_{\sigma} E_\omega u(\sigma(\beta), s),$$

or equivalently, we would solve for each belief-perception β:

$$\sigma^*(\beta) = \arg\max_{a} E_{\omega(\cdot|\beta)} u(a, s).$$

In this model, the agent has a belief-perception β, but he does not take it at face value. Rather than maximizing the naive expectation

$$u^{naive}(a, \beta) = E_\beta u(a, s),$$

he behaves as if he knew the process that generates beliefs. He behaves as if his belief was $\omega(\cdot \mid \beta)$. This is precisely the reason why, in the complex die problem, the misperception $\hat{\rho}$ had no effect on behavior. The posterior probability $\omega(\cdot \mid \hat{\rho})$ is concentrated on the true value of ρ, whatever the perception.

Direct strategy restrictions such as those discussed above allow for an intermediate ground between a fully knowledgeable agent – who behaves as if he knew $\omega(\cdot \mid \beta)$ – and a naive agent taking his belief at face value. Such an agent faces a reality check, but not to the point where he can fully undo perception errors.

10. Beliefs are a part of everyday language and would seem to be an essential ingredient in decision making. We form opinions about the problems that we face, and we seemingly use these opinions to make decisions. This is precisely what we mean by belief-perceptions.

In the investment problem, we modeled the perception $z (= \eta s)$ as a (noisy) point estimate of the return s. One could ask for more "realism." One could argue that a point estimate is not a realistic description because it does not capture the agent's doubt about his own estimate. A more "realistic" model could be that he instead holds a belief β over the possible returns.

Whichever model one finds attractive, if one wants to avoid predictions that exploit too finely the structure of the model, an issue remains, namely, to define direct strategy restrictions, i.e., a set of admissible mappings from signals to actions.

Formally, with the point estimate z, we used

$$\sigma^\lambda(z) = \lambda z$$

as a way to model various degrees of caution in taking into account the point estimate.

If the signal z is a probability distribution (e.g., $z = \beta$), there are many candidates to describe what taking one's belief with caution might mean, including defining the point estimate $E\beta$ associated with β and applying the strategy σ^λ to that point estimate. One standard possibility is to consider a belief distance d, and define, for any $\theta > 0$, a $\theta-prudent$ utility:

$$v^\theta(a,\beta) = \min_{\beta'} E_{\beta'} u(a,s) + \frac{1}{\theta} d(\beta,\beta').$$

This is not a worst-case scenario, but it captures the idea that the agent should explore the possibility that the belief β is not correct and consider the consequences of these errors. For any θ, one may then consider the strategy σ^θ that maximizes that $\theta-$prudent utility:

$$\sigma^\theta(\beta) = \arg\max_a v^\theta(a,\beta).$$

Each σ^θ defines a particular way to deal with beliefs. When θ is close to 0, $\sigma^\theta(\beta)$ gets close to a naive behavior that would take β at face value. As θ increases, the agent gets more cautious. When θ is very large, investment must get close to 0, as any positive investment yields a negative $\theta-$corrected utility.

These definitions allow one to endogenize the degree to which the agent trusts his beliefs, given the process ω that generates them:

$$\theta^* = \arg\max_\theta E_\omega u(\sigma^\theta(\beta),s).$$

So, under both assumptions (point estimates or beliefs), the analyst endogenizes the degree to which the agent exerts caution in employing his signal: either through an optimal shading factor λ^*, or through an optimal prudence parameter θ^*.

11. Which modeling strategy is more appealing is a matter of taste – our taste is parsimony. In general, we see no need to enrich the mathematical description of signals if a simpler model already conveys the main insights or if the more complex model does not add new insight.

> **To summarize**: (i) A representative situation has been defined as a distribution ω over situations (z,s), where z refers to the agent's perception of current situation s. (ii) The agent is not assumed to know

the characteristics of that representative situation, nor have perceptions of it, otherwise these perceptions should be included in the definition of z. (iii) Each strategy, when applied to that representative situation, provides an aggregate performance measurement, and the comparison of these aggregate measurements across the strategies available defines in implicit ways what the agent knows about ω (i.e., what works for him and what does not). (iv) A direct strategy restriction Σ limits the extent of this implicit knowledge. Both ω and Σ are primitives of our model: they jointly define the degree to which the agent can adjust to his environment. (v) The beliefs that standard models define are not perceptions. We view them as distributions that help us compute aggregate performance measurements. But they should not be thought of as perceptions, for if they were, they would have to be included in the definition of z, and both ω and Σ would have to be redefined.

Further Comments

Prudent strategies. Robust control theory attempts to find optimal decision rules, considering the possibility that the environment changes (or that it is not certain) and the θ-prudent strategy defines a particular way of achieving that, with θ capturing the degree to which the environment might differ from what was originally thought. Another formulation could apply a maxmin criterion over a set of priors (Gilboa and Schmeidler (1989)). For example, for any prior β that the agent might have, define $B^\theta(\beta)$ as the set of priors that reflects the agent's doubt about β, where $B^\theta(\beta) = \{\beta', d(\beta, \beta') \leq \theta\}$. Applying a maxmin criterion to this set defines a strategy

$$\sigma^\theta(\beta) = \arg\max_a \min_{\beta' \in B^\theta(\beta)} Eu(a, \beta').$$

See Hansen and Sargent (2001) for a discussion of the connections between the two approaches.

As if. The notion of "as if" that we use is weaker than the traditional one. Our assumption is that the agent's behavior is the same as that of an agent who knows the model, but is constrained to use that knowledge to compute the best-performing strategy among a limited set of strategies. In standard models, the agent's behavior is the same as that of an agent who knows the model and makes exact inferences from his knowledge of the structure of the model,[3] and

---

[3] Analysts often think of agents making these inferences, not simply that they behave as if they were making them.

subsequently, chooses a strategy with no a priori restriction on the degree to which he can exploit his inferences.

There is a long tradition in economics (dating back to Friedman (1953) and Savage (1953)) of leaving aside the process by which people make decisions. A billiard player manages to sink a ball without knowing the laws of motion and friction. He has simply learned to hit the ball using the right trajectory, speed and spin. As outsiders we may use these laws to compute the likelihood of success as a function of trajectory, speed and spin, and find the triple that maximizes chance of success (taking into account subsequent play, along with making it difficult for the other to succeed in case of miss). But the player need not go through these computations; we just describe or predict his behavior as if he did.

Sometimes, ordinary people play billiards, and an outsider may want to explain the data that he sees, i.e., the pairs (s,a) where s is the position of the balls and a the observed trajectory along with speed and spin. One path would consist of representing the decision problem as if the agent had a prior (or a ball of priors) about the laws of motion and friction, and then adopted a $\theta-$prudent strategy given this prior (Hansen and Sargent) or a maximin strategy given this ball of priors (Gilboa and Schmeidler). Alternatively, one may argue that the agent misperceives s, i.e., that he gets a noisy estimate z of the positions of the balls, according to some signal distribution $\omega(z,s)$, and that we can represent his decision as if he computed Bayesian updates $\omega(s \mid z)$ and then maximized expected utility given his knowledge of the laws of motion and friction. Or, following Sims and rational inattention models, one may argue that the latter model gives too much freedom to the analyst in choosing the structure of the noise, and that there should be constraints on how attention is allocated across the various positions of the ball, possibly paying more attention to the position of the ball you hit first than to the position you will find yourself in should you miss, or if you succeed.

In this environment, our approach would be quite different. We would be inclined to think that players miss sometimes just because any particular trajectory, speed and spin is difficult to implement with precision, and that, for example, choosing a greater speed may impair the implemented trajectory, or that some trajectories are more prone to errors than others. Given these basic assumptions on noisy targeting, we would argue that from experience, agents have learned which speed suits them, or given their lack of talent, which angles are better avoided.

Eventually, this learning operates without an agent's precise knowledge of the stochastic relationship between the targeted and realized action. He learns the best target speed (for him), and this optimal speed is the same as if he had known with precision the assumed relationship between targets and actions, and was only allowed to change speed.

As-if continued. External and internal validity. *In modeling the saving decision of a representative agent in a changing environment (the underlying* *state s varies), analysts generally find it convenient to express the agent's policy as a function of his belief about the underlying state. Beliefs are determined as if the agent was aware of the stochastic structure. While the policy function may look simple within that representation, the mapping from history to beliefs is a complex object, out of reach to agents. The "as-if" methodology then assesses models based on the quality of the predictions (external validity), rather than on the plausibility of the mechanism by which predictions are obtained, hence ignoring a legitimate concern – how policies might actually be implemented (internal validity).*

It may be that predictions (external validity) would improve if we asked for internal validity as well, and imposed behavioral restrictions, using the quality of predictions to assess which behavioral restrictions are more reasonable.

***Bayesian methodology** asks that one makes precise what is not known. According to that methodology, if ω is an element of the model that is not known, one should model precisely what the agents know and do not know about ω. We depart from the Bayesian methodology in that we argue that it is fine to simply assume that ω is unknown to the agent. One need only assume that the agent can compare strategies, and this does not require his knowing ω. There is no need to make precise the beliefs that he could entertain about ω, unless we have reasons to think that these beliefs influence decision making, and that interesting insights can be drawn from a more precise modeling. Rather than trying to model how an agent "thinks" when there is ignorance, one may instead go directly to "how he behaves" when there is ignorance.*

We depart from the Bayesian methodology, but we do not depart substantially from the way empirical work is done, either in our interpretation of distributions as a typical situation that agents face, nor when we impose direct strategy restrictions. As already pointed out, real data is used to estimate the typical situation an agent faces, and estimation of behavior is typically done by adding a priori constraints on admissible mappings from observables to actions. Thinking about what restrictions to consider can be done at the modeling stage, guided by plausibility considerations given the environment considered, rather than delayed until empirical analysis.

References

Gilboa, I. and Schmeidler, D. (1989). Maxmin expected utility with non-unique priors. *Journal of Mathematical Economics*, 18, 141–153.

Hansen, L. P. and Sargent, T. (2001). Robust control and model uncertainty. *The American Economic Review*, 91(2), 60–66.

Legends and Myths

Legend: *A story in which a kernel of truth is embellished to an unlikely degree.*
Myth: *A fiction or half-truth, especially one that forms part of an ideology.*[1]

One goal of game theory is to provide insights into strategic behavior, categorize situations and formalize the strategic concerns that agents face in such situations. Most often, the basic insight is very simple, and can be captured in words, or formalized through an elementary model.

That a basic insight can be conveyed in plain language could already be taken as a signal of its robustness or relevance. Most often however, our inclination as theorists is to test the limit of that basic insight, with the legitimate motivation that this should permit one to assess the scope of the elementary intuition.

In this quest for stronger mathematical foundations, one generally ends up with highly sophisticated models that make precise the conditions under which the basic insights can be further embellished. This may give theorists reassurance. Unfortunately, the embellishments are often obtained at the cost of strong and implausible cognitive assumptions, with agents being endowed with arbitrarily many tools to exploit the structure of the model itself, casting doubt, we believe, on the conclusions obtained in these models, and more generally, on the relevance of the exercise.

---

[1] American Heritage® Dictionary of the English Language, Fifth Edition. Copyright © 2011 by Houghton Mifflin Harcourt Publishing Company. Published by Houghton Mifflin Harcourt Publishing Company. All rights reserved.

Information Aggregation

diego aranega

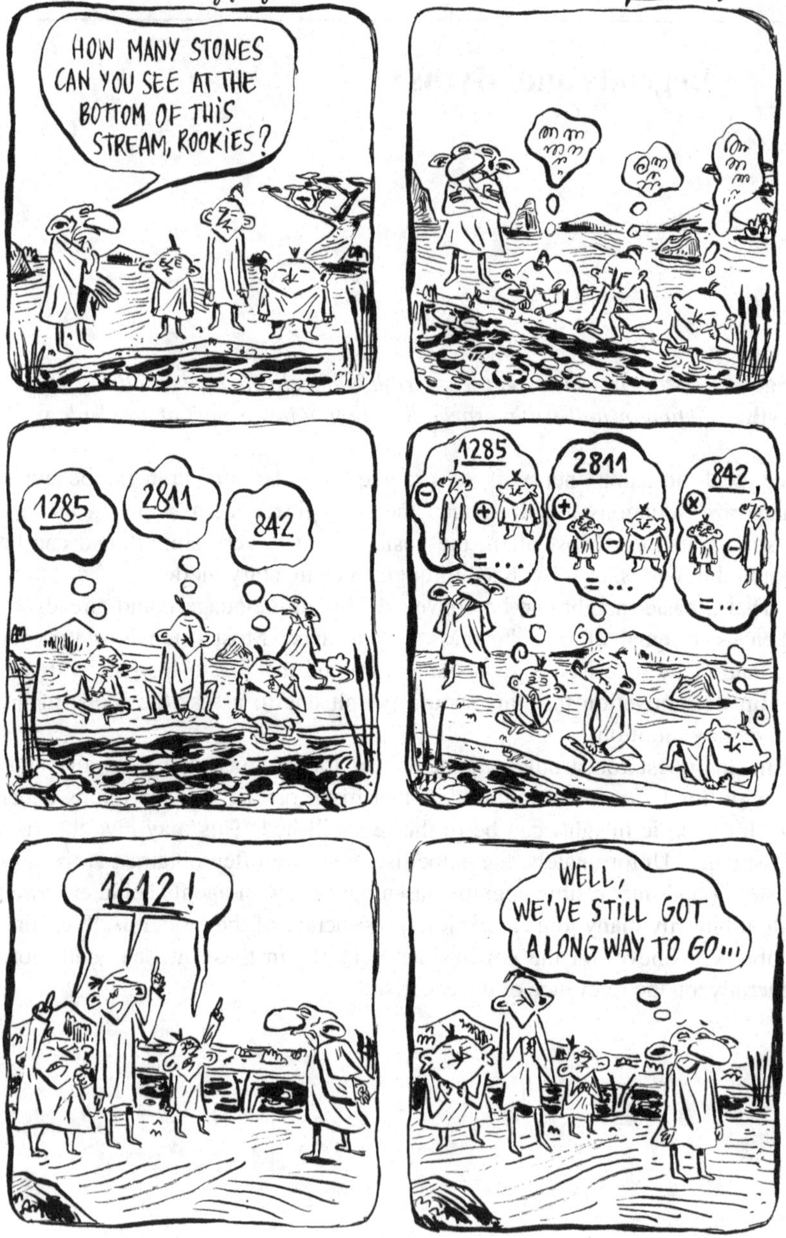

CHAPTER 6

Information Aggregation

1. A common theme in economic theory is that markets aggregate information well: the price reflects all the information available to the agents participating in the market. The result is surprising. Given the number of dimensions on which uncertainty could bear, how can a price mechanism, a one-dimensional instrument, achieve this *tour de force*? The truth is that in general it cannot.

2. Information aggregation is a challenge because in modeling a market, one assumes that there is no direct information sharing between participants. Participants make bids, based on possibly poor estimates of the value of the item for sale, and the transaction price is determined by market rules as a function of bids. How, then, can information transmission come about? We explain below the logic behind information aggregation. Following this, we shall explain the logic behind information aggregation in markets, and in nonmarket mechanisms such as voting.

3. *An urn example.* Think, first, of an urn filled with coins of various sizes and colors. Your objective is to determine the total value of the coins present in the urn, and come up with a point estimate of that value. Your problem is that you cannot be sure of the number of coins, nor of the nominal value of each coin.

An object for sale is like this urn. You don't know with certainty all its characteristics. Once you acquire the object, you learn its true value but, before that, you have only an estimate of that value. That estimate may be overly optimistic or overly pessimistic.

Now imagine a group of people, all staring at the same urn and willing to guess the total value of the coins in the urn. Also imagine that you are told that, among all participants, you have the most optimistic estimate. This information is likely to undermine your faith in your estimate, and it is plausible that you revise it to a more conservative figure. And presumably, one can expect that the larger the group, the larger the change in your estimate.

Information aggregation is precisely about this adjustment. Others have estimates or perceptions that are related to some degree to the actual value of the urn. Being told something about others' estimates could, in principle, improve mine.

4. A critical question is the extent of the adjustment. If I adjust too much, I may end up being too pessimistic. If I don't adjust enough, I may remain overly optimistic. The literature on information aggregation generally portrays agents who misperceive the value of an asset, but who manage to perfectly undo their initial misperceptions when confronted with information about others' estimates. This information about others' estimates may differ depending on context (the number of assets for sale, the number of buyers, the mechanism by which assets are sold). But across these variants, the objective is the same – to explain or show that markets lead to the asset being sold at a price that is close to the true value of the asset, despite the fact that each agent starts with a misperception of that value. We explain below the logic of these papers.

5. *A stylized illustration.* We denote by v the true value of the urn. We consider n agents staring at the urn. We model ignorance about v by assuming that each one gets a perception z_i of that value, and by defining a particular joint distribution ω over the value v and the perceptions z_i. Specifically, let us assume that

$$z_i = \eta_i v$$

where v is drawn from an exponential distribution, and where each η_i is an estimation factor drawn independently from the same distribution having positive support on $[0.9, 1.1]$. Roughly, this means that agents make an estimation error, but this error, when positive, cannot exceed 10 percent of the value of the urn.

Imagine now that n is very large, that you have the highest estimate, and that you are informed of this. You are asked your best prediction of v, based on your estimate z. Call b that best prediction.[1] Since there are many agents, the estimate of the most optimistic agent exceeds v by a factor that is, most likely, very close to 1.1: that is, $z \simeq 1.1v$. If told that you have the highest estimate, then, knowing the structure of the model, you can infer that you are very likely to be optimistic by a factor close to 1.1, so your best prediction is:

$$b \simeq \frac{z}{1.1} \simeq \frac{1.1v}{1.1} = v$$

Thus, being told that you are most optimistic among a large group of people permits you to almost perfectly infer the error in your perception. You end up with an almost perfect prediction of the value.

---

[1] Call I the event where you are the most optimistic agent. For an agent who fully exploits the structure of the model, the best prediction is by definition the number that minimizes $E((b-v)^2 \mid z, I)$, or equivalently, $b = E(v \mid z, I)$.

The example is a caricature, but it explains the process of information aggregation in models. That one should take his initial estimate with caution sounds right. The degree to which one ought to shade one's estimate would seem to be a difficult matter in practice. Knowing the structure of the model, the task becomes trivial: you may infer almost exactly your initial estimation error.

6. *Unbounded errors.* Consider an example that is less of a caricature, in which errors are possibly unbounded. For example, assume that η_i is lognormally distributed. Then, being told that you are the most optimistic bidder does not permit you to perfectly infer the size of the estimation error.

Consider for example the case where $\log \eta_i$ is distributed normally with expectation 0 and standard deviation $\sigma = 0.2$. With a thousand participants, the maximum estimate may vary substantially. The following graph plots the empirical distribution of the largest estimation factor $\eta^0 = \max_i \eta$, obtained through 10,000 independent trials, each involving 1,000 participants.

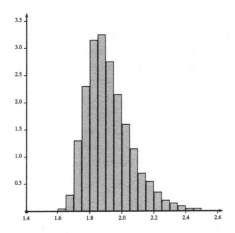

On average across these trials, the largest factor is 1.92, and the standard deviation is 0.14. This means that when you are told that your estimate is highest, you should adjust your initial estimate downward, dividing it by a factor close to 2. The resulting estimate, however, remains a noisy approximation of value, because the distribution over the highest factor is not concentrated on a particular number.

Assume, now, that you are told that among all participants, your estimate is not the highest, but that it coincides with the 10th percentile: only 10 percent of bidders have an estimate higher than yours.

Then, this information, jointly with the knowledge of the distribution over errors, permits you to almost perfectly infer the size of your error when the number of participants is large. Call $\eta^{0.1}$ the estimation factor of the participant for whom 10 percent of participants have a larger estimation factor than his. For a population of 1,000 participants, this means that his estimate is ranked

101st. The following figure shows the empirical distribution of $\eta^{0.1}$ (obtained through 10,000 independent trials, each involving 1,000 participants).

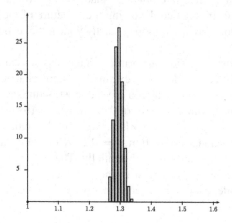

The graph shows that $\eta^{0.1}$ is much more concentrated than $\bar{\eta}$. The average value of $\eta^{0.1}$ is 1.29, and the standard deviation is 0.014.

Of course, the conclusions above draw heavily on the presumption that the agent knows the distribution from which estimation errors are drawn. Different values for the variance σ^2 would generate quite different predictions for the factor $\eta^{0.1}$. With $\sigma = 0.3$, the average value of $\eta^{0.1}$ increases to 1.47.

Information aggregation works insofar as the distribution over errors is known with precision. With uncertainty about the distribution over errors, being told about the ranking of one's estimate does not pin down with precision the size of one's error.

7. Markets. In a market, nobody tells you how your estimate compares with others', if it is the highest, or if it coincides with the 10th percentile. However, with bidders that differ only in their estimate z_i but are otherwise identical, one expects that higher estimates will translate into higher bids. So if there is a single good for sale, we expect the most optimistic bidder to win. And if there are 130 identical objects being sold to 1,300 bidders, each willing to acquire only one object, we expect the bidders having the highest 130 estimates to win.[2] In particular, the least optimistic bidder among those who win has an estimate that coincides with the 10th percentile.

One contribution of theoretical models has been to prove that for an agent bidding in a uniform auction,[3] it is optimal for him to behave as if he was pivotal, that is, as if he was winning by a zero margin. The reason is that in

---

[2] This is a simple market setup inspired by Pesendorfer and Swinkels (2000). In practice, and for most markets, agents would be allowed to bid for more than one unit.

[3] In a uniform auction, all winning bidders pay the same price, equal to the highest bid among losers.

other events, small changes to his bid are of no consequence to his chance of winning or losing, nor to the price he pays in the event he wins.

This means that he should behave as if he was approximately the least optimistic among the winners (or most optimistic among the losers). With many participants, this precisely pins down how he ought to correct his initial estimate: when he knows the distribution over perception errors (his own and that of others), being the least optimistic among the winners tells with precision the size of the mistake that he makes.

To illustrate simply why transaction prices must be close to v in a uniform auction, assume that each potential bidder i chooses to bid a fraction λ_i of his estimate:

$$b_i = \lambda_i z_i.$$

Look for a symmetric equilibrium in which all bidders use the same shading factor λ^*.[4] With 130 goods sold to $1,300$ participants, the price must settle on the 131st largest bid, that is, on a bid equal to $\lambda^* \eta^{0.1} v$. If $\lambda^* \eta^{0.1}$ happens to be above 1 for most realizations, winners pay too much, providing each bidder an incentive to forgo participating in the auction or to decrease λ_i to win less often. If the quantity $\lambda^* \eta^{0.1}$ happens to be below 1 for most realizations, winners pay too little, and some bidders will find that a larger λ_i profitably increases the chance of winning. With a large number of bidders, $\eta^{0.1}$ is concentrated on the expectation $E\eta^{0.1}$ and, in a symmetric equilibrium, it must be that:

$$\lambda^* \simeq \frac{1}{E\eta^{0.1}},$$

and the price, equal to $\lambda^* \eta^{0.1} v$, must thus be concentrated on v.

8. *Partial versus complete information about estimates.* The information revealed in a price mechanism is partial: bidders don't have access to the estimate that *each particular participant* receives. Why isn't this an issue?

This is not an issue because by construction, we built a model in which there is a stable relationship (i.e., "almost one-to-one") between the value of the asset v and the μ_0-largest estimate, for $\mu_0 = 0.1$. The inference that one makes from observing the μ_0-largest estimate is thus perfect, and observing the whole empirical distribution over estimates (which amounts to observing the μ-largest estimate for all values of μ) cannot further improve this inference. Many factors can alter this conclusion. We mention two.

Variations in dispersion of errors. Depending on the characteristics of the asset, the variance of the error term might differ substantially. Agents could,

---

[4] We only provide below a necessary condition on λ^*. Proving that such a symmetric equilibrium exists is more involved. We shall come back to this issue in Chapter 16.

of course, be aware of that possibility. But having a precise idea of these variations across assets seems unrealistic.

Heterogeneity. Gauging the quality of one's estimate and how it compares to others' is a second key issue in markets. The model circumvents these difficulties by assuming symmetric agents. Departing from that benchmark likely creates further difficulties, as agents' perceptions of the characteristics of the asset may be correlated, partially driven by their own reading of these characteristics, with variations in readings across assets generating further sources of dispersion and bias of the estimates.

9. *Aggregating many versus few estimates*. Aggregating two expert opinions is difficult. If I ask a young French demographer and a renowned Congolese historian about life expectancy in Congo, I might get two quite different responses. Deciding how to weigh these expert opinions is a challenge, because the quality or bias of any given expert opinion is difficult to assess with precision. Why would this issue mysteriously disappear once we move to a large number of opinions, expert or not. Do we believe that getting a million opinions would improve our assessment of life expectancy in Congo?

The same issue arises in markets. For a given asset, some experts are presumably better qualified than others at estimating its value. I care about whether those participating actively in the market are those actually getting better estimates. And I also care about the fraction of optimistic bidders participating in the market, as their participation may affect prices. Do we believe that as the number of participants increases, the fraction of optimistic bidders will remain stable across different kinds of sales?

10. *The wisdom of crowds*. Notwithstanding previous comments, the belief that large crowds make it easy to get to the truth is widespread, and it is often referred to as the *wisdom of the crowd*. The usual story behind the idea stems from a single field experiment by Francis Galton at a cattle market. Galton asked participants to estimate the weight of a given cow. Most quotes were off track by a substantial amount. However, the median quote got it (almost) right.

One could take the lack of replication of the Galton experiment as suggesting that the wisdom of crowds is perhaps not so prevalent. Of course, it may simply be that few have attempted to replicate it. As always, inference is difficult.

11. *Voting under majority rule*. An implication of the wisdom-of-crowds logic is that majority voting aggregates information nicely. Imagine that a group considers the possible adoption of a new alternative A, comparing it to the status quo S. All group members are assumed to have the same preferences: the problem is not one of aggregating preferences, but of aggregating information.[5]

---

[5] This is a simple voting setup inspired by Feddersen and Pesendorfer (2000).

Define u as a measure of the difference in value between A and S and let $v = \exp u$. The group would like to select A if and only if u is positive or, equivalently, if and only if v is above 1. However, members are ignorant of the exact value of v. We model this by assuming that v is a random variable, and that each member gets a noisy estimate of v:[6]

$$z_i = \eta_i v.$$

This means that when η_i is above 1, the member is optimistic, and when η_i is below 1, he is pessimistic.

This simple model illustrates what is behind the wisdom of crowds. If each η_i is independently drawn from the same distribution and if $\Pr(\eta_i > 1) = 1/2$, a large group will always get it right. In a large group, optimists (i.e., $\eta_i > 1$) and pessimists (i.e., $\eta_i < 1$) are in almost equal numbers. Whenever A is better ($v > 1$), not only the optimists vote for A, but also the mildly pessimistic as well, and the alternative A gets majority support.

The wisdom-of-crowds hypothesis may seem suspicious, as one can think of many reasons why crowds' judgements would be subject to systematic biases. Nevertheless, the typical voting model in economics goes one step beyond. It portrays agents who behave as though they knew with precision the distribution over the errors that each member makes. We examine the consequence of this assumption below.

12. *Voting under qualified majority rules.* We now have in mind that the new alternative A passes if and only if it gets sufficient support. "Sufficient" can mean different things. We consider qualified majority rules: A passes if a fraction q of the population votes for it.

At first glance, a more stringent majority rule should make alternative A more difficult to pass, because it then takes fewer people to reject A. The contribution of economics models has been to point out that individuals adjust (or should adjust) their decisions to the qualified majority rule considered: somebody willing to support S under the majority rule might be less inclined to do so if a very large support is needed to get A through. A negative vote carries more weight, and one may be reluctant to cast a negative vote unless the evidence that one receives against A is strong enough.

The problem is similar to the urn question. Think of the case where unanimity for A is required, so that any individual has the option to veto A through a single vote for S. I might have received evidence against A, but if all others received evidence more favorable to A than I did, I may want to reconsider my position, and avoid vetoing A.

As for the urn, the difficulty is the degree to which one should adjust the decision. When will I think that my evidence against A is strong enough that it justifies voting for S? *What exactly does strong enough mean?*

---

[6] An alternative formulation could be $z_i = u + \varepsilon_i$. We adopt the multiplicative formulation to make the comparison with earlier formalizations easier.

Economic models provide a clear-cut answer. A sophisticated voter should adjust his behavior to the voting mechanism, tailoring the adjustment to the distributions over errors. The optimal adjustment induces perfect information aggregation: *A* passes if and only if it is worthwhile, irrespective of the particular voting rule considered.

13. *A formal illustration.* Consider the qualified majority rule q in which adopting *A* requires support by at least a fraction q of voters (with $q < 1/2$). Assume agent i supports *A* if and only if his signal is strong enough, that is:

$$z_i > \lambda_i.$$

The threshold λ_i characterizes agent i's strategy, and one can compute the expected gains associated with the strategies $(\lambda_1, \ldots, \lambda_n)$ and look for a symmetric equilibrium λ^*. The insight that the voting rule affects voting behavior will be reflected in the fact that the equilibrium threshold λ^* decreases when the majority requirement q increases.

Assume all voters other than i use the same strategy λ^*. To voter i, the only event he cares about is when he is pivotal, that is, when his choice determines the outcome. This happens when among all other voters, exactly $k - 1$ vote for *A*, where k satisfies $(k - 1)/n < q < k/n$, which roughly means that the q-highest estimate is close to λ^*, hence that $v\eta^q \simeq \lambda^*.$[7]

With a large number of voters, η^q is concentrated on the scalar $\overline{\eta}^q$ for which $\Pr(\eta_i > \overline{\eta}^q) \equiv q$. So in the event that i is pivotal, one may infer the value of v almost perfectly: $v \simeq \lambda^*/\overline{\eta}^q$. If voter i infers that v almost certainly exceeds 1, he should vote for *A* (unless z_i is extremely low). If he infers $v < 1$, he should vote against *A* (unless z_i is extremely high). The only case when his optimal threshold is not extreme is when the inference is $v \simeq 1$, hence equilibrium requires $\lambda^* \simeq \overline{\eta}^q$, which decreases when q increases.

To illustrate this numerically, assume $\log \eta_i$ is normally distributed with standard deviation equal to $\sigma = 0.2$. When the majority rule is 1/2, the equilibrium threshold λ^* is 1. When the necessary majority q increases to 0.7, the equilibrium threshold λ^* decreases to 0.9.

The graphs on the next page illustrate the latter case (i.e., $q = 0.7$ and $\lambda^* = 0.9$), showing the extent of actual support when $v = 1$ and when $v = 1.1$. In these graphs, the curve defines the density over estimates when $v = 1$ (on the left) and when $v = 1.1$ (on the right).[8] All group members getting an estimate above $\lambda^* = 0.9$ vote in favor of *A*. The shaded area indicates the probability that a given individual gets a draw above 0.9. With large numbers, the support for *A* approximately coincides with that probability. The threshold λ^* is precisely set so that when $v = 1$, support exactly coincides with 0.7. When $v = 1.1$, support is 0.87, above the required majority 0.7.

---

[7] Recall that η^q designates the estimation factor of the participant for whom q percent of participants have a larger estimation factor than his.

[8] In both cases, v is the median estimate – half of the voters get an estimate above v.

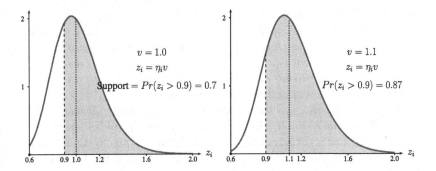

14. Perfect information aggregation across various voting systems can be seen as an embellishment of the wisdom of crowds. As for the urn and markets, it builds on the assumption that not only the fraction of optimists remains the same across instances, but also that, for any given x, the degree of optimism of the x-percent-most-optimistic agents remains stable as well.

Rephrasing this in terms of Galton's cow experiment, one could tell a farmer the following:

"You know what, among all the many estimates that I have received, there are exactly 13 percent of estimates that are more optimistic than yours...";

With the farmer soon replying:

"Ah, okay, my mistake. I know what the correct figure is then. Thanks."

15. While much emphasis is generally put on the performance of institutions in aggregating information, the literature recognizes that when uncertainty bears on more than one dimension, a price or voting mechanism will often not aggregate information well, opening the path for understanding how performance differs across institutions.

One interpretation of our critique is that information aggregation results hinge on the presumption that uncertainty bears on a single dimension. In general however, there is no reason to think that uncertainty would only bear on one dimension. For mathematical convenience, we describe precisely the distribution from which a given variable is drawn. Once we recognize that there is no reason that this distribution should be known, we need to introduce the possibility that uncertainty bears on more than one dimension, and as a result, institutions will generally fail to aggregate information well.

Further Comments

Galton. We referred to Galton's cow experiment[9] because it sometimes lends support to the idea that the median opinion would be the wisest, closest to the

---

[9] Galton (1907).

*truth. Note, however, that Galton's main interest was not to elicit some "truth,"
but to improve how a jury would assess damages, with the objective of finding
a method that would select the fairest compromise between necessarily diverse
opinions.*[10] *His idea was that a fair compromise would be better achieved by
eliciting the median estimate among jury members, rather than by asking each
jury member his estimate and computing the average.*

*Part of his objection was that reporting a precise figure for damages is too
difficult,*[11] *and interestingly, Galton proposed a method to elicit the median
estimate which does not rely on agents reporting such a precise figure. Based
on the presumption that estimates are normally distributed around the median,
he advocates choosing two numbers x and y > x, and asking jury members
to report whether they think damages should be below x, between x and y
or above y. Fitting these answers to a normal distribution, one can elicit the
median estimate (simultaneously with the dispersion of opinions).*

*Condorcet. Formal analysis comparing voting institutions, with the aim of
producing better decisions (say judicial ones) goes back at least to Condorcet.
In relation to the ideas developed in this chapter, and the issue as to whether
larger crowds would help, Condorcet comments that larger consent that a
proposition is true may only prove this fact (that the consent is larger), without
bringing new certitude to the truth of the proposition itself.*[12]

*Market efficiency hypothesis. In the 1970's, with the development of infor-
mation economics, a number of authors addressed the question of whether
markets could be efficient, with prices perfectly revealing the value of the
underlying assets. The issue often takes the form of analyzing a stylized
market composed of a set of identically informed and a set of identically
uninformed agents, and determining whether prices reflect the information
held by informed agents.*[13] *In these stylized models, price is a simple function*

---

[10] With respect to the question of finding "the most suitable amount of money to be granted for
any particular purpose" [such as compensation of damages], Galton (1899, page 638) asks:
"How is the medium amount to be ascertained, which is the fairest compromise between many
different opinions?" So it is not the "true" level of compensation but the fairest, that one is
looking for.

[11] His other objection to using the average opinion is that this leaves undue influence or voting
power to those coming up with absurdly large or small ones.

[12] Condorcet, Essai sur l'application de l'analyse à la probabilité des décisions (page 148 (cxlviii):
"le jugement de tous les hommes, en faveur de cette proposition, ne peut produire une probabilité plus grande [...] Si ceux qui y croient se bornent aux preuves données avant eux, et n'en
cherchent pas de nouvelles, leur consentement, en supposant qu'il put produire une certitude,
prouverait seulement qu'il est certain que ce fait, que cette proposition sont probables."
[The [unanimous] judgment of all men in favor of this proposal cannot produce a larger
probability [...] If all that believe in it restrict attention to the existing evidence, without looking
for new ones, their [unanimous] approval, if it ever were to produce a certitude, could only
prove one, that it is certain that the proposal is probable].

[13] See, for example, Kihlstrom and Mirman (1975) and Green (1973).

of the information held by the informed traders, and of some other parameter reflecting "market conditions." To the extent that this extraneous market parameter remains unknown to agents, prices cannot reveal perfectly the information held by informed traders. Grossman and Stiglitz (1980) pointed out that the existence of some residual uncertainty is critical to the functioning of markets, because otherwise no trader would have an incentive to pay the cost of acquiring information in the first place.

In this chapter, we also ask whether prices can reflect the underlying value of the asset in the presence of a population of diversely informed agents. Our emphasis, however, is not on the theoretical impossibility of markets that perfectly reveal prices, but on the practical difficulty/impossibility of determining what to make of each and everyone's opinion even if it were freely available. Said differently, "market conditions" include the particular way that information and opinions are dispersed across agents, and one suspects that these market conditions (hence prices) are subject to shocks unrelated to underlying values.

References

Condorcet, N. de (1785). *Essai sur l'application de l'analyse à la probabilité des décisions*, Paris.

Feddersen, T. and Pesendorfer, W. (1997). Voting behavior and information aggregation in elections with private information. *Econometrica*, 65(5), 1029–1058.

Galton, F. (1899). The median estimate. *Report of the British Association for the Advancement of Science*, 638–640.

Galton, F. (1907). Vox Populi, *Nature*, 1949(75), 450–451.

Green, J. (1973). Information, efficiency, and equilibrium. Discussion Paper No. 284, Harvard: Harvard Institute of Economic Research.

Grossman, S. J. and Stiglitz, J. E. (1980). On the impossibility of informationally efficient markets. *The American Economic Review*, 70(3), 393–408.

Kihlstrom, R. E. and Mirman, L. J. (1975). Information and market equilibrium. *The Bell Journal of Economics*, 6(1), 357–376.

Pesendorfer, W. and Swinkels, J. M. (1997). The loser's curse and information aggregation in common value auctions. *Econometrica*, 65(6), 1247–1281.

diego aranega

CHAPTER 7

Mechanism Design

1. You own an object that you intend to sell through an *ascending-price* auction, an auction where the price rises until a single potential buyer is still interested in buying at that price. A friend comes and says:

"This doesn't look like a good idea to me. I recently bought a nice Art Deco bronze through a similar auction: I was ready to bid up to $1,000 and got it for under $400. What you should do is run *a first-price* auction: all participants simultaneously make bids and the highest bidder gets the object and pays his bid. You'll get what the object is worth to the winner, not what it is worth to the last guy who drops out!"

A second friend, who is well versed in selling mechanisms, jumps into the conversation and brings up an intriguing idea:

"I know what you should do. Run an *all-pay* auction: it looks like first price, but with a twist: every bidder pays his bid, whether he wins or not. You can multiply your gains by whatever number of bidder participates!"

Sounds like a scam... But tempting.

2. Your friends' suggestions are worth considering, but of course, they leave an important issue aside. *Auction rules affect behavior.* How much would your friend have bid in the first-price auction? Quite plausibly, he would have tried to take a chance, bidding somewhat below $1,000, betting on the possibility to get the bronze at a lower price. With the all-pay auction, you might trick people who do not understand the rules, but for bidders who do, there is an obvious risk of paying one's bid and getting nothing in return, a disheartening prospect likely to chill one's willingness to participate.

In brief, the comparison is not an obvious one. When you modify the rules that determine the prices paid by winners and losers, you modify bidders' incentives.

3. *Mechanism design* aims at comparing selling protocols. Imagine you own an object that you wish to sell. Should you post a price and wait for a buyer, or should you design an auction? If you negotiate with a buyer, should you make an offer or should you wait for the buyer to quote a price? If the object can

be divided, are you better off selling the undivided object or selling separately parts of the object, possibly of different sizes?

Comparisons are based on making behavioral predictions in each of these selling mechanisms. By examining the consequences of each possible procedure on behavior, i.e., the allocation (who eventually owns the object) and the prices paid or received by winners and losers, mechanism design may rank procedures according to the desired objective (e.g., maximize the seller's revenue or efficiency).

4. An obvious limit to the exercise is that many "procedures" are informal. A negotiation is not an auction with transparent unalterable rules. We can portray it as a precise protocol in which players alternate in making offers, but by doing so, we may be omitting important features of real-life negotiation – its malleable or flexible nature.

Nevertheless, even focusing on well-defined selling protocols, mechanism design is a real challenge for two reasons: understanding the strategic issues behind a single mechanism seems difficult, and the number of possible selling procedures is virtually unlimited.

Providing a formal framework in which these evaluations can be done in a systematic way has been one of the important accomplishments of economic theory, and the techniques involved are indispensable tools.

5. *Revenue equivalence.* One celebrated insight of the mechanism design literature is *revenue equivalence.* In essence, it compares a wide variety of selling rules and argues that, if these rules produce the same allocation, the seller's revenue must be the same.

There are conditions, of course, as the result builds on a specific way of modeling what agents know and ignore. At first glance, the conditions seem relatively weak. In essence, behavioral predictions are made assuming that each participant knows his own value, but does not know the values of others. Ignorance is modeled by assuming that each participant has a value drawn independently from the same distribution f.

This chapter examines this result, and argues that the predictions above fail to capture important strategic differences among the auction formats.

To fix ideas, when needed, numerical simulations will be made assuming that values are drawn from lognormal distributions. We assume that there are n participants and that each participant $i = 1, \ldots, n$ has a value v_i for the object:

$$v_i = \eta_i v_0$$

where v_0 is a fixed scalar and η_i is drawn from a lognormal distribution, with $\log \eta_i$ distributed as $\mathcal{N}(0, \sigma^2)$.

6. *An informal discussion.* Before any computations we explain informally the main strategic differences between the three auction formats described above.

In the *ascending-price* auction, bidders don't have much to think about, just watch the price and drop out when the price reaches one's value.[1]

Bidding in the *first-price* auction is more involved. A bidder would like to shade his bid below his valuation, but this decision involves a tradeoff: the more he shades his bid below his value, the larger his gain when he wins, but the smaller the chance of winning.

Bidding in the *all-pay* auction seems substantially more involved.[2] A single participant wins while others pay their bids and get nothing in return. Winning probably requires some aggressive or serious bidding (i.e., bidding a significant fraction of one's valuation). But with many bidders, it cannot be that they all bid seriously, because then at least some of them would incur an expected loss. It also cannot be that no bidder bid seriously, because then bidding seriously would be a sure win. So, while one expects that most potential bidders remain cautious, one also expects that *some of them* will bid seriously.

But who should be the serious bidder(s)? Assessing one's chance of winning before bidding would help. But how would one know what his chances of winning are?

This suggests that all-pay auctions involve a coordination problem, as it may not be obvious for an agent to know *a priori* whether and when to bid aggressively. We also expect that, if coordination is an issue, the performance of these auctions might be quite poor, particularly if there is a large number of potential bidders. If there are few serious participants, competition is effectively reduced to those serious participants.

To summarize, the ascending-price auction involves no strategic difficulty. The first-price auction involves one strategic issue – how much to shade. The all-pay auction seems to involve at least two strategic issues – deciding on whether to bid aggressively and deciding on a bid level when aggressive.

Notwithstanding these differences in bidding complexity, the literature finds that in each auction, the highest valuation bidder makes the highest bid and wins the auction (so all auctions allocate the object efficiently), and that the three formats generate the same expected revenue for the seller. In particular, the performance of the all-pay auction is no worse (or better) than the two others. Why?

7. *Assessing one's chance of winning.* In defining precisely the nature of what the agents ignore, and in assuming that bidders find the optimal bid function, the analyst endows the agents with precise knowledge of the relationship between their value and their actual chance of winning. This allows the agents to avoid wasting money when their chances of winning are slim. This is crucial in the all-pay auction, which we analyze below.

---

[1] We consider here the Japanese version where the price rises continuously until only a single bidder is interested. At that point, the object is awarded to the remaining bidder at the current price.

[2] Recall that in the all-pay auction, each participant makes a bid, the seller collects all bids (including the losing bids) and the object is awarded to the highest bidder.

Formally, if a bidder has value v, he can behave as though he knew the probability $q(v)$ that he has the highest value among all other participants. That probability has the following expression:

$$q(v) = [F(v)]^{n-1}.$$

In particular, under our symmetry assumption, if all bidders participating in the all-pay auction use the same increasing bid function $b(v)$, a bidder with value v gets an expected gain equal to:

$$u(v) = q(v)v - b(v).$$

Since $u(v)$ cannot be negative, this provides a useful upper bound on the bid function $b(v)$:

$$b(v) \leq q(v)v \text{ or equivalently } \frac{b(v)}{v} \leq q(v).$$

The next figure plots $q(v)$ for two standard deviation levels, $\sigma = 0.2$ and $\sigma = 0.3$, setting $v_0 = 1$ and $n = 10$.

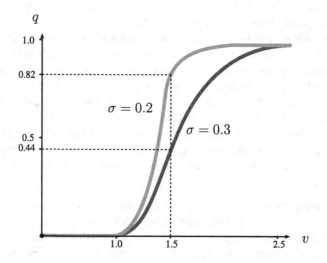

In both cases, the function is S-shaped, and a bidder is likely to fare better when he happens to be in the top part of the curve. The two curves however illustrate that for a given value $v = 1.5$, the chance of being the highest value bidder are quite sensitive to σ: $q(1.5) = 0.44$ when $\sigma = 0.3$ and $q(1.5) = 0.82$ when $\sigma = 0.2$. More generally, shifts in v_0, changes in n, or alternate distributions would alter the S−function, shifting it or affecting its steepness.

8. *Equilibrium bidding.* Assessing $q(v)$ is not the end of the story because an agent might be willing to shade his bid below $q(v)$ in hopes of gaining a positive expected surplus. We explain in the Appendix of this chapter how "equilibrium shading" is derived. [3] One obtains the following bid function:

$$b(v) = v\lambda(v) \text{ with } \lambda(v) = q(v) - \frac{1}{v}\int_0^v q(x)dx.$$

λ is a shading parameter, and the function $\lambda(v)$ defines how shading is adjusted to each value realization v. The expression reflects how bidding is tuned to distributions, and based on a precise assessment of the chances of winning conditional on all possible valuations. We illustrate below $\lambda(\cdot)$ for $n = 10$ and $\sigma = 0.5$.

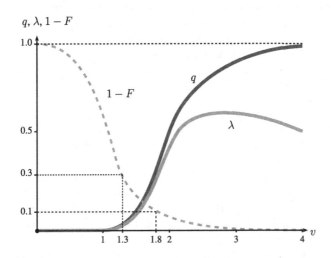

In the figure above, the dotted curve is the probability $1 - F(v)$ that a given bidder has a value above v. This curve provides clues on how coordination is achieved. From this curve, one can see that 70 percent of the time, a bidder's value is below 1.3, and he bids a negligible fraction of his value (below 4 percent). One can also see that 90 percent of the time, a bidder's value is below 1.8, and his shading then almost coincides with $q(v)$ (remaining below 30 percent).

---

[3] Equilibrium means that when all bidders adopt that strategy, none can profit from adopting a different strategy.

There are two consequences of this:

- Serious bidding is relatively rare and a serious bidder is unlikely to face strong competition: one can calculate that the expected number of bidders bidding at least 30 percent of their value is 1.2.
- For most realizations of v, $q(v)$ offers good guidance on how to bid in the auction.

In other words, the knowledge of v, and implicitly F, endows agents with a powerful coordination device, enabling them to avoid wasting money in instances where chances of winning are insubstantial.

That might be a useful idealized benchmark, but it fails to capture the difficulties that most would face when bidding in such an auction. We most likely would have no clue about our chances of being the highest bidder. Or if we did, or thought that we did, chances are that our clues are erroneous.

9. *No clues.* The remainder of this chapter explores the case when agents do not have access to a precise assessment of the chances of winning conditional on valuation, or equivalently, when agents cannot finely adjust their strategy to behave as if they had such a precise assessment.

To this end, we assume that bidders may only evaluate (and compare) linear bidding rules of the form:

$$b^\lambda(v) = \lambda v$$

where λ is a scalar.

One interpretation is that upon seeing their own valuation, bidders cannot make reliable inferences about how their own valuation ranks compared to others'. A high valuation reflects a highly valuable good, and agents cannot disentangle how much their valuation stems from their own private taste and how much is common to all bidders. If they thought that bidding a fixed fraction λ_0 of their value was a good idea for some realizations of v, this remains true for other realizations of v.

Note that the constraint imposed on bidding strategies does not *a priori* rule out the possibility that the object is allocated efficiently: if all bidders adopt the same strategy λ^*, the highest valuation bidder wins.

However, as we demonstrate below, such an outcome (with all bidders adopting the same λ^*) is impossible when there are many bidders. Bidding a significant fraction of your value is costly because there are many instances in which you lose, and you lose more often when there are more bidders. So, assuring non-negative expected gains requires a low λ, more so with many bidders. But then bidding more aggressively becomes a near-certain gain.

The non-negative profit condition. The total amount to be shared across bidders is at most

$$S_n = E[\max_{i=1,\dots,n} v_i].$$

When all bidders use the same shading factor λ, a bidder's gain is bounded by $S_n/n - \lambda Ev$.

Since equilibrium profits must be non-negative, this provides an upper bound on λ:

$$\lambda \leq \overline{\lambda}_n \equiv \frac{S_n}{nEv}.$$

The ratio S_n/Ev increases with the number of bidders n, and it also increases with the dispersion parameter σ. However, $\overline{\lambda}_n$ quickly falls: when n is "high enough," competition is tempered, and a bidder would rather set λ above $\overline{\lambda}_n$ and cheaply acquire the object with high probability. We shall see below what high enough means.

The incentive condition. To check incentives, we define, for any x and λ, the gain $G(x,\lambda)$ that a bidder would derive by using the bidding rule $b^{\lambda x}$ while others use bidding rule b^λ:

$$G(x,\lambda) = \int vf(v)[F(xv)]^{n-1}dv - \lambda xEv.$$

For it to be optimal to set $x = 1$, it must be that $\frac{\partial G}{\partial x}(1,\lambda) = 0$, implying a tentative equilibrium shading λ_n^*:[4]

$$\lambda_n^* = \int v^2 f(v)[(n-1)f(v)[F(v)]^{n-2}]dv/Ev.$$

This tentative value λ_n^* is unfortunately incompatible with the non-negative profit condition above ($G(1,\lambda) \geq 0$ or, equivalently, $\lambda \leq \overline{\lambda}_n$) when n rises. For $\sigma = 0.5$, $\lambda_2^* = 0.53$ and the ratio $\lambda_n^*/\overline{\lambda}_n$ remains below 1 for $n = 2$ only. This shows that there can be at most two serious bidders, each bidding approximately half his value!

With higher dispersion (say $\sigma = 0.6$), $\overline{\lambda}_n$ does not decrease as quickly with n and there can be three serious bidders, but no more.[5]

In any case, since this entails many bidders forgoing the auction, the efficiency loss and the loss in revenue to the seller are substantial, compared to the ascending price auction.

10. *Erroneous clues.* Our assumption on bidding is by no means the only way to restrict an agent's ability to precisely adjust to the underlying distribution.

---

[4] One may also write $\lambda_n^* = E[v^2 f(v) \mid v = v^{(1,n-1)}]/Ev$, where $v^{(1,n-1)}$ denotes the highest realization among $n - 1$ draws.

[5] When $\sigma = 0.6$, $\lambda_3^* = 0.51$, the three "serious" bidders each bid approximately half their value. Even though each bidder has an ex ante chance 1/3 of winning, his expected gain is positive because in events where he loses, his value is lower and he bids less.

One could assume that each agent has a misspecified perception of q, which we denote $\widehat{q}$, and look for an equilibrium in which participants bid a fraction of $v\widehat{q}(v)$:

$$b^\lambda(v) = \lambda v\widehat{q}(v).$$

Alternatively, since there is no reason to believe that misperceptions are perfectly correlated across bidders, one could assume that a bidder's perception is random, say:

$$\widehat{q}_i(v) = \widehat{q}(\theta_i v)$$

where θ_i is a random variable, with $\log \theta_i$ normally distributed.

This might increase the potential number of participants in equilibrium, in the same way that a larger dispersion of values does. However, this would create another difficulty, reducing efficiency by introducing errors in the allocation, thus reducing the participants' expected gain upon winning below S_n.

11. *Equivalence revisited.* In the all-pay auction, the linear restriction has a substantial effect on bidding, reducing the number of bidders who may bid seriously. Our analysis however has left aside one issue. When there are many bidders, who will bid seriously? How is coordination achieved?

In standard analysis, coordination is achieved through valuations, with only higher valuation bidders bidding seriously. With linear bidding, bidding depends on value, but this does not allow for enough self-selection. Further coordination must emerge through other means such as past experience, which possibly creates randomness in the number of serious bidders, and, in any event, undoes the connection between the highest value participants in a given auction and those who make a serious bid.

In contrast, in the first-price auction, the linear restriction has only a minor effect on bidding. Shading in the first-price auction exploits the dispersion of bids: the more dispersed the bids are, the larger the incentives to shade. The difference is that in the standard model, shading incentives are analyzed separately for each value realization, leading to a shading function $\lambda_{fp}(v)$; while with the linear restriction, this incentive is examined on average across possible value realizations, leading to a shading factor λ_{fp}^*.

The following figures summarize equilibrium bidding in the all-pay and first-price auctions in the case of lognormally distributed values ($\sigma = 0.5$), for the case of $n = 10$ bidders.[6]

---

[6] In the all-pay auction, with linear shading, at most two bidders participate, and the figure gives the equilibrium shading for the case $n = 2$.

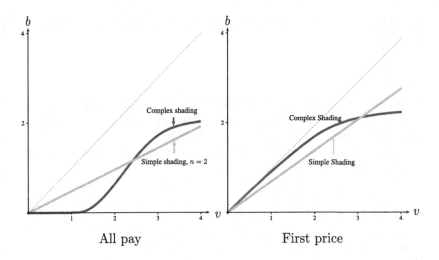

All pay   First price

It can be verified that in the first-price auction the overall effect of the linear restriction is to slightly reduce the seller's rent (by less than 3 percent when $\sigma = 0.5$ and $n = 10$. But, unlike in the all-pay auction, there is no negative effect on participation.

12. *Back to mechanism design.* When one moves from ascending-price to first-price auctions, or to all-pay auctions, the seller's revenue need not improve because buyers become strategic: if buyers pay their bids when they win, they will shade their bids below their value. If they pay their bid even when they don't win, then they will shade their bids even more.

Both models (the unconstrained and constrained models) illustrate that strategic phenomenon. But the consequence for behavior and revenues is quite different across models.

Equivalence is an elegant result, but it sweeps under the rug the cognitive demands on agents. Most analysts are conscious of that difficulty, and live with the legitimate precautionary statement that one should not have too much faith in models. But precautionary statements are warnings that lack a formalized treatment that can be passed on simply to the next generation of analysts. The myth of equivalence may get passed on without the warning.

The obstacle could be primarily technical. If we could solve auctions in which there is randomness in the underlying distribution (random v_0 for example), and in which agents also receive signals about that distribution, then we could introduce both difficulties: decreased ability to determine the actual $q(v)$ (because $q(v)$ depends on v_0 and v_0 is unknown), and differences in assessments across bidders. These models however prove difficult to solve with standard techniques. The constrained model achieves precisely that, with parsimony, and provides a simple tool that limits the cognitive demands placed on agents.

Further Comments

Mechanism design goes back, at least, to Hayek (1945), and the debate over the comparison between decentralized and centrally planned economies. Hayek argued that markets and other institutions are mechanisms that: "serve an essential role of communicating dispersed information about the desires and resources of different individuals in society."[7]

The abstract formulation of this idea goes back to Hurwicz (1960,1972). In reduced form, each agent takes actions based, at least partially, on his own information, within limits defined by the institutions. With this view in mind, an economic institution, along with the behavior that it generates, may be reduced to an abstract mechanism, i.e., a mapping from information (on which choices are conditioned) to outcomes. Any institution thus has an abstract centralized twin in which each agent communicates his information to a central planner who implements the appropriate outcomes given all the information revealed.

One advantage of this formulation is that it makes the incentive issue within each institution more transparent: changing the institution may modify the agent's strategic choices, in the same way that changing the rules that govern its centralized twin would modify each one's incentives to report or misreport his own information. It also simplifies the analysis of these incentives. Whatever the institution under scrutiny, and the behavior supposedly induced by it, one may derive the properties of the behavior induced by the institution by studying incentives in its centralized twin.[8]

The main theme of this chapter is that this move to the centralized twin is not innocuous. From the centralized twin perspective, an auction associates to each value v a probability $q(v)$ of getting the object, and an expected transfer $t(v)$. From that perspective, the second-price auction, in which each bidder bids his value ($b^{sp}(v) = v$)) and the all-pay auction, in which each bidder bids $b^{allpay}(v) = v\lambda^*(v)$, are equivalent: for each individual with value v, or behaving as if he had value v, both institutions induce the same expected chance of getting the object, and the same expected transfer ($t(v) = v\lambda^*(v)$).

That view however misses the fact that the all-pay auction outcome described above is difficult to implement. The assumption about agents' behavior is questionable – a bid function finely tuned to model parameters. From a theoretical standpoint, we may say that both auctions implement the same allocation. Practically, our analysis casts doubts on the equivalence.

---

[7] Quoted from Roger Myerson's Nobel lecture (2007). The importance of information and communication feedbacks has been central in the study of (self)regulatory processes in the 1940's, and led to the development of Cybernetics (Wiener (1948)).

[8] This step is called the revelation principle (Gibbard (1973) and Myerson (1979)).

Our view of implementability is closer to that of Leonid Hurwicz in his Nobel lecture (2007), who talked about "genuine implementation," and worried about the "modus operandi" – what it takes for the mechanism to work in practice.

This concern for practicality is related to the old planned/decentralized economy debate and the size of the message space required to mimic a decentralized economy (Mount and Reiter (1974)), as well as the more recent debate emerging in computer science on computational and communication complexity.[9] Two mechanisms may be formally equivalent in terms of the mapping from information to outcomes, yet the cognitive burden placed on agents or the institution to implement these mappings may differ substantially.[10]

In this chapter, we have attempted to address the cognitive burden placed on the agents who participate in an auction,[11] with a cognitive limitation taking the form of a restriction to linear strategies.[12] That restriction makes it impossible to produce the same reduced form $(q(v),t(v))$ for all auction formats.[13] Given this restriction, second-price, first-price and all-pay auctions cannot have the same centralized twin.

Appendix

We derive below equilibrium bidding in the all-pay auction, as well as in other mechanisms. Whatever mechanism, in a symmetric equilibrium, we may define $b(v)$ as the expected payment incurred by a bidder who behaves as if his value was v. In the case of the all-pay auction $b(v)$ just corresponds to the bid. Assuming this function is strictly increasing, the bidder with the highest value wins (the equilibrium considered is symmetric), and we may define

$$u(v) = vq(v) - b(v) \tag{7.1}$$

as the equilibrium gain.

Also define $U(v,\widehat{v})$ as the expected gain of a bidder with value v who behaves as if his value was $\widehat{v}$.

We have $U(v,\widehat{v}) = vq(\widehat{v}) - b(\widehat{v})$. Incentives require that the bidder with value v finds it optimal to behave as if his value was v, implying that $\frac{\partial U}{\partial \widehat{v}}(v,v) =$

---

[9] See Blume et al. (2015) for a review.

[10] One generally worries about the complexity of the mapping between the information revealed and the outcome, or the size of the message space.

[11] There is no burden placed on the designer, as all auctions considered are simple to carry out.

[12] This may also be interpreted as a way to impose a limit on the agent's ability to parse or classify the environments, that is, to determine which strategy is best in which environment. By limiting the set of strategies, one simplifies the classification of environments, and one also increases the chance of correct classification. This link between confidence in the classification and the family of functions used for classification purposes has been formalized in computer science, by characterizing the VC dimension (Vapnik and Chervonenkis (1971)), or the power or capacity, of a given family.

[13] In addition, while one can still define the pair $(q(v),t(v))$ for a given auction and a given candidate strategy, this reduced form can no longer be used to check incentives.

0. This implies $u'(v) = \frac{\partial U}{\partial v}(v,v) = q(v)$, hence, since a bidder with value 0 gets no gain,

$$u(v) = \int_0^v q(x)dx.$$

Given (7.1), this completely characterizes $b(v)$ and $u(v)$ as a function of q. This also means that a bidder's expected gain is unchanged across selling mechanisms. The revenue of the seller is also unchanged.

For the first-price auction, a bidder only pays his bid $b^{fp}(v)$ when he wins, so $b(v) = q(v)b^{fp}(v)$, hence $b^{fp}(v)$ is characterized as well:

$$b^{fp}(v) = v(1 - \frac{1}{vq(v)} \int_0^v q(x)dx).$$

The following figure plots equilibrium bid functions for each format, assuming $n = 5$ and $\sigma = 0.5$, and v_0 normalized to 1.

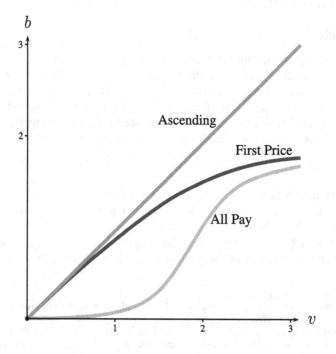

References

Blume, L., Easley, D., Kleinberg, J., Kleinberg R. & Tardos, É. (2015). Introduction to computer science and economic theory. *Journal of Economic Theory*, 156, 1–13.

Gibbard, A. (1973) Manipulation of voting schemes: a general result. *Econometrica*, 41, 587–601.

Hayek, F. A. (1945). The use of knowledge in society. *American Economic Review*, 35(4), 519–530.

Hurwicz, L. (1960). Optimality and informational efficiency in resource allocation processes. In Arrow, Karlin & Suppes, eds., *Mathematical Methods in the Social Sciences*. Stanford: Stanford University Press.

Hurwicz, L. (1972). On informationally decentralized systems. In C. B. Maguire and R. Radner, eds., *Decision and Organization*, North-Holland, Amsterdam.

Hurwicz, L. (2007). Nobel lecture. But who will guard the guardians. In K. Grandin, ed., *The Nobel prizes 2007*. Stockholm.

Mount, K. and Reiter, S. (1974). The informational size of message spaces. *Journal of Economic Theory*, 8: 161–192.

Myerson, R. (1979). Incentive-compatibility and the bargaining problem. *Econometrica*, 47, 61–73.

Myerson, R. (2007). Nobel lecture. Perspective on mechanism design in economic theory. In K. Grandin, ed., *The Nobel Prizes 2007*. Stockholm.

Vapnik, V. and Chervonenkis, A. (1971). On the uniform convergence of relative frequencies of events to their probabilities. *Theory of Probability and its Applications*, 16(2), 264–280.

Wiener, N. (1948). *Cybernetics: Or Control and Communication in the Animal and the Machine*, Paris: Hermann & Cie & Cambridge, Massachusetts: MIT Press.

CHAPTER 8

Surplus Extraction

1. A seller has an object that he would like to sell to a buyer. He would like to get the highest possible price above his own valuation for it. Obviously he won't be able to sell it at a price that exceeds the buyer's valuation. But he might be able to sell it at a price close to the buyer's valuation, in which case we say that the seller fully extracts the available surplus (that is, the difference between the buyer's and seller's valuation, if positive).

If the seller knew the buyer's valuation, surplus extraction would be simple. The seller could simply make a take-it-or-leave-it offer, leaving the buyer with arbitrarily small rent. When the seller does not know the buyer's valuation however, extraction is more difficult as there is a risk that the seller's offer will not be correctly targeted: too high results in no trade (an inefficient outcome) and too low results in rents to the buyer.

2. One insight of the literature is that despite the seller's ignorance, clever selling mechanisms may improve surplus extraction, and even yield near full surplus extraction. The more general idea is that with appropriate tools, the agent having bargaining power can appropriate all rents, without generating inefficiencies.

This "insight" should come as a surprise. How can one extract what one doesn't know? How can the buyer be induced to provide information (his value) that will subsequently be used at his expense?

The truth is that these clever mechanisms build on buyers and sellers knowing details of a model that one cannot realistically expect them to know.[1]

3. Full surplus extraction is typically achieved by letting the seller propose (and commit to) *a menu of contingent price offers.*

A contingent price offer means that, rather than making a simple price offer, the seller offers a *contract* that specifies a price to be paid, as a function

---

[1] These mechanisms extensively exploit the signal structure, in particular, the correlations between the signals that agents receive (Cremer and McLean (1985)). Following Neeman (2004), the literature has questioned the generality of the correlation structure assumed.

of some yet-to-be-realized signal or observation. To fix ideas, we will think of that signal as an estimate of the object to be provided by a panel of experts.

A menu of contingent price offers means that the seller offers a set of such contracts, and lets the buyer choose the contract he likes best. Note that in some ways, this standard theoretical exercise is of limited practicality. One suspects that a buyer confronted with such an offer is likely to be quite suspicious, possibly questioning secret influence that the seller might have on the process which eventually determines prices. Our interest, here, is not the practical value of the idea, but rather its theoretical underpinnings.

4. Formally, we denote by v the buyer's value, and normalize to 0 the seller's value. We also denote by w the estimate that will be provided by the panel of experts.

A seller could propose a price p, with two possible consequences: missed trade if $p > v$, or surplus left to the buyer if $p < v$. Alternatively, the seller may propose a contingent price offer, or *contract*, that is a function P that specifies a price $P(w)$ to be paid by the buyer if the panel's estimate is w.

A contract is a potentially powerful tool to extract surplus. If there was a deterministic relationship between w and v, say:

$$w = \alpha v \tag{8.1}$$

then offering the contract

$$P(w) = w/\alpha$$

would permit the seller to extract all the rent: by construction, the price to be paid is v; the buyer gets no rent but does not lose from accepting.

Of course, the point is trivial. In essence, it says that rent extraction poses no difficulty even when v is not known at the time of contracting, as long as this value is subsequently known perfectly.

5. A seemingly more challenging situation is one in which the relationship between v and w is uncertain.

As a first illustration, consider the case in which the relationship is as described above (Equation (8.1)), except that α is now assumed to be an independent random variable, say drawn from some distribution f. In spite of this randomness, one may define the expectation

$$\alpha_0 \equiv E\alpha,$$

and consider the contingent price offer:

$$P(w) = w/\alpha_0.$$

The price eventually paid by the buyer depends on the realization w. In expectation however, the gain from accepting this contract when one's value is v satisfies:[2]

$$v - E[P(w) \mid v] = 0.$$

The buyer thus does not lose from accepting the offer, and the seller can extract all the surplus. This example illustrates that lack of knowledge of the coefficient α does not, per se, create a difficulty. The exact value of α is not known at the time of contracting; however, the locus of the distribution, characterized by α_0, is perfectly known to both the seller and the buyer. Given this precise knowledge of α_0, the seller can carefully design the contract P so that, regardless of the value v, the expected gain from accepting is zero. Additionally, because the buyer knows α_0 as well, he can predict that he is making no losses (in expectation) from accepting the offer.

6. *Using a menu of contracts.* There are two ingredients that make the contract P useful: the fact that f is known to both agents, and the simple linear structure assumed. For more complex relationships between v and w, a single contract will not work, but a menu of contracts may. We illustrate below how this can be done.

Assume the following nonlinear relationship:

$$w = \phi(v) + \varepsilon,$$

where ε is an independent random variable with expectation 0 and variance σ^2.[3]

Given these assumptions, we define a menu of contingent prices, parameterized by some $\widehat{v}$:

$$P^{\widehat{v}}(w) = \widehat{v} + M[(w - \phi(\widehat{v}))^2 - \sigma^2].$$

Assume that the seller proposes such a menu, and that the buyer is free to choose the contingent price he likes best. Picking contract $P^{\widehat{v}}$ is equivalent to paying $\widehat{v}$ up front, and then receiving a reward or getting a penalty as a function of the distance between w and $\phi(\widehat{v})$. The value $\widehat{v}$ can be interpreted as the buyer's statement about his own value. Given this statement, $\phi(\widehat{v})$ is the stated expected value of w. If, indeed, w turns out to be sufficiently close to its stated expected value, the buyer receives a reward. Otherwise he receives a penalty.

From the buyer's perspective, the expected price from accepting the contract $P^{\widehat{v}}$ is :

$$E[P^{\widehat{v}}(w) \mid v] = \widehat{v} + M[\phi(v) - \phi(\widehat{v})]^2.$$

---

[2] This is because $E[P(w) \mid v] = \frac{Ew}{\alpha_0} = \frac{E\alpha}{\alpha_0} v = v$.

[3] For example, $\phi(v) = v^a$ with $a < 1$.

The buyer has the option to choose $\widehat{v} = v$, in which case his expected gain is zero. But he might want to reduce the expected price paid by stating that the good is worth less than its actual value (i.e., choosing $\widehat{v} < v$). The consequence, however, is that in expectation, the buyer incurs positive penalties.

By setting M sufficiently large, the seller can ensure that penalties from picking $\widehat{v} \neq v$ are very large, and the buyer must then report a value $\widehat{v}$ very close to v: the seller, therefore, extracts almost all the rent, regardless of the realization of v. Through this clever mechanism, the seller manages to construct a reward/penalty scheme that simultaneously ensures participation (the buyer gets non-negative gains) and provides incentives to report a value close to the true value.

As in the previous example, the construction of this menu relies on both agents having precise knowledge of the model, the functional form ϕ and the variance σ^2.

7. In both cases examined above, the seller knows neither the buyer's value v nor the experts' value w. He can only speculate that some relationship must exist between these two objects, since whatever makes an object valuable to an agent likely makes it also valuable to others (at least to some degree). The modeling tool that we use to describe mathematically this relationship is to define a joint distribution over the pair (v, w).

Defining this distribution is just a modeling tool that makes precise the relationship between v and w. However, we simultaneously endow the seller with instruments (i.e., contracts) that can be used to exploit, to an unrealistic degree, features of the model (i.e., the distribution) that we don't really expect the agents to know. The proposal made by the seller hinges on that distribution, as does the buyer's decision to accept (or reject) the proposal.

8. When the seller offers a price, he is subject to the possibility that his offer is ill-informed (because he doesn't know the exact value v). When the seller makes a contingent price offer, he could also be subject to the possibility that his offer is ill-informed, because he typically does not know the exact relationship between v and w (characterized by α is the first example).

However, by an artifact of modeling, these difficulties do not give rise to missed trade, nor surplus left to the buyer. Intuitively, there is no reason that an agent would have a good idea about the ratio α. The fact that neither agent has a good idea of α is modeled by assuming that α is a random variable. Unfortunately, a consequence of the usual modeling strategy is that both are assumed to know the distribution from which α is drawn, hence the expectation α_0. In particular, they have identical assessments of the benefits from the contract, making it easy for the seller to target a contract that extracts all surplus.

9. In offering a contract rather than a price, the seller actually faces the two following difficulties: the possibility that he misperceives α_0 and the possibility that the buyer also misperceives α_0.

Strategically, the seller's own misperceptions of α_0 ought to play the same role as his misperception of v – cautiousness in choosing the offer, whether that offer is a single or contingent price. As for price offers, this caution is synonymous with rents to the buyer and, sometimes, missed trade when he has not been cautious enough.

In addition to this standard strategic consideration, the buyer's acceptance decision is now at stake: deciding whether to accept a price p is an easier decision than deciding whether to accept a contract based on some yet-to-be-realized value w.[4] The buyer's possibly optimistic misperceptions may give the seller additional opportunities to extract surplus. However, misperceptions may also induce the buyer to be cautious in his acceptance decision, either protecting himself against his own possibly pessimistic misperception by being bolder in his acceptance decisions, or protecting himself against the seller's conflicting objective by being more prudent in his acceptance decisions.

Thus, contracts potentially open new strategic considerations, without resolving the original problem (lack of knowledge of v), and there is no reason to expect, in general, that inefficiencies (missed trade) and rents to the buyer would be reduced.

10. To conclude, we formalize the discussion above. We provide a model in which lack of knowledge of α does not translate into identical expectations. We begin by describing the simple price offer case.

We assume that whenever the buyer's value is v, the seller's perception of that value is $\tilde{v} = \gamma v$ where γ is assumed to be a random variable independent of v drawn from some density f, say $\log \gamma \sim \mathcal{N}(0, \sigma^2)$.

A price offer by the seller must depend on what the seller knows, that is, $\tilde{v}$. If the seller naively believed his perception, he would attempt to extract all rents by offering $p = \tilde{v}$. Yet, a seller who understands that his perception may be erroneous might want to be more cautious. To this end, we allow the seller to pick a shading factor λ optimally, offering:

$$p = \lambda \tilde{v}.$$

Normalizing the expectation Ev to 1, the seller's expected payoff can be written as:

$$G_S(\lambda) = \lambda \int_{\lambda \gamma < 1} \gamma f(\gamma) d\gamma.$$

By shading, the seller increases the chance of trade, but reduces his gain in the event of a sale. The optimal threshold λ^* solves this tradeoff.

---

[4] Simpler because in the first case, one need only compare p and v; while in the second, one has to determine the consequences of the contract.

11. We next explore the case where the seller proposes a contingent price. Consider as before the simple structure ($w = \alpha v$) and define each player's perception of α as:

$$\alpha_i = \alpha/\mu_i$$

where μ_i is drawn from some distribution f_i, for example, a lognormal distribution (i.e., $\log \mu_i \sim \mathcal{N}(0, \sigma_i^2)$). One may interpret a noisier perception (i.e., a larger σ_i) as less information.

For the seller, we assume that a contingent price offer must depend on what he knows (his perception α_i). A naive seller who takes his perception α_i at face value could attempt full surplus extraction by offering the following contingent price, $P_0(w) = w/\alpha_1$. As before however, a more sophisticated seller might prefer to be cautious and offer:

$$P^{\lambda_1}(w) = \lambda_1 P_0(w) = \lambda_1 w/\alpha_1.$$

In contrast to the price-offer case, the buyer's acceptance decision may be difficult because he also may not know α. He may form a naive estimate of the expected price offered by the seller, based on his perception α_2 of α, namely, $P^{\lambda_1}(\alpha_2 v)$. As is the case for the seller, he might want to be cautious in his acceptance decision, and set an acceptance threshold λ_2, accepting only when[5]

$$P^{\lambda_1}(\alpha_2 v) < \lambda_2 v \text{ or, equivalently, } \lambda_1 \mu_1 < \lambda_2 \mu_2.$$

To summarize, the seller wants to maximize:

$$G_S(\lambda_1, \lambda_2) = \int_{\lambda_1 \mu_1 < \lambda_2 \mu_2} \lambda_1 \mu_1 f_1(\mu_1) f_2(\mu_2) d\mu_1 d\mu_2,$$

choosing λ_1 optimally (given λ_2). The buyer wants to maximize:

$$G_B(\lambda_1, \lambda_2) = \int_{\lambda_1 \mu_1 < \lambda_2 \mu_2} (1 - \mu_1 \lambda_1) f_1(\mu_1) f_2(\mu_2) d\mu_1 d\mu_2$$

choosing λ_2 optimally (given λ_1).[6]

12. *Discussion.* For the special case where the buyer has an accurate perception of α (i.e., $\mu_2 \equiv 1$), the buyer has no reason to be strategic ($\lambda_2 = 1$ is optimal), and the problem is formally equivalent to the simple price offer.

---

[5] The condition $P^{\lambda_1}(\alpha_2 v) < \lambda_2 v$ is equivalent to $\lambda_1 \frac{\alpha_2 v}{\alpha_1} < \lambda_2 v$ hence, since $\alpha_i = \alpha/\mu_i$, to $\lambda_1 \mu_1 < \lambda_2 \mu_2$.

[6] To compute an equilibrium $(\lambda_1^*, \lambda_2^*)$, one can let $x = \lambda_1/\lambda_2$, $G(x) = \Pr(x\mu_1 < \mu_2)$ and $H(x) = G(x)E[\mu_1 \mid x\mu_1 < \mu_2]$. We have $G_S = \lambda_2 x H(x)$, which determines x^*, and $G_B = G(x) - \lambda_1 H(x)$, which implies $\lambda_1^* = G'(x^*)/H'(x^*)$ for an interior equilibrium.

Whether the seller prefers the simple price offer or the contingent price offer depends on the relative accuracy of his signals on v and on α. To the extent that we think that the seller has more accurate signals about $\alpha (= w/v)$ than about v, then indeed a contingent offer may be worthwhile. It is difficult to think why one's perception of α would be more accurate than perceptions of v. In fact, if one thinks that the seller constructs a signal of w/v from his perception $\tilde{v}$ of v and his perception $\tilde{w}$ of w, (that is $\alpha_1 = \tilde{w}/\tilde{v}$) then the opposite will be true.

In addition, in the likely case that the buyer's perception is inaccurate (μ_2 is a random variable), offering contracts raises more complex strategic issues, with the buyer setting λ_2 optimally. In particular, if the seller has relatively accurate perceptions of v and α, while the buyer has an inaccurate perception of α (i.e., μ_2 noisy), offering the contract is a bad idea because letting the buyer decide whether he wishes to accept the contract will generate more missed trades.[7]

13. *Summary.* Beyond the first observation that contracts and possibly menus of contracts might sometimes help, there is a question of how much the original theoretical exercise improves our understanding. This exercise takes seriously our modeling tool – a distribution over valuations/signals to characterize uncertainty, and grants both agents precise knowledge of this distribution. Imprecise knowledge of distributions however would restore rents to buyers. The original model suggests that contracts can be powerful tools, but it masks the strategic concerns that agents would inevitably face in attempting to propose or deciding whether to accept such contracts, notwithstanding the practical concern mentioned earlier – the inevitable suspicion that a complex contract generates. We elaborate on this suspicion in Chapter 21.

Further Comments

The surplus extraction literature originates from an example by Myerson, which shows that when a seller faces two buyers with correlated values, running an auction may not be the mechanism that generates the highest revenue. By exploiting the correlation structure in a clever way, a seller may be able to obtain full surplus extraction, that is, obtaining a revenue equal in expectation to the highest valuation. That idea was later generalized by Cremer and McLean (1985).

Myerson's aim was to express caution about the conclusion that auctions are optimal mechanisms: if one applies the standard mechanism design methodology to environments in which values are (slightly) correlated, as

---

[7] One can check that if σ_1 is small, then as σ_2 gets large, x^* grows very large, while λ_1^* remains bounded (because if not the buyer would have negative gains). The reason that x^* grows large when σ_2 is sufficiently large is that, for the distributions considered, the seller prefers to bet on a large mistake by the buyer. This in turn implies that in equilibrium, λ_2^* vanishes when σ_2 is large, as does the seller's expected gain.

opposed to being statistically independent, it is no longer the case that simple auctions are optimal. Although the example could already be seen as a critique of the mechanism design methodology itself, with conclusions being too sensitive to small changes in model specifications, Cremer and McLean's extension led to the broader concern that mechanisms themselves should not rely "too heavily" on the model specification; ideally they should be detail or prior free.[8]

We are of course sympathetic to that view, although we do not see "prior free" as an ideal benchmark. A take-it-or-leave-it offer is a mechanism that seems simple enough, yet the optimal offer cannot be unrelated to the model specifications. The modeling difficulty is in making sense of "not too heavily." Our answer has been to put a limit on the ability of players to exploit the underlying structure of the model, and to model this limit through strategy restrictions. It is fine if a seller wants to propose a contingent contract rather than a price, but his ability to calibrate that contract is limited to a one-dimensional variable.

We also emphasize that while the literature would like to avoid mechanisms that rely too heavily on model specifications, we point out not only the difficulty that a designer faces in constructing such a mechanism, but also the difficulty that the agents involved in these mechanisms face in determining how to behave (how to bid in the all-pay auction, whether to accept a contingent contract, etc.).

Beyond the surplus extraction literature, this chapter may also give a different perspective on contractual incompleteness, and question the practical scope of some theoretically attractive contracts. For the sake of mathematical tractability, one often limits heterogeneity in perceptions, introducing variables that are candidates for the basis of a contractual agreement, but which are generated according to a commonly known process. The expert assessment in this chapter played that role, being a yet-to-be-realized signal and providing an easy tool to design contracts that are acceptable to both parties. However, signals often come with heterogenous perceptions about what might generate them, thus making their use in a contract difficult.[9]

---

[8] The caution was formulated by Wilson (1987), and the literature often refers to Wilson's doctrine to motivate the use of detail-free design, ex post incentive compatibility or dominant strategy implementation. See for example Bergeman and Morris (2005) and Chung and Ely (2007) for detailed discussions.

[9] One reason for contractual incompleteness often invoked in the economics literature (see Tirole (1999) for a review) is that the "state of the world" on which parties might contract may not be observable/verifiable by the courts, hence these contracts would not be enforceable (an idea that has been challenged by the implementation literature).

A second reason is that some states may be unforeseen. Dealing with unforeseen contingencies is a challenge, because models often make precise these unforeseen contingencies and associate payoffs to them. Tirole (1999, page 756) writes: "with rational agents contingencies are never unforeseen; they are at worst, indescribable."

Tirole suggests that rational agents, by definition, must foresee the payoffs (implicitly because otherwise computations and comparisons of alternatives would be impossible). And if payoffs are foreseen, this leaves a large range of contractual possibilities.

Said differently, many models "find" that contracting under the veil of ignorance is easy, because under the veil of ignorance there are no asymmetries of information, hence (in these models) no differences in perceptions. However, any non-economist would probably find it implausible that ignorance would eliminate differences in perceptions.

References

Bergemann, D. and Morris, S. (2005). Robust mechanism design. *Econometrica*, 73(6), 1771–1813.

Chung, K. S. and Ely, J. (2007). Foundations of dominant strategy mechanisms. *Review of Economic Studies*, 74, 447–476.

Cremer, J. and McLean, R. (1985). Optimal selling strategies under uncertainty for a discriminating monopolist when demands are interdependent. *Econometrica*, 53, 345–361.

Myerson, R. (1981). Optimal auction design. *Mathematics of Operations Research*, 6, 58–73.

Neeman, Z. (2004). The relevance of private information in mechanism design. *Journal of Economic Theory*, 117, 55–77.

Tirole, J. (1999). Incomplete contracts: where do we stand? *Econometrica*, 67(4), 741–781.

Wilson, R. (1987). Game-theoretic approaches to trading processes. In T. Bewley, ed., *Advances in Economic Theory: Fifth World Congress*, pp. 33–77, Cambridge: Cambridge University Press.

We do not object to the possibility that agents contract on jointly observable payoff realizations. However, while the analyst may conveniently specify the details of what is unforeseen by the agent and the details of the links between actions and payoff contingencies, it is questionable that agents can fully exploit these presumed links. The range of contracts compared by the agent should be reasonably limited and anchored on their (possibly noisy) perceptions of the environment.

Even if the set of possible payoffs may be described, the perceived link between actions and future payoffs may be incorrect, shaping the set of potential contracts without the agent being able to undo the effects of these incorrect perceptions.

Tirole (1999, page 764) acknowledges this difficulty: "There is a serious issue as to how parties form probability distributions over payoffs when they cannot even conceptualize the contingencies and actions that yield those payoffs, and as to how they end up having common beliefs ex ante." This chapter addresses this issue.

CHAPTER 9

Folk Theorems

1. Long-term relationships have been extensively studied, aimed at understanding how repeated interaction can foster cooperation. The basic idea is simple. By conditioning future behavior on the outcome of current interactions, one can induce cooperative behavior today via future consequences. If an agent foresees that uncooperative behavior today translates into less profitable interactions tomorrow, his incentive to cooperate today increases.

This discipline is easy to implement when actions are observable, as deviations from cooperative behavior can be immediately and perfectly detected. If players put sufficient weight on future outcomes, the prospect of disrupting future cooperation is a stick that each wishes to avoid, resulting in disciplined behavior today.

However, actions are often not directly observable. When a firm secretly undercuts a competitor, this may eventually affect market shares. But changes in market shares could also have resulted from a temporary shift in demand. In a repeated bilateral interaction, when I put in effort in choosing a gift, the effort is not observable. It could be that, at times, a gift is appreciated even if little effort was expended and, at other times, a gift is not especially appreciated even when effort was put in. Actions are not directly observable, and the aim of the literature has been to understand how the nature and quality of observations affect the possibility of cooperation.

2. The literature has primarily focused on Folk theorems, characterizing when and how appropriate behavioral arrangements/agreements can provide the necessary carrots and sticks to support jointly desirable outcomes. Some behavioral arrangements are surprisingly effective: even when participants obtain poor information about each other's strategy, the usual conflict between self-interest and social efficiency can be overcome.

Yet, the plausibility of these behavioral arrangements is questionable. As in previous chapters, a weakness of the results is that the design of "strategies that work" often hinges on details of a model that one would not expect players to know or easily learn.

Repetition certainly helps, and the ability of players to foresee the likely consequence of their action fosters cooperation. But the general message conveyed by these results is that with sufficiently patient players, the nature and quality of information agents get about each other's behavior is not that critical. To the extent that the underlying behavioral assumptions are implausible, this message may be misleading. One would like to understand better the scope of cooperation *in practice*, and the extent to which given strategies work well in a variety of environments.

3. Actions taken by others may not be directly observable, but they have consequences on payoffs. The first challenge is to model the link between the actions taken and the observations made. This is done by assuming a *probability distribution* over outcomes contingent on the players' actions.

Imagine two firms selling similar products and posting identical prices. Consumers arrive sequentially. When a consumer arrives, each firm has the option to send him a secret price cut. The consumer's decision to buy depends on the prices offered and on his taste. Joint profit maximization can be achieved via collusion between the firms: it requires that there be no price cuts.

To simplify the problem further, assume that each firm i has a single way to undercut, so only two possible actions – *undercut* or *not* undercut the posted price agreement, $a_i \in \{u, n\}$. Also assume that given the posted price, the consumer always buys, so the outcome is the firm to which the consumer goes, firm 1 or firm 2: $y \in \{1, 2\}$.

A difficulty is in defining the relationship between the actions taken (a_1, a_2) and the outcome observed (y), and the usual assumption is that this relationship is stochastic, reflecting some uncertainty about the taste of consumers. Formally, the analyst defines what is called a monitoring structure, specifying a probability distribution over y for each action pair (a_1, a_2). For example:

$$p \equiv \Pr(y = 1 \mid a_1, a_2) = 1/2 \quad \text{if } a_1 = a_2 \tag{9.1}$$

and

$$\Pr(y = i \mid a_i, a_j) = 1 \quad \text{if } a_i = u \text{ and } a_j = n.$$

This means that, in the absence of undercutting (or if both undercut), firms share the market equally in expectation, while a firm that undercuts when the other does not gets the consumer. Assume also that the probability p does not vary over time.[1]

As discussed in Chapter 2, these distributional assumptions are a modeling convenience to capture in a parsimonious way, the idea that a firm that doesn't

---

[1] The interpretation is that consumers are heterogenous, tastes are symmetrically distributed across consumers, and that consumers are drawn sequentially from an arbitrarily large pool (justifying the non-varying probability $p = 1/2$).

get a consumer cannot be sure why: is this because of consumer taste, or because the other firm stole the consumer through secret undercutting?

4. The monitoring technology is a modeling tool that incorporates a firm's uncertainty about why it did not get a consumer. However, it can play a key role in constructing tacit agreements between the firms.

In the long run, if firms manage to avoid undercutting, the fraction of consumers that each gets on average over time should be close to $1/2$. So this seemingly innocuous assumption implies that although deviations are not perfectly detectable in the short run, even infrequent deviations become perfectly detectable in the long run: if a firm undercuts the other a tiny fraction α of the time, her market share will be arbitrarily close to $(1-\alpha)\frac{1}{2}+\alpha=\frac{1}{2}+\frac{\alpha}{2}$ in the long run, making the deviation perfectly detectable.

This is obviously a modeling artifact. There is no reason that market shares would be immune to permanent or long-lasting shocks. Observing a 40 percent market share is not necessarily evidence that one firm took advantage of the other. It may simply be evidence that consumer tastes shifted in that period. Much of the Folk theorem literature that deals with imperfectly observable actions hinges on the modeling artifact that, in the long run, even mildly profitable deviations are perfectly detectable.[2]

This logic is similar to that pointed out in the information aggregation chapter. With many occurrences of the same problem, a firm's overall market share is no longer subject to shocks. With many draws of noisy value estimates $z_i = \mu_i v$, the fraction of optimistic agents (i.e., those for which $z_i > v$) is also not subject to shocks.

5. We now formally illustrate the obstacle to sustaining a fully collusive agreement in the long run, when the monitoring technology is subject to permanent shocks. In a few words, if this were the case, a player could undercut some of the time, acting as though market conditions were better than they are for him. If this had no adverse consequences on the fraction of the time that (n,n) is played, that would be a profitable deviation. So this must reduce the fraction of the time that (n,n) is played, and an agreement cannot remain fully collusive when market conditions shift. Full details appear in Compte and Postlewaite (2013). We provide here a "slightly formalized" intuition.

The monitoring technology is characterized by the parameter p, that defines expected market shares when no undercutting takes place. Define a tacit agreement as a strategy that maps past observations of y to current play. A tacit agreement is an equilibrium if neither player can gain by behaving differently from the tacit agreement. We ask whether there exists

---

[2] Recent work somewhat mitigates the assumption that the monitoring structure is known, assuming an initial draw among a few well-defined distributions (see Fudenberg Yamamoto (2010) for example). These models however share the feature that most deviations (even infrequent ones) are perfectly detectable in the long run.

an equilibrium tacit agreement that generates the cooperative outcome most of the time independently of p, assuming that p remains in an interval $[\underline{p},\overline{p}]$ such that $\underline{p} < 1/2 < \overline{p}$.[3]

The answer is that this is not possible. Consider p and α such that

$$\alpha + (1 - \alpha)p < \overline{p}.$$

Firm 1, by undercutting firm 2 with probability α in any period where (n,n) ought to be played, generates an outcome that coincides with the one that would result from the monitoring technology $p' = \alpha + (1 - \alpha)p$ and no undercutting taking place. Since in the latter case, (n,n) is played most of the time, the same must be true when the monitoring technology is p and firm 1 undercuts with probability α. So, undercutting must be a profitable deviation for firm 1. This contradicts the hypothesis that a tacit agreement would generate the cooperative outcome (n,n) most of the time, for all $p \in [\underline{p},\overline{p}]$.[4]

6. To illustrate further the difficulty in sustaining cooperation, we exhibit a particular collusive equilibrium in which sufficiently patient players choose (n,n) most of the time when $p = 1/2$. Following that, we explain the consequences of a shift in p.

Toward this end, we first complete the description of the game by assuming that in any particular period, players may agree on a temporary exclusion: only one of them posts a price. That firm becomes a monopoly for one period, without running the risk that the other undercuts. To fix ideas, assume that when no undercutting occurs, they both get the same payoff in expectation, and that undercutting or exclusion both generate an efficiency loss (L).

Exclusions are inefficient, so they should be used parsimoniously. The question is whether they can be rarely used, and yet provide adequate incentives not to undercut when both post prices.

There is a very simple mechanism that achieves this. Define Δ to be the current balance between the number of consumers obtained by each firm:

$$\Delta = \#\{y = 1\} - \#\{y = 2\}.$$

We define strategies parameterized by the maximum value K that the spread $\mid \Delta \mid$ can take. If $\mid \Delta \mid < K$, both firms are allowed to post prices and they

---

[3] Alternatively, one may assume that p is drawn from a distribution that is continuous on $[0,1]$ and strictly positive on $(\underline{p},\overline{p})$.

[4] The argument implicitly considers a deviation α as though firm 1 had relatively precise knowledge of p, thereby avoiding the possibility that her expected share $\alpha + (1 - \alpha)p$ exceeds $\overline{p}$: the tacit agreement cannot be adjusted to p, but deviations can. Note however that; (i) such knowledge comes about quickly given the assumed stationarity; and (ii) under the distributional assumption of Footnote 3, even if p is unknown, there is a loss from the deviation only when p is close to $\overline{p}$, hence second-order in α, while the gain is first-order in α.

are both supposed to play n (no undercutting). When the balance becomes too favorable to a firm, say firm 1 (i.e., $\Delta = K$), that firm is excluded for two periods (after that $\Delta = K - 2$), and symmetrically for firm 2.

It is easy to verify that this is an equilibrium when players are sufficiently patient. In essence, this mechanism ensures that market shares remain close to $1/2$. A firm could decide to undercut today (stealing one consumer), but eventually, the market share constraint will force her to give back whatever she stole from the other firm (giving back a consumer) hence overall at least incurring the efficient loss L. The length of time it takes to give back the consumer depends on K, but if players are patient enough, this is not an issue and K can be set large, meaning that the maximum spread K is rarely reached. The equilibrium is close to being efficient.

Of course, the mechanism is finely tuned to the hypothesis that $p = 1/2$. Should consumer tastes shift so that $p < 1/2$, the spread $| \Delta |$ will drift toward K, and inefficiencies will be unavoidable.

In fact, the only way that one can ensure a 50/50 market share when $p = 40$ percent is to exclude a firm $1/6$ of the time![5]

7. *Concluding comments.* By defining a particular monitoring structure, the analyst implicitly assumes that in the long run, deviations are easily detectable. An interesting insight of the literature is that in spite of this assumption, which should seemingly make it easy to support cooperation, resorting to mutual punishments to sustain cooperation necessarily generates inefficiencies.[6]

Another interesting insight of the literature is that the inefficiencies above may be reduced when punishments are not mutual – punishing one player means rewarding the other.[7] The example above illustrates this, with the temporary exclusion of one player benefiting the other to some degree. What the example shows, however, is that the adequate balancing of sticks and carrots is a difficult matter. Doing it in ways that support efficient outcomes requires adjusting strategies to the process that determines observations, hence to aspects of the model that we shouldn't expect players to know.

Further Comments

Simplifying the environment that we analyze is a natural tendency for theorists. Our aim is often to illustrate a basic phenomenon, disentangling it from other effects that may obfuscate the main insight. Often however, the models may

---

[5] If f is the fraction of the time firm 2 is excluded, the market share of firm 1 is $p(1 - f) + f$. Equal market shares in the long run requires $p(1 - f) + f = 1/2$, that is $f = (1/2 - p)/(1 - p)$.

[6] Intuitively, punishments must have the same order of magnitude as gains from deviating, and be triggered with significant probability in case of deviation. The problem is that, to be triggered with significant probability in case of deviation, they must also be triggered with significant probability even when no deviation occurs (Radner, Myerson and Maskin (1986)).

[7] See Fudenberg, Levine and Maskin (1994).

become so simplified that their structure can be exploited too easily, or in unrealistic ways, by the agents that we wish to model.

For example, the analysis of finitely repeated games reveals that sustaining cooperation is not as obvious as it may seem. Since there is no incentive to cooperate in the last period, there cannot be any incentive to cooperate either at the next to last date, and so on backwards. That there may exist an end date effect is a valid insight. That it contaminates behavior at all dates prior to the last one, preventing any cooperation whatsoever, seems to be a modeling artifact that illustrates more about our models and their shortcomings than about behavior in real interactions. The move to models in which the game does not end, or ends stochastically, have proved useful in that respect.[8]

Another example is the analysis of games in which agents receive public signals imperfectly correlated with the actions played. These models achieve cooperation by relying on coordination, built around these public signals that players simultaneously receive, triggering phases of non-cooperation and phases of cooperation whose length are finely tuned to special characteristics of the game being played.

While the construction allows us to show that through adequate coordination, sustaining cooperation is theoretically feasible even when actions cannot be perfectly observed, we seldom address the practicality of these behavioral arrangements (if agents were not able to perfectly tune their behavior to the public signal received, such coordination would become impossible), or whether public signals and coordination are central to cooperation in practice.

This chapter began with a basic intuition that is important, if not central, to cooperation in practice: incentives to cooperate arise when one anticipates that "bad" behavior today leads to bad experiences that translate into less profitable interactions tomorrow. There may be obvious reasons why such a link (between bad behavior and reduced profitable interactions in the future) exists, that do not rely on fine coordination of agents' strategies. When the environment changes stochastically, with some persistence, there is some value to using current experience to assess whether attempting to cooperate is worthwhile. This willingness to learn from experience, in turn, may generate enough dependence on past signals to create incentives to cooperate. Said differently, it could be that models which are based on coordination overemphasize the role played by public signals in practice. After all, it seems that we often manage to cooperate without them, or without ever being certain of the degree to which the seemingly public signals that we pay attention to have been noticed or taken into account by others.[9]

---

[8] See Rubinstein (1991), who provides another defense for studying infinitely repeated games: the infinite version captures better the agent's perception of a long game. We share that view but our argument above is slightly different. It may be fine to consider a finite game, but then the ability of agents to exploit that finite length ought to be limited. See Chapter 19.

[9] This is the path followed in Chapter 14. We propose a model in which the underlying parameters vary, providing agents with obvious incentives to adjust behavior to past experience.

The lesson that we draw is that if we wish to address real-world problems, our models must maintain a balance: the environment should remain complex enough, or the strategic variables sufficiently limited, to ensure that intuitions are not driven by the inner workings of our tools.[10]

Finally, we point out that many results in repeated game theory have a mechanism design flavor. We fix a particular game specification and then aim to find the best ways to achieve cooperation for that particular specification. This is useful for understanding the power and limits of our mathematical tools and models to achieve or support cooperation. We should be judicious about transporting insights from analyses of these models to real-world problems: do they contribute to a better understanding of how real-world agents behave or cooperate?

This same observation applies to other branches of economic theory. As analysts, we pose a contracting problem as though agents had the luxury of comparing arbitrarily many contracts. Whether the optimal contract obtained in this way is useful in understanding real contracts might be questioned. The form of optimal contracts will rarely take the form that we see in practice, unless one starts with special assumptions on the form of the environment under study. And even when it does take a form that we see in practice, one cannot help but wonder whether optimization across all possible contractual forms is behind the contracts that we see.

References

Fudenberg, D., Levine, D. and Maskin, E. (1994). The folk theorem with imperfect public information. *Econometrica*, 62(5), 997–1039.

Fudenberg, D. and Yamamoto, Y. (2010). Games where the payoffs and monitoring structure are unknown. *Econometrica*, 78(5), 1673–1710.

Radner, R., Myerson, R. and Maskin, E. (1986). An example of a repeated partnership game with discounting and with uniformly inefficient equilibria. *The Review of Economic Studies*, 53(1), 59–69.

Rubinstein, A. (1991). Comments on the interpretation of game theory. *Econometrica*, 59(4), 909–924.

---

[10] As yet another illustration, comparative statics made on mixed strategy equilibria often have a counterintuitive favor, because the mixing is tuned to a very special payoff structure.

CHAPTER 10

Comparative Statics

1. A recurrent question in economic theory concerns the effect of changes in information on economic decisions, and further, the incentives to reveal or hide information. Is an employer better off withholding or sharing (some) information about the job he proposes to a prospective employee? Does information produce more or less competitive behavior? What kind of information should a seller disclose? Does information promote or hinder coordination?

A frequent insight from theoretical models is that one is better off when the others are "uninformed": it is easier to take advantage of poorly informed agents. The conclusion generally finds its genesis in the fact that when an agent is uninformed, it is easy for others to predict what the agent believes. This is obviously a surprising statement. If you have no idea what a logarithm is, and if I force you to give me your best guess of the logarithm of 132, predicting your answer would seem to be difficult.

2. As with previous chapters, a weakness of the "insight" is that it is mostly a modeling artifact. It stems from the special way in which information or lack of information is modeled in games. In modeling a game in which agents lack information about some underlying state, agents are assumed to know (or behave as if they knew) the underlying distribution over states. In addition, agents may not be equally informed, and some may receive further information about the realized state. In these models, an "uninformed" agent is an agent who gets no further specific information on which he might condition his behavior. Despite this lack of specific information, the uninformed agent is assumed to be perfectly informed of the distribution, and others thus know what he knows, or what drives his decisions.[1]

3. *Back to dice.* Two dice are thrown. A five and a one show up. Our agent does not see which faces are shown, but he is asked to report his best prediction of

---

[1] Some solution concepts do not necessarily have this property. We shall discuss these at the end of this chapter (see point 11).

the sum $s = s_1 + s_2$.[2] The state s can be seen as a realization of a random variable taking values in $\{2, \ldots, 12\}$. The current realization is $5 + 1 = 6$, but its expectation is 7. That expectation coincides with the agent's best prediction, and an outside observer, whether he knows or does not know s, has no difficulty predicting that answer.

Now assume that our agent is given *partial information*; that is, he gets to see one of two thrown dice, say $s_1 = 5$. His prediction is then modified to $5 + 3.5 = 8.5$. The information that the agent receives ($s_1 = 5$) improves his prediction of the sum. For example, the maximal error is reduced from $12 - 7 = 5$ to $11 - 8.5 = 2.5$. To an outsider who does not see the dice, that information makes it more difficult to guess the prediction of the agent, because the prediction of the agent is a function of what the agent sees: the prediction is $s_1 + 3.5$. And even to an outsider who *sees* the dice (five and one) but cannot see which face (five or one) was observed by the agent, guessing the agent's prediction is difficult: will it be $5 + 3.5$ or $1 + 3.5$?

4. We have described above the standard way of modeling an "uninformed" agent. Despite his apparent lack of information, our agent is rather well informed: he knows what a die is, he knows that it has six faces, and that each of these faces is equally likely. In the language of Chapter 2, the agent ignores the current situation s, but he has a very good idea about the characteristics of the generic situation that he faces. He is characterized by local ignorance, but global knowledge. This way of modeling ignorance is at the heart of our concern. In games, all players know the generic situation, so they know perfectly what "uninformed" players know, and therefore they can anticipate their behavior perfectly.

5. One could imagine an agent with less information than that described above, an agent with less knowledge of the generic situation. It could be that the agent has never heard of a die, or that he is not completely sure that it has six faces, or that he is not sure about its shape – whether it is a cube or not. Showing an agent what a die is *is* information. Without this information, the agent's best prediction of the sum s need not be seven and, indeed, guessing the agent's prediction seems difficult.

Similarly, if one is asked to report $\phi(x) \equiv (\log x)^2$ for various values of x, knowing what a logarithm is, or even having access to a logarithmic table is valuable information, because it allows one to report figures that are closer for each x to the actual value of $(\log x)^2$. On the other hand, as mathematical skills decrease, one expects greater deviations from correct values. One can only speculate whether these departures from correct answers exhibit a systematic optimistic or pessimistic bias across values of x. It is not unreasonable to expect that whatever these biases are, departures will vary across agents. In particular,

---

[2] By best prediction, we mean the real number a that minimizes the expected loss $(a - s)^2$.

to an outsider who knows the correct responses and whose job is to guess the reports, the job seems easier if a logarithmic table is available to the agent, more difficult if the agent has never heard of logarithms.

The general message of these examples is that lack of information not only undermines a player' predictions, but also adversely affects the accuracy of others' guesses about these predictions.

6. *A typical estimation problem.* The model below formalizes this. Consider an agent who is asked to report a message or take an action as close as possible to some underlying state s, where s is a real number. If the report a and the state s do not coincide, the agent is assumed to experience a quadratic loss, that is, $L(a,s) = (a-s)^2$. One could think of this as a jar problem. A jar is filled with coins and you are asked to report a number as close as possible to the value of the coins in the jar.

The agent does not see the state s. His information is modeled by assuming that a signal z is observed and by assuming a particular probability distribution ω over state and observation (s,z). Specifically, assume that

$$z = s + \varepsilon$$

with s and ε drawn from independent normal distributions centered on s_0 and ε_0, with variance v^2 and σ^2 respectively.[3]

Under these assumptions, the optimal action/report consists of choosing:

$$a^*(z) = E_\omega[s \mid z] = \rho(z - \varepsilon_0) + (1-\rho)s_0 \text{ where } \rho = \frac{v^2}{\sigma^2 + v^2}.$$

The agent corrects for estimation errors in two ways. He avoids systematic estimation errors (ε_0), and then takes an average between $z - \varepsilon_0$ and the mean s_0, putting weight ρ below 1 on his signal. This is a "regression to the mean." As the agent's signal gets noisier (σ^2 higher), the coefficient ρ decreases and more weight is put on the mean (s_0).

In other words, the agent behaves as if he were given *two pieces of information*: the signal z, and the prior information on distributions, which may be conveniently summarized (given the assumed structure of the problem) by a *prior estimate* s_0 and a *quality parameter* ρ of the signal z. As the signal z becomes noisier, the agent puts more weight on his prior estimate s_0. And he does so because whenever the agent gets a signal, he behaves as if he were also implicitly informed of the quality of that signal.

---

[3] We allow for $\varepsilon_0 \neq 0$ to account for the possibility of systematic estimation errors. Note that the mathematical model presented here allows for negative s, mostly to simplify the mathematical computations to come. We could describe a similar model in which both s and z are positive random variables.

7. *Predictability.* The estimation problem above illustrates the effect of the accuracy of the estimate (measured by $1/\sigma$) on the discrepancy between informed and uninformed choice, and on the variance of the agent's choice. As one expects, when quality decreases, the variance of the error (i.e., $E(s - a^*(z))^2$) increases.[4] In contrast, however, the variance of the agent's choice is reduced:

$$E(a^*(z) - Ea^*(z))^2 = E(a^*(z) - s_0)^2 = \rho^2\sigma^2 = (\frac{v^2}{\sigma^2 + v^2})^2\sigma^2 \searrow 0.$$

Intuitively, our poorly informed agent receives a signal z, but he knows enough about the process that generates these signals to understand that he should ignore them. The consequence is that to an outsider, when the noise gets very large, the agent's choice becomes more predictable, and guessing the agent's report becomes easier.

The conclusion is surprising. One could expect that a less informed agent might not know that the signal z should be ignored. The consequence might be that for such an agent, behavior remains partially driven by z, and the behavior of even poorly informed agents remains hard to predict.

8. *A guessing game.* To illustrate further, call the agent player 1, the outsider player 2, and assume that player 2 knows the state and reports his optimal guess of player 1's prediction a. Call that guess b, and assume that player 2 tries to minimize $(b - a)^2$, where a is the report of player 1.

There are two instances in which player 2's guessing job is easy: when player 1 is completely informed (z very precise), and when player 1 is uninformed (z very noisy). Between those polar cases, the signal that player 1 gets creates, from the perspective of player 2, randomness in behavior (because player 2 does not see player 1's signal) that makes guessing more difficult.

9. *Further examples.* Lack of information reduces randomness in behavior: it becomes tuned to the exogenously fixed prior distributions. Many models exploit this idea. We provide below three examples, which we formalize in Section 12.

When a seller makes an offer to a buyer, it is easier for a seller to tailor his offer to a buyer who remains uninformed of the characteristics of the object. Information creates heterogeneity in possible values, and this heterogeneity is a source of rent for the buyer.

When two such buyers compete for an object in an auction, and when they do not care about the same characteristics of that object, information about the characteristics creates dispersion in values. This weakens competition and hurts the seller.

---

[4] One can check that $E(s - a^*(z))^2 = \rho^2\sigma^2 + (1 - \rho)^2v^2 = \frac{v^2}{1 + v^2/\sigma^2}$, which increases when σ^2 increases.

When two agents care about adjusting behavior to some underlying state, and about coordinating their behavior, lack of information may improve their ability to take coordinated actions, because actions become tailored to the priors (which are identical), rather than driven by agent-specific (and possibly diverse) information over the state.

In these three examples, the intuition is misleading because it builds on a questionable premise:

Lack of information $\implies$ *No heterogeneity*

10. *Regressing to the mean. But which mean?* Optimal behavior calls for regression to the mean. In some applications, this sounds reasonable. If my son tells me that he just saw a man about 10 feet tall, I will probably think that the man was quite tall but opt for a more realistic figure – one that would look closer to "normal." In many applications, however, there may not exist a "normal" estimate.

If faced with a die that does not look like a cube, being told that out of 40 throws, 20 were six, may not seem abnormal: this event (call it A) may just be seen as an indication that the die is biased in favor of six. Of course, being told that 2 out of 4 throws were six also provides information. But, this event (call it B) appears to be weaker evidence that the die is biased in favor of six: it is not an unlikely event, even for unbiased dice.

Put differently, imagine that after seeing event A (or event B), you are asked to bid for the right to win \$1,000 if the number you pick shows up on the next draw of the die. Then, it is likely that you bet that a six will come up, and that your bid will be higher under event A than under event B. One way to model this problem is to assume that all possible biases are equally likely. This generates a joint distribution over $p = (p_1,\ldots,p_6)$ (the bias) and $X \in \{A,B\}$. One may then compute the conditional expectations $E[p_6 \mid X]$ and observe:

$$E[p_6 \mid A] > E[p_6 \mid B].$$

In this example, the assumption that all possible biases are equally likely is made for convenience. We make it, not because we think that in the world of biased dice, all biases are equally probable: but, rather, we make it because it is a convenient way to capture how the strength of the evidence changes with the number of draws, and possibly also because other distributions would seem difficult to justify.

This way of modeling ignorance (i.e., all biases equally probable) produces a force in the direction of $1/6$, and this force is stronger when there are fewer draws. There isn't really a "population of biased dice." Nevertheless, for agents who see only a few draws, it seems reasonable that their estimates of p_6 remain close to $1/6$.

Many problems, however, do not map neatly to the die example above. There may exist nothing equivalent to the uniform draw over biases, which could generate a force toward some mean prediction, and on which all agents would agree. If one must estimate a quantity of oil in an oil field, it could be that many estimates seem normal. If I think of a point estimate for a number of coins in a jar, there may be nothing that would make me think the estimate is extreme, and similarly when asked about $(\log x)^2$ for various values of x. As with the biased die, I may not have great confidence in my estimates. The reason may be that I know that my mathematical skills are not great, or that I know from experience that predictions of oil fields are rarely accurate. But while for the biased die it did not seem crazy to assume a uniform draw over all biases, it is hard to come up with a natural "mean" or "generic" situation. There is no such thing as a typical oil field, a typical jar, or a typical response to $(\log x)^2$.

11. *Heterogenous versus common priors.* A prevailing approach in economic modeling is that the distribution ω over (z, s) enables us to represent the ignorance that an agent faces, and that ω should be thought of as being subjective. With that subjective view in mind, there is no reason that the distribution ω should be common to all participants. It can be thought of as being agent-specific, say characterized by a specific mean of the underlying state, s_0^i for agent i. Lack of precise information about s (i.e., a noisy signal z_i) then translates into more weight being put on priors, hence more weight on s_0^i. In particular, lack of precise information need not translate into less heterogeneity in reports, as they will reflect heterogeneity in priors – each agent regresses to the mean, but each has in mind a different mean.

While this heterogenous prior approach may sometimes be valuable, particularly when predictions can be made irrespective of the priors, analysts generally favor models in which more structure is put on priors: standard modeling typically assumes common priors.

A first difficulty with heterogenous priors is that decisions are not necessarily connected to actual consequences for the agent. If we are interested in the extent to which buyers and sellers miss trading opportunities, a theory that profitable trades are missed because each side entertains bizarre ideas about the actual surplus is limited. Agents should eventually consider that their behavior is misguided, and adjust it in ways that could make trade more likely. Defining a unique prior, common to all players, and reflecting the typical situation that agents face, may be viewed as a disciplining device that we impose on ourselves, so that "insights" are not generated by absurd assumptions about subjective priors, and so that the evaluation of strategies truly reflects the typical consequences for the agents.

Another issue with the subjective approach is that it becomes difficult to model game situations where interests are intertwined. To illustrate, consider a modified version of the guessing game, in which the agent who makes the first prediction has a stake in the quality of the second agent's guess. With a purely subjective view, one may want to describe beliefs entertained by the second about the first. And the belief that the first entertains about the beliefs of the second, etc. Eventually, a player's decision could be based on a complex hierarchy of beliefs.

Harsanyi's contribution was to propose a shortcut that dispenses with these complex belief hierarchies. A player's belief, however complex, is summarized by a type, and the game is solved as if types and states were drawn from a common joint distribution, as if there were no heterogeneity in higher-order beliefs. This technique has enabled the huge development of information economics since the 1970's. However, it has some undesirable consequences. The consequence emphasized in this chapter is the lack of heterogeneity in beliefs as players become less informed: their beliefs necessarily converge to the hypothetical common prior distribution over underlying states.

What we propose is an alternate device, one that maintains the assumption of a single underlying distribution (over states and observations), but that limits agents' ability to exploit that distribution. This distribution is not meant to describe what is in the agents' mind, but, rather, a way of connecting decisions to actual consequences. We thus retain a force toward welfare maximization by each player, without simultaneously introducing common views in the agents' minds and commonly known beliefs for uninformed agents.

12. *Comparative statics. Three detailed examples.* We present three examples of insights obtained using standard modeling techniques, following which we critique that method. In each example, we analyze the comparative statics with respect to information, starting from one or several uninformed agents, and next endowing them with further information.

Rent extraction. The first insight is that it is easier for a seller to fine tune his offer to a buyer who remains uninformed. When the buyer acquires information, he sees whether there is a good fit between the object and his preferences. This is detrimental to the seller because the buyer only buys when there is a good fit, and the seller (who does not observe whether or not the fit is good) can no longer adjust his offer to the buyer's preference.

Formally, assume the seller's value is 0 and the buyer's value is $v > 0$. The buyer's value depends on characteristics of the object that are relevant to the buyer. Specifically, we assume

$$v = w\theta,$$

where θ is a positive random variable with expectation 1 and w is a positive scalar. The parameter θ reflects how the object's characteristics affect the buyer's value. When the buyer knows these characteristics, his value is $w\theta$. When he is uninformed, his expected value is w. The seller does not observe θ.[5]

---

[5] The seller may know the characteristics of the object, but we assume that he does not know how characteristics affect the buyer's value.

If the potential buyer is uninformed, the seller may obtain a gain arbitrarily close to w.[6] Since w is also the total surplus available, the seller cannot hope to do better if the potential buyer gets more information.[7,8]

A similar insight holds in a strategic interaction between a firm and a prospective employee, with the firm making a take-it-or-leave-it wage offer. Under similar assumptions, the firm is better off if the prospective employee does not have easy access to the requirements or duties that come with the job.[9]

The logic is the same: it is easier to hold the employee to his reservation level if he is uninformed. Information that an agent gathers or possesses creates an asymmetry in information that (typically) generates rents to one who acquires information (the buyer or the employee).[10]

In a model where priors do not play such a key role, we would expect two strategic effects (as in Chapter 8): a poorly informed buyer could be cautious in his acceptance decisions, and a seller could face difficulties in predicting the acceptance decision of a poorly informed agent. Indeed, what makes the seller's decision more difficult is not information per se, but lack of predictability. It just happens that the model tends to equate lack of information with greater predictability.

Second-price auction. When two bidders participate in a second-price auction,[11] the seller's revenue is the minimum of the two bids. Consequently increased dispersion in values tends to diminish the seller's revenue. Because information tends to increase dispersion, information can also decrease the seller's revenue, and a seller may thus prefer that bidders remain uninformed.[12]

Formally, consider two bidders participating in a second-price auction. Values to the bidders are modeled as in the rent extraction problem above. Specifically, the value is:

$$v_i = w\theta_i,$$

---

[6] When the seller makes an offer below but arbitrarily close to w, the buyer accepts (and gets almost 0 gain).

[7] One can further check that for any price $p > w$ offered to an informed buyer, his expected gain is $G = p \Pr(\theta > \frac{p}{w})$, and that for any non-degenerate distribution $\tilde{\theta}$, $G \leq w \max_x x \Pr(\theta > x) < w$.

[8] We do not suggest that the seller is always better off when the buyer is uninformed. If the seller had another prospective buyer to whom he could sell at price w, information acquisition by the buyer always increases the seller's gain, because it provides the seller with an opportunity to sell at $p > w$ without the risk of losing a trade.

[9] Whether the candidate is an insider or an outsider to the firm may be the source of the difference in information.

[10] For example, see Cremer and Khalil (1992), who uses that insight to show that "the optimal contract [should] never induce precontractual observation or precontractual investigation [by the agent]."

[11] In a second-price auction, the object is allocated to the highest bidder, at a price equal to the second highest bid.

[12] See for example Ganuza (2004) for a model that exploits this idea.

where θ_1 and θ_2 are positive, and independently and identically distributed, with, say, expectation 1.[13]

When the agents do not know the characteristics, each bids his expected value for the object (that is, $wE\theta_i = w$). The seller gets a revenue w. When the agents know the characteristics of the object, each one bids v_i, and the seller's revenue decreases to $wE\min\theta_i$.

In this example, there are efficiency gains from information acquisition (unlike in the previous take-it-or-leave-it example). From the seller's perspective, however, these efficiency gains are offset by the increase in rent that (both) buyers get in expectation.

From each buyer's perspective, lack of information comes with certainty about priors, hence certainty about one another's expected values. The symmetry assumption then reduces rents to 0 for both. In contrast, information generates a dispersion in value, and dispersion creates rents.

In other words, rents are linked to the dispersion in value estimates. Value estimates are more concentrated when agents are less informed. This, again, happens because the model equates lack of information with no dispersion in estimates.

In a model in which priors would not play such a key role, we could expect another strategic effect: a poorly informed bidder could be cautious in his bidding strategy, correcting for the estimation errors he might be making, considering the fact that he wins only because he is overly optimistic (see Chapter 11).

Coordination. Consider an organization with two divisions. Each division cares about the fit of its choices to the environment. The organization cares about the fit of the divisions' choices to the environment, *as well as the coordination of choices between divisions.*[14] The organization has information that could improve the divisions' assessments of the environment. Should it provide that information? We illustrate below that because information may increase variance in behavior, the organization may have incentives to withhold information.

Preferences of each division $i = 1, 2$ are defined as follows:

$$L_i(a_1, a_2, s) = (a_i - s)^2.$$

Preferences of the organization are defined by

$$L_0(a_1, a_2, s) = m(a_1 - a_2)^2 + L_1(a_1, a_2, s) + L_2(a_1, a_2, s).$$

---

[13] Independence might stem from agents caring about different characteristics. It implies that in a second-price auction, it is optimal for each player to bid his own expected value for the object.

[14] The setup in the example below is inspired by Dessein and Santos (2006).

Observations are modeled as noisy signals z_1 and z_2 that divisions privately receive:

$$z_i = s + \varepsilon_i$$

with the state s and noise terms ε_i assumed to be normally and independently distributed, with variances respectively equal to v^2 and σ^2. In the limit where signals are very noisy (i.e., $\sigma = \infty$, divisions are uninformed), the divisions both choose $a_i = s_0$, and the organization's loss is

$$L_0^{un} = 2v^2.$$

When signals are less noisy, divisions choose $a_i = \rho z_i + (1 - \rho)s_0$ where $\rho = v^2/(v^2 + \sigma^2)$, and the organization's loss is:

$$L_0^{inf} = 2m\rho^2\sigma^2 + 2\rho^2\sigma^2 + 2(1 - \rho)^2 v^2.$$

Comparing these losses, we get:[15]

$$L_0^{inf} - L_0^{un} = 2\sigma^2\rho^2(m - 1 - \frac{v^2}{\sigma^2})$$

which implies that if $m > 1$ and if σ^2/v^2 is sufficiently large, the organization is better off withholding information, for fear that this information would impair coordination.

The logic of the example is thus similar to that pointed out earlier. Lack of information ($\sigma = \infty$) makes agents sensitive only to the prior distribution assumed, and, somewhat artificially, this facilitates coordination. As agents get more information, their behavior becomes less coordinated.[16]

In a model in which priors do not play this role, lack of information would make both coordination and consistency with the state more difficult. The organization and the divisions would all be unambiguously better off if the signals' noise was reduced.

Comments. The examples above analyze the comparative statics with respect to information. In so doing, we start with an *uninformed agent* and endow him with some information in the form of signals correlated with the underlying state. This additional information generates behavior that looks more random, and less predictable than either uninformed or perfectly informed agents/outsiders.

One could consider an alternative model in which the starting point is a perfectly informed agent, and compare this with the situation where he is slightly less informed. In comparison with a perfectly informed agent, the behavior of a slightly less informed agent would look less predictable.

[15] Observe that $v^2 - (\rho^2\sigma^2 + (1 - \rho)^2 v^2) = v^4/(\sigma^2 + v^2) = \rho^2(\sigma^2 + v^2)$.
[16] See Dessein et al. (2016) for a model with a similar flavor, in which poor information of each division on their own task makes coordination across divisions easier.

So we do not claim that standard models always have the property that reduced information makes behavior more predictable. Rather, we point out that *some* models have this property, and they have it because agents are implicitly assumed to know the model and priors.

Further Comments

Regression to the mean. The idea originates from Francis Galton's study of height,[17] his observation that offsprings' deviation from the mean is a fraction of their own parents' deviation from the mean population. Of course, transmission of traits is now better understood. Still, in relation to Galton's question, one can ask, as we did in this chapter: How does one define the mean? What's the relevant population?

In the context of signal processing, regression to the mean suggests that one should not take signals at face value. When one treats observed performance as a signal about ability, one should be cautious: observed performance may contain an element of luck, an idiosyncratic element specific to the current instance. To determine true ability, or to predict the next draw, one should regress the signal to the mean.

Our primary message has been that "mean performance" may be difficult to define. Performance might depend on the particular circumstances in which the task was undertaken. "Mean performance," then, becomes an ambiguous term, even for the statistician who observes performance (but not the circumstances).

In a story told by Daniel Kahneman, the observation that very good performance of prospective pilots tends to be followed by a decrease in performance is attributed to a purely statistical effect (the idea that the initial good outcome is due to luck). An equally convincing story is that in a later trial, when one tries to reproduce what led to good performance, one may have erroneous ideas of what has led to it, not realizing that new circumstances call for different responses. The reason for the decline might not be purely statistical, but, rather, overconfidence in what caused good performance in the previous trial, with the consequence that praising good performance, hence reinforcing one's confidence, could be counter productive, as the flight instructor in Daniel Kahneman's story suggested.

Base-rate neglect. Our discussion is also related to the idea that people would be subject to base-rate neglect, overemphasizing the signals related to the specific case at hand, and not properly taking account of the statistical information or aggregate data that concerns the category of cases to which that specific case (seemingly) belongs.

The degree to which agents might neglect base rates has been extensively studied. Among the plausible reasons suggested about why aggregate statistical information has reduced influence on perceptions, a recurrent

---

[17] Galton (1886)

suggestion, consistent with our view, is that assessing the reliability or the relevance of aggregated data is difficult.[18]

Our emphasis however is not in explaining base-rate neglect, but in drawing attention to the logic underlying most economic models, and the fact that in these models, the prior distribution is akin to a base rate that sometimes get too much influence on predicted behavior, not too little: (i) standard models artificially define two components of information, one that relates to the specific case under consideration (through a signal z) and another that relates to the broader category of cases to which it belongs (through a distribution ω); (ii) comparative statics modify the quality of the first component only, assuming that the second component remains accurately known and common to all players (changes in signals' quality are thus perfectly assessed), with the consequence that standard models may overemphasize the role of base-rates/priors.

Our view is that it is productive to study models in which agents do not have an accurate or reliable perception of the category of cases to which the current problem belongs (e.g., the quality of the signals they get). A consequence of a less reliable perception of the category would likely be a greater dispersion in the behavior of uninformed agents.

Information measures. Economists' approach to modeling information or comparing information structures is similar to that developed in information theory by Shannon (1948), which characterizes the degree to which a coding system and a noisy communication channel transmit information from a given source. These measures quantify the reduction in uncertainty induced by the code and the channel,[19] *building on the engineer's knowledge of the characteristics of the source (English sentences) and the channel (chances of losses in transmission).*[20]

While the exercise is natural for the engineer who knows the general characteristics of the data to be transmitted, and the characteristics of the transmission channels and of the code that he uses, the enlistment of these measures to economic agents deserves scrutiny: the economic environment does not speak a well-defined language with known and unchanging characteristics; nor can we ascertain the relationship between the environment faced and our perception of it.

---

[18] See Koehler (1996) for a review.

[19] If s is the state and z the message received (both modeled as random variables $\tilde{s}$ and $\tilde{z}$), one measures the expected entropy reduction induced by observing z rather than "nothing": $I \equiv H(\tilde{s}) - H(\tilde{s} \mid \tilde{z}) \equiv -E_s \log \omega(s) + E_z E_s \log \omega(s \mid z)$ where $\omega(z,s)$ is the joint distribution over z,s and $\omega(s)$ the marginal distribution over states.

[20] The comparison of information structures, due to Blackwell (1951), also proceeds from the assumption that both structures share the same marginal distribution over states, and that agents behave as though they knew that marginal distribution, along with the processes that generate the signals.

In particular, from the perspective of this chapter, these measures imply that for the lowest level of information transmission (that is even if the source (English sentences) is completely opaque), the receiver still knows that English sentences are being transmitted, hence he can predict accurately the chance that the words "elephant" and "regressing" are being transmitted in the same sentence. The consequence is that models that measure the agent's information with these techniques[21] share with standard Bayesian models the feature that we have questioned throughout this chapter – complete lack of information never exacerbates differences in perceptions across agents, but rather homogenizes them.

Public versus private signals. *We have emphasized in this chapter that, in standard models, lack of information can facilitate coordination by concentrating beliefs on a common prior distribution. Public signals play a similar coordinating role. One property of public signals in many models is not only that the realized signal is observed by all, but the process that generates it is also assumed known to all, implying common beliefs. Hence, while models often distinguish between public and private signals, emphasizing the coordinating role of public signals, it is likely that in real life, public signals come with heterogenous assessments of their quality, or heterogenous interpretations, and that this heterogeneity translates into lesser coordination than that obtained in models.[22]*

References

Blackwell, D. (1951). Comparison of experiments. *Proceedings of the Second Berkeley Symposium on Mathematical Statistics and Probability*, 93–102.

Crémer, J. and Khalil, F. (1992). Gathering information before signing a contract. *The American Economic Review*, 82(3), 566–578.

Dessein, W. and Santos, T. (2005). Adaptive organizations. *Journal of Political Economy*, 114(5), 956–995.

Galton, F. (1886). Regression towards mediocrity in hereditary stature. *Journal of the Anthropological Institute*, 15, 246–263.

Ganuza, J.-J. (2004). Ignorance promotes competition: an auction model with endogenous private valuations. *The RAND Journal of Economics*, 35, 583–98.

Kahneman, D. (2002). Biographical. Nobelprize.org.

Koehler, J. J. (1996). The base rate fallacy reconsidered: descriptive, normative, and methodological challenges. *Behavioral and Brain Sciences*, 19, 1–53.

Morris, S. and Shin, H. S. (2002). Social value of public Information. *American Economic Review*, 92(5), 1521–1534.

Shannon, C. (1948). A mathematical theory of communication. *Bell System Technical Journal*, 27: 379–423 & 623–656.

Sims, C. (2003) Implications of rational inattention. *Journal of Monetary Economics*, 50(3), 665–690.

---

[21] Including, for example, rational inattention models following Sims (2003).

[22] See Morris and Shin (2002) for a model that exploits the coordinating role of signals, and in which that coordinating role may have adverse welfare consequences.

Applications

This part reviews some of the most well-studied strategic problems. In each chapter, the objective is threefold: provide a parsimonious treatment of the application considered; highlight the strength of standard assumptions; and suggest a different path in which agents are assumed to be less able to exploit the structure of the model.

The suggestions proposed build on direct strategy restrictions, with substantially fewer strategic variables. A benefit is a parsimonious and relatively robust treatment of these problems, parsimonious because by construction there are fewer strategic variables, and robust because when agents are less able to exploit the structure of the model, their behavior is less sensitive to changes in the parameters of the model.

Of course, with restrictions, few dimensions of behavior are endogenized, and this raises difficult modeling questions. Which dimensions should one endogenize? Are some restrictions more appropriate than others?

We discuss this in the Miscellanea. For now, we simply say that we do not have a definitive answer to these questions and that we do not aim to be exhaustive about possible modeling choices. Our aim is to identify what is plausibly the agent's first-order strategic concern for a class of games, and ignore what is plausibly second-order. Others may choose other strategy restrictions, generating different insights. We view this as complementary to our treatment.

CHAPTER 11

Auctions

1. *Shading in first-price auctions.* A first-price auction is a selling mechanism in which each potential buyer places a bid, the highest bidder wins the object for sale and pays his bid. A key aspect of bidding in first-price auctions is in deciding on appropriate shading. The tradeoff is a simple one. If the object is worth a value v to you, bidding v results in no profit. Shading your bid will result in a profit if you win, but your chance of winning likely decreases. So, there is a tradeoff between a higher profit conditional on winning, and a lower chance of winning.

To model this tradeoff, denote by b the agent's bid, and by p the maximum bid among other bidders. The agent cannot know p for sure. For now, let us define f as the distribution over the possible maximum bid made by others, and by

$$\phi(\lambda) \equiv \Pr\{v - p > \lambda\} \equiv \int_{p < v - \lambda} f(p)dp$$

the probability that our bidder wins when shading his value v by a fixed amount λ. His expected gain is:

$$\lambda\phi(\lambda).$$

The function ϕ is a decreasing function. The tradeoff is that higher λ increases profit in the event of winning, but lowers the chance of winning. The derivation of the optimal shading is analogous to a standard *monopoly pricing* problem in which $\phi(\lambda)$ is interpreted as a demand function.

2. *Equilibrium shading.* A key aspect of an analysis of auctions is that it describes an equilibrium phenomenon in which each potential buyer solves the tradeoff above, and in which the price p, the distribution f and the function ϕ defined above are determined endogenously. The problem is no longer a

127

monopoly pricing problem, but an *oligopoly pricing* problem, as the demand ϕ that each bidder faces depends on the behavior of others.[1] Intuitively, if others shade a lot, one should have little competitive pressure and find shading a relatively safe strategy. On the other hand, if others are aggressive competitors who shade little, substantial shading might lead to very little chance of winning, in which case a more aggressive strategy might be preferable. Equilibrium analysis aims to endogenize the level of shading that each bidder finds optimal, given the behavior of others. Equilibrium shading reflects the degree to which the environment is competitive. It also determines how surplus is shared between the seller and buyers: smaller shading generates higher revenue for the seller and lower expected rents for buyers.

What follows is a simple model that captures the forces involved in determining equilibrium shading.

Define $(v_1, \ldots, v_n)$ as a vector of valuations. Uncertainty is modeled by assuming that the vector is drawn from a (symmetric) distribution.

Bidding is assumed to be characterized for each bidder i by a *uniform* shading level λ_i. That is, bidder i bids

$$b_i = v_i - \lambda_i$$

whenever his value is v_i.[2] Given this behavioral assumption, we can associate, to each vector of shading levels $\lambda = (\lambda_1, \ldots \lambda_n)$ and each bidder i, an expected gain $G_i(\lambda)$:

$$G_i(\lambda) = \lambda_i \Pr(v_i - \lambda_i > \max_{j \neq i} v_j - \lambda_j).$$

Bidders are symmetric, and we look for a symmetric equilibrium. That is, we look for a shading level λ^* such that when all bidders shade by the same amount λ^*, no one finds it profitable to modify his shading λ^*. This implies

$$\lambda^* = \arg\max \lambda_i \phi(\lambda_i - \lambda^*)$$

where

$$\phi(x) = \Pr(v_i - \max_{j \neq i} v_j > x).$$

---

[1] See Caplin and Nalebuff (1986) for an analysis of price competition in an oligopolistic environment.

[2] We emphasize that the shading level λ_i is applied uniformly to any value v_i in the range of values considered (given the type of object considered). Clearly, acquiring a firm or a used car are different matters, and would likely lead to different shading levels in practice. If we were to look for a shading rule that applies universally, a multiplicative shading (as the one assumed in Chapter 7) would be more plausible. We discuss this further at the end of this chapter.

Looking at first-order conditions, we can characterize the only possible candidate for a symmetric equilibrium λ^*:

$$\lambda^* = \frac{\phi(0)}{|\phi'(0)|} = \frac{1}{n\,|\phi'(0)|}$$

3. *The effect of dispersion.* Intuitively, equilibrium shading depends on the proportional change in the winning probability for a bidder when he increases his bid. This proportional change is high (hence shading is small) when there are many bidders (because in this case each has a small chance $\phi(0) = 1/n$ of winning), or when values are not very dispersed (i.e., $|\phi'(0)|$ is large). This is a standard Bertrand competition effect. When valuations are more dispersed or bidders less numerous, the effect is weaker, and shading is larger.

The simple expression that we obtain (characterizing equilibrium shading) relies on the particular restriction on strategies that we assumed. Had we opted for a multiplicative formulation, the mathematics would have been more complex, and dispersion would not be captured by the slope $|\phi'(0)|$ alone.

Nevertheless, the qualitative statement would be analogous. More dispersion in valuations reduces competition. Both models establish a similar link between value dispersion and competitive forces.

To formalize the effect of dispersion, assume the following structure:

$$v_i = \alpha + d\,\theta_i$$

with all variables drawn from independent distributions. α reflects characteristics of the object affecting the preference of all participants, θ_i reflects a private characteristic, and d is a dispersion parameter. Also define

$$\phi_0(x) \equiv \Pr(\theta_i - \max_{j \neq i} \theta_j > x) \text{ and } \lambda_0^* = \frac{\phi_0(0)}{|\phi_0'(0)|}.$$

For a fixed d, the condition $v_i - \max_{j \neq i} v_j > x$ is equivalent to

$$\theta_i - \max_{j \neq i} \theta_j > x/d,$$

and we obtain $\phi(x) = \phi_0(x/d)$; hence

$$\lambda^* = d\,\lambda_0^*.$$

In words, the smaller the dispersion parameter, the stronger the competitive forces, and if d is a random variable, we obtain:

$$\lambda^* = \frac{1}{E[1/d]}\lambda_0^*.$$

4. *Objections to standard modeling.* The model departs from standard modeling of auctions in that the strategy is characterized by a single parameter λ, while in standard modeling, one would model agents who optimally adjust bidding, *for each separate realization* v_i.

A possible motivation for the standard model is that, given the distribution from which values are assumed to be drawn, values convey information about the chance of being the highest valuation bidder, and about the dispersion of values below one's own value in the event one wins. Agents should have an opportunity to use that information if it is available.

To illustrate, assume that bidder values are independently drawn on an interval, say $[100, 120]$. For a bidder with value 120, all other bidders have valuations dispersed below his on the whole interval $[100, 120]$. For a bidder with value 101, if he has the highest value, it must be that all others are concentrated between 100 and 101. Competition must thus be much fiercer at the bottom of the interval. The consequence is small shading at the bottom of the interval, higher shading at the top.

An obvious objection is that, in real auctions, one doesn't observe the distributions from which values are drawn. In many situations, it seems difficult to judge, based solely on one's valuation, whether the valuation is high or low compared to others'. When attending an auction for a painting that I like, I might have a personal estimate of $1,000; or possibly $1,100. Whichever figure comes to mind, the specific number seems second order in assessing the chances of being the highest value bidder.

It could of course be that one gets more direct information about one's own chances. If the painting is of my mother or if I am a collector of the artist, I may be quite sure that I'm likely to have the highest value. But, value itself often seems to be a poor instrument. The logic of our simplified model is to disregard this poor instrument altogether. The parameter λ captures a systematic way in which shading occurs (not optimally tailored to each value realization given the particular distribution assumed).

5. *A strategic issue: significant shading.* In bidding in a first-price auction, an agent faces a tradeoff between two types of strategies:

(i) Trying to beat competition by being aggressive, which gives a reasonable chance of winning but a small gain in the event of winning.

(ii) Betting on having a high value compared to others, and shading significantly, which possibly reduces the chance of winning, but generates large gains in the event of winning.

What the equilibrium behavior describes is a smooth resolution of this conflict, in which all bidders find it optimal to settle on the *same* shading level λ^*. An attractive consequence of that smooth resolution is efficiency: the bidder with the highest valuation wins the object.

There are conditions, however, under which no such smooth resolution is possible. When valuations are most likely concentrated, the equilibrium shading level λ^* must be small. Competition is fierce and leaves little rent to bidders. Imagine now that there is a small chance that valuations are dispersed. A bidder may be better off gambling on this being the case and shading significantly: he will only win if in addition he turns out to have a valuation substantially higher than others', but when he wins he gets a substantial gain.

Formally, profits under our tentative equilibrium are equal to $\lambda^*\phi(0)$. This profit must be compared to the gain from shading by a larger amount, say Δ. If the following condition (E) holds:

$$\max_{\Delta} \Delta\phi(\Delta - \lambda^*) > \lambda^*\phi(0), \tag{E}$$

then at least one player prefers to deviate.

Dispersion uncertainty. To better understand circumstances under which (E) might hold, assume that the parameter d takes two values, $\underline{d}$ with probability $1 - p$, and value $\overline{d} > \underline{d}$ with probability p. Then, under minor conditions on ϕ_0, it is sufficient that:

$$\frac{p(1-p)}{4} > \underline{d}/\overline{d}$$

for condition (E) to hold.[3] This means that if p is small, but large compared to relative dispersion $\underline{d}/\overline{d}$, at least one bidder prefers to engage in significant shading, gambling that his valuation is quite high relative to others'.

Intuitively, for any fixed $p > 0$, it is sufficient that $\underline{d}$ is small to drive λ^*, and hence profits, to 0. The reason is that a small change in shading then has a strong effect on the winning probability. And as $\overline{d}$ increases, the gains from the large shading strategy increase.

6. *Revenue comparisons.* We now compare revenues generated by first-price and second-price auctions. Bidding in a first-price auction is not as obvious as it may seem. For the winner, the best strategy is to bid just above the second highest bid. But the winner cannot anticipate what this second highest bid will be. In contrast, in the second-price auction, the winner precisely pays the second highest bid, so he need not adjust his bid to the second highest.

The consequence is that, in the first-price auction, optimal shading depends on a tradeoff between various circumstances; sometimes, it would have been optimal to shade little; and, sometimes, it would have been optimal to shade significantly. Depending on the relative weight of these low- and high-shading

---

[3] A sufficient condition on ϕ_0 is that for all positive Δ, $|\phi_0'(\Delta)| \leq |\phi_0'(0)|$. Since $E[1/d] \geq (1-p)/\underline{d}$, the tentative equilibrium shading satisfies $\lambda^* \leq \lambda_0^*\underline{d}/(1-p)$.

When the bidder opts for a large shading Δ, he wins with probability at least $p\phi_0(\Delta/\overline{d})$. His expected gain is thus at least equal to $\max_{\Delta} \Delta p\phi_0(\Delta/\overline{d}) = p\overline{d}\max_{\Delta} \Delta\phi_0(\Delta)$. Under the condition above on ϕ_0, $\Delta\phi_0(\Delta) \geq \Delta(\phi_0(0) + \Delta\phi_0'(0)) = \phi_0(0)\Delta(1 - \Delta/\lambda_0^*)$, implying that $\max_{\Delta} \Delta\phi_0(\Delta) \geq \phi_0(0)\lambda_0^*/4$. The optimal deviation thus gives an expected payoff at least equal to $\phi_0(0)p\overline{d}\lambda_0^*/4$. When the latter payoff exceeds $\phi_0(0)\lambda_0^*\underline{d}/(1-p)$, (E) holds.

situations, bidders may end up finding that "somewhat" small shading is optimal, or that "somewhat high" shading is optimal. In the former case, we can expect the first-price auction to generate more revenue, and, in the latter case, we can expect the opposite.

To illustrate, let us return to our low/high dispersion example. If there is a significant chance that values are concentrated (small d), this may be enough to generate fierce competition. In this case, competition is tough even in events where dispersion is large (high d), that is, even in events where rents could potentially be quite high for the buyers. Rents remain small for buyers because they cannot tailor shading to dispersion: shading remains small whether dispersion is small or large, and this is a source of increased revenues for the seller.[4]

Formally, in a second-price auction, the winner, say player i, gets $y = \theta_i - \max_{j \neq i} \theta_j$ in events where y is non-negative. Since y is distributed according to the density $-\phi'(y)$ (by definition of ϕ), a bidder's expected gain, which we denote G^{II}, is therefore:

$$G^{II} = \int_{y \geq 0} -y\phi'(y)dy = \int_{y \geq 0} \phi(y)dy,$$

which can be compared to a bidder's expected gain G^I in the first-price auction: $G^I = \lambda^* \phi(0)$. The following figure illustrates graphically the gains G^I and G^{II} in the case of two bidders ($\phi(0) = 1/2$).

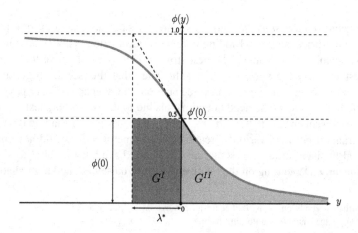

---

[4] The opposite argument works, of course, when the chance of a large dispersion drives shading to high levels. There are events where dispersion turns out to be small and yet buyers get large rents.

Call ρ the ratio between G^{II} and G^{I}:

$$\rho = G^{II}/G^{I},$$

and ρ_0 this ratio when the dispersion parameter d is equal to 1.[5] Since the allocation does not change across formats, the seller's revenue is highest when the bidder's expected gain is smallest. So *the first-price auction generates more revenue than the second-price if and only if* $\rho > 1$, and we have:

$$\rho > 1 \Leftrightarrow \int_{y \geq 0} \frac{\phi(y)}{\phi(0)} dy > \frac{\phi(0)}{|\phi'(0)|}. \tag{P}$$

Our main observation is that *dispersion uncertainty* makes it easier to satisfy inequality (P). Indeed, we have:[6]

$$\rho = \kappa \rho_0 \text{ where } \kappa = E(1/d) * Ed,$$

and the coefficient κ is equal to 1 if d is certain, larger than 1 otherwise. So for a fixed distribution ϕ_0, dispersion uncertainty increases ρ.

Said differently, the first-price auction is better for the seller when the "demand" function *combines* high concentration and substantial dispersion: concentration (i.e., high $|\phi'(0)|$) implies a strong Bertrand competition effect, hence low gains for buyers in the first-price auction, while substantial dispersion implies high rents in the second-price auction. Dispersion uncertainty makes it easier to satisfy these two conditions.[7]

7. Misperceptions and misadjustments. In an ascending-price auction, the best strategy is obvious – dropping from the auction when the price reaches one's value. Bidding optimally in a first-price auction is less obvious as it depends on the degree to which the environment is competitive, on the number of bidders, and on the dispersion of values.

Said differently, we have characterized equilibrium shading λ^*, and in so doing, we have proposed a model that links properties of the distribution over values to behavior. Distributions, however, are not meant to be observable by participants. The model is a shortcut that leaves unmodeled the process by which people conform to equilibrium behavior: we can only hope that agents eventually figure out that behaving in this way is optimal, and, for example,

---

[5] $\rho_0 = \int_{y \geq 0} \frac{\phi_0(y)}{\phi_0(0)} dy / \lambda_0^*$.

[6] This is because for any given d, $\phi(y) = \phi_0(y/d)$.

[7] Note that dispersion uncertainty may also generate incentives for large shading (strategic issue). It can be checked, however, that (P) may hold without generating such incentives. The technical reason is that $\int_{y \geq 0} \phi(y) dy > \max_y y\phi(y)$.

that they will shade less when there are more bidders or when values are less dispersed.

So, although the model does not explain or describe the agents' thought process, it suggests features of the environment that agents should consider when deciding how to bid, such as the number of bidders or the dispersion of values (i.e., $\phi'(0)$).

Standard models thus portray agents as *adjusting perfectly and instantaneously* to these features of the environment. This is a useful modeling simplification; but in a world in which one cannot presume such an immediate and perfect adjustment, strategies are bound to diverge from the "correct" equilibrium outcome. Sources of discrepancies are numerous, as an agent may possibly rely on poorly informative or irrelevant signals about the environment without realizing their strength or lack of relevance.

Our aim, in what follows, is to describe the consequences of these misperceptions or misadjustments.

8. *Noisy shading and misperceptions.* A simple way to model misperceptions/misadjustments is to assume noisy shading, with agents having only imperfect control over shading. A mechanical consequence of noise is that we are bound to lose on efficiency, hence on the surplus to be shared. Another consequence, which we analyze below, is that noise modifies incentives to shade, possibly altering the way that surplus is shared between the seller and the buyers.

Formally, we model misperceptions by assuming bid strategies that take the following form:

$$b_i = v_i - \lambda_i + \varepsilon_i. \tag{11.1}$$

The parameter ε_i is meant to be a (small)[8] noise parameter, which we take to be centered on 0, and that prevents each bidder i from perfectly adjusting shading to the underlying distribution over values. We keep, however, the assumption that bidder i controls λ_i and tries to find the optimal *target shading*. This ensures that despite his errors, his behavior is driven by relevant welfare comparisons, in expectation over the mistakes that he might make.

---

[8] We keep ε_i small to ensure that shading remains positive despite the noise. There are many ways to introduce errors, and other ways to correct for errors that we could imagine. For example, we could assume: $b_i = v_i - \lambda_i/(1 + \eta_i)$ where η_i is a positive random variable. This way of modeling noise and strategies would introduce a more direct motive for shading less (and possibly other comparative statics with respect to noise), as smaller shading is a way to reduce mistakes. Our objective however is not to be exhaustive about possible strategic effects, but to illustrate two different forces that may affect bidding.

An alternative interpretation of the model is that the agent has access only to a noisy estimate of value, denoted z_i:

$$z_i = v_i + \varepsilon_i$$

and that bidding takes the form assumed earlier:

$$b_i = z_i - \lambda_i.$$

Of course, we are not suggesting that misadjustments to the environment and misperceptions of one's own value are always equivalent. We just point out that (11.1) encompasses both interpretations.

9. *Strategic consequences.* Misperceptions can have two effects: they may increase the dispersion of bids, and may generate a selection bias (as a bidder with a positive noise term ε_i has a greater chance of being selected). Higher dispersion weakens competition. The selection bias is potentially favorable to sellers, though bidders may try to compensate for it by increasing shading.

Given our behavioral assumption, we can compute the gain $G_i(\lambda_i, \lambda)$ that bidder i obtains when he shades by λ_i and others shade by λ. To do this, we define

$$y_i = v_i + \varepsilon_i - \max_{j \neq i}(v_j + \varepsilon_j)$$

as the margin by which player i wins when all use the same bid strategy. Next, define

$$\phi_\varepsilon(y) \equiv \Pr(y_i > y); \quad \psi(y) \equiv E[\varepsilon_i \,|\, y_i > y] \quad \text{and} \quad \Psi(y) = E[\varepsilon_i \,|\, y_i = y].$$

$\psi(y)$ (and $\Psi(y)$) are thus the expected error that bidder i makes when he wins by a margin at least equal to y (exactly equal to y). Note that $\psi(y)$ is positive and increasing because bidder i tends to win more often when ε_i is positive. This is a selection bias, and the selection bias is stronger when you are winning by a larger margin.

If other bidders shade by λ, we have:

$$G_i(\lambda_i) = (\lambda_i - \psi(\lambda_i - \lambda))\phi_\varepsilon(\lambda_i - \lambda).$$

A symmetric equilibrium shading λ_ε^* must thus satisfy:

$$\lambda_\varepsilon^* + \psi(0) = \frac{\phi_\varepsilon(0)}{-\phi_\varepsilon'(0)}(1 - \psi'(0)),$$

or equivalently:[9]

$$\lambda_\varepsilon^* = \frac{\phi_\varepsilon(0)}{-\phi_\varepsilon'(0)} + \Psi(0).$$

This formula captures the two strategic consequences of noise on incentives. Noise creates greater dispersion in bids, which typically increases shading (because $-\phi_\varepsilon'(0)$ typically decreases). It also generates a selection bias of size $\psi(0)$, which bidders only partially offset by shading an additional $\Psi(0)$.[10] For bidders, the consequence for profits is:

$$G_i(\lambda_\varepsilon^*) = \phi_\varepsilon(0) \left[\frac{\phi_\varepsilon(0)}{-\phi_\varepsilon'(0)} + \Psi(0) - \psi(0) \right],$$

where we see that the partial offsetting of the selection bias may reduce profits ($\Psi(0) < \psi(0)$); while the dispersion of bids generally makes the environment less competitive (smaller $-\phi_\varepsilon'(0)$), hence conducive to higher profit.

For normal distributions and two bidders, total welfare and total profits can be characterized in closed form. Assume v_i and ε_i are normal distributions with mean and variance respectively equal to (v_0, η^2) and $(0, \sigma^2)$. Let $\rho = \sigma^2/\eta^2$. We provide below the exact formula for total welfare (W) and total profits (G):[11]

$$W = v_0 + \frac{\eta}{\sqrt{\pi(1+\rho)}} \text{ and } G = \frac{\eta}{\sqrt{\pi}}(\frac{1}{\sqrt{1+\rho}} + \sqrt{1+\rho}(\pi - \sqrt{2}).$$

Thus, as ρ increases above 0, welfare decreases (because the object is no longer necessarily allocated to the highest value bidder), but total profits for buyers nevertheless increase. The reason for this is that, due to noise, competition is weaker (smaller $-\phi_\varepsilon'(0)$), and this effect dominates the fact that the selection bias is only partially offset ($\Psi(0) < \psi(0)$). The immediate consequence is that the seller is worse off.

To summarize, a bidder is more likely to win when optimistic about his own valuation. This is a selection bias, which creates a gap between the

---

[9] This follows because $\Psi = \frac{(\psi\phi)'}{\phi'} = \psi + \psi'\frac{\phi}{\phi'}$.

[10] Intuitively, the reason that bidders only partially offset the selection bias is that at the optimal shading, bidders implicitly consider what happens when they win by a zero margin; while, on average, they win by a larger-than-zero margin. They, thus, face a selection bias of magnitude $\psi(0)$ (larger than $\Psi(0)$).

[11] To simplify notation, denote by $h = -\phi_\varepsilon'$ the density over y_i. Note that $y_i \sim \mathcal{N}(0, \sigma_y^2)$ with $\sigma_y = \sqrt{2}\sqrt{\sigma^2 + \eta^2}$. Define $M = E[z_i - v_0 \mid z_i > z_j]$. We observe that $W = v_0 + M - \psi(0)$ and that by symmetry,

$$M = \frac{1}{2}E[z_i - z_j \mid z_i - z_j > 0] = \int_{y_i > 0} y_i h(y_i) dy_i = E\max(0, y_i) = \sigma_y/\sqrt{2\pi}.$$

Also observe that $\Psi(y) = E[\varepsilon_i \mid y_i = y] = \alpha y$, with $\alpha = \frac{\sigma^2}{2\sigma^2 + 2\eta^2}$, hence $\psi(0) = 2\alpha \int_{y_i > 0} y_i h(y_i) dy_i$. To obtain G, we observe that $G = W - S$ where S is the seller's gain. To compute S, we observe that $S = M - \gamma_\varepsilon^*$ and, since $y_i \sim \mathcal{N}(0, \sigma_y^2)$, $\lambda_\varepsilon^* = \sqrt{\pi}\sigma_y$.

estimated value and the realized value conditional on winning. This gap is called the winner's curse, and profit-maximizing bidders ought to bid in a way that takes into account this selection bias. The analysis above highlights that in equilibrium, the offsetting of the selection bias is incomplete, which is detrimental to bidders. But, it also highlights that the dispersion in bids that misperceptions create may sufficiently weaken competition that bidders may nevertheless benefit from the noisier environment. It is not increased information that is a source of rents, but increased dispersion.

Further Comments

Independence and correlation. A standard division in studying auctions is whether values are independent or correlated. *Technically the distinction means that in the former case, values should be thought of as being drawn from independent distributions, while in the latter case, one should think of a random parameter affecting all values.*

The distinction seems awkward. The object for sale is the same for every potential buyer, it has characteristics that each one can observe. These characteristics may not be valued in the same way, but to any potential buyer, the value of a car surely differs substantially from the value he attaches to a plant. This justified our representation

$$v_i = \alpha + d\,\theta_i,$$

where α is a shift parameter that captures the "typical" value of the object for sale.

So there should be no question that values are correlated across auctions. The idea that the analyst can nevertheless focus on the case where values are independent stems from the fact that, if bidders know α, d and the structure of the model, they can infer the value of the independently drawn characteristic $\theta_i \equiv (v_i - \alpha)/d$, and use it as an instrument to derive optimal/equilibrium bidding $b^*(v_i) = v_i - \lambda^*(\theta_i)$. From this perspective, the independent value is the more cognitively demanding, as it requires knowing α and d, and determining how to condition bids on three variables $(v_i, \alpha$ and d).

Nevertheless, whether bidders condition behavior on v_i or on (v_i, α, d), both formulations are quite demanding cognitively. In both formulations, bidders may exploit the structure of the model and, for example, adjust their shading strategy using information on the difference $D = v_i - \max_{j \neq i} v_j$ conveyed by v_i (or v_i, α and d).

What we have proposed is a drastic simplification in which v_i is used in bidding, but where the information about D potentially provided by v_i is not. This provides a more parsimonious auction model. It also opens the path to intermediate models in which bidders get "some" information about D, in the form of coarse signals about rank that they could condition behavior on, *without necessarily embodying the level of sophistication assumed in standard models.*[12]

Dispersion rents or information rents? *The literature often refers to "information rents" to describe the gains that an "informed" player gets. In auctions, a more appropriate terminology might be "dispersion rents": bid dispersion generates rents, and private information in standard models generates rents insofar as it creates bid dispersion. Our model illustrates that poor information (i.e., noisier estimates) may translate into higher bid dispersion, and that improving an agent's information (i.e., less noisy estimates) may induce less bid dispersion, hence smaller rents.*[13]

This effect of noise on bid dispersion would not hold in a standard model – the opposite would actually be true. Noisier estimates would translate into less dispersed posteriors (by a regression to the mean effect), and therefore greater competition when symmetry is assumed. The latter conclusion, however, is (in our view) an artifact of the standard model, and of the implicit assumption that agents know (or behave as if they knew) all distributions: as noise increases, value estimates decrease in importance and more weight is put on priors,[14] *as explained in Chapter 10.*

Common values, interdependence and estimation errors. *In modeling auctions, the distinction between private and common values is often seen as a key dividing line. In common or interdependent value auctions, the bids of others' reveal information about one's own valuation, and, in bidding, a rational bidder ought to take into account those inferences. An omniscient bidder will indeed find this advice useful. To most bidders, however, the precise ways in which preferences are interdependent are likely obscure, and the appropriate inference likely out of reach.*

From a less sophisticated bidder's perspective, a more useful dividing line may be whether he is subject to estimation errors or not. If a bidder is subject to estimation errors, he faces selection bias: he is more likely to win when the error is positive. This selection bias has been identified first by Capen et al. (1971), and the optimal response to it is caution.[15] *This phenomenon is not specific to auctions or the presence of interdependencies in valuations: it may arise in any decision problem where an agent compares an alternative that is easy to evaluate (not buying) to one that is more difficult to evaluate hence subject to estimation error.*[16]

---

[12] This is the path taken in Compte and Postlewaite (2012). In this paper, we investigate whether and when some rank related signals promote or diminish competition.

[13] Note that the motive invoked here as to why poor information hurts the seller is different from that invoked in Milgrom and Weber (1982), which relies on affiliation.

[14] That logic is pursued in Ganuza (2004) for example.

[15] See Compte (2001), which examines the effect of increasing the number of bidders on this selection bias, in the context of the second-price auction.

[16] See Compte and Postlewaite (2012) and Chapter 21.

Now, the level of caution depends on context, and indeed, the degree of interdependence then matters. If idiosyncratic components are less dispersed (small d), which can be interpreted as values being more interdependent, the estimation errors carry more weight and caution should increase.

Efficiency in first price. In a symmetric environment with independent values, an equilibrium in monotonic strategies is guaranteed to exist, implying an efficient allocation of the object.[17] *With our focus on a restricted set of strategies, this is no longer guaranteed, and we explained in Section 6 when it may fail to exist.*[18] *Since our model may be interpreted as one in which players are unable to draw precise inference about rank given their values, as in a correlated value model, our model also gives hints as to when there may be nonexistence of an equilibrium in monotonic strategies in a standard correlated value model.*

In any event, one reason that first-price auctions are likely to generate inefficient outcomes is that symmetry in perceptions of the environment is likely to fail, hence differences in shading levels are likely to arise, generating inefficient allocations. Whether these inefficiencies are large in practice remains, however, an important applied question.

Additive versus multiplicative shading. Technically, one difference between additive and multiplicative shading is that the latter mechanically incorporates into bidding some information about rank that the former does not: in the multiplicative version, shading is stronger for higher value realizations. For some auction formats such as the first-price auction, the qualitative effects are similar under both assumptions. For other auction formats such as the all-pay auction, an additive shading assumption could drastically modify the analysis and make existence of an equilibrium an issue even with few bidders. To us, however, failure of existence is not a weakness of the additive formulation, but an illustration of what is necessary to generate stable predictions under that particular auction format.

Suggestions for further research/applications. Through strategy restrictions, one obtains a more parsimonious treatment of auctions, with only one, or few, dimensions of behavior being endogenized. This, in turn, may help deal with problems that are technically difficult to address within the standard framework, or at least simplify their analysis. In the spirit of Chapter 7, it may also help assess the robustness of existing

---

[17] See Milgrom and Weber (1982).
[18] In essence the reason is similar to why competition for differentiated goods may not generate a pure strategy equilibrium. See Caplin and Nalebuff (1986).

models in which players' knowledge of their rank in the distribution plays a key role.

Specific topics and relevant references: (i) auctions in which buyers get other signals beyond their own valuation (Fang and Morris (2006)); (ii) auctions in which multiple units or slots are sold;[19] (iii) dynamic selling problems in which the seller faces a sequence of buyers (Lauermann and Wolinski (2016)); (iv) contests in which one or several prizes are offered (Moldovanu and Sela (2001)),[20] and more generally, matching problems;[21] (v) auctions in which the seller chooses a reserve price strategically, as a function of his perception of the buyers' valuations.[22]

References

Capen, E. C., Clapp, R. B. and Campbell, W. M. (1971). Competitive bidding in high risk situations. *Journal of Petroleum Technology*, 23, 641–653.

Caplin, A. and Nalebuff, B. (1986). Multi-dimensional product differentiation and price competition. *Oxford Economic Papers*, 38, 129–145.

Compte, O. (2001). The winner's curse with independent private values, mimeo.

Compte, O. and Postlewaite, A. (2012a). Simple auctions, mimeo.

Compte, O. and Postlewaite, A. (2012b). Cautiousness, mimeo.

Fang, H. and Morris, S. (2006). Multidimensional private value auctions. *Journal of Economic Theory*, 126, 1–30.

Ganuza, J.-J. (2004). Ignorance promotes competition: an auction model with endogenous private valuations. *The RAND Journal of Economics*, 35(3), 583–598.

[19] One could for example study the performance of a product-mix auction (Klemperer (2010)), as compared with a sequential auction of each good. More generally, many selling procedures are possible, each allowing bidders to express their preferences to varying degrees, and each having different rules for selecting winners and transfers. Comparing the performance and efficiency properties of these formats is a challenge which can be easily surmounted if the set of bidding strategies examined is reduced (e.g., by assuming linear shading across all units).

[20] These games typically have the structure of an all-pay auction, as that analyzed in Chapter 7.

[21] One part of the matching literature deals with the matching of students to various schools. In that literature, students behave as if they had perfect assessments of their chance of being admitted to each school. One might reconsider these models, by assuming either that agents get only noisy signals of their position (in the queue for schools), or that the intensity of their preferences does not give them accurate information about how that intensity compares to others'. A second segment of the matching literature considers matching of buyers and sellers to understand how surplus in matching will be shared. One can think of such models as one side of the market suggesting shares to agents on the other side. Equilibria of such games implicitly assume that each agent's suggested shares are precisely calibrated to his relative ranking within his side and to characteristics of the other side. Strategy restrictions could model situations where agents are less able to discern their relative ranking on the basis of their own characteristics, and less able to precisely target each agent on the other side.

[22] In standard terms, these are called "informed principal problems" and they are notoriously difficult to solve. From our perspective, we are only adding a single strategic variable. See Chapter 17.

Klemperer, P. (2010). The product-mix auction: a new auction design for differentiated goods. *Journal of the European Economic Association*, 8, 526–536.

Lauermann, S. and Wolinsky, A. (2016). Search with adverse selection. *Econometrica*, 84, 243–315.

Milgrom, P. and Weber, R. (1982). A theory of auctions and competitive bidding. *Econometrica*, 50, 443–459.

Moldovanu, B. and Sela, A. (2001). The optimal allocation of prizes in contests. *The American Economic Review*, 91, 542–558.

CHAPTER 12

Learning

1. *Learning.* Learning is central to many economic decisions. Any economic environment is subject to change, and good decision making requires that one adjusts to these changes. A supplier may provide high-quality products at a particular point in time, justifying the interaction with that supplier. But, if perceived quality drops, and if that perception is reasonably accurate, one may want to reassess the relationship.

Technically, learning takes the form of a dynamic strategy: it describes how an agent adjusts, or should adjust, his behavior over time to his observations and perceptions. A strategy that prescribes disrupting the relationship with a supplier whose perceived quality drops is a dynamic strategy that adjusts to current conditions.

We are interested in dynamic strategies because they can affect incentives in interesting ways. A supplier who faces clients that react to quality has incentives to produce higher quality. In a partnership, dynamic strategies may promote cooperative behavior, as one may fear that lower effort will reduce incentives for others to do their part. These incentives are studied in the next two chapters.

Before proceeding, we note that we are not interested in *arbitrary* dynamic strategies. A strategy that prescribes a halt to dealing with a supplier whose perceived quality rises is a dynamic strategy, but not one that does a good job at adjusting to current conditions. Eventually, we are interested in dynamic strategies that are *optimal*, in a sense to be made precise.

2. *Limited learning.* A difficulty stems from the fact that the number of possible dynamic strategies rises exponentially with the length of interaction. This often makes the search for an optimal dynamic strategy challenging. Each new date potentially brings a new experience (e.g., whether the product was good enough), and one must determine at each date how each possible combination of past experiences should be aggregated before deciding whether to continue buying from that supplier.

Beyond the technical challenge that the task represents, the quest for optimality raises a conceptual issue. As emphasized earlier, game theory

143

methodology typically ignores or avoids making precise how optimal behavior is reached. Computing the optimal strategy is a shortcut that bypasses learning issues.

The same methodology is employed in dynamic situations: the aim is to describe learning through the characterization of an optimal dynamic strategy, leaving aside how a player comes to play according to that optimal strategy. This omission is problematic – and more so when the number of available strategies is huge.

This conceptual issue motivates what follows. In the simple dynamic model proposed in this chapter, we restrict attention to a *reduced* set of (dynamic) strategies, and assume that the agent follows an optimal strategy within that limited set. Our model is thus intermediate between an exogenously given (learning) strategy and a standard Bayesian strategy. Learning is limited.

3. *Permanent and temporary shocks.* We describe below a standard dynamic decision problem with two purposes in mind. First, to illustrate strategy restrictions in a dynamic setting. Second, to formalize simply a classic issue that economic agents face in dynamic settings – the difficulty to discriminate between temporary and permanent shocks to the environment. In particular, we investigate how the degree of permanence in the environment and signal accuracy affect optimal behavior.

To understand the economic issue, consider a buyer trying to track the quality of the product that he gets from a supplier. The buyer may try to assess the supplier's quality based on a sample of products previously bought from that supplier. The problem is that the sample may not be representative of the quality of the seller's products, either because the sample is too small or because a large sample may include products over a range of time that may not accurately reflect the quality of *currently* produced goods. In other words, quality may be subject to both temporary and permanent shocks, and it may be difficult for the agent to assess whether perceived quality changes, if any, are transitory or permanent.

Despite this difficulty, one expects two insights: if shocks are mostly temporary, current and past observations, however accurate they are, will be of little help in adjusting behavior; one should then expect optimal behavior to be independent of observations. If shocks have sufficient permanence, and if observations are reasonably accurate, one should expect dependence.

4. *A simple model.*
Payoffs. In any period, the agent has the choice between two actions, which we shall refer to as *arms*.[1] One arm is safe with a known payoff, normalized to 0.[2] The other arm is risky and yields an expected benefit s.

---

[1] The environment corresponds to a multi-arm bandit problem.
[2] This is a simplification of some environments studied in the multi-arm bandit literature. In the general case, both arms can yield an unknown payoff.

The agent would like to select the risky arm if and only if s is positive. However, he faces two difficulties. The state may change from one period to the next, so past experience may become irrelevant. Additionally, even when he picks the risky arm, he cannot observe perfectly the current value of s.

In line with the buyer-seller example above, and anticipating the next chapter, we think of the agent as a buyer who either (I)nteracts with a seller (the risky arm) or does (N)ot interact (the safe arm).[3]

Process. The underlying state s changes over time. For simplicity, we assume that at the start of each period, a new state is drawn with probability α from a distribution with density h. A small value of α means that the state has significant permanence. Throughout, it will be convenient to let $s_0 = Es$, and to think of the following structure for the new draw:[4]

$$s = s_0 + \mu$$

where μ is normally distributed (i.e., $\mu \sim \mathcal{N}(0, \sigma^2)$). One interpretation of s_0 is that it is the long-run benefit of using the risky arm.

Comment 1. Let us emphasize the following. We model the fact that the agent ignores the exact date at which the state changes by assuming a particular stochastic process, characterized by specific transition probabilities. These transition probabilities do not change, however. This is a modeling convenience. In principle, as explained in Chapter 3, there is no reason to expect such stability in transition probabilities.

Observations. The second friction that we introduce is that the current state cannot be observed perfectly (even after picking the risky arm). We model this by assuming that when he picks the safe arm, the agent observes nothing, and when he picks the risky arm, the agent gets one of two possible signals, $y = \bar{y}, \underline{y}$, with the (good) signal $\bar{y}$ being more likely when s is higher.[5,6] Formally, we denote by $\pi(s)$ the probability of a good signal ($\bar{y}$) when the state is s. In numerical simulations below, we assume:

$$\pi(s) = \exp \beta s / (1 + \exp \beta s)$$

---

[3] The state s may be interpreted as the current quality of the good produced by the supplier, or the current fit between the seller's product and the buyer's preference.

[4] This representation will be used to assess the effect of (additive) distribution shifts, thus varying s_0.

[5] One may want to interpret y as the realized benefit, but it need not be. The signal y is meant to summarize whatever information the agent uses when deciding which arm to take in the future. This information could be much coarser than the actual realized benefit.

[6] In more complex environments in which both actions lead to uncertain payoffs, the agent would also get a signal about the expected benefit s when taking the safe arm.

for some $\beta > 0$. The parameter β reflects the quality of the signal that the agent gets in any period in which he chooses the risky arm. The signal allows him to discriminate (imperfectly) between s positive and s negative.

Agent's objectives. The agent would like to take the risky arm if and only if s is positive. If he could, he would obtain an expected payoff

$$V \equiv E\max(s,0) \equiv \overline{P}\,\overline{w},$$

where $\overline{P} = \Pr(s > 0)$ and $\overline{w} = E(s \mid s > 0)$.[7] The agent's problem is that he does not know s. However, he can use past experience to decide when to choose the risky arm. The aim of what follows is to assess when using past experience is indeed a good idea.

5. *Objections to standard modeling.* The standard approach defines a strategy σ as a mapping from any history of actions and observations to a decision, and, given the parameters of the model, it determines a *dynamic strategy* σ^* that is optimal among *all* such mappings.

Along the same line as Comment 1 above, our point of view is that it is implausible that the agent would know precisely the model (process and distributions), or that the agent would know which mapping performs best among all possible mappings. Instead, we limit the agent to a plausible set of learning strategies and assume that the agent behaves as though he could only compare the performance of strategies in that limited set. We suggest below one plausible restriction. We do not suggest that this is the most realistic way to constrain the strategy set, only that it captures a strategic consideration that is central to bandit problems (i.e., the degree to which one tries the risky arm).

6. *Static strategies.* Static strategies define a particular decision (safe or risky), irrespective of the signals received. We evaluate these. If the agent always takes the safe arm, he gets 0. If he always takes the risky arm, what he gets in the long run depends on the frequency with which he is in each state s. Denote that frequency by $h(s)$. The long-run gain from buying is:

$$Es = \sum_s h(s)s = s_0.$$

The best static strategy therefore yields $\max(0, s_0)$.

7. *A simple dynamic strategy.* A dynamic strategy uses past experience, and we define below a family of such strategies. First consider a basic strategy σ_0 that starts by interacting (i.e., choosing the risky arm), continues doing so as

[7] Similarly we define $\underline{P} = \Pr(s < 0)$ and $\underline{W} = E(s \mid s < 0)$.

long as good signals are received, and discontinues interaction (i.e., chooses the safe arm) permanently after the first bad signal.[8]

Then for any fixed $\lambda \in [0, 1]$, we define the strategy σ^λ that restarts σ^0 with probability λ at the beginning of any period. In other words, the agent may be in one of two possible *behavioral states* θ ((I)nteract or (N)ot interact), and the strategy σ^λ defines transitions over these behavioral states as a function of the history of signals received:[9]

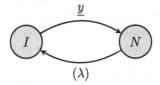

$$(\lambda)$$

The parameter λ may be interpreted as the degree to which the agent tries or *experiments* the risky arm once in state N, checking whether interacting is indeed not good. It may also be interpreted as the agent's propensity to interact, as $\lambda = 1$ means that bad signals have no effect – he interacts at all dates.

Each strategy σ^λ induces a long-run distribution over (s, θ), and we shall denote by $q^\lambda(s)$ the long-run frequency with which he chooses the risky arm when the state is s. We define v^λ as the *long-run value* that the agent obtains when following σ^λ. We have:

$$v^\lambda = \sum_s h(s)q^\lambda(s)s = Eq^\lambda(s)s.$$

In words, by conditioning his behavior on signals, the agent generates a frequency of interaction that varies with s. Since the dynamic strategy has the property that only bad signals generate interruptions, one expects q^λ to be increasing in s.

For example, in the limit case where α is arbitrarily small, this frequency has the following simple expression:

$$q^\lambda(s) = \frac{\lambda}{1 - (1 - \lambda)\pi(s)}.$$

And in the limit case where β is arbitrarily large (perfect signals), q^λ takes only two values, $\underline{q}$ when $s < 0$ and $\bar{q} > \underline{q}$ when $s > 0$ (see the Appendix

---

[8] One could elaborate on strategy σ_0 and consider review periods, modifying the condition that triggers quitting the risky arm forever. We briefly discuss this possibility at the end of this chapter.

[9] This means that if the agent is in state I in a given period, he interacts. If he receives a bad signal y, he moves to state N. At the start of next period, he transits back to I with probability λ, in which case the bad signal has no effect on the relationship. With probability $1 - \lambda$, he remains in N and thus does not interact for that period. In every subsequent period, he transits back to I with probability λ.

for closed-form expressions). In both cases, the dynamic strategy acts as a selection device that makes interaction more likely when it is worthwhile ($q^\lambda(s)$ is increasing with s), and this is where the potential benefit from a dynamic strategy lies, as we verify below.

8. *Optimality of a given dynamic strategy.* Fix $\lambda_0 \in (0,1)$. Can the dynamic strategy σ^{λ_0} improve upon the static strategies?[10]

If interacting is seldom worthwhile, sampling that risky action may not be such a good idea. Similarly, if interacting is almost always a good idea, reacting to bad signals by discontinuing the interaction for very long cannot be good either. When the ex ante gains from interacting and not interacting are more balanced (i.e., s_0 not too far from 0), the dynamic strategy may be better.

When $s_0 = 0$, for example, the dynamic strategy *always* improves over the static strategies. To see why, observe that, since $q^{\lambda_0}(s)$ is increasing, $Eq^{\lambda_0}(s)(s - Es) > 0$.[11] Defining $Q^{\lambda_0} = Eq^{\lambda_0}(s)$, we thus have:

$$v^{\lambda_0} > Q^{\lambda_0} s_0,$$

implying that the dynamic strategy *strictly* improves upon the static strategies when $s_0 = 0$.

More generally, the stochastic process that generates states and observations is characterized by s_0, σ, α and β, and one can attempt to characterize the set of parameter models for which the dynamic strategy dominates static strategies,

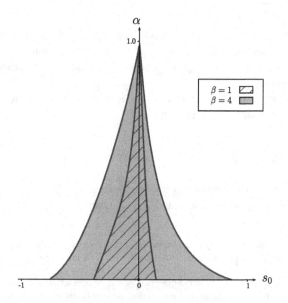

---

[11] Define $G(x) = \int_{s>x}(s - Es)h(s)ds$. We have $G(x) \geq 0$ for all x and $Eq(s)(s - Es) = \int q'(s)G(s)ds$, which is positive because q is increasing.

as illustrated above. The figure plots the domain over α and s_0 for which the dynamic strategy is best, for two values of β ($\beta = 1$ and $\beta = 4$), fixing $\lambda_0 = 1/10$ and $\sigma = 1$. It illustrates that the domain expands when the signal is higher quality (higher β), or when persistence increases (smaller α). Plotting the set of pairs (α, β) for which the dynamic strategy is best for various values of s_0 would also show that the domain shrinks when the long-run benefit of one of the options relative to the other increases (i.e., when s_0 increases above 0 or decreases below 0).

9. *Comparison with first best and stochastic response functions.* Ideally, the agent would like to track perfectly whether $s > 0$ or $s < 0$. If he could freely choose the probabilities of interaction $q(s)$ contingent on s, he would pick q^* satisfying $q^*(s) = 1$ if $s > 0$, and $q^*(s) = 0$ otherwise; and he would obtain the maximum feasible payoff V. Our agent, however, cannot track perfectly the underlying state. Consequently, he makes mistakes, characterized by a stochastic response function q that differs from q^*. We plot below one such response.

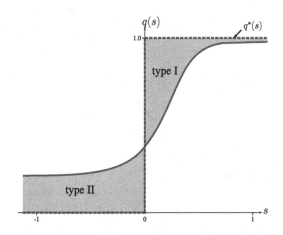

On the right side, $s > 0$ and yet he takes the safe arm with positive probability $1 - q(s)$ (refer to them as type I errors). On the left side, $s < 0$ and yet he takes the risky arm with positive probability $q(s)$ (refer to them as type II errors). These mistakes have a cost, negligible when s is close to 0, but substantial for larger s.

Formally, compared to the maximum feasible payoff V that a player obtains by perfectly tracking the current state, the agent incurs a loss $L(q)$, which one can write as:

$$L(q) \equiv \underline{P}\, E[\,|s|\, q(s)\ |\ s < 0\,] + \overline{P}\, E[\,(1 - q(s))\, s\ |\ s > 0].$$

10. *Optimal learning.* In our setup, optimal learning means that the agent follows a strategy that maximizes his long-run value among the strategies that he is assumed to compare. We considered the simplest case in which, in addition to the static strategies, the agent has the option to use a *single* dynamic strategy σ^{λ_0}.

We consider below a more complex model in which the agent is given the option to use *any* dynamic strategy σ^λ for $\lambda \in [0,1]$, and in which the agent is assumed to play the dynamic strategy λ^* that generates the highest long-run value v^λ, or equivalently that generates the minimum loss L among all σ^λ. The parameter λ^* characterizes the optimal degree to which the agent tries the risky arm.

Intuitively, high λ's reduce type I mistakes but generate more type II mistakes. The following figure plots stochastic responses for two different values of λ, assuming α close to 0.

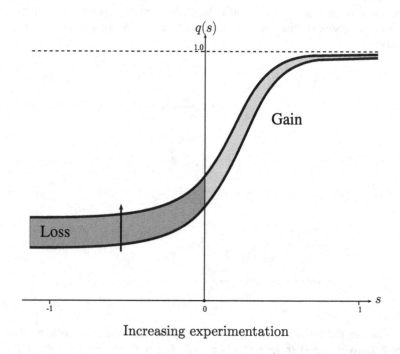

Increasing experimentation

When λ increases, the stochastic response function shifts *upward*, reducing the probability of type I mistakes (gains on the right side), but increasing the probability of type II mistakes (losses on the left side). There are costs associated with each type of mistake. The sum of these costs is $L(q^\lambda)$, and the optimal level of λ^* strikes the right balance between these two costs.

Clearly, the optimal level depends on the underlying distribution. For example, when $s_0 = 0$, the suggested increase in λ generates more losses than gains, hence an expected loss. When s_0 is sufficiently large, realizations of s

fall mostly in the gain region, and in expectation, the suggested increase in λ generates a gain.

11. *Effect of distribution shifts.* We explore the effect of shifts of the distribution on the agent's optimal response. As just explained, when s_0 increases, realizations of s shift to the right, hence the weight on type I mistakes increases: the agent has incentive to increase λ to reduce their likelihood.[12]

In the figure below, we set $\sigma^2 = 1$ and show how the optimal λ^* changes with s_0 for various values of β, and refer to $S_0^{(\beta)}$ as the interval of values of s_0 for which optimal experimentation is interior (i.e., $\lambda^* \in (0,1)$).

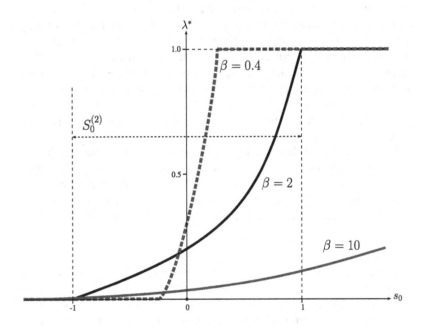

Outside the interval $S_0^{(\beta)}$, the agent prefers to ignore the signals that he gets: he either always interacts (for low s_0) or never interacts (for high s_0). The size of the interval $S_0^{(\beta)}$ thus reflects the agent's ability to use signals to discriminate between states. In addition to the quality of signals (β), various other factors contribute to determine this ability: the strategy restriction (which affects the agent's ability to tailor his behavior to the stochastic process), the lack of persistence (α), and the underlying uncertainty (i.e., the size of σ^2), as, if all states look alike, they are more difficult to distinguish.

When discrimination is easier (e.g., $\beta = 10$), optimal experimentation is flat on a large range of values of s_0, meaning that it is not very sensitive to the underlying distributions.

---

[12] For some non-uniform distributions, a non-monotonic dependence could be obtained.

When discrimination becomes difficult (the steep dashed line, $\beta = 0.4$), optimizing on λ amounts to determining whether the expectation Es is positive (in which case $\lambda^* = 1$) or negative (in which case $\lambda^* = 0$): the locus of s_0 (whether s_0 is positive or negative) dominates in determining the agent's behavior, and for most values of s_0, the agent is not sensitive to the signals that he receives.

12. *A caution.* The prediction of our model as β gets small might be taken with caution, as it may be seen as an artifact of our modeling assumptions – we explain why.

The model aims to characterize the behavior of an agent tracking a moving target (whether the state s is positive or negative). For mathematical convenience, we introduce a stochastic process assumed to be unchanging. For small values of β, behavior is mostly driven by the locus of s_0. This is because through optimization, the agent implicitly manages to determine that the signals he gets are poor, and he appropriately disregards them in favor of the prior "information" (i.e., the stochastic process itself and the exact locus of s_0), even though this prior was merely introduced for mathematical convenience.

In practice, the quality of the signals that one gets is probably subject to shocks and difficult to assess. In addition, the locus of s_0 might be subject to shocks. This suggests that despite our simplified strategy set, allowing the agent to tailor λ to β and s_0 is an assumption that may be too strong: for some range of parameter values, the optimal response becomes overly sensitive to model parameters.[13]

13. *Belief states and belief revisions.* One interpretation of our model is that the behavioral states θ are mental states, or "belief states." When $\theta = I$, the agent believes that interacting is beneficial, and when $\theta = N$, he believes that not interacting is better. Each value of λ defines how the agent revises beliefs as a function of experience, and the optimal λ^* then defines the revision that performs best in the long run. It endogenizes the optimal way to revise belief states, given the constraints on feasible revisions. There are many ways to generate richer behavior, either by endogenizing the response to bad signals or by adding more behavioral states. This would generate a richer set of beliefs, and more complex belief revisions. Ultimately, this would allow the agent to better track the underlying state. However, this better tracking would hinge on the specific process assumed, and the benefits (to the analyst) of following this path deserves further scrutiny, or may depend on the application at hand.

---

[13] For that range of parameters, the concern expressed in Chapter 10 thus applies to our model: predictions seem to be too much driven by priors.

Further Comments

Macroeconomics. *The proposed learning model can be the foundation of a macroeconomic model in which agents try to adjust consumption decisions optimally as a function of past observations. The model obtained would neither be a naive model of learning in which agents compute an optimal choice based on a mechanically constructed (but misspecified) prediction of future prices (e.g., Bray (1982)), nor a rational expectations model in which agents implicitly manage to optimally use the data they get, given the stochastic process that jointly generates prices and observations. Our agents would behave "optimally" given that stochastic process, but "optimally" would mean, among the dynamic rules that the agent compares.*

Bandit problems. *The bandit problem was first formulated by Thompson (1933), in the context of the comparison of the performance of various clinical treatments, with the question of whether and when to abandon a seemingly low-performance treatment. The question of how to optimally accumulate data on each of the treatments available was formulated in more general terms by Robbins (1952). Optimal learning is precisely about optimal data accumulation (which arm/treatment one should choose as a function of existing data). Note that these clinical problems have a structure that differs from the one studied in this chapter: the welfare levels associated with each treatment (measured as the expected cure to an individual drawn randomly from a large pool of sick individuals) are unknown, but they are assumed not to vary over time. In many economic problems, the environment, or the perceptions that we have of it, may be subject to shocks that are more or less persistent.*

Learning, sophistication and mechanism design. *Optimal learning has a mechanism design flavor. Much effort is made to tailor the learning strategy to a presumed stochastic process.*[14] *This chapter has been an attempt to provide a simple relationship between characteristics of the stochastic process (summarized by s_0, σ^2, β, α) and characteristics of the behavioral response (summarized by λ). Increased sophistication would obviously help the agent. Instead of triggering an interruption after a single bad signal, the agent might consider modifying his choice every T periods, and, for example, trigger an interruption when the fraction of bad signals exceeds a threshold ϕ. This would potentially improve the quality of the interruption decision, but this would be at the cost of lowering effective permanence (modifying his choice every T periods amounts to a higher α), hence diminishing the agent's ability to exploit this improved interruption decision.*[15] *While the optimal tailoring of T*

---

[14] In computer science, this sometimes takes the form of finding an algorithm that does well against a given *class* of stochastic processes (adversarial bandits), rather than a given process.

[15] The probability that there is a change of state between t and $t + T$ is equal to $1 - (1 - \alpha)^T$, which is approximately equal to αT when α is small and T not too large.

and ϕ could be of interest in some applications, understanding the relationship between λ and s_0 may be good enough.

> **Suggested research/application.** We have examined a single agent who tries to determine when to choose the risky arm. In the spirit of the literature on strategic experimentation,[16] one could examine an extension involving two agents with similar preferences. For example, one could assume that when in state N, an agent now receives a signal, say $y' \in \{0,1\}$ correlated with the other player's current experience or activity. Each agent could then be endowed with two strategic variables: λ as in this chapter, reflecting one's propensity to experiment independently of the other's experience/activity, and λ', reflecting the propensity to experiment conditional on the other getting a good experience, or being active.
>
> The strategic variable λ' is potentially useful in that it may lead a player to experiment in the presence of good signals from the other (while he would have set $\lambda = 0$ in the absence of any signals). This may lead to at least *some* experimentation taking place (rather than none).[17] But, as players start sharing the burden of experimentation, a player may have an incentive to free ride on the other's experimentation activity (choosing a smaller λ). Within this simple model, one could thus examine conditions under which players jointly win or lose when they observe each other's experience, or if asymmetric communication helps. One could also examine the possible (in)stability of symmetric equilibria: at least one of them must initiate experimentation ($\lambda > 0$), hence if y' is reliable, the second agent might prefer to always let the first bear the cost, either by imitating him (interacting if he does) or by free riding on his experience (i.e., setting $\lambda = 0$).

Appendix

Closed-form expressions. The following Lemma provides a closed-form expression for the stochastic response q^λ induced by σ^λ.

Lemma: *Define ρ_λ such that $\rho_\lambda = E(\frac{1-(1-\lambda)\pi(s)}{1-(1-\alpha)(1-\lambda)\pi(s)})$. We have:*

$$q^\lambda(s) = \frac{\lambda}{\rho_\lambda} \frac{1}{1-(1-\alpha)(1-\lambda)\pi(s))}$$

[16] See for example Bolton and Harris (1999), Keller et al. (2005), or Horner and Skrzypacz (2016) for a review.
[17] Following Bolton and Harris (1999), this phenomenon has been called the "encouragement effect": each player's (conditional) experimentation is an encouragement for the other to (conditionally) experiment as well.

Proof: Let $\phi(s) = 1/(1 - (1 - \alpha)(1 - \lambda)\pi(s))$, $Q_\lambda = Eq^\lambda(s)$ and $\phi_0 = E\phi(s)$. Also define $\tilde{q}^\lambda(s)$ as the end of period probability that $\theta = I$. We have: $\tilde{q}^\lambda(s) = (1 - \lambda)\pi(s)q^\lambda(s) + \lambda$, and $q^\lambda(s) = (1 - \alpha)\tilde{q}^\lambda(s) + \alpha E\tilde{q}^\lambda(s)$. The latter equality implies $Q_\lambda = Eq^\lambda(s) = E\tilde{q}^\lambda(s)$, and combining the two equalities yields $.q^\lambda(s) = (\lambda(1 - \alpha) + \alpha Q_\lambda)\phi(s)$. Taking expectations we get $Q_\lambda = (\lambda(1 - \alpha) + \alpha Q_\lambda)\phi_0$, which implies $q^\lambda(s) = Q_\lambda\phi(s)/\phi_0$ and $(1 - \alpha\phi_0)Q_\lambda = \lambda(1 - \alpha)\phi_0$, which further implies, since $(1 - \alpha)\rho_\lambda = 1 - \alpha\phi_0$, $\rho_\lambda Q_\lambda = \lambda\phi_0$ and $q^\lambda(s) = \lambda\phi(s)/\rho_\lambda$.**Q.E.D.**

This lemma has the following corollary, obtained for the limit case where signals are (almost) perfect $(1/\beta \simeq 0)$:

Corollary: *When $1/\beta \simeq 0$, q^λ takes only two values, $\underline{q}$ (when $s < 0$) and $\overline{q}$ (when $s > 0$), $\underline{q} = \lambda/\rho_\lambda$ and $1 - \overline{q} = \frac{(1-\lambda)\alpha\underline{P}}{\lambda+(1-\lambda)\alpha\underline{P}}$, where $\rho_\lambda = \frac{\lambda+(1-\lambda)\alpha\underline{P}}{\lambda+(1-\lambda)\alpha}$.*

The loss can then be written as

$$L(\lambda) = \underline{q}\,\underline{P}\,\underline{W} + (1 - \overline{q})\overline{P}\,\overline{W}.$$

Finally, with strong persistence $(\alpha \simeq 0)$ and imperfect signals, $q^\lambda(s) = \frac{\lambda}{1-(1-\lambda)\pi(s)}$, and the loss function can be written as

$$L(\lambda) = E\frac{\lambda}{1 - (1 - \lambda)\pi(s)}s.$$

Optimal learning with perfect signals. The optimal learning rule strikes the right balance between the two possible types of mistake. When α is small and signals perfect, the loss can be approximately written as

$$L(\lambda) \simeq \lambda\,\underline{P}\,\underline{W} + \frac{\alpha}{\lambda}\frac{\underline{P}}{}\,\overline{P}\,\overline{W}$$

and optimal λ^* is given by:

$$\lambda^* \simeq k\sqrt{\alpha} \text{ with } k = \sqrt{\frac{\overline{P}\,\overline{W}}{\underline{W}}}.$$

That is, while state changes occur at rate α, experimentation occurs at a higher rate, comparable to $\alpha^{1/2}$, with a higher rate when the ratio $\frac{\overline{P}\,\overline{W}}{\underline{W}}$ increases.

References

Bolton, P. and Harris, C. (1999). Strategic experimentation. *Econometrica*, 67(2), 349–374.

Bray, M. (1982). Learning, estimation, and the stability of rational expectations. *Journal of Economic Theory*, 26(2), 318–39.

Horner, J. and Skrzypacz, A. (2016). Learning, experimentation and information design. Working paper.

Keller, R., Rady, S. and Cripps, M. (2005). Strategic experimentation with exponential bandits. *Econometrica*, 73(1), 39–68.

Robbins, H. (1952). Some aspects of the sequential design of experiments. *Bulletin of the American Mathematical Society*, 58(5), 527–535.

Thompson, W. R. (1933). On the likelihood that one unknown probability exceeds another in view of the evidence of two samples. *Biometrika*, 25(3–4), 285–294.

CHAPTER 13

Reputation

1. Reputation usually refers to the assessments that people make about an agent's abilities or his moral qualities such as honesty, or about the general way he handles particular situations or behaves in particular circumstances. These assessments are typically based on past signals, experiences or observations, and one finds them useful because, to the extent that the qualities which one attributes to a reputable agent might be persistent, they are a predictor of the benefits from future interactions, helping one determine whether such an interaction is desirable. In short, one prefers to deal with a reputable agent and avoid interactions with disreputable agents.

Discrimination between reputable and disreputable agents has another important benefit: it creates an incentive for the agent under scrutiny to behave according to standards that promote his reputation, even if doing so is costly.

Reputation thus has two ingredients: one side learns from past experience, trying to discriminate between profitable and unprofitable encounters; the other side is concerned about his reputation, and tries to influence the agent's perception through his actions or efforts.[1]

We build a simple model with precisely these ingredients, in the context of a buyer/seller relationship.[2] On one side, a seller (whom we refer to as player 2) attempts to build or preserve a reputation for good conduct (say, providing high quality), and is concerned about the possibility that he loses his reputation if he does not meet the other side's expectation. On the other side, a buyer (whom we will refer to as player 1) attempts to discriminate between good and bad conduct, and has the option to discontinue buying for a while if he becomes convinced that the prospects from the interaction are currently not good.

---

[1] The literature often distinguishes between situations where one side is short-lived, and interactions in which both sides are long-lived (see Mailath and Samuelson (2006) for a review). Our model will focus on the case where both agents are long-lived. Extensions to the case where one agent is short-lived are possible, but more involved technically. We come back to this issue at the end of the chapter.

[2] Some aspects of the model borrow from Mailath and Samuelson (2001).

2. *A reputation game.*
Payoffs. The buyer decides in each period whether or not to interact with the seller. Payoffs to the buyer are 0 from no interaction, and w from interaction. The payoff w depends on some underlying state $s \in R$, and the effort level $e \in [0, 1]$ made by the seller. There are many ways that effort can affect gains, with effort for example affecting w for some states and not for others. We consider a simple version where effort affects w uniformly:

$$w = e + s.$$

The value w measures the current quality of the interaction. One may interpret the state s as a characteristic of player 2, reflecting an intrinsic, yet variable, quality of the production. One may also interpret the state s as an (unobservable) preference parameter for player 1, defining the current fit between the good produced and player 1's characteristics.

We assume that player 2 benefits from the interaction. He gets a payoff equal to 1 when player 1 interacts, minus the cost of effort.[3] We denote by $g(e)$ the cost function. We assume convex costs and $g'(0) = 0$.

Process and observations. The process over states and observations is defined as in the previous chapter. The state changes with probability α in every period. When the state changes, it is drawn from a distribution h. Letting $s_0 = Es$, it will be convenient to think of the following structure for the new draw:

$$s = s_0 + \mu$$

where s_0 is fixed and μ a random variable with 0 expectation. In addition, in numerical simulations below, μ will be assumed to be normally distributed with variance σ^2. Thus, when the seller makes a constant effort e when interacting, he just shifts s_0 upward by e.

As in the previous chapter, whether the value w from interacting is positive or negative cannot be observed perfectly. This friction is modeled by assuming that when the buyer does not interact, he observes nothing, and when he interacts, he gets one of two possible signals, $y = \bar{y}, \underline{y}$, with the (good) signal $\bar{y}$ being more likely when w is higher. This allows him to discriminate (imperfectly) whether w is positive or negative.[4] Formally, we denote by $\pi(w)$ the probability of a good signal ($\bar{y}$) when the expected benefit is w. In numerical simulations to come, we shall assume:

$$\pi(w) = \exp \beta w / (1 + \exp \beta w)$$

---

[3] The cost of effort is incurred only if interaction occurs.
[4] One may want to interpret y as the realized benefit, but it need not be so. The signal y is meant to summarize whatever information the agent is processing for the purpose of deciding which decision to take in the future. This information could be much coarser than the actual realized benefit.

for some positive parameter β. The parameter reflects the quality of the signal that the agent gets in any period in which he chooses to interact.

Stackelberg effort. A relevant benchmark in reputation models is the level of effort that the seller would make if he could credibly commit to that level, called the Stackelberg effort, denoted e^{**}. Formally, define

$$Q(e) \equiv \Pr(w > 0 \mid e) = \Pr(s + e > 0).$$

This is the transaction volume that player 2 would get if he were facing an agent who interacts if and only if w is positive. Defining $\pi(e)$ as the seller's profit, and assuming that π is concave,[5] we have:

$$e^{**} = \arg\max_e \pi(e) \equiv (1 - g(e))Q(e).$$

The Stackelberg effort plays a key role in reputation models because if player 2 could build a reputation for sustaining a particular effort level, and if he could choose which reputation he wanted to sustain, then, against a player who observes w (or learns it quickly), he would choose an effort level equal (or close) to e^{**}. Of course, because of the two frictions, limited permanence ($\alpha > 0$) and imperfect observations ($1/\beta > 0$), his choice will generally diverge from e^{**}.

3. *Strategic variables.* One side attempts to learn from experience, and we model learning as in the previous chapter – limiting the set of dynamic strategies considered by the buyer. Define first the basic strategy σ^0 that starts by interacting, and continues doing so as long as good signals are received, permanently foregoing interaction after the first bad signal.

For any fixed $\lambda \in (0, 1]$, we define the strategy σ^λ that restarts σ^0 with probability λ at the beginning of any period. In other words, the agent may be in one of two possible *behavioral/belief states* θ ((I)nteracting or (N)ot interacting), and the strategy σ^λ defines transitions over these belief states as a function of the history of signals received:

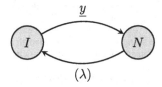

(λ)

---

[5] Concavity ensures a unique solution. However, a unique solution would also obtain under weaker conditions, for example if $\log Q$ is concave (which is the case when μ is a normal distribution).

The parameter λ may be interpreted as the degree to which the agent experiments with the risky arm when in state N, checking whether interaction is profitable.[6]

On the other side, the seller chooses the effort level e that he applies throughout the relationship, in events in which he interacts.[7,8] Our reputation game thus has two (and only two) strategic variables: the *propensity to interact* λ,[9] and the *effort level* e.[10]

4. *Reputation equilibrium.* As long as player 1 is sensitive to the signals that he faces ($\lambda \neq 0$ and $\lambda \neq 1$), player 1's behavior potentially constitutes an incentive mechanism for player 2: player 1 has two belief states, and higher effort increases the chance that player 1 remains in the high belief state, thereby increasing the chance of interaction. The strength of this incentive/reputation mechanism depends on the parameters of the model. We analyze this next.

Formally, as before, any pair (e, λ) induces a long-run distribution over states (θ, s), and we refer to $\phi^\lambda(e, s)$ as the fraction of the time that the buyer interacts when in state s. Given the assumed process and structure of signals, the frequency $\phi^\lambda(e, s)$ depends only on $e + s$, and it coincides with the frequency $q^\lambda(s + e)$ where q^λ has been defined in the previous chapter:

$$\phi^\lambda(e, s) = q^\lambda(s + e).$$

The frequency function $q^\lambda(.)$ is increasing, meaning that the agents interact more frequently when the state is higher, or when the effort is higher. Finally, define $Q^\lambda(e)$ as the expected volume that player 2 gets when his effort is e:

$$Q^\lambda(e) \equiv E_s q^\lambda(e + s).$$

---

[6] Note that $\lambda = 1$ means that the agent interacts at all dates, while $\lambda = 0$ means that the state in which there is no interaction is absorbing.

[7] Effort is thus, by assumption, identical in every period in which he interacts.

[8] The payoff and signal structure of the model that we propose is in the spirit of Mailath and Samuelson (2001), with, here, a continuum of effort levels allowed for the seller. The stochastic environment is different. Mailath and Samuelson assume that in every period, with small positive probability, the seller is replaced by a new seller who behaves in a predetermined way (behavioral types with limited permanence). We do not introduce behavioral types, but our assumption that there are exogenous changes in the benefits (s) from interaction provides the buyer with a motive for learning similar to that in Mailath and Samuelson. The substantial simplification in our model comes from the strategy restrictions imposed, on both the buyer and seller sides.

[9] The propensity to interact, λ, may also be interpreted as a propensity to experiment after bad experiences.

[10] Our reputation model thus imposes a strategy restriction on player 1 as in the learning problem (Chapter 12). It also imposes a strategy restriction on player 2, who ignores the possibility of adjusting effort as a function of the history of his signals (past effort and whether interaction occurred). We discuss this assumption below.

A *reputation equilibrium*, when it exists, is defined as a pair (λ^*, e^*) with $\lambda^* \in (0, 1)$ and $e^* > 0$ that solves:

$$e^* = \arg\max_e (1 - g(e))Q^{\lambda^*}(e)$$

$$\lambda^* = \arg\max_\lambda E_s(e^* + s)q^\lambda(e^* + s).$$

5. *The seller's incentives.* The degree to which player 1 experiments after bad experiences affects player 2's incentives to make an effort. When λ is very small, a bad signal generates a long period with no interaction, and the seller has incentives to avoid this by making high effort. Analogously, when λ is close to 1, a bad signal is of almost no consequence on the probability of interaction, and player 2 has almost no incentives to make effort.

Said differently, experimentation by the buyer is like volume that comes for free, and this tends to reduce the incentives to make effort.

To illustrate this effect, consider the limit when imperfections (α and $1/\beta$) are both very small. We have:[11]

$$Q^\lambda(e) = Q(e) + \lambda(1 - Q(e)) + O(\lg\beta/\beta) + O(\alpha/\lambda).$$

This means that, if λ is small (but large compared to α and $\lg\beta/\beta$), the two last terms of the above expression can be ignored,[12] and the optimal effort solves:

$$e^* = \max_e (1 - \lambda)\pi(e) + \lambda(1 - g(e)). \tag{13.1}$$

Since $\pi - \frac{\lambda}{1-\lambda}g$ is concave, this implies that effort decreases with λ.

6. *Equilibrium.* We illustrate the construction of equilibrium in three cases, varying the level of imperfections (β) while keeping α very small (high permanence). We choose parameters so that, in the absence of effort, interactions are not profitable on average (i.e., $Es = s_0 < 0$). To derive the graphs below, we also choose a quadratic cost function $g(e) = e^2/2$, and choose $s_0 = -0.4$ and $\sigma^2 = 1$. The Stackelberg effort is $e^{**} \simeq 0.575$.

We start with an intermediate case where noise is neither very small nor very large ($\beta = 2$). The experimentation strategy for the buyer (player 1) is given by an upward slopping curve as in the bandit problem. The seller's response is a downward sloping curve: when λ increases, incentives to make an effort

---

[11] This follows from observing that: (i) except for w such that $|w| \leq K(\lg\beta/\beta)$, the agent's error is comparable to at most $1/\beta^K$; and (ii) errors also stem from the agent's foregoing interaction while w is positive, but the effect of these errors is comparable to α/λ (because the agent is trying every $1/\lambda$ periods on average, while the state changes every $1/\alpha$ periods on average).

[12] These two terms can also be ignored when we consider the marginal effect of a small change in effort, because a change in effort is equivalent to a shift in the distribution h, and the distribution h has bounded derivatives.

disappear. The intersection of these two curves characterizes the reputation equilibrium.

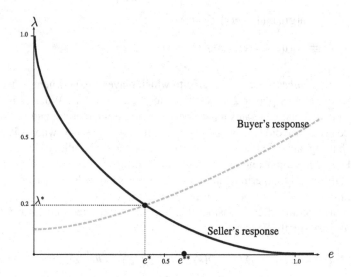

Small and large noise. When frictions (α and $1/\beta$) are small, the equilibrium effort e^* is close to the Stackelberg effort e^{**} because optimal experimentation must be small, and yet large compared to α.[13] This implies that optimal effort solves (13.1) with λ close to 0, hence e^* must be close to e^{**}: in equilibrium, effort is close to the Stackelberg effort.

For sufficiently large noise levels ($1/\beta$ large), incentives to put in effort are poor even if λ is close to 0 because on the relevant range (e such that $g(e) < 1$), effort has little effect on the probability of a good signal. As a result, effort must be small. But then interactions are not profitable on average ($Ew < 0$), and with poor signals, the agent prefers to avoid interaction altogether: $\lambda^* = 0$; there cannot exist an equilibrium in which players interact in the long run.

These two cases are summarized in the following figures, which plot best responses for each player, assuming α arbitrarily small, with large and small noise ($1/\beta = 2.5$ and $1/\beta = 0.1$).

With large noise, the buyer's response is to set $\lambda = 0$ until $e + s_0$ gets close to 0, [14] at which point the response increases sharply. In addition, the seller's incentives are poor even when λ is close to 0. With small noise, the buyer's response is flat and small over the relevant range of effort. In addition, when λ gets small, the seller's incentives become strong.

---

[13] Formally, for any interval of effort $[0, \bar{e}]$, there exists k such that $\lambda^* \geq k\sqrt{\alpha}$. This is because the distribution over s has unbounded support, so the events $w < 0$ and $w > 0$ have probability bounded away from 0 for all $e \in [0, \bar{e}]$.

[14] With even larger noise, there would be a step at $e = -s_0 = 0.4$.

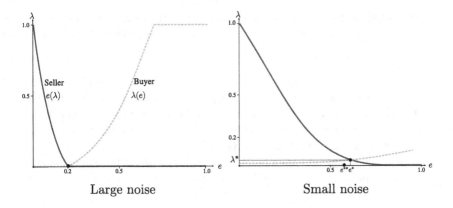

Large noise   Small noise

7. *Imperfections and seller's incentives.* We parameterized two kinds of imperfections: (i) noise $(1/\beta)$ and (ii) lack of permanence (α). With almost no imperfections, the seller would make the Stackelberg effort e^{**}, and there would be almost no inefficiencies in expectation.[15] As imperfections grow, inefficiencies increase:

(i) conditions continue to be good $(w > 0)$ but the buyer stops interacting, or conditions have become bad $(w < 0)$ and the buyer continues to interact;

(ii) conditions have become good but the buyer is still not interacting (under small λ), or conditions continue to be bad but the buyer tries to interact (under high λ).

Through their choices (λ and e), the buyer and the seller modify the frequencies of different kinds of errors. By increasing experimentation (higher λ), the buyer examines whether, despite a bad signal, conditions are in fact good, or if conditions have become good since the last encounter. By increasing effort (higher e), the seller reduces the likelihood of no interaction phases.

The strategies (λ and e) are neither complements nor substitutes: more experimentation reduces the seller's incentives to make effort but lower effort by the seller reduces the buyer's incentive to experiment. Consequently, in general, the effect of imperfections on equilibrium behavior is ambiguous: it depends on the extent to which each side benefits or is hurt by the respective errors.

---

[15] There would still be some inefficiencies, because the buyer can only detect whether the state changes from bad $(w < 0)$ to good $(w > 0)$ by experimenting. But these inefficiencies are small in expectation because the buyer experiments often enough to quickly track these changes, and yet not too often to avoid a large number of unprofitable trials.

We illustrate this in a limit case where values have closed-form expressions ($1/\beta \ll \alpha \ll 1$) and examine whether and when the equilibrium effort level e^* lies above or below e^{**}.

8. *The limit case where* $1/\beta \ll \alpha \ll 1$. Under the above conditions, there are essentially two sources of errors: if the buyer experiments little, he may remain in the No interaction state although the underlying conditions for trade have become favorable ($w > 0$). Or the buyer experiments frequently, and he tries to interact while conditions are still bad ($w < 0$).

The seller would obviously prefer that the buyer experiments more often, as these are never costly to the seller, but the buyer is concerned about the cost and benefits of experimentation. In particular, let

$$\underline{W}(e) = E[-w \mid w < 0, e] \text{ and } \overline{W}(e) = E[w \mid w > 0, e].$$

When $\underline{W}(e)$ is large or $\overline{W}(e)$ is small, experimenting is costly, so experimentation is low. To compensate for a low level of experimentation by the buyer, the seller may prefer to increase his effort above the Stackelberg effort, so as to reduce the probability that they get stuck in lengthy (and costly to him) "No interaction" phases. The following proposition makes this precise.

Proposition 1: *If at* e^{**}, $Q(e) > \overline{W}(e)/\underline{W}(e)$ *then for small* α *and* $1/\beta \ll \alpha$, *the equilibrium effort* e^* *lies above the Stackelberg effort* e^{**}.

In essence, when the right-hand side is low, experimentation by the buyer is rather small. It is worthwhile for the seller to compensate for low experimentation by increasing effort, but only if $Q(e) = \Pr(w > 0 \mid e)$ is sufficiently large. Otherwise, he is just making an extra effort that is most often not worthwhile (because w is often low despite the extra effort, and the buyer likely stops interacting anyway).

A detailed proof is in the Appendix. Intuitively, when α is small, but large relative to $1/\beta$, the buyer optimally tracks whether conditions have become good again by setting λ comparable to $\sqrt{\alpha}$ (i.e., $\lambda = k\sqrt{\alpha}$), and the volume of trade can be expressed as follows:

$$Q^\lambda(e) = Q(e) + \sqrt{\alpha}\Delta(e,k)$$

where $\Delta(e,k)$ represents the net effect of errors made by the buyers on the volume of trade. This term has two components: a positive component resulting from the agent experimenting in bad states ($w < 0$); and a negative component resulting from the agent's getting stuck not interacting while the state is good. Whether e^* exceeds e^{**} depends on whether $\Delta(e,k)/Q(e)$ is increasing or decreasing around e^{**} (see Appendix).

When, for example, $\overline{W}(e)/\underline{W}(e)$ is very large, experimentation is frequent (k is large), and the positive component predominates. The seller benefits from these errors, and the benefit is smaller when effort is larger (because the event ($w < 0$) is less frequent when effort is larger). Consequently, $\Delta(e,k)/Q(e)$ is decreasing, and e^* is below e^{**}.

9. *Sustaining or exploiting one's reputation?* Proposition 1 implies interesting comparative statics. When $\underline{W}$ is high, experimentation tends to be low. If one interprets the state $\theta = I$ as a state where the seller has good reputation, this means that there exists a mechanical tendency for reputation to disappear, and when it disappears, it does so for a long period of time. As a result, to sustain his reputation, the seller needs to be aggressive.

In contrast, when $\underline{W}$ is small, experimentation is naturally high, so, despite occasions in which the reputation disappears, it does not disappear for long. The strategic consequence for the seller is that he may exploit his reputation by reducing his effort level below Stackelberg levels without being affected in the long run: in order to generate a high volume, he only needs to be good enough.

10. *Degrees of sophistication. The buyer's side.* The tradition in game theory calls for endogenizing the buyer's experimentation strategy. We have done this, but have put limits, however, on this endogenization. According to the usual standards, our endogenization might appear overly restrictive. Still, one may find that our assumption is too strong: it assumes that the buyer can perfectly calibrate λ to the distribution ω. In particular, when signals are noisy (low β), we are led to the conclusion that the buyer either always buys (in case $e + s_0 > 0$) or never buys (in case $e + s_0 < 0$). Quite plausibly, the buyer might only be able to reliably compare few values of λ (each distinct from 0 and 1).

Going in the direction of further sophistication, one could enlarge the set of strategies. By allowing for strategies that trigger "no interaction" under different conditions, one could introduce a different/additional strategic variable characterizing experimentation duration (how long one keeps on trying the risky arm before moving to "No interaction." One could gain insights about the optimal duration, namely the usual tradeoff between exploration and exploitation (with an optimal length of experimentation comparable to $\ln \alpha$ periods).

There is a (modeling) issue, however, in introducing more strategic variables: it generates insights that may be quite sensitive to the model specification (here, the presumption that α does not vary). Taking α as fixed is a mathematical convenience. Tailoring the optimal length of experimentation to that particular feature of the model may lead us to overemphasize the relevance of that strategic variable.

The seller's side. Similar issues arise concerning the seller's strategy set. We have implicitly assumed that the seller had no information, or was not exploiting any information, related to the underlying state s. Obviously, there could be an incentive for the seller to decrease effort if he believes that $s + e$ is well above 0, for example. And although he is not assumed to receive any direct signal related to s, the mere fact that the interaction is uninterrupted is evidence that $s + e$ might be high. Along these lines, one could enrich the set of strategies for the seller: one could introduce a second strategic variable, the extent to which the seller diminishes or increases effort during a given interaction phase. The same comment applies, however. One may end up overemphasizing these strategic effects, as they are tailored to the underlying process assumed. The optimal direction (increase or decrease) may be clear for the particular model we considered, but not necessarily so with more general payoff and process specifications.

Further Comments

Historical note and related literature. Reputation effects were first studied in the context of finitely repeated games, as a response to the fact that equilibrium predictions in such games could be counterintuitive (Kreps, Milgrom, Roberts and Wilson (1982)).[16] *Their idea is as follows. By adding a grain of uncertainty, either about long-lasting parameters of the game (the payoff structure, for example) or about behavior (with some small probability, one player is a "commitment type" who plays in a predetermined way), one may introduce an incentive for players to learn, i.e., to use past observations to better predict the future.*[17]

This paper has had a considerable influence on modeling reputation, with most reputation papers adopting the "commitment type" modeling strategy.[18] *These papers have been useful in identifying weaknesses in some equilibrium constructions, yet they are subject to a number of criticisms.*

First, they rely on a number of special assumptions: the presence of commitment types that are sometimes hard to justify, restrictions on the set of commitment types,[19] *and optimal dynamic strategies that adjust finely to some hypothetical distribution over these presumed commitment types. From an ex ante perspective, the analyst is essentially putting arbitrary restrictions on behavior,*[20] *and the motivation for these particular restrictions is often unclear.*

---

[16] In a finitely repeated prisoner's dilemma, the only equilibrium involves defecting at all dates. In these games, one might expect that cooperation is possible when the interaction is long enough. Yet the end game behavior (i.e., defection) unravels to all previous dates. We shall examine this question in Chapter 19, and provide another response.

[17] In the latter case for example, the presence of commitment types modifies the incentives of a player in events where his behavior is not predetermined: he may choose to behave as though he had a predetermined behavior – with the hope of influencing the beliefs of the other side (to the extent that he finds an advantage to that), thus modifying, possibly drastically, the equilibrium outcome.

[18] The reason is primarily technical. Introducing uncertainty about the payoff structure becomes difficult to handle as time goes on. Mailath and Samuelson (2006) refer to the "commitment type" modeling strategy as the "adverse selection approach to reputation."

[19] Technically, the force of these reputation effects comes from the fact that there is a limited number of commitment types that a player can mimic. If there were as many commitment types as possible dynamic strategies, past observations would be of little help in predicting the future.

[20] That is, with some probability ε, play is exogenously given.

Another criticism of these models is their sophistication. On one side, a player, say player 1, faces a possibly committed agent, and any possible history of observations that he might make translates into a posterior distribution or posterior belief over commitment types. On the other side, player 2 must consider all possible ways to exploit or manipulate these beliefs. This tailoring is complex, and depends on the nature of signals that players receive: if signals are public, player 2 can perfectly track player 1's beliefs; while if signals are private, player 2 keeps track of a distribution over player 1's possible beliefs – for each sequence of observations that player 2 makes. These computations are intractable in most cases, and would not seem particularly relevant to applied situations in which one expects that agents may only have rough perceptions of what the other side is up to.

Finally, while these models are meant to capture how one side's behavior may influence the other side's beliefs, the standard equilibrium construction fails to reflect this influence: in Fudenberg and Levine (1989) for example, one side behaves in a way that looks like a particular "commitment type," but in equilibrium this does not modify the posterior probability (or belief) that the player is a "commitment type."

This chapter can be seen as an effort to avoid having agents enter into overly complex computations, to propose a model in which one side's behavior truly influences the other side's beliefs (with beliefs summarized simply by a belief state I or N), and to provide a path to understand how greater or lesser sophistication would affect outcomes.

Short-lived and long-lived players. *It is a standard assumption in the literature to consider short-lived agents. We could in principle use our model to analyze a sequence of short-lived agents whose belief state θ_i evolves over time as a function of the entire history of signals. This path would introduce heterogenous beliefs and concomitant technical difficulties that are not present in the standard model.[21] This heterogeneity is a substantive issue that in our view deserves scrutiny: it is often difficult to judge whether the outcomes or behavior seen in other interactions are relevant to our interactions, hence potentially subject to heterogenous assessment.[22] One might thus want to*

---

[21] Our behavioral assumption implies that each short-lived agent experiences private state changes (even if the sequence of signals is the same). Consequently, our model with short-lived agents creates heterogeneous belief states and is more difficult to solve. This contrasts with the standard model (with short-lived agents) in which all short-lived are assumed to see the same history, and to react in exactly the same way to the sequence of signals they observe. Both assumptions seem questionable.

[22] Said differently, the issue is whether behavior observed in one interaction is relevant to later interactions, or if the set of circumstances under which the initial behavior was observed should be considered special, and not representative of typical circumstances. Whether the resolve of the EU in dealing with Brexit signals a similar resolve with other countries potentially considering exit is an open question. Similarly, the weak response of the U.S in dealing with

reconsider the usual assumption that all short-lived agents have perfectly correlated beliefs.

Reputation and commitment. *An interesting insight of the literature is the link between reputation and commitment.*[23] *When one side (player 2) adjusts to what he sees, the other side (player 1) can obtain the best possible payoff, as if he could commit to a particular course of play and expect player 2 to adjust. This cannot work for both sides simultaneously and has been a motivation for studying interactions with short-lived players for whom commitment has no value. One may wonder why our model with two long-lived agents does not become a battlefield between two desires to establish commitment, as in Kreps and Wilson (1982). The reason is that we have limited the seller's strategy space. With a more sophisticated seller, who, for example, chooses his effort level as a function of the observed propensity of player 1 to interact, one would obtain a strategic reason for player 1 to diminish interactions, so as to induce higher effort from player 2.*

Learning without commitment types. *Learning is at the heart of any reputation mechanism. In traditional models, learning takes the form of belief revisions summarized by posterior probability distributions over "commitment types" and a strategic "noncommitted" type.*

In our model, there are no "commitment types" nor "noncommitted" types. The presence of commitment types is not essential to a reputation mechanism. Eventually what matters is that the buyer learns from experience. In the model proposed, the environment changes, and these changes have serious enough consequences, enough permanence, and are detected with sufficient accuracy, to produce history-dependent strategies for the buyer, and this history dependence in turn generates incentives for the seller to improve the quality of its product.

Our seller is strategic, yet not fully uncommitted: he chooses among a limited number of strategies. The limitation may stem from a lack of sophistication, or the agent's inability to compare more complex strategies. But at least technically, the limitation may be interpreted as a partial commitment: the seller behaves as if he was committed to using a strategy within a predetermined set.[24]

Equilibrium stability. *With rather noisy signals, the agent's strategy may become quite sensitive to the underlying process (i.e., the locus of s_0*

the 2013 chemical attacks in Syria does not necessarily signal a similar weak response in the future if the issue arises again or with respect to other countries.

[23] This link was pointed out early on in Schelling (1960).

[24] Note that from an ex ante perspective, introducing commitment types can also be interpreted as a strategy restriction: with small probability, a seller behaves in a predetermined way. We have been studying a different kind of strategy restriction.

for example). An implication is equilibrium instability under best response dynamics, because the buyer's optimal response $\lambda^*(e)$ becomes too sensitive to the effort level e. Thus, even in our simplified framework, stability under best response dynamics cannot be taken for granted. This issue of equilibrium stability is seldom addressed in these types of environment, because even best responses are often impossible to characterize. A benefit of our simplified environment is thus that this issue can be addressed, and that one can express caution with respect to predictions obtained in corners of the model in which stability is not guaranteed.[25]

Suggested research/applications. Based on the discussion above, we see various possible extensions: one could introduce more sophistication (on either side), with the hope of understanding which side, if either, benefits from greater sophistication;[26] another extension could model heterogeneous buyers, each of whom tries to learn from the others' experience, in the spirit of the suggested research of Chapter 12. Finally, the model could handle short-run buyers whose beliefs are not perfectly aligned. One difference with our basic model is that a buyer may receive a signal even at dates when his belief state is N: so, as in the heterogenous buyers case just mentioned, belief transitions could be usefully enriched, allowing transitions to belief state I conditional on the signal y received by the current buyer, if any.

Appendix

Proof of Proposition 1. Observe that under the conditions of the proposition, the buyer optimally tracks whether conditions have become good again by setting λ comparable to $\sqrt{\alpha}$. Specifically, letting $\overline{P}(e) = Q(e)$ and $\underline{P}(e) = 1 - \overline{P}(e)$, we have: $\lambda^*(e) = k(e)\sqrt{\alpha}$ where $k(e) = (\overline{P}(e)\overline{W}(e)/\underline{W}(e))^{1/2}$ (see Chapter 12, Corollary).

To check the seller's optimal response to λ, set $k = \lambda/\sqrt{\alpha}$. Omitting negligible terms, one gets

$$Q^\lambda(e) = Q(e) + \sqrt{\alpha}\,\Delta(k,e) \text{ where}$$

$$\Delta(k,e) = -\frac{P(e)}{k}\overline{P}(e) + k\underline{P}(e).$$

[25] Instability does not mean that we should not expect reputation mechanisms to work. Rather, the instability obtained seems more of an artifact of the model, which invites us to modify it (through more randomness in s_0 for example, or less ability to pin down the best response λ^*).

[26] A plausible effect of the seller's sophistication could be a reduction in the variance of w in equilibrium (as sellers are trying to target effort that leaves positive but small rents to buyers), hence plausibly diminished incentives to experiment for the buyer.

The term $\Delta(k, e)$ represents the net effect of the buyer's errors on the volume of trade.[27] Let $\phi(e) = \Delta(k, e)/\overline{P}(e)$, and write $\pi(e, \alpha) = (1 - g(e))Q(e)(1 + \sqrt{\alpha}\phi(e))$. The optimal effort $e^*(\alpha)$ satisfies $\frac{\partial \pi}{\partial e} = 0$, and $\frac{de^*}{d\alpha}$ has the sign of $\pi(e, \alpha)\sqrt{\alpha}\phi'(e)$. It is easy to check that $\phi'(e) = \overline{P}'(1/k - k/\overline{P}^2)$. Using $k^2 = \overline{P}\,\overline{W}/\underline{W}$, we see that $\phi'(e) > 0$ when $k^2 < \overline{P}^2$, as desired.

References

Fudenberg, D. and Levine, D. (1989). Reputation and equilibrium selection in games with a patient player. *Econometrica*, 57, 759–778.

Kreps, D., Milgrom, P., Roberts, J. and Wilson, R. (1982). Rational cooperation in the finitely repeated prisoners' dilemma. *Journal of Economic Theory*, 27, 245–252.

Kreps, D. and Wilson, R. (1982). Reputation and imperfect information. *Journal of Economic Theory*, 27, 253–279.

Mailath, G. and Samuelson, L. (2001). Who wants a good reputation? *The Review of Economic Studies*, 68(2), 415–41.

Mailath, G. and Samuelson, L. (2006). *Repeated Games and Reputations: Long-Run Relationships*, Oxford: Oxford University Press.

Schelling, T. C. (1960). *The Strategy of Conflict*, Massachusetts: Harvard University Press.

---

[27] To check the expression for $\Delta(k, e)$, note that, compared to the perfect case where the volume is $Q(e)$, the net volume $Q^\lambda(e) - Q(e)$ coincides with $\underline{q}\underline{P} - (1 - \overline{q})\overline{P}$, where the expressions for $\underline{q}$ and $\overline{q}$ are given in Chapter 12 (Corollary).

CHAPTER 14

Cooperation

1. Through the course of a relationship or partnership, incentives to invest vary: at times, we may be upset over the way the partnership goes, with low expectations about sustained cooperation and little hope that making effort would increase prospects. At other times, we feel good about prospects, ready to invest again in the relationship and worried that decreasing effort might undermine cooperation. We are interested in building a simple model that explains conditions under which cooperation (i.e., high effort level on both sides) can be sustained, at least periodically.

A partnership bears some resemblance to the strategic interaction studied in the previous chapter. When I choose an effort level, I affect whether the other side (my partner) will be satisfied or dissatisfied. The consequence is as in the reputation problem: if my partner follows a dynamic strategy influenced by her satisfaction (reducing effort when dissatisfied), this creates an incentive for me to cooperate (that is, to continue high effort); and doing so may prevent my partner from reducing effort.

There is a difference, however: sustained cooperation requires that *both sides* put in high effort. In particular, if one player's incentives to put in effort are so strong that he prefers to remain cooperative at all times, the incentive for the other side to put in effort is eliminated; both players must thus be provided with incentives to use a dynamic strategy, that is, a strategy that sometimes cooperates and sometimes defects depending on observations.

This chapter explains how this might be done. In essence, there are many reasons why one might want to condition behavior on observations. One is that the benefits of cooperation may vary over time, and that players attempt to use recent experience to determine whether cooperation is currently productive. We formalize this idea in a simple exchange game.[1]

---

[1] In contrast to the repeated game literature, which often assumes that the exact same game is repeated, we introduce the possibility that the payoff structure is subject to persistent shocks. The presence of these shocks will provide a motive for using dynamic strategies, as these may generate higher welfare than a constant strategy that would cooperate always, irrespective of current conditions.

2. *A gift exchange game.* There are two players who exchange gifts each period. Each has two possible actions, one that corresponds to not making an effort in choosing a gift, and a second corresponding to making a costly effort. Gifts may or may not be perceived as "thoughtful," and a gift is more likely perceived as thoughtful when the other puts in costly effort.

Payoff structure. Actions are $\{C,D\}$ with C representing costly effort. C stands for "cooperation" and D stands for "defection." The cost of effort is γ. The expected payoff that player i receives from the interaction is 0 when the other does not put in effort, and it is x when the other puts in effort.[2] The players' expected payoffs are thus:

	C	N
C	$x-\gamma,x-\gamma$	$-\gamma,x$
N	$x,-\gamma$	$0,0$

We refer to x as the *benefit of cooperation.*

Process. The benefits of cooperation are assumed to vary, and to model the variations, we assume that x follows a stochastic process. For simplicity, we assume that in each period, with small probability α, there is a new draw of x. We also assume that $x \in \{0,g\}$, with $g > \gamma$, and we designate $Q = \Pr(x=0)$. This means that effort is either valuable for both players, or unprofitable. One interpretation is that there are times when each player's understanding of the other's needs decreases, and effort becomes useless.[3] Ideally, agents should cooperate in good times (when $x = g$) and defect in bad times (when $x = 0$). Agents, however, do not observe x perfectly.

Observations. Agents do not observe whether times are good or bad, nor the action of the other player. Rather, each receives a private signal $y_i \in Y_i = \{\underline{y},\bar{y}\}$ which (imperfectly) reflects the other's effort and the benefits x.[4] Specifically, we assume:

$$p = \Pr\{y_i = \bar{y} \mid a_j = C, x_i = g\} \text{ and}$$
$$q = \Pr\{y_i = \bar{y} \mid (a_j,x_i) = (a,x)\} \text{ for all } (a,x) \neq (C,g),$$

---

[2] Our analysis would carry over to cases where the benefits of cooperation are agent-specific, i.e., equal to x_i for agent i.

[3] For ease of exposition, we model these changes as perfectly correlated shocks, both in time and value across players. Our analysis would carry over to more general noise structures. In particular it would carry over to cases where benefits are private (i.e., x_i for player i) and where changes in benefits are not necessarily synchronized.

[4] It may be convenient to think of y_i as the realized payoff for player i, in which case one would assume the following relationships: $g = p\bar{y} + (1-p)\underline{y}$ and $0 = q\bar{y} + (1-q)\underline{y}$.

with $p > q$ so that one can refer to $y_i = \underline{y}$ as a "bad" signal and $y_i = \bar{y}$ as a "good" signal. In words, the main difficulty that a player faces is that a bad signal may either reflect bad luck, bad times (low x), or times perceived as bad by the other side (who plays D).

Dynamic strategies. One option for an agent is to ignore signals and follow a constant strategy, playing C at all dates (strategy σ^C) or playing D at all dates (strategy σ^D). Alternatively, an agent may attempt to adjust his effort level to circumstances (ideally whether times are good and whether the other cooperates) and adopt a dynamic strategy whereby his effort level is a function of past experience. We follow the path set out in previous chapters: we restrict attention to a few simple dynamic strategies, and assume that agents adopt the optimal dynamic strategy within a limited set, to be defined next.[5]

To define the dynamic strategies we consider, we assume that each player i may be in one of two possible belief states $\theta_i \in \{H, L\}$, high or low, and that he plays C in belief state H, and plays D in belief state L. Next, we describe how a player's belief state changes over time. For any given $k \in (0, 1)$ and $\lambda \in [0, 1]$, we define the strategy $\sigma^{\lambda,k}$ where player i's belief state changes over time based on past experience according to the following transitions:[6]

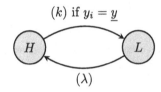

In other words, when $\theta_i = H$ in a given period, player i transits to L with probability k when he receives a bad signal, and he remains in H if he receives a good signal. When in state L at the end of a given period, he transits back to H next period with probability λ.[7] We refer to λ as an individual's *propensity to cooperate*.

The dynamic strategies proposed illustrate a plausible way that agents might use past experience. They echo the family of strategies that our agent used in Chapter 12 to learn about his environment: the agent is uncertain as to when effort is worthwhile; and, when pessimistic (i.e., in state L), he nevertheless *experiments* with cooperation, going back to state H with probability λ. The environment is strategic, but we assume that he considers the same set of strategies as in Chapter 12.

---

[5] As always, endowing an agent with a richer set of strategies allows him to adjust to circumstances more finely. A simple set will be sufficient for our purpose.

[6] In previous chapters, the probability k was assumed to be 1.

[7] Note that λ induces a dynamic strategy that remains nontrivial in the long run only when $\lambda \in (0, 1)$. When $\lambda = 1$ for player i, this player cooperates at all dates; when $\lambda = 0$, he defects at all dates in the long run.

One might argue that the current environment differs from that of Chapter 12 in that signals are received even when he defects, and these signals might be usefully employed to modify how he transits back to state H. We see no objection to following that path, and later in this chapter, we investigate another family of strategies in which player i transits back to state H with probability λ_i, but only does so in events where he receives a good signal (see Section 9). We denote by $\overline{\sigma}^{\lambda_i,k}$ such strategies.

Nevertheless, it is useful to investigate the strategic interaction between less sophisticated agents, not knowing (or not attempting to evaluate) whether the signal observed when in state L should prompt different courses of play.

Strategy restrictions. For the first part of this chapter, we fix particular values for $k \in (0,1)$ and $\lambda \in (0,1)$, define $\widehat{\sigma} \equiv \sigma^{\lambda,k}$, and assume that each player i compares three possible strategies:

$$\sigma_i \in \Sigma_i = \{\sigma^D, \sigma^C, \widehat{\sigma}\}.$$

Next, in Section 6, we continue to fix k but assume that each player i compares all possible strategies $\sigma^{\lambda_i,k}$ as λ_i varies:

$$\Sigma_i = \{\sigma^{\lambda_i,k}\}_{\lambda_i \in [0,1]}.$$

Finally, in Section 9, we continue to fix k and assume that each player i compares all possible strategies $\overline{\sigma}^{\lambda_i,k}$ as λ_i varies:

$$\Sigma_i = \{\overline{\sigma}^{\lambda_i,k}\}_{\lambda_i \in [0,1]}.$$

We shall see how this latter family affects incentives and the scope for cooperation.

Long-run values and equilibrium. When players adopt nontrivial dynamic strategies, they typically alternate between *cooperative phases* in which both players cooperate, and *punishment phases* where at least one player defects. For example, if they both adopt $\sigma^{\lambda,k}$ with λ small, one expects that punishment phases will be of long duration, with players missing many opportunities for profitable cooperation. On the other hand, if λ is high, their propensity to cooperate may be so large that they attempt to cooperate in many events where cooperation is not profitable (when $x = 0$).

Thus, adjustment to the underlying condition x cannot be perfect, even if agents could jointly choose λ_1 and λ_2 to maximize their joint interest. Our aim below is to examine the strategic consequences of letting each player follow the dynamic strategy σ_i that suits best his own interest. Toward this end, we define the long-run payoff $v(\sigma)$ induced by $\sigma = (\sigma_1, \sigma_2)$, and then define equilibrium behavior.

Define the state s as the triplet (θ_1, θ_2, x), where $\theta_i \in \{H, L\}$ is the current belief state of player i and $x \in \{0, g\}$ is the current benefit. Denote by S the set of possible such states. For any pair of strategies $\sigma = (\sigma_1, \sigma_2)$, and any state $s \in S$, one may define the long-run frequency of state s induced by σ.[8] Call $\phi^\sigma(s)$ that long-run frequency. Also denote by $u(s)$ players' expected gain in a period where the state is s. We associate to each σ the long-run value $v(\sigma)$ induced by σ:

$$v(\sigma) = \sum_{s \in S} u(s)\phi^\sigma(s).$$

Given the simple structure of the game, a player, say player 1, only cares about two events: the event A where $\theta_2 = H$ and $x = g$; and the event B where $\theta_1 = H$. Defining ϕ_z^σ as the long-run frequency of event z,[9] we have:

$$v_1(\sigma) = g\phi_A^\sigma - \gamma\phi_B^\sigma.$$

This expression reflects the main tradeoff: a more cooperative strategy by player 1 is more costly (higher ϕ_B^σ), but it may increase the chances of profitable cooperation (higher ϕ_A^σ).

We say that σ is an *equilibrium* if for each player i and each strategy $\sigma_i' \in \Sigma_i$:

$$v_i(\sigma_i', \sigma_{-i}) \leq v_i(\sigma).$$

We are interested in finding the model parameters for which cooperation occurs in equilibrium.

3. *Incentives to cooperate.* A key aspect of dynamic strategies is that they create incentives to cooperate (that is, put in effort), for reasons similar to those in the previous chapter. Assume that player 2 follows the dynamic strategy $\widehat{\sigma}$. Then, through his choice of action, player 1 can influence the belief state (and behavior) of player 2. If player 1 puts in high effort, he makes it more likely that player 2 will remain in the good belief state, and this generates incentives to put in effort if the cost of effort γ is not too high. We make this precise next.

To simplify notation, we let ϕ_z^D (respectively ϕ_z^C and $\widehat{\phi}_z$) denote the long-run probability of the event z when player 1 follows σ^D (respectively σ^C and $\widehat{\sigma}$). We have:

$$v_1(\sigma^D, \widehat{\sigma}) = \phi_A^D g$$
$$v_1(\sigma^C, \widehat{\sigma}) = \phi_A^C g - \gamma$$
$$v_1(\widehat{\sigma}, \widehat{\sigma}) = \widehat{\phi}_A g - \widehat{\phi}_B \gamma.$$

---

[8] We adopt the convention that if player i adopts the constant strategy σ^C (respectively σ^D) he remains in state H (respectively L).

[9] $\phi_z^\sigma = \sum_{s \in z} \phi^\sigma(s)$.

Because player 2 is responsive to signals (he follows $\widehat{\sigma}$), and because $p > q$, greater effort by player 1 increases the frequency with which player 2 puts in effort. As can be easily verified:

$$\phi_A^C > \widehat{\phi}_A > \phi_A^D.$$

The consequence is that if γ is not too large, player 1 has incentive to cooperate. The condition that σ^C improves over σ^D is:

$$\gamma < (\phi_A^C - \phi_A^D)g,$$

and the condition that $\widehat{\sigma}$ improves over σ^D is:

$$\gamma < \frac{\widehat{\phi}_A - \phi_A^D}{\widehat{\phi}_B}g.$$

In words, incentives to cooperate require that effort induce a sufficiently large increase in the probability of cooperation.[10]

4. *Incentives to use a dynamic strategy.* That player 1 is willing to cooperate is not the end of the story. If the consequence is that player 1 is willing to cooperate all the time (i.e., use σ^C), then player 2 will have no incentive to use the dynamic strategy $\widehat{\sigma}$. An equilibrium involving cooperation requires that *both* sides use the dynamic strategy $\widehat{\sigma}$. Formally, this requires:

$$v_1(\widehat{\sigma},\widehat{\sigma}) > v_1(\sigma^C,\widehat{\sigma})$$

that is:

$$\widehat{\phi}_A g - \widehat{\phi}_B \gamma > \phi_A^C g - \gamma$$

or equivalently

$$\gamma > \frac{\phi_A^C - \widehat{\phi}_A}{1 - \widehat{\phi}_B}g.$$

Intuitively, under the above condition, a player has incentive to use the dynamic strategy (which implies making no effort, sometimes) rather than the cooperative strategy because this allows him to economize on costs in events where effort is not worthwhile. If the other player is persistently in belief state L, or if the benefit x is persistently low, it is unnecessarily costly to put in effort. By using a dynamic strategy, player 1 may hope to reduce effort,

[10] Alternatively, for fixed probabilities $\phi_A^C, \widehat{\phi}_A$ and ϕ_A^D ranked as above, incentives to cooperate require that gains for defecting against a cooperative partner be not too large – a standard insight.

putting forth effort only when it is profitable (i.e., when $(\theta_2, x) = (H, g)$).[11]
One difficulty, of course, is that player 1 does not observe (θ_2, x) in the current
period, and he may choose not to put in effort in events when it would,
in fact, be profitable. The effect is a decrease in cooperation: $\widehat{\phi}_A$ is smaller
than ϕ_A^C.

There is thus a tradeoff between reduced cooperation and lower expenses,
and this tradeoff tilts behavior in favor of the dynamic strategy when the cost
of effort γ is sufficiently high.

5. *Equilibrium.* Combining previous inequalities, the dynamic strategy $\widehat{\sigma}$
improves upon both σ^D and σ^C when

$$\frac{\phi_A^C - \widehat{\phi}_A}{1 - \widehat{\phi}_B} g < \gamma < \frac{\widehat{\phi}_A - \phi_A^D}{\widehat{\phi}_B} g.$$

Checking the compatibility of these inequalities is easy when p is close to 1
and α sufficiently small. Then, when $x = g$, bad signals are rare, so using $\widehat{\sigma}$
rather than σ^C cannot hurt much. In contrast, when $x = 0$, the strategy σ^C is
very bad because it involves effort with zero expected payoff in return: the
strategy $\widehat{\sigma}$ is better because it reduces the number of periods in which effort is
made. Further details are in the Appendix.

The following figure provides the region of parameters (p, γ) where $(\widehat{\sigma}, \widehat{\sigma})$
is an equilibrium, when $q = 0.1$, $\lambda = 0.1$, $k = 0.2$, $Q = 1/2$ and α is very

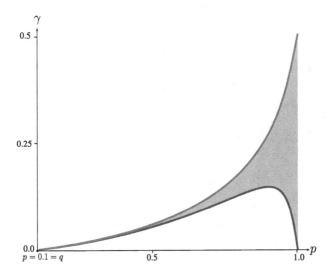

---

[11] This incentive to use a nontrivial dynamic strategy potentially exists even in a standard repeated
game where x doesn't vary, because one wishes to adjust to the behavior of the other player.
Variations in x amplify that incentive, enabling cooperation as an equilibrium phenomenon in
our model (see Footnote 12 on next page).

small.[12] The range of values of γ for which $(\widehat{\sigma}, \widehat{\sigma})$ is an equilibrium expands when p approaches to 1.

6. *More sophisticated players.* We assumed that players can only compare few strategies. This makes it relatively easy to check for incentives. Our objective below is to understand whether cooperation can still be obtained when players consider more strategies, with the aim of endogenizing players' propensities to cooperate λ_1 and λ_2, that is, the degree to which players experiment with cooperation when in state L. Toward this end, we fix k and assume that players use the rule $\sigma^{\lambda_i, k}$ that maximizes their long-run payoff, among all possible values of $\lambda_i \in [0, 1]$.

Computations are similar. Simplifying notation, we now refer to $\phi_z^{\lambda_1, \lambda_2}$ as the long-run frequency of event z when the strategy pair (λ_1, λ_2) is used. We have:

$$v_1(\lambda_1, \lambda_2) = \phi_A^{\lambda_1, \lambda_2} g - \phi_B^{\lambda_1, \lambda_2} \gamma.$$

Player 1 faces the following tradeoff. By increasing λ_1, he increases $\phi_A^{\lambda_1, \lambda_2}$ because this increases the likelihood of cooperation in events where player 2 is in, or about to be in, belief state H. However, he also increases the frequency $\phi_B^{\lambda_1, \lambda_2}$.

The thick curve below shows the best response of player 1 as a function of λ_2, for specific values of the parameters.[13]

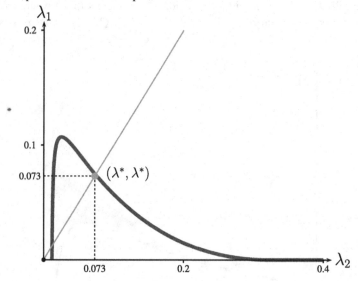

[12] The existence of a set of parameters for which cooperation is possible contrasts with Compte and Postlewaite (2015), who show that this type of strategy cannot support equilibrium cooperation. The difference is that, here, we consider a setup in which the benefits of cooperation vary over time, which makes it worthwhile to use $\sigma^{\lambda, k}$ rather than either constant strategy.

[13] We use $p = 0.95, q = 0.1, k = 0.2, \gamma = 0.3$ and $Q = 0.5$.

The thick curve illustrates that when λ_2 is too small, there is no point in trying to cooperate. The probability of reciprocal cooperation is too low, and player 1's best response is to set λ_1 to 0. It also illustrates that when λ_2 is too high, player 1 is better off taking advantage of his cooperative-minded partner, and his best response is again to set λ_1 to 0.

For intermediate values of λ_2, the best response of player 1 is to experiment somewhat with cooperation ($\lambda_1 \in (0,1)$). At $\lambda_2^* \simeq 0.073$, the best response of player 1 is to set $\lambda_1^* = \lambda_2^*$: a symmetric equilibrium. At this equilibrium, the propensities to cooperate are substitutes: the larger λ_2, the smaller player 1's incentives to cooperate.

We have exhibited an equilibrium involving cooperation, but we do not suggest that cooperation could be obtained for all parameter values. When signals are noisier ($p = 0.9$), the best response has a similar shape, but the two curves do not cross. The response of player 1 is never strong enough, and the only equilibrium is that both remain in state L.

7. *Punishment and recoordination.* When players use nontrivial dynamic strategies, behavior alternates between phases of cooperation and phases of defection (in which at least one player defects). The defection phase may be interpreted as a *punishment* phase that ends once players manage to *recoordinate.* We describe this alternation below.

A defection phase begins when a player receives a bad signal and reacts to it by moving to belief state L. He then starts defecting, good signals become less likely, and it becomes likely that the other player will soon move to belief state L as well: both players remain in belief state L for some time. The defection phase is initiated by one player reacting to a bad signal that may have two causes: either bad luck (both players put in effort and yet a bad signal occurs $-p < 1$); or a change in the underlying benefits from cooperation ($x = 0$). In the former case, it is a bad idea to trigger a defection phase, while in the latter case, it is a good idea to stop attempting to sustain cooperation that is no longer worthwhile.

Once both players are in belief state L, the return to cooperation may take time. The dynamic strategy calls for occasionally checking (i.e., with probability λ) whether the time is ripe to cooperate again. The difficulty is that these attempts need not be simultaneous, so players may remain in the defection phase for quite some time if λ is low. When these attempts happen to be simultaneous (or close to simultaneous if k is not too close to 1), players may start a cooperative phase again, possibly a very long phase if p is close to 1 and $x = g$.

In summary, the dynamic strategy plays two roles.

(i) It acts as *a punishment device* that moves behavior to a defection phase when the state is low or a player defects. This is an incentive mechanism similar to that in reputation. Potentially, this incentive mechanism is more powerful for player 1 when the punishment is likely to last long, that is, when λ_2 is low.

(ii) It acts as a *recoordinating mechanism* that brings behavior back to a cooperative phase when cooperation is profitable. When λ_2 is too low however, recoordination is sufficiently difficult that attempts to move cooperation back on track are too likely to fail – incentives to cooperate vanish.

8. *A static perspective.* Even though the interaction is dynamic, the game can be described as a simple static game in which each player i chooses his propensity to cooperate λ_i. The higher λ_i, the more costly the strategy is (because ϕ_B increases with λ_1), but the more one can expect the other to reciprocate (because ϕ_A increases with λ_1).

More precisely, for low (but not too low) values of λ, propensities are strategic complements, meaning that a higher propensity of one's partner to cooperate generates a higher propensity for oneself. For higher values of λ, propensities become strategic substitutes. At the equilibrium we obtain, propensities are strategic substitutes, and players would be better off if they could jointly commit to a higher level λ_i^{**}. For the parameters that we chose, if players could jointly set the pair (λ_1, λ_2), they would optimally set them at a higher level $(\lambda_1^{**} = \lambda_2^{**} = 0.21)$.

The degree to which players cooperate in equilibrium depends on the exact shape of the functions ϕ_A and ϕ_B. The exact shape of these functions depends on the family of strategies considered. Other families may generate different shapes, but with a similar tradeoff (with higher effort translating into high costs and more reciprocation). Some families of strategies, however, could do a better job at inducing higher equilibrium effort, for example by facilitating recoordination back to cooperation. We investigate this next.

9. *Recoordination made easier.* To illustrate that some families of strategies may be more conducive to cooperation, we investigate a family in which each player i goes back to state H with probability λ_i upon receiving a good signal.

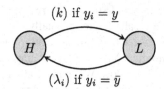

(k) if $y_i = \underline{y}$

(λ_i) if $y_i = \bar{y}$

Compared to previous transitions, attempts to recoordinate to cooperation are only made in events where $y_i = \bar{y}$. An essential difference is that once a player, say i, attempts to cooperate, and if the underlying state happens to be good $(x = g)$, there is a greater chance that the other player (j) observes the good signal $(y_j = \bar{y})$ when the state happens to be good. In particular, if p and λ_j are large, recoordination is likely to be successful. Thus, one virtue of the transitions above is that recoordination attempts may be infrequent (if $q\lambda$ is small), and yet successful when $x = g$ (if $p\lambda$ is large). This is in contrast with previous transitions where recoordination attempts had to be relatively frequent to be successful.

The thick curve below shows the best response of player 1 as a function of λ_2, for the same parameter values as before.[14]

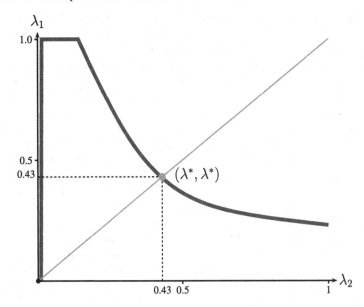

The figure illustrates as before that when λ_2 is too small, there is no point in trying to cooperate. For high values of λ_2, incentives decrease because each player would prefer that the other incur the cost of attempting to recoordinate. Indeed, the current state might be $x = 0$, and in such events, an attempt to recoordinate is bound to fail.

At $\lambda_2^* \simeq 0.43$, the best response of player 1 is to set $\lambda_1^* = \lambda_2^*$, a symmetric equilibrium. Note that in equilibrium, if both players are in state L, a player attempts to recoordinate with probability $q\lambda_2^* = 0.043$. So these attempts are less frequent than before, but they succeed more frequently. As a result, players' expected values are higher in this equilibrium (0.3, compared to 0.2 before).

Another consequence is that there are many parameter values for which cooperation was impossible before, but become possible under this new family.

Further Comments

Public and private signals. Much of the literature has been concerned with distinguishing between cases where signals are public and cases where signals are private. This is largely for technical reasons. Equilibrium construction has

---

[14] Again, $p = 0.95, q = 0.1, k = 0.2, \gamma = 0.3$ and $Q = 0.5$.

mostly relied on dynamic programming techniques, and these are easier to implement when at any point in time, players are in complete certainty about each other's continuation strategy.[15]

There are several difficulties with this:

(i) *Descriptively, it is not very compelling that players would be certain, at any point of time, of each other's current action. Our everyday experience is that we are rarely certain about how others behave.*

(ii) *A primary role of signals is to enable players to learn about what others are doing. By focusing on equilibria in which each knows others' plans of action, theory neglects this role. Learning is then absent from equilibrium behavior.*

(iii) *The theory might suggest that since it is technically easier to deal with public signals, it should also be easier for agents to cooperate when signals are public. One lesson from our exercise is that the seeds for cooperation lie in a simple ingredient (the fact that players use dynamic strategies for simple learning reasons), and that the public or private nature of signals is not necessarily a help or a hindrance to players conditioning behavior on their observations.*

(iv) *Whether signals are public or private, how one reacts to signals is likely to be private in practice, that is, partially influenced by other unmodeled private elements or perceptions.*[16] *So the distinction between public and private signals is likely to be irrelevant, or at least less important than what theory suggests.*

Tit for Tat. *Tit for Tat is a strategy in which a player echoes his opponent's latest actions: a Tit-for-Tat player cooperates after seeing cooperation, and defects after seeing a defection. The dynamic strategies that we considered in Section 9 have a Tit-for-Tat flavor (with a hysteresis twist): they produce stochastic reactions that trigger a cooperative mood*[17] *after good signals (with probability λ, the degree to which one is forgiving), and a noncooperative mood after bad signals (with probability k, the degree to which one reacts promptly to bad signals). These strategies are natural generalizations of Tit for Tat in environments in which one cannot observe perfectly the actions of others. In the spirit of Axelrod's tournaments, one could examine which*

---

[15] With public signals, dynamic programming techniques typically summarize the future by a continuation value vector (see for example Abreu, Pearce and Stacchetti (1990), and Fudenberg, Levine and Maskin (1994) for the case of very patient players). With private signals, dynamic programming techniques are more difficult to implement because future play is uncertain, and potentially depends on each player's belief about signals received by others. Attempts to use dynamic programming techniques in this context have produced "belief free equilibria," the fragility of which we discuss in Compte and Postlewaite (2013).

[16] See also the comments in Chapter 10, page 141.

[17] The mood is potentially long lasting. Behavior is not solely driven by the latest signal observed (hence the hysteresis twist).

of these strategies would be selected by evolution. Our analysis provides a
partial answer to that question, endogenizing forgiveness for a given stochastic
environment and a given k.[18]

Further research/applications. Through strategy restrictions, one
obtains a more parsimonious treatment of repeated relationships, which
enables us to represent them as static games with few strategic
variables. This makes it possible to establish a connection with a classic
static contribution game, in which one's propensity to experiment the
cooperative arm can be interpreted as a contribution to the relationship.
In that spirit, one may investigate the existence and stability of
asymmetric equilibria between a sophisticated player who conditions
experimentation on receiving a good signal, and a less sophisticated
player who experiments unconditionally. One might also investigate
equilibria in which each player has both strategic variables available
(i.e., the propensity to experiment unconditionally, and the propensity
to experiment after a good signal), and examine the connection with
strategic experimentation models in which players share a common
interest (see Chapter 12).

Another interpretation of our strategy restrictions is that we constrain
each agent to hold a limited number of belief states, and (partially)
endogenize belief revisions by focusing on a few stochastic transitions
and finding the agent's optimal transition probabilities.[19] We believe
this technique could be useful in many contexts, in particular when
one wishes to represent agents as alternating between a few states of
mind (convinced or unconvinced, suspicious or trustful, attentive or
inattentive) as a function of the evidence or the messages received, rather
than representing them as holding precise probabilistic beliefs (derived
from the knowledge of the model and the application of Bayes rule).

Appendix

We consider the limit case where α is arbitrarily close to 0. Under this
assumption, we can compute long-run frequencies as if there were an initial
draw of x that did not change. We also examine the case where p is close to 1.

Consider first the event where $x = g$. If player 1 uses either $\hat{\sigma}$ or σ^C and if p
is sufficiently close to 1, both players seldom exit from the belief state (H, H).
This means that conditional on $x = g$, they both remain in state (H, H) most of

---

[18] Our equilibrium is locally stable, as the best response function $\lambda_1(\lambda_2)$ is relatively flat near the
equilibrium value that we identified.

[19] Other work along this line includes Wilson (2014).

the time. It follows that

$$\widehat{\phi}_A \simeq \phi_A^C \simeq \Pr(x = g) = 1 - Q.$$

Consider now the event $x = 0$. Whatever actions are being used, each player receives the good signal $\bar{y}$ with probability q in every period. When player 1 uses $\widehat{\sigma}$, he thus returns to H periodically, and in the long run, he is in belief state H with frequency ϕ_0 that solves $\phi_0 = (1 - (1 - q)k)\phi_0 + \lambda(1 - \phi_0)$, or equivalently, $\phi_0 = \frac{\lambda}{\lambda + (1-q)k}$. To compute $\widehat{\phi}_B$, we aggregate both events ($x = 0$ and $x = g$) and obtain

$$\widehat{\phi}_B = \Pr(x = g)\widehat{\phi}_A + \Pr(x = 0)\phi_0$$
$$\simeq (1 - Q) + Q\phi_0$$

implying that $1 - \widehat{\phi}_B \simeq Q(1 - \phi_0)$.

References

Axelrod, R. (1984). *The Evolution of Cooperation*, New York: Basic Books.
Abreu, D., Pearce, D. and Stacchetti, E. (1990). Toward a theory of discounted repeated games with imperfect monitoring. *Econometrica*, 58, 1041–1063.
Compte, O. and Postlewaite, A. (2013). Belief free equilibria, mimeo. University of Pennsylvania, 13–020.
Compte, O. and Postlewaite, A. (2015). Plausible cooperation. *Games and Economic Behavior*, 91, 45–59.
Fudenberg, D., Levine, D. and Maskin, E. (1994). The folk theorem with imperfect public information. *Econometrica*, 62, 997–1039.
Wilson, A. (2014). Bounded memory and biases in information processing. *Econometrica*, 82(6), 2257–2294.

CHAPTER 15

Influence

1. There are numerous situations in which we rely on others' opinions to make a decision. We appeal to others because we believe that they might have a better grasp of the situation we face, or better information than we have about the decision we should take. When we appeal to others, however, we grant them power to influence our decision, and we cannot ignore the possibility that they might use this influence to serve their interest, rather than ours – possibly manipulating or distorting what they believe or know to their advantage. We should be cautious about taking their advice at face value.

In short, influence results from two opposing forces: one side distorts what he reports to affect decision making while the other tries to determine how much he should rely on the advice he is given.

We provide below a simple model of influence, building on these two ingredients (distortion and skepticism), characterizing the degree to which one side (the adviser) distorts what he knows, and the degree to which the other side (the decision maker) exerts skepticism. Both are potential obstacles to good decision making, and the model quantifies the inefficiencies and how value is shared between the decision maker and the adviser.

2. *A sender-receiver game.* Our game involves two players, a decision maker (player 1) who is to take a decision, and an adviser (player 2) who first gives advice to the decision maker about what should be done. We describe, in turn, the preferences, the players' observations, and the strategies that each player compares.[1]

Preferences. The decision maker's objective is to choose a decision d as close as possible to a given ideal point $s \in S$. We assume that S is the real line, and that preferences are quadratic – the loss from choosing $d \neq s$ is $(d - s)^2$.

The decision maker seeks advice from an agent. The preferences of the agent are biased *upward*: his preferences over decisions are quadratic as well,

---

[1] The preferences assumed follow Crawford and Sobel (1982); observations and strategy sets differ.

185

but his ideal point, denoted θ, is greater than the decision maker's ($\theta > s$). We denote by $b(> 0)$ the difference between the two ideal points, and refer to b as a bias:

$$b \equiv \theta - s.$$

Observations. We model a class of situations in which the adviser knows θ, and in which neither player knows with precision s nor the bias b.[2]

Specifically, the decision maker gets an estimate of s, denoted x, and each player i gets an estimate or perception b_i of b, and we refer to the ratio b_i/b as η_i:

$$x = s + \varepsilon$$
$$b_i = \eta_i b.$$

Throughout this chapter, s, b, ε and each η_i are independent random variables. We also assume $E\eta_i = 1$ and let

$$\varphi_i \equiv E\eta_i^2.$$

This parameter will play a key role, and $1/\varphi_i$ characterizes player i's ability to perceive the bias b accurately, hence also the degree to which player i can adjust his behavior to the underlying bias b.

In later numerical simulations, we further assume that ε is normally distributed ($\varepsilon \sim \mathcal{N}(0, \sigma^2)$), and that b is lognormally distributed:

$$b = b_0 z \text{ with } \log z \sim \mathcal{N}(0, \sigma_z^2) \text{ and } b_0 > 0.$$

Timing. The timing of the interaction is simple. Based on θ and b_2, the agent suggests decision y, and we denote by σ_2 the agent's strategy:

$$y = \sigma_2(\theta, b_2).$$

Next, based on y, x and b_1, the decision maker takes a decision d, and we denote by σ_1 the decision maker's strategy:

$$d = \sigma_1(x, y, b_1).$$

Each strategy profile $\sigma = (\sigma_1, \sigma_2)$ generates an expected loss $L_i(\sigma)$ for each agent i, which agent i wants to minimize through his strategy choice σ_i.

---

[2] This is in contrast to Crawford and Sobel (1982) who assume that the adviser knows perfectly not only his own preferences, but also the bias (hence also the decision maker's preferences). We allow instead for the possibility that the adviser knows imperfectly the bias. Said differently, in Crawford and Sobel, the uncertainty bears only on s and the adviser knows s. In our model, the uncertainty bears on the pair (s, θ), and neither the adviser nor the decision maker knows that pair perfectly.

3. *Signal aggregation and strategy restrictions.* When we receive signals or opinions from different sources, we face a difficult issue: how to aggregate these signals or opinions, and even before asking about aggregation, how much to rely on various opinions.

Formally, when an agent receives two signals x and y about the underlying state s characterized by a joint distribution ω on (s,x,y), the traditional approach consists of assuming that the agent can compare all possible ways of using the signals x and y. With quadratic preferences, this leads to the seemingly simple decision function:

$$d(x,y) = E_\omega[s \mid x,y].$$

Much of our earlier criticism again applies. The behavior obtained is more complex than the mathematical expression above suggests, calibrated to model parameters (ω), as though the agent had precise and reliable information about ω. This characterization seems implausible: in ordinary life, even the simpler problem of comparing the reliability of two different sources of information can be challenging.

Again, our approach consists of limiting the agent's ability to exploit his signals by limiting the strategies he compares. For example, consider an agent limited to two strategies:

$$d^N(x,y) = x \text{ or}$$
$$d^T(x,y) = y.$$

This agent is implicitly endowed with the ability to determine which source he should trust – which source is more reliable. But, the agent is unable to exploit signals beyond that global reliability comparison.

Obviously, they are many ways to restrict the strategies compared, essentially because there are many ways to weaken a strong assumption. The purpose of what follows is to illustrate various restrictions that are qualitatively interesting or, at a minimum, capture simple notions of distortion on one side, and of trust or skepticism on the other side.

Before proceeding, we note that some strategy restrictions may be too crude to generate interesting insights or, for example, capture the idea that there might be various degrees of trust. In the example above in which the strategy set is restricted to $\Sigma_1 = \{d^T, d^N\}$, the decision maker either fully trusts or never trusts y. The consequence is that, *by construction*, influence is either absent (d^N) or complete (d^T).

In what follows (Sections 5 and 7), we introduce richer sets of strategies for the decision maker, with the aim of capturing various degrees of cautiousness regarding the suggestion y received. Before doing this, we start with the adviser's strategy set.

4. *Distortion.* For the adviser, one possibility is to report his ideal decision θ, hoping that the decision maker will follow his suggestion. An adviser who thinks strategically could consider other options: he could distort his suggestion away from the decision maker's supposed preference, or he could be considerate and distort his suggestion toward the decision maker's supposed preference.

Formally, for any μ, we define the strategy σ_2^{μ} whereby he suggests:

$$y = \theta + \mu b_2.$$

$\mu > 0$ means that the adviser distorts his suggestion away from the decision maker's supposed optimal choice, while $\mu < 0$ means that he distorts his suggestion in the direction of what he thinks is the preference of the decision maker (he is considerate).[3] Throughout the chapter, the strategic choice of the adviser is μ:[4]

$$\Sigma_2 = \{\sigma_2^{\mu}\}_{\mu \in \mathcal{R}}.$$

5. *Filtering.* For the decision maker, one option is to take at face value the suggested decision, taking it as a suggestion of what he should do. Another is to filter it, taking into account the fact that the suggestion might be biased away from his own preference, and using his perception b_1 of the bias b to debias the suggestion:

$$d = y - \lambda b_1.$$

The parameter λ captures the degree to which he suspects manipulation and filters the suggestion. We denote by σ_1^{λ} this strategy, and endow the decision maker with the ability to choose λ optimally:

$$\Sigma_1^F = \{\sigma_1^{\lambda}\}_{\lambda \in \mathcal{R}}.$$

Accordingly, the decision maker relies solely on (y, b_1) to take a decision, not using any "prior opinion" x. He might do this if he thinks his prior opinion is too noisy to be useful, for example.

In the second part of this chapter, we investigate another family of strategies where x is used by the decision maker as a benchmark to assess whether the suggestion is reliable.

---

[3] We suggest that a non-strategic adviser reports his preferred decision. Alternatively, a naive adviser might report what he thinks is best for the agent, i.e., $y = \theta - b_2$, while a strategic adviser would bias his report (most likely upward): $y = \theta - b_2 + \gamma b_2$ for some γ. Both versions are formally equivalent.

[4] As in previous chapters, the strategic variable is assumed to apply uniformly across realizations (θ, b_2).

6. *Equilibrium with filtering.* We examine the interaction where players are restricted to Σ_1^F and Σ_2 respectively. The analysis is remarkably simple. For each pair (λ, μ), the decision implemented is

$$d = s + b + \mu b_2 - \lambda b_1 = s + b(1 + \mu\eta_2 - \lambda\eta_1).$$

Expected losses for each player are thus

$$L_1 = Eb^2(1 + \mu\eta_2 - \lambda\eta_1)^2 \text{ and } L_2 = Eb^2(\mu\eta_2 - \lambda\eta_1)^2.$$

For the decision maker, the decision differs from s, and he can use λ as an instrument to generate decisions that are closer to s. For the adviser, the decision differs from $\theta = s + b$, and he can use μ to nudge the decision toward θ. Since η_1 and η_2 are noisy, both instruments are imperfect.

Qualitatively, even when the adviser does not distort ($y = \theta$), the suggestion is biased ($\theta > s$), so the decision maker treats it with caution ($\lambda > 0$). Now, the larger the caution exerted λ, the more the adviser wishes to distort ($\mu > 0$). Conversely, greater distortion by the adviser (higher μ) increases the decision maker's caution (higher λ).

Formally, using $E\eta_i = 1$ and $\varphi_i = E\eta_i^2$ (> 1), best responses have a simple expression:

$$\lambda(\mu) = \frac{1 + \mu}{\varphi_1} \text{ and}$$

$$\mu(\lambda) = \frac{\lambda}{\varphi_2}.$$

The slopes are both positive, confirming the intuition above. We plot the best responses below, setting $\varphi_1 = 2$, for various values of φ_2.

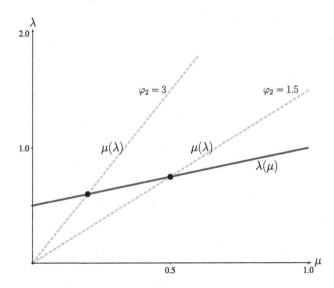

As mentioned earlier, $1/\varphi_2$ reflects the adviser's ability to perceive accurately the bias. The larger φ_2, the more difficult it is for the adviser to make a suggestion that is tuned to the actual bias b. This explains why the optimal response $\mu(\lambda)$ of the adviser remains weak when φ_2 is large: his estimate b_2 of the bias is noisier, hence he puts less weight on b_2, which means a smaller μ.

The equilibrium level of distortion and skepticism is characterized by the intersection of the lines, (λ^*, μ^*).[5] The figure above shows that when the adviser's ability decreases (higher φ_2), both the equilibrium distortion and skepticism are reduced.

Plugging the equilibrium values (λ^*, μ^*) into the loss function,[6] and normalizing Eb^2 to 1, one obtains a simple expression for the equilibrium losses:

$$L_1 = 1 + \frac{2 - \varphi_2}{\varphi_1 \varphi_2 - 1} \text{ and } L_2 = \frac{\varphi_2}{\varphi_1 \varphi_2 - 1}. \tag{15.1}$$

This implies that

$$L_1 + L_2 = 1 + \frac{2}{\varphi_1 \varphi_2 - 1},$$

meaning that increases in abilities by either player (i.e., a decrease in $\varphi_1 \varphi_2$) hurts at least one player. The figure below summarizes how L_1 and L_2 are affected when φ_1 changes, for different levels of φ_2.[7]

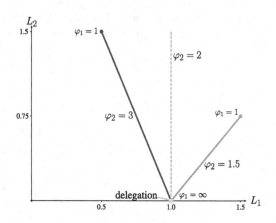

[5] These points have a simple expression as a function of the abilities φ_1 and φ_2. Normalizing Eb^2 to 1, we have: $\lambda^* = \frac{\varphi_2}{\varphi_1 \varphi_2 - 1}$ and $\mu^* = \frac{1}{\varphi_1 \varphi_2 - 1}$.
[6] $L_1 = 1 + L_2 + 2(\mu - \lambda)$ and $L_2 = \mu^2 \varphi_2 + \lambda^2 \varphi_1 - 2\lambda\mu$.
[7] Equation (15.1) implies $L_1 - \frac{2 - \varphi_2}{\varphi_2} L_2 = 1$, with $L_1 = 1$ when $\varphi_2 = \infty$ and $L_1 = 1/(\varphi_2 - 1)$ when $\varphi_1 = 1$.

The figure illustrates that there are two different regimes:

(i) $\varphi_2 < 2$. Here, player 2 has *high* ability to influence the decision, and greater ability by player 1 hurts both players. In that region, the decision maker (player 1) would actually *benefit from delegating* the decision to player 2.[8]

(ii) $\varphi_2 > 2$. Here, player 2 has *little* ability to influence the decision, he makes less distorted suggestions, and the decision maker's ability to assess the bias accurately benefits him (and hurts the adviser). In this region, *communication is better than delegation.*

The model also illustrates that the bias of the decision maker is not necessarily an impediment to efficient communication:[9] when $\varphi_1 \varphi_2$ is large, communication is close to being efficient, and surplus sharing favors the player with better knowledge of the bias. The bias becomes an impediment when both players have a good perception of it and attempt to use that perception to their advantage.

Finally since L_1 (and L_2) decrease with φ_2,[10] the model illustrates simply why a decision maker may be better off asking advice without revealing his preferences precisely – lower precision raises φ_2, hence diminishes losses. It also illustrates why, when we fear manipulation (or do not have a reasonable benchmark x in mind initially), we may prefer to seek advice from people who do not try to learn what the advice will be used for.[11]

7. Skepticism/trust under competing opinions. We proposed above a model in which the decision maker's initial opinion x is deliberately ignored. We next examine a model in which the two opinions (x and y) compete, and in which b_1 is ignored. We mentioned earlier two basic strategies, d^T and d^N, according to which the decision maker either fully trusts the suggestion, or ignores it. We consider below a richer set of strategies in which the decision maker attempts to use the difference $|y - x|$ as a gauge of y's reliability. For any $\rho \geq 0$, we define the strategy σ_1^ρ as follows:

$$d = \begin{cases} y & \text{if } |y - x| < \rho \\ x & \text{otherwise} \end{cases}$$

---

[8] Delegation would amount to committing to choosing $d = y$ (i.e., $\lambda = 0$) and player 2's best response is then to set $\mu = 0$. The losses from delegation would thus be $L_1 = 1$ and $L_2 = 0$.

[9] This is in contrast to Crawford and Sobel (1982). This chapter suggests that the limit on the amount of information transmitted (measured by the total welfare reached) is not necessarily determined by the size of the bias. One obstacle to information transmission is the degree to which players know the bias, and the strategic consequence (exaggeration and suspicion) that this knowledge generates.

[10] $\frac{\partial L_1}{\partial \varphi_2}$ has the same sign as $1 - 2\varphi_1$ (< 0).

[11] Said differently, a commitment from the adviser not to investigate in detail what the receiver cares about (i.e., a commitment to keep b_2 noisy, hence φ_2 high) is valuable to both. The value of commitment in communication games has been examined in Kamenica and Gentzkow (2011). Our model provides another motive for commitment.

The scalar ρ captures the degree to which the decision maker trusts the suggestion y. When $|y - x|$ exceeds ρ, he views the suggestion as unreliable. When $\rho = 0$, the agent always follows his own estimate, d^N. When $\rho = +\infty$, the agent always trusts the external opinion, he follows d^T. By allowing other strategies where $\rho \neq 0, \infty$, we endow the agent with some limited ability to make inferences about reliability.[12]

In what follows, we assume that the decision maker can choose the degree of trust/skepticism ρ optimally:

$$\Sigma_1^S = \{\sigma_1^\rho\}_{\rho \geq 0}.$$

Obviously, one could think of strategies that combine filtering and skepticism, with σ_1^ρ applied to the filtered suggestion $y - \lambda b_1$, rather than to the unfiltered one (i.e., y). We could also assume that player 1's strategy set is $\Sigma_1^S \cup \Sigma_1^F$ and thereby endogenize which regime (trust or filtering) arises in equilibrium. We leave aside these possibilities in order to focus on the strategic effect associated with skepticism (ρ).

8. *Optimal trust/skepticism: the decision maker's incentives.* To examine the decision maker's incentive, consider first the case where the adviser does not distort the suggestion ($\mu = 0$, $y = s + b$). Ideally, the decision maker would like to follow the suggestion y if and only if the bias b is smaller than the magnitude of the error $|\varepsilon|$, and choose x otherwise. His problem is that he has access to neither b nor ε. Still he may use the difference $\Delta = |y - x|$ as an instrument to decide which opinion to follow: his own (x) or the external suggestion (y).

The reason why Δ may be a useful instrument is simple. Imagine that b is either small compared to σ, or large compared to σ. Then observing that Δ is not too large indicates that b is likely small, and observing that Δ is large indicates that b is likely large. Taking y in the former case is preferable to taking x.

The figure on the next page illustrates the best response of the decision maker when b is lognormally distributed (i.e., $b = b_0 z$ with z lognormal). It describes how the optimal response ρ varies with b_0, setting $\sigma_z = 1$. When b_0 is large (above 1.5), the best response is to ignore completely the suggestion ($\rho = 0$). As b_0 decreases, the decision maker has an incentive to consider the suggestion insofar as $\Delta < \rho(b_0)$, and the extent to which the suggestion is considered expands as b_0 decreases.

Our model parameterizes the degree to which the suggestion is trusted as a function of the bias b_0, and randomness in b plays a key role: the response becomes steeper when the variance σ_z^2 is smaller, and in the limit where σ_z^2

---

[12] In the spirit of previous chapters, one interpretation is that the agent has two mental/belief states N or T, and the observation of x and y generates a deterministic transition to one or the other state, parameterized here by ρ. One could also imagine a less powerful ability to discriminate by considering a family of stochastic transition: be trustful (T) if and only if $|y - x| < \eta \rho$ where η is a random variable.

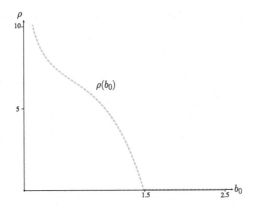

vanishes, there are only two possible best responses, complete distrust ($\rho = 0$) if $b_0 > \sigma$, and full trust ($\rho = \infty$) if $b_0 < \sigma$.

9. *Optimal distortion and equilibrium.* For a given level of trust $\rho > 0$, the adviser faces the possibility that his suggestion will be ignored. For example, if he simply reports $y = \theta$ without distortion, he will not be trusted if $\varepsilon < b - \rho$ or if $\varepsilon > b + \rho$, and the final decision will differ from θ.

Whatever the value of $b > 0$, slightly distorting the suggestion in the direction of the decision maker's presumed preference generates a first-order increase in the probability $P = \Pr(\Delta < \rho)$ that the suggestion will be trusted, hence a first-order gain.[13] There is a loss because, when the suggestion is trusted, the decision lies further from his ideal decision, but when the distortion is small this is a second-order loss: there is thus a first-order gain in distorting in the direction of the decision maker's presumed preference (i.e., $\mu < 0$).

Of course, incentives to distort depend on ρ. If ρ is very large, the adviser is trusted most of the time in any case, so incentives to distort vanish. Incentives are more powerful for lower values of ρ.

The next figure illustrates how the adviser's incentive to distort varies with ρ for specific values of the parameters, assuming that η_2 is concentrated on 1.[14] The adviser's response $\mu(\rho)$ is described by the solid line. It illustrates that, as expected, the more trusting the decision maker (high ρ), the less the adviser distorts (small μ). When ρ decreases, his only chance to affect the decision is to distort significantly in the direction of the decision's maker's preference: in the limit as ρ gets close to 0, he chooses μ close to -0.9, hence he almost

---

[13] Formally, denote by F the distribution over ε, assumed symmetric around 0. We have $P = F(b + \rho) - F(b - \rho)$, and $\frac{dP}{db} = f(b + \rho) - f(b - \rho) < 0$, hence reducing y (or acting as if b was smaller) generates a first-order increase in the probability P that the suggestion is trusted.

[14] We set $b_0 = 3$, $\sigma_z = 1$, $\sigma_\varepsilon = 2$.

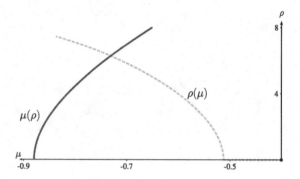

offsets completely his bias: his suggestion is close to the decision maker's most preferred decision.

The figure also shows the decision maker's best response function (the dashed line).[15] The point where the two curves cross is an equilibrium (μ^*, ρ^*) that characterizes the degree to which the adviser takes into account the decision maker's preference (μ^*), and the degree to which the decision maker trusts the suggestion (ρ^*).

To conclude, we observe that when $b_0 > \sigma_\varepsilon$, the equilibria that we construct necessarily yield a better outcome for the decision maker, compared to delegation. Indeed, when $b_0 > \sigma_\varepsilon$, delegation is worse than the strategy that ignores the adviser's suggestion $(\rho = 0)$. Since $\mu < 0$ and since ignoring is always an option, he must have a higher payoff in equilibrium (otherwise he would ignore it).

10. Communication helps because the adviser wants to affect the decision, and to do this he must distort his suggestion in the direction of the decision maker's preference. The larger b_0, the stronger this distortion must be.

Said differently, the adviser is *competing* with the decision maker's initial opinion, forcing the adviser to leave the decision maker with a substantial fraction of the rent.[16] When the decision maker does not initially have a (somewhat reliable) benchmark in mind, his only option may be to debias the adviser's manipulation attempts (as in our first model), and we have seen how this can be detrimental to both players when perceptions of the bias are somewhat accurate.

---

[15] Given that $\eta_2 = 1$, $y = s + (1 + \mu)b_0 z$, the distortion μ is equivalent to a change in b_0. Thus the dashed curve has a shape similar to the decision maker's best response drawn in the previous figure: ρ increases above 0 when $(1 + \mu)b_0$ is around 1.5, that is, since $b_0 = 3$, when μ is around -0.5.

[16] Of course, when the decision maker's signal becomes noisier (larger σ_ε), we can expect trust to increase (larger ρ) and, hence, the adviser to leave smaller rents to the decision maker. In addition, if the adviser's perception of the bias becomes noisier, then (at least for small noise) we may expect greater caution from the adviser, hence a larger $|\mu|$ and higher rents left to the decision marker. We leave these conjectures for further research.

Further Comments

There are numerous situations in which, before making a decision, one needs to aggregate signals from different sources. We may have formed an opinion about the appropriate course of action, but someone offers a different opinion. What should we do? Whose opinion should we trust? In addition, one cannot dismiss the possibility that the opinions that we are exposed to stem from strategic considerations, whereby others try to influence our opinions and, consequently, affect our decisions. How should one take into account this strategic concern?

Aggregating opinions is difficult in practice, because we seldom have access to, nor a good understanding of, the process that generates opinions. Standard models implicitly assume that agents have a perfect understanding of the process that generates opinions, and the structure of the equilibria in this literature is often driven by this implausible assumption.

For example, in the classic sender-receiver game (Crawford and Sobel (1982)), the structure of the model is simple enough that the sender (our adviser) has a very precise idea of how his message will translate into a decision, and this potentially allows him to substantially manipulate the receiver (our decision maker), to the advantage of the sender and the detriment of the receiver. Much of the technical effort in Crawford and Sobel then consists of endogenizing how this ability can be reduced in equilibrium – one finds that pooling should occur, with only a finite number of different messages sent in equilibrium. The structure of these equilibria draws heavily on each player's ability to tailor his behavior to parameters of the model (the bias, and the prior distribution over states).[17] Equilibria can be qualitatively different if that ability is reduced, as well as some of the conclusions about the (in)efficiency of communication.

This chapter has suggested a path toward decreasing agents' sophistication, limiting their ability to perceive the bias accurately, and putting constraints on how they use these perceptions.[18,19]

Beyond the simplification that we propose, it also forces one to think first of classes of strategies that make intuitive sense. We see two benefits. First, this

---

[17] In particular, the fact that states are known to lie in a given interval plays a key role.

[18] The strategy restriction prevents agents from finely exploiting not only the distribution over perceptions, but also the underlying distribution over the decision maker's preferences s. By construction, the latter distribution plays no role in the analysis.

[19] We proposed a direct strategy restriction that limits the number of strategic variables to one. Other ways to reduce the sender's ability have been proposed in the literature. One may assume that the receiver gets a noisy signal of the underlying state; that the sender does not know precisely the preference of the receiver (Seidmann 1990); or that the sender's message is transmitted through a noisy channel (Blume, Board and Kawamura (2007)).

There are also models in which direct strategic restrictions have been proposed, whereby, with some exogenous probability the receiver behaves naively and trusts the sender (see Crawford (2003) for an example in a different communication game, and Kartik, Ottaviani and Squintani (2007)).

produces models that we believe are more focused on intuition or economics, and less centered around technical issues that surface primarily due to the somewhat implausible assumption one starts from. Second, these restrictions may capture the agent's a priori thinking about the class of problem that he faces, a plausible simplifying step that agents undergo when facing complex problems; this chapter provides an illustration of how this a priori thinking may shape predictions and intuitions.[20,21]

Disentangling strategic effects. *The model proposed in this chapter is richer than that in Crawford and Sobel (1982) and could be analyzed using standard tools, with unlimited strategy sets. In comparison with Crawford and Sobel, we have added variability in the bias and noisy perceptions of it, as well as noisy perception for the decision maker of the underlying state. These assumptions alone would limit the extent to which the sender could condition his message on the exact bias realization, and they would also reduce the sender's ability to predict the receiver's response. Without direct restrictions, however, an equilibrium of this enriched model is a complex object, often intractable or difficult to interpret. Our view is that direct strategy restrictions allow the disentangling of various strategic effects that one might expect in the unrestricted model. Additionally, it may give hints about when one of the effects identified in the simpler model might prevail in the richer model.*

Suggested research/applications. It would be natural to examine the case in which the decision maker solicits reports from several senders.[22] With two senders (2 and 3) having the same bias $b > 0$, but noisy perceptions of it (say b_2 and b_3), the first model has a simple extension in which the decision maker takes into account the lowest suggestion $y = \min y_2, y_3$ and filters it as before with an appropriate coefficient λ: $d = y - \lambda b_1$. Two effects can be expected. For a given degree of manipulation by advisers ($\mu = \mu^2 = \mu^3$), the incentive to filter is

---

[20] See Arad and Rubinstein (2017) for a related view in a different class of games.

[21] The level-k literature (see the introduction of Costa-Gomez and Crawford (2006) for a review) can be seen as a way to model this thinking, and to propose a description of agents with varied levels of sophistication. At level 0, agents are naive. At level 1, agents best respond to level 0, etc. In some respects, the definition of naive players in the level-k literature, and the definition of a basic strategy in our framework are similar, and both serve as an anchor to define other strategies: in the level-k literature, the family of strategies considered is obtained by applying iteratively subjective best responses (starting from the naive one), while in our case, the naive one is modulated through a plausible behavioral alteration.

   The main difference between this approach and ours is that we next endogenize which strategy within the family is selected: sophistication is not modeled as an extra step of thinking, but as a richer set of strategies to compare.

   It might be interesting to build on the level-k family to endogenize which of these levels is selected in equilibrium, in a given strategic environment.

[22] See Battaglini (2002) for a model with multiple senders.

diminished (lower λ). However, for a given λ, the incentive to exaggerate is amplified, because the exaggeration only has an effect in events where one has the lowest estimate of the bias. With lognormal noise, it is easy to check that the latter effect dominates: the presence of the other sender reduces the penalty for lying, and all players are worse off in equilibrium.

With two senders having opposite biases (say b and $-b$), we may expect that competition between senders would help, and that the presence of another sender may be used to increase the penalty for distorting the advice away from the decision maker's preference. Without the use of a benchmark signal x to which the decision maker can compare the advisers' suggestions y^2 and y^3, such penalties seem hard to construct. Allowing the use of x, however, one could assume that the agent follows $y^2 - \lambda b^1$ or $y^3 + \lambda b^1$ depending on which advice (y_2 or y_3) is closer to x.

References

Arad, A. and Rubinstein, A. (2017). Multi-dimensional reasoning in games: framework, equilibrium and applications, working paper.

Battaglini, M. (2002). Multiple referrals and multidimensional cheap talk. *Econometrica*, 70, 1379–1401.

Blume, A., Board O. J. and Kawamura K. (2007). Noisy talk. *Theoretical Economics*, 2, 395–440.

Costa-Gomes, M. A. and Crawford, V. P. (2006). Cognition and behavior in two-person guessing games: an experimental study. *American Economic Review*, 96(5), 1737–1768.

Crawford, V. (2003). Lying for strategic advantage: rational and boundedly rational misrepresentation of intentions. *American Economic Review*, 93(1), 133–149.

Crawford, V. and Sobel, J. (1982). Strategic information transmission. *Econometrica*, 50, 1431–1451.

Kamenica, E. and Gentzkow, M. (2011). Bayesian persuasion. *American Economic Review*, 101(6), 2590–2615.

Kartik, N., Ottaviani, M. and Squintani, F. (2007). Credulity, lies, and costly talk. *Journal of Economic Theory*, 134(1), 93–116.

Seidmann, D. (1990). Effective cheap talk with conflicting interests. *Journal of Economic Theory*, 50, 445–458.

CHAPTER 16

Information Aggregation in Markets

1. A common theme in economics is that markets aggregate information well. Despite having heterogenous views about the value of the asset to be sold, an auction may generate a price that coincides with the true value of the asset. This is surprising as there are many possible sources of uncertainty, each of which would seem to be an obstacle to information aggregation. Once we introduce heterogeneity in agents' assessments, other sources of uncertainty seem natural. Across markets, heterogeneity might vary without agents being fully aware of the variations. Some agents might have a reasonably correct estimate of value, while others might have only a vague idea of the degree to which agents are heterogenous. Even the proportion of agents of each kind might vary across markets, without agents being aware of the variation of that proportion.

Given all these potential sources of uncertainty, how can a simple price mechanism achieve perfect aggregation? We illustrate in a simple formal model why prices will generally no longer reflect value once other dimensions of uncertainty are introduced (beyond the uncertainty about the value of the asset). We assume heterogenous estimates of the underlying value of the asset, and consider two additional sources of uncertainty, one coming from variations in demand (*demand uncertainty*), and one coming from variations in the dispersion of agents' assessments (*dispersion uncertainty*). We go on to explain how price fluctuates as a function of these variations, away from the true value of the asset.

As emphasized in Chapter 6, this insight should not come as a surprise. The literature has long recognized that when uncertainty bears on more than one dimension, a price mechanism will generally not aggregate information well. One message from this chapter is that even in environments in which uncertainty would seem to bear on a single dimension (the [common] value of the asset), the "one-dimension" assumption may be unrealistic. A second message is that demand and dispersion uncertainty have quite different strategic consequences.

2. This chapter examines an auction model in which a large number of identical objects are to be sold, and in which all interested agents have the same value for

the object (but possibly different perceptions of that value) and wish to acquire only one object. We focus on two sources of uncertainty/variability – demand uncertainty, where the number of agents interested in the object is a random variable, and dispersion uncertainty, where the heterogeneity of perceptions is also a random variable.

We will see that demand and dispersion uncertainty have quite different strategic consequences. Under demand uncertainty, winning the auction is good news: winning is more likely to happen when demand is low, in which case prices tend to be below value. This creates an incentive to participate in the auction, and to bid higher when the perception of value is higher, even though perceptions are noisy. Under dispersion uncertainty, and if the object is relatively scarce, perceptions of winners (hence prices) tend to be higher when dispersion is large. The consequence is that a higher perception may become a signal of higher dispersion (hence also higher prices), thereby weakening the incentive to participate. We will show that because of these countervailing incentives, dispersion uncertainty is likely to generate demand uncertainty.

3. *A simple auction model.* We consider a basic auction setup. There are k identical objects for sale, and n bidders each with unitary demand ($n > k$). We assume that all bidders have the same value v for the object. We model lack of information by assuming that each buyer receives a noisy estimate z_i of the underlying value v. Specifically, we assume that

$$z_i = \eta_i v,$$

where the η_i's are positive random variables drawn from independent and identical distributions. We denote by g^μ this distribution, with μ characterizing the dispersion of estimates. For the sake of illustration, we assume that η_i has a lognormal distribution:

$$\log \eta_i \sim \mathcal{N}(0, \mu^2).$$

Finally, without loss of generality, we set $v = 1$.[1]

The selling mechanism that we consider is a uniform auction (with price set equal to the $(k + 1)^{th}$ bid). We are interested in the limit case in which k and n are very large, and we let $y \equiv k/n$. In our symmetric environment, y will represent the ex ante probability that a given bidder is served (on average across the realizations of the estimates).[2]

We start our analysis by considering cases where μ and y are fixed, but later take these parameters to be random variables. Randomness in μ means there is uncertainty about the dispersion of estimates. Randomness in y means there is some aggregate uncertainty about the number of active bidders (with y low

---

[1] Given the assumptions made in this chapter, all payoffs will be proportional to v.

[2] The setup is thus analogous to that of Pesendorfer and Swinkels (1997).

whenever demand is high). Aggregate demand uncertainty will be considered exogenous, but we will explain why dispersion uncertainty likely generates aggregate demand uncertainty.

4. *Strategy restriction.* We restrict attention to a particular class of bidding strategies, characterized by a shading factor:

$$b_i^{\lambda_i}(z_i) = \lambda_i z_i.$$

This may be viewed as an imposed restriction on the strategy space that captures the idea that an agent is unable to determine whether his estimate is high compared to others' based on his estimate; he cannot (or is prevented from) condition(ing) his shading behavior (λ_i) on z_i.[3]

One interpretation of z_i is that it models player i's opinion about v. Each player i however is aware that his estimate is noisy. He thus does not take z_i at face value, and attempts to correct for noise in his estimate through his choice of λ_i, setting it optimally on average across possible realizations of z_i.[4]

5. *Analysis.* We look for a symmetric pure strategy equilibrium, characterized by some common shading level λ^*. With a very large number of bidders, any given player's behavior has a negligible influence on prices. From a given player's perspective, the price is determined by the highest losing bid, which means that when he wins, the price is determined by the estimation error of the kth most optimistic bidder among the $n - 1$ other bidders, and the shading behavior λ^*.

Specifically, for any y and μ, define $z^{(y,\mu)}$ as the *threshold estimate* for which

$$\Pr_\mu(z_i > z^{(y,\mu)}) = y,$$

that is, letting $G_\mu(z) = \Pr_\mu(z_i > z)$,

$$z^{(y,\mu)} \equiv G_\mu^{-1}(y).$$

When all bidders follow the same strategy λ, and given our large number approximation, $z^{(y,\mu)}$ is the estimate above which bidders are served. The

---

[3] It can also be thought of as resulting from optimal bidding when the value v is drawn from a diffuse prior.

[4] Although we consider a family of simple shading strategies, we believe that this assumption is not central to the results of this chapter. The difficulties that we point to (in particular when dispersion uncertainty is introduced) would survive in any attempt to construct a symmetric monotonic equilibrium (in which bids increase with estimates), as these monotonic strategies would define a threshold estimate (above which bidders win) similar to the one we shall construct.

202   **Ignorance and Uncertainty**

highest losing bid is thus $\lambda z^{(y,\mu)}$, and it determines the price:[5]

$$p(y,\mu) = \lambda z^{(y,\mu)}.$$

From a bidder's perspective, a single bid does not affect the price, but it affects the probability of being selected. Formally, define

$$\alpha \equiv \lambda_i/\lambda.$$

Bidder i gets an object only in events where αz_i exceeds $z^{(y,\mu)}$, and we can express bidder i's payoff as a function of λ and α:

$$V^{\mu,y}(\alpha,\lambda) = (1 - \lambda z^{(y,\mu)})G(z^{(y,\mu)}/\alpha). \tag{16.1}$$

We can thus examine for each λ the bidder's optimal response, and look for a symmetric equilibrium, that is, a shading level λ^* such that bidder i's optimal response is to set $\alpha = 1$.

When there is no uncertainty about (μ, y), the expression (16.1) implies:
 – if $\lambda < 1/z^{(y,\mu)}$, it is optimal to get the object (hence set α very high);
 – if $\lambda > 1/z^{(y,\mu)}$, it is optimal to abandon the auction (hence set $\alpha = 0$).

So, the only candidate equilibrium is that all bidders choose:[6]

$$\lambda^* = 1/z^{(y,\mu)}.$$

This captures the intuition of the typical "information aggregation" result. In equilibrium, an agent behaves as though he could determine the estimation error made by the kth most optimistic bidder (which will be him if he is the marginal winning bidder), and as though he could appropriately adjust his bid.

6. *Aggregate demand uncertainty.* In the previous analysis, we were silent about each agent's private incentive to use his signal. We can make precise each agent's benefit of using his signal when we introduce aggregate demand uncertainty.

Specifically, assume that y takes two values, say y_L (low demand) and y_H (high demand), with equal probability.[7] Define z_L and $z_H > z_L$ to be the

---

[5] For any given k,n, the actual price is a random variable. Denote by $z^{(k,n,\mu)}$ the kth highest estimate out of $n - 1$. From a given bidder's perspective, conditional on events where he wins, he pays $p = \lambda z^{(k,n,\mu)}$. At the limit where k,n get large with $k/n = y$, the mean of $z^{(k,n,\mu)}$ tends to $z^{(y,\mu)}$ and its variance tends to 0.

[6] This gives a necessary condition. Checking incentives for a fixed (k,n) requires taking into account the fact that the price is a random variable. We omit these questions here and next study cases where there is non-negligible aggregate demand uncertainty.

[7] Note that under low demand, the ratio $y = k/n$ is large, so $y_L > y_H$. The bidder has a greater chance of getting the object when demand is low.

corresponding thresholds.[8] The price paid by winners is either λz_L or λz_H depending on realized demand, and we have:

$$V_\mu(\alpha,\lambda) = E_y V^{\mu,y}(\alpha,\lambda)$$
$$= (1/2)[(1 - \lambda z_L)G_\mu(z_L/\alpha) + (1 - \lambda z_H)G_\mu(z_H/\alpha)].$$

For $\lambda < 1/z_H$, getting the object is profitable in both events, so the best strategy is to set α arbitrarily high. For $\lambda > 1/z_L$, winning is a certain loss, so the best strategy is to set $\alpha = 0$.

In between, when $\lambda \in (1/z_H, 1/z_L)$, the agent faces a standard tradeoff. He would like to increase the chance of getting the object when the price is low $(z = z_L)$, and simultaneously decrease it when the price is high $(z = z_H)$. But, through changes in α, he cannot change his chance of winning in different directions. For λ close to $1/z_H$ or $1/z_L$, his best response is still to either set $\alpha = 0$ or $\alpha = +\infty$. However, as λ gets close to λ^m, with λ^m defined as:

$$\lambda^m = 1/z^m \text{ where } z^m = (z_L + z_H)/2,$$

some interior α must be optimal.

Indeed, at λ^m, the expected price of the object is $\lambda^m z^m = 1$, hence it equals the value of the object. Thus, never buying or always buying yields 0 gain. Now, by choosing $\alpha = 1$, he makes a strictly positive gain (i.e., $V_\mu(1, \lambda_m) > 0$): he wins with higher probability $G_\mu(z_L) = y_L$ when demand is low (hence when the price is low), and with a lower probability $y_H < y_L$ when demand is high (hence when price is high).

The following figure illustrates how the agent responds to λ, for $\mu = 1$ and $y = 0.2$ or 0.3.

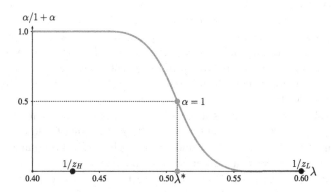

When λ is small (i.e., others shade significantly), the agent wants to get the object (i.e., bid high and set α high), and when λ is large, he wants to avoid

---

[8] That is, $z_L = z^{(y_L,\mu)}$ and $z_H = z^{(y_H,\mu)}$. Note that by definition, $G^\mu(z_L) = y_L$ and $G^\mu(z_H) = y_H$. Since $y_L > y_H$ and G^μ is decreasing, $z_H > z_L$: price is smaller when demand is lower.

winning (i.e., set α low). There is a smooth tradeoff for the model parameters chosen: there exists a shading factor λ^* for which it is optimal for the agent to choose $\alpha = 1$ (or equivalently $\alpha/(1 + \alpha) = 0.5$ in the figure). This shading λ^* is the equilibrium shading.

7. *Dispersion uncertainty.* We next consider uncertainty about the dispersion parameter μ. Specifically, fix the demand parameter y and assume that μ_L and $\mu_H > \mu_L$ are equally likely. As before, the thresholds defining the winning bidders depend on the realization (L or H). They are now given by:

$$z_L \equiv G_{\mu_L}^{-1}(y) \equiv z^{(\mu_L, y)} \text{ and } z_H \equiv G_{\mu_L}^{-1}(y) \equiv z^{(\mu_H, y)}.$$

Note that when objects are relatively scarce compared to the number of players (y small), the more dispersed distribution (μ_H) generates a higher price, that is $z_H > z_L$. Under that assumption (y small), event L is the more favorable: the price (λz_L) is smaller and a player would like to buy more frequently under that event.

Formally, the expression for expected gain is similar to the previous one, except that the expectation is now taken with respect to μ.

$$V_y(\alpha, \lambda) = E_\mu V^{\mu, y}(\alpha, \lambda)$$
$$= (1/2)[(1 - \lambda z_L)G_{\mu_L}(z_L/\alpha) + (1 - \lambda z_H)G_{\mu_H}(z_H/\alpha)].$$

There are important differences, however.

Under aggregate demand uncertainty, a buyer gets the object more frequently when demand is low (this is why we had $V_\mu(1, \lambda^m) > 0$).

Under dispersion uncertainty, a player wins with the *same* probability y under either event, so, by definition of λ^m, $V_y(1, \lambda^m) = 0$. So, choosing $\alpha = 1$ will only be strictly profitable if bidders shade more ($\lambda < \lambda^m$). The problem, however, is that the marginal effect of a change in bidding on the probability of getting the object is *larger* in the *low dispersion* state. Therefore, when $\alpha = 1$ and $\lambda = \lambda^m$, a player benefits by increasing α, because this makes the favorable state L more likely.

The following figure plots a player's best response as a function of λ, assuming $\mu_L = 0.8$, $\mu_H = 1$ and $y = 0.2$.[9] It indicates that for low values λ, it is optimal to bid high as before, and for high values of λ it is optimal to stay out of the auction. The main difference with the previous case is as explained above: at λ^m, increasing α has a larger effect on the chance of winning in the good state L than in the bad state. So the bidder prefers to set α above 1. When λ increases above λ^m, the incentive to outbid others diminishes, because even winning in the low state is not that attractive. But it does not decrease

---

[9] The discontinuity occurs at some λ for which $\max_\alpha V_y(\alpha, \lambda) = 0$, hence at some λ for which it is optimal to stay out of the auction.

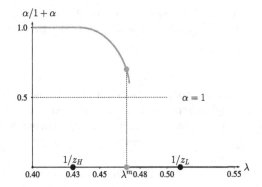

fast enough. Slightly above λ^m, λ reaches a point where staying out ($\alpha = 0$) becomes a better option.

Intuitively, when there is dispersion uncertainty, then, conditional on winning, a higher estimate z signals higher dispersion, hence a higher price. In this case, bidding more when the estimate is higher is not a good idea. There is no symmetric equilibrium in this case.

8. *Combined dispersion and aggregate demand uncertainty.* We now illustrate the combined effect of dispersion and aggregate demand uncertainty in our numerical example, assuming independent draws of y and μ. The main difference is that when there is sufficient aggregate demand uncertainty, the incentives to increase α at $\alpha = 1$ are dampened sufficiently, and as a result, a symmetric equilibrium exists. We check this under the same distributional assumption, with $y \in \{y_L, y_H\}$ and $\mu \in \{\mu_L, \mu_H\}$ and all pairs (y, μ) equiprobable. The following figure illustrates the bidder's optimal response to λ, assuming values $0.2, 0.3$ for y and $0.8, 1$ for μ.

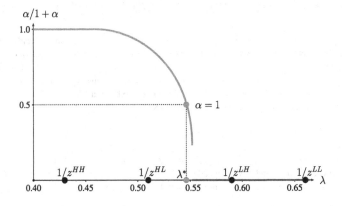

In equilibrium, the realized price is $p = \lambda^* z^{y\mu}$, and it thus varies as a function of the realization (y, μ), taking values ranging from $\lambda^* z^{LL} = 0.93$ to $\lambda^* z^{HH} = 1.08$.

9. *Discussion.* Dispersion uncertainty creates an incentive to set one's bid above the others, even as expected prices get close to the underlying value of the good, and a higher expected price in turn creates incentives to drop out. Thus, dispersion uncertainty creates the seed for demand uncertainty, and it is only when aggregate demand uncertainty is sufficiently large that these conflicting incentives disappear.

For pedagogical reasons, we analyzed the case in which aggregate demand uncertainty is exogenous, rather than endogenizing it through strategic choices. But, in the presence of dispersion uncertainty, many factors or signals could fuel demand uncertainty.

When there is dispersion uncertainty, even very noisy signals about the dispersion of estimates can be valuable: dispersion uncertainty gives rise to variation in prices, and in our examples where supply is relatively scarce, one would want to participate and bid high only in events where dispersion is believed to be low. In particular, agents who get very poor estimates of value and a not too inaccurate signal of dispersion would prefer to use the latter signal rather than the former to bid/participate. Aggregate uncertainty about the distribution over these signals, or aggregate uncertainty about the fraction of agents getting that type of signal, will inevitably translate into aggregate demand uncertainty.[10]

Further Comments

In Parts I and II, we voiced the following caution: in a model where players have too many instruments, they may too easily adjust behavior to special features of the model. This chapter provides an example where, in the absence of aggregate uncertainty, strategy restrictions alone (at least the one we considered) may not be sufficient to prevent players from adjusting to the assumed distribution over estimates. Sometimes, finding the right balance between the richness of the environment and the richness of the strategy space

---

[10] To express the last point formally, assume that a fraction y_0 of agents observe only a signal about the dispersion μ, say $\widehat{\mu} \in \{\widehat{L}, \widehat{H}\}$. Call $\pi_{\widehat{\mu}, \mu} = \Pr(\widehat{\mu} \mid \mu)$. The signal is valuable, for example, if $\rho \equiv \pi_{\widehat{L}, L} / \pi_{\widehat{L}, H} > 1$ and these bidders will want to participate if and only if $\widehat{\mu} = \widehat{L}$. In particular, in large markets where gains remain close to 0 on average and are yet subject to significant variations in price, ρ need not be far above 1 to be valuable.

Now, the actual supply that the other bidders face is

$$\widehat{y}(\mu) = \frac{y - y_0 \pi_{\widehat{L}, \mu}}{1 - y_0}, \text{ with } \mu \in \{L, H\}.$$

Demand is thus correlated with the actual dispersion parameter. But this correlation is small when ρ is close to 1, and any independent shock on y_0 (or on π) would generate the kind of conditions we have analyzed, with independent draws of y and μ.

is better achieved by enriching the environment (e.g., introducing aggregate uncertainty).

Indeed, one could try the following: keep the basic model with no aggregate uncertainty, but reduce the power of the agents' instruments by restricting agents to noisy strategies. Noisy strategies, however, amount to adding a source of independent noise on the estimate, and without aggregate uncertainty, perfect information aggregation would still be obtained. Noisy strategies are not effective, because strategy choices are assumed to be independent, and with a large number of players, the noise introduced in the individual strategies has a deterministic effect in the aggregate: agents may, again, adjust their behavior as if they knew that systematic effect.

The latter observation applies to any game with a large number of players. Equilibrium analysis typically neglects the process by which equilibrium is reached. If we were careful in modeling the adjustment process and dealt with a varying environment, there would likely be a lag before the population adjusts, this lag would likely be longer when the population is larger. One could interpret aggregate uncertainty in this chapter as a way to capture an unmodeled yet imperfect adjustment process.

Suggested research/application. In the spirit of Feddersen and Pesendorfer (1997) (see also Chapter 6), one could examine voting problems over two alternatives A and B, and introduce dispersion uncertainty on the estimates of the benefit of B over A. Dispersion uncertainty would prevent perfect information aggregation, and allow for a comparison between various voting rules.

The auction framework studied belongs to a class of participation games with arbitrarily large number of players. In participation games for which players pay an exogenous participation cost and gain a fixed prize (with fewer prizes than players), the exogenous cost often serves as a self-selection device (only lower cost agents participate).[11] Aggregate uncertainty about cost levels (or the dispersion of costs) will inevitably make self-selection more difficult, and potentially make existence of a monotone equilibrium problematic unless aggregate uncertainty about the number of players is also introduced.

Dynamic versions of this game (in which participation decision could be modeled through a family of simple learning strategies) would potentially address the issue raised above, with aggregate uncertainty arising from an imperfect adjustment process.

---

[11] As in the all-pay auction examined in Chapter 7, cost realizations may play a strong coordinating role.

208   Ignorance and Uncertainty

References

Feddersen, T. and Pesendorfer, W. (1997). Voting behavior and information aggregation in elections with private information. *Econometrica*, 65(5), 1029–1058.
Pesendorfer, W. and Swinkels, J. M. (1997). The loser's curse and information aggregation in common value auctions. *Econometrica*, 65(6), 1247–1281.

CHAPTER 17

Bargaining

1. A typical question which one faces in bargaining is whether one should make an offer or let the other side make an offer. When selling an object, making a take-it-or-leave-it offer puts one in good position to extract surplus. However, a second issue seems relevant as well: choosing which offer to make is more difficult than deciding whether to accept or reject an offer,[1] possibly leading one to prefer that the other make an offer.

Abstracting from dynamic issues,[2] we ask whether a seller is better off making a take-it-or-leave-it offer, or letting the other side make a take-it-or-leave-it offer, and we illustrate that ignorance may tilt the comparison in favor of letting the other make the offer.[3]

2. Intuitively making a take-it-or-leave offer allows for maximum rent extraction, as one may push the other side down to his reservation level. But, one also risks missing the reservation level, with two possible consequences: missed trade, or excess surplus left to the other side, depending on the sign of the mistake when making an offer.

What if, as a seller, we let the other side make a take-it-or-leave-it offer? *A priori*, it is not obvious that this helps: the buyer may exploit his "bargaining power" and extract most or all of the surplus. Yet, one could imagine that the buyer also makes an error that leaves us with a large part of the surplus.

3. We will provide conditions under which it is better to let the other make the offer. In the model proposed, the source of mistakes is that proposers get noisy estimates of surplus. Overly optimistic estimates may lead to missed trade and pessimistic estimates may lead to excess surplus left to the other. One may

---

[1] If rejecting means no trade, the later decision only requires that one compares the proposed price with one's value for the object.
[2] Dynamic issues are relevant as well. In practice, bargaining may involve many rounds of offers, and current offers may shape each side's aspirations.
[3] We also assume agents know perfectly their own valuation (private values). If this were not the case, one might let the other side make an offer in order to learn about one's own valuation.

mitigate these losses through the choice of the offer, either by shading one's estimate of the surplus (cautiousness) to avoid missed trade, or by inflating it to improve the terms of trade when trade occurs, betting that one's estimate is pessimistic.

When noisier estimates translate into increased cautiousness, the terms of trade deteriorate for the one making the offer, and an ill-informed player may prefer to let the other make the offer.

4. *The model.* We consider a strategic interaction between a seller and a buyer, and assume that each knows his value for the object. The seller has value v_1 for the object and the buyer has value $v_2 > v_1$ for the object. We denote by S the surplus to be shared:

$$S = v_2 - v_1.$$

Without uncertainty, and with the ability to fully optimize, an agent can tailor his offer to the surplus that can be extracted. A seller would, for example, offer $p = v_1 + S$ and extract all surplus. The standard way to model ignorance and prevent full surplus extraction is to make S a random variable. Then, any given price either satisfies $p - v_1 > S$ (in which case no trade occurs), or $p - v_1 < S$ (in which case surplus is left to the buyer).[4]

We choose a different route that does not introduce randomness in surplus. We treat S as a fixed scalar, and define $\tilde{S}$ as a random variable that reflects the agent's noisy perception of S. Strategies are functions of the perception $\tilde{S}$, but we assume that the agent compares only a limited set of such functions.[5]

Formally, we define the ratio

$$x = \tilde{S}/S$$

and assume that it is distributed according to a continuous density g^{μ}, where the parameter μ reflects noise in perception. In the numerical computations below, we assume that $\log x$ is normally distributed:

$$\log x \sim \mathcal{N}(0, \mu^2).$$

The degree to which $\tilde{S}$ is noisy will play a key role. By varying the noisiness in the seller's perception, we will vary the seller's ability to extract surplus.

---

[4] If the uncertainty is modeled by assuming that S is a random variable characterized by a continuous density f over possible surplus realizations, then under full optimization, the seller chooses $p = v_1 + \Delta^*$ where:

$$\Delta^* = \arg\max_{\Delta} \Delta(1 - F(\Delta)).$$

Setting p exactly equal to $v_1 + S$ and fully extracting surplus is impossible because the agent cannot tailor the markup Δ to the surplus S. The optimal markup Δ^* reflects a standard tradeoff between increased share of the surplus and reduced chance of trade.

[5] The technique is similar to the investment example in Chapter 4, and the rent extraction game in Chapter 8.

Accordingly, we also interpret μ as an ability parameter, i.e., the ability of the seller to adjust his offer to the underlying surplus S (with smaller μ amounting to greater ability).

Next, for any $\lambda \geq 0$, we define the price-offer strategy p^λ:

$$p^\lambda(\widetilde{S}) = v_1 + \lambda\widetilde{S}.$$

The parameter λ can be interpreted as a scale adjustment parameter,[6] and we assume that the agent behaves as though he could optimize that scale parameter.

5. *Values and optimal behavior.* For a seller characterized by a perception parameter μ, and for a strategy p^λ, one can compute the seller's expected payoff, denoted $v(\lambda, \mu)$. Since trade occurs in events where $\lambda\widetilde{S} < S$, we have

$$v(\lambda, \mu) = \lambda S \int_{\lambda x < 1} x g^\mu(x)dx.$$

For the seller, the tradeoff is standard. A more cautious strategy (i.e., smaller λ) translates into smaller gains when trade occurs, but makes trade more likely.

We are interested in the relationship between μ and agents' expected payoffs when the seller sets the scale parameter λ optimally. Toward this end, for any ability level μ of the seller, we denote the optimal shading by $\lambda^*(\mu)$, and the expected payoff by

$$v^*(\mu) = v(\lambda^*(\mu), \mu).$$

We also denote by $Q(\lambda, \mu)$ the probability of trade, and define $Q^*(\mu) = Q(\lambda^*(\mu), \mu)$. Finally, we denote by $\widehat{v}(\lambda, \mu)$ the buyer's expected payoff when he faces a seller with ability μ who adopts strategy λ:

$$\widehat{v}(\lambda, \mu) = S \int_{\lambda x < 1} (1 - \lambda x) g^\mu(x)dx,$$

and we denote by

$$\widehat{v}^*(\mu) = \widehat{v}(\lambda^*(\mu), \mu)$$

the buyer's expected payoff when he faces a seller of ability μ who chooses λ optimally. Since all payoffs are proportional to S, we normalize S to 1.[7]

---

[6] An alternative interpretation is that the seller picks a convex combination of his estimate of v_2 and his value. Alternative specifications where the seller picks a geometric average would yield similar insights. Also note that the seller makes an offer that incorporates a (noisy) perception of the surplus, so our formulation is akin to an "informed principal" problem.

[7] Note that this means that, given our restrictions, our analysis would be unchanged if S was a random variable (drawn independently of x).

6. *Analysis.* We make several observations based on numerical computations. Our distributional assumption plays a role in the conclusions, and we return to that in Section 7d.

a. When μ is very small, the distribution is concentrated near $x = 1$, and approximate full rent extraction is possible. When μ increases, the seller's ability to extract rent decreases. The following figure plots expected gains $v(\lambda, \mu)$ for $\mu = 0.2$. Optimal λ^* is 0.74, resulting in an expected payoff of 0.68.

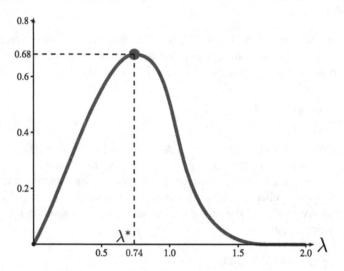

b. Low ability (high μ) makes it difficult to target the appropriate price mark up S through the scale adjustment λ. The next figure plots the seller's gain (v^*: lower curve), the probability of trade (Q^*: upper curve) and the expected seller's share of the surplus conditional on trade ($s = v^*/Q^*$: middle curve) as a function of μ. These functions are all decreasing in μ.

The vertical dashed line defines the ability parameter μ^* ($\mu^* \simeq 0.67$) for which the buyer and seller equally share the surplus. For μ larger than μ^*, the buyer's expected payoff is larger than the seller's.

c. The seller faces the risk of missed trades, leading to cautiousness (i.e., reducing λ). But the seller also faces a selection bias. His offer is accepted only when he is sufficiently pessimistic about the surplus to be shared, which implies an expected price upon trading bounded away from v_2. Formally, for any λ, trades occur only if $\lambda \widetilde{S} < S \equiv 1$, implying that:

$$\Delta^{\lambda,\mu} \equiv E[p^\lambda - v_1 \mid trade] = E[\lambda \widetilde{S} \mid \lambda \widetilde{S} < 1] < 1.$$

In principle, this selection bias gives the seller an incentive to increase λ to obtain a larger share upon trading – and more so for high μ since the selection

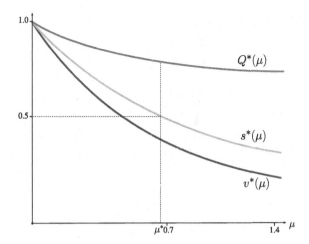

bias gets worse as noise increases.[8] But attempts to mitigate the selection bias are potentially costly in terms of missed trades, and, under our distributional assumption, the combined effect is that the expected share $s^*(\mu)$ decreases with μ. The risk of no trade is the dominant effect.[9]

d. When the buyer makes the offer, he is subject to the same difficulty, determining the optimal offer. We model the buyer's decision problem analogously to the seller's. The buyer gets a noisy perception $\tilde{S}$ of the surplus to be shared, independent of the seller's, and considers strategies of the form $p^\lambda = v_2 - \lambda\tilde{S}$. He is thus subject to the same maximization program that the seller faced.[10] If endowed with ability μ^b, he chooses $\lambda^*(\mu^b)$, obtains $v^*(\mu^b)$ and leaves $\widehat{v}^*(\mu^b)$ in expectation to the seller.

Now, building on the possibility that the seller and the buyer have different abilities μ and μ^b, the following figure plots the set of pairs (μ, μ^b) for which

$$v^*(\mu) < \widehat{v}^*(\mu^b).$$

That is, the set of pair (μ, μ^b) for which the seller is better off when the buyer makes the offer (the shaded area).

The following figure illustrates that a seller with low ability (high μ) is better off when the buyer makes the offer, unless the buyer has overly high ability (μ^b too low). When the buyer and the seller have identical abilities

---

[8] For a given λ, $\Delta^{\lambda,\mu}$ decreases when μ increases. Even if one defines $\widehat{\lambda}(\mu)$ so that $E\widehat{\lambda}(\mu)\tilde{S}$ remains constant, $\Delta^{\widehat{\lambda}(\mu),\mu}$ decreases when μ increases.

[9] Other distributional assumptions could lead to a different conclusion, as we explain in Section 7d.

[10] This is because trade occurs when $v_2 - \lambda\tilde{S} > v_1$, hence when $\lambda\tilde{S} < S$. Note that $v_2 - \lambda\tilde{S}$ may be negative under our lognormal assumption, without this affecting incentives. Rather than the additive form analyzed, one could also study a multiplicative version.

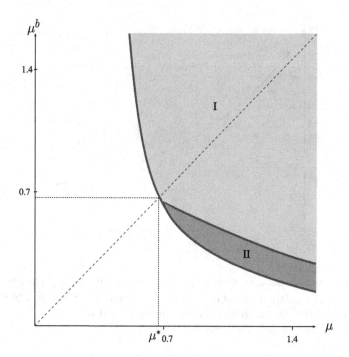

$(\mu = \mu^b$: this is the $45°$ line in the figure), there is a threshold μ^* above which each side prefers that the other side makes the offer.[11]

Finally, the figure also illustrates when, conditional on trading, the seller's expected share of the surplus increases (region I) or decreases (region II) when he lets the buyer make the offer. The first region is preponderant, and it illustrates that the main motive for letting the other make the offer is seldom efficiency, but rather, benefiting from the other's cautiousness in making offers.

7. Discussion.

a. Perception and ability. One interpretation of μ is that it reflects noise in perception. An alternative interpretation is that it reflects the agent's ability to tailor his offers to the underlying surplus, with smaller μ reflecting higher ability. Another interpretation is that the seller targets a markup λS over his value v_1, but trembles in executing this strategy, generating an actual markup equal to $x\lambda S$: the variance of x (i.e., μ) then captures the degree to which he trembles.[12]

---

[11] There is actually a large set of pairs (μ, μ^b) for which both sides prefer to let the other make the offer. This is the set of pairs for which $v^*(\mu) < \widehat{v}^*(\mu^b)$ and $v^*(\mu^b) < \widehat{v}^*(\mu)$. Graphically, it consists of the intersection of the shaded area with its symmetric image around the $45°$ line.

[12] Trembles have been proposed by Selten (1975), as a way to distinguish between more reasonable and less reasonable Nash equilibria. Trembles, here, are not meant to be necessarily small, but a consequence of (possibly large) noise in perceptions.

Our modeling device is reminiscent of the notion of execution skill discussed in Larkey, Kadane, Austin and Zamir (1997), and interpreted there as an ability to execute a planned

Whichever interpretation is preferred, one can think of the agent as endowed with a set of instruments to parse the environment and adjust to it. From an ex ante perspective, the pair (λ, μ) defines a mixed strategy $\sigma^{\lambda,\mu}$ over possible offers, and one can define $P^{\lambda,\mu}(y)$ as the probability that the seller makes an offer below yS, under $\sigma^{\lambda,\mu}$. The family

$$\mathcal{P}^\mu = \{P^{\lambda,\mu}\}_{\lambda \geq 0}$$

defines the set of instruments available to the agent, with the understanding that he manages to pick the one that maximizes expected utility. This family can be seen as a *joint strategy restriction*, stemming from a distributional assumption (on x), and a direct strategy restriction (the parameterized family p^λ).

When $\mu = 0$, the functions $P^{\lambda,0}$ are step functions and the agent can perfectly adjust to S – the optimal instrument is $\lambda^*(0) = 1$, leading to full extraction. For μ close to 0, the family $\mathcal{P}^\mu$ remains close to a family of step functions. The figure below plots the functions $P^{\lambda,\mu}(x)$ for $\mu = 0.5$, with λ taking values ranging from $\lambda = 0.6$ up to $\lambda = 1$.

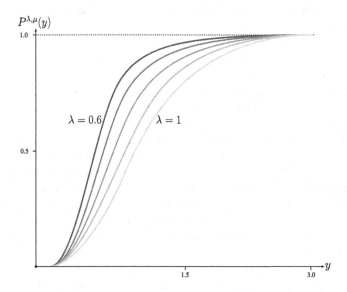

The functions are flatter, implying lower ability to adjust offers to the underlying surplus S.

strategy. Our noise term μ plays a similar role, preventing exact execution of a planned offer. See also Archibald and Shoram (2011), who measured skill in terms of the minimum tremble that one makes.

b. Comparison with a standard Bayesian model. The proposed modeling strategy differs from a standard Bayesian model in that the agent does not make a Bayesian inference after observing $\widetilde{S}$. Would he do so, since there is no actual uncertainty on S, he would be able to extract full surplus by offering $p = v_1 + S$. In the proposed model, the exact surplus scale S is fixed, but the agent has a poor instrument, characterized by the family of strategies p^λ. To understand the role of this restriction, consider a more complete set of instruments, say:

$$p^{\lambda,k}(\widetilde{S}) = v_1 + k + \lambda\widetilde{S},$$

where k is a shift adjustment parameter, and λ is a scale adjustment parameter, just as before. With such a set $\{p^{\lambda,k}\}_{\lambda,k}$, given that S is not random, the agent would learn to put no weight on signal $\widetilde{S}$ and calculate the offer that extracts the whole surplus S, optimizing on the shift parameter only (i.e., $k^* = S$, $\lambda^* = 0$). In contrast, we assume no shift adjustment ($k = 0$): we prevent the agent from learning the appropriate scale S through *shift adjustments*, and only allow him to approach S through *scale adjustments*. We make this assumption not because we believe that agents would never attempt shift adjustments, but because we believe that it is difficult for agents to learn the exact locus of S, and we therefore use the restriction as a technical device to prevent perfect adjustment to S.[13]

c. Comparison with a subjective Bayesian model. The proposed model also differs from a subjective Bayesian model, in which agents' offers are solely driven by a subjective prior. In our model, subjective perceptions matter (through $\widetilde{S}$), but the agent is endowed with some ability to optimize, and the optimal choice λ^* is driven by the actual surplus S to be shared. To see better how this differs from a subjective Bayesian model, one could interpret $\widetilde{S}$ as the (subjectively) optimal offer that an agent would make if endowed with some subjective prior belief $\widetilde{\beta}$, and think of the distribution over $\widetilde{S}$ as reflecting a distribution over possible prior beliefs. Our model then goes one step further. It takes $\widetilde{S}$ as an input in decision making, treating it as a signal, and assumes that agents attempt to exploit this signal, but can only imperfectly do so: the agent cannot optimize over all functions of $\widetilde{S}$, but rather only over a restricted set.

d. Other distributional assumptions. Our conclusions are based on a *joint strategy restriction*, stemming from a distributional assumption (on x) and a direct strategy restriction (the parameterized family p^λ). Modifying the distributional assumption amounts to an alternative joint strategy restriction,

---

[13] An alternative modeling strategy is to assume that S is a random variable. Then, even allowing for shift adjustments would not eliminate errors. This modeling strategy, however, would require that one define a particular distribution over possible values of S, and allow the agent to adjust k to that particular distribution.

under which our conclusion (that higher variance of x would translate into greater caution and smaller shares for the seller) would not necessarily hold.

To illustrate with an extreme example, assume x takes only two positive values, $x_0 < 1$ with probability q and $x_1 > 1$ with probability $1 - q$. Given our strategy restriction, the agent would optimally choose either $\lambda = 1/x_0$, getting full surplus with probability q, or $\lambda = 1/x_1$, avoiding missed trades but getting only a fraction $1/x_1$ of the surplus with probability q. For q sufficiently large, the first option is preferable: $\lambda^* = 1/x_0$; the seller is essentially betting that his estimate $\tilde{S}$ is pessimistic, and he manages to secure the maximum surplus S upon trading.[14]

In the end, our conclusion depends on whether, under the joint restriction, players manage to determine with precision the value of $\lambda\tilde{S}$ upon trading. If pessimistic estimates are sufficiently dispersed, it is hard to improve the terms of trade without simultaneously decreasing the chance of trade. If error terms x are sufficiently concentrated when pessimistic and sufficiently frequent, as in the above example, then "it is not difficult" for the seller to offset this pessimism without risking much in the probability of trading. It is not difficult, but it amounts to assuming that the seller can finely exploit the distribution over his errors in ways that are questionable.

e. Comments on mechanism design. The comparison that we make can be interpreted as a simple mechanism design exercise, in which only two mechanisms are available (one in which the seller makes the offer and another in which the buyer makes the offer), and where the comparison between these mechanisms is made at an ex ante stage. The mechanism design literature typically examines a more general issue – that of finding the optimal mechanism out of all possible mechanisms (Myerson (1981)). Applied to our question, this literature would conclude that, when valuations are private and drawn from independent distributions, the seller's optimal mechanism consists of making take-it-or-leave offers.[15] One essential difference with our approach is that once the distribution over valuations is defined, there is a lower bound on agents' ignorance. Agents act as though they knew with precision this distribution, and *in that world*, it is not optimal to let the other side make the offer. Our proposed model yields a qualitatively different outcome.

Suggested research/applications. A natural extension would be to investigate the classic problem where the object is divisible: a seller with production cost $c(q)$ faces a buyer with valuation $v(q)$.[16] A useful

---

[14] Indeed, setting $x_1 = \mu$ and $x_0 = 1/\mu$, and letting μ get large, one finds that the larger μ, the larger the variance of the estimate, and the larger the share and value for the seller.

[15] See Williams (1987). The result can also be seen as a simple extension of Myerson (1981).

[16] The problem can be framed either as a seller facing a buyer with unknown demand function (Mussa and Rosen (1978)), or as a buyer facing a seller with unknown cost function (Baron and Myerson (1982)).

benchmark is the efficient level of production q_e and the margin m_e (over total cost $c(q_e)$) for which the seller would appropriate all welfare gains.[17] With noisy estimates $(\widehat{q}_e, \widehat{m}_e)$,[18] the seller might prefer to be cautious, possibly adjusting his fixed quantity/price offer to a quantity $q^\lambda = \lambda \widehat{q}_e$ and a margin $m^\mu = \mu \widehat{m}_e$. By looking for the optimal contract (q^λ, m^μ) within that simplified family, one could examine the degree to which the seller prefers to adjust quantities or prices.

Also, the seller might prefer to leave some control to the buyer, offering a contract where the buyer has the option to pick a quantity q within a range Q^λ (say $Q^\lambda = \{q, q \geq q^\lambda\}$),[19] at a price equal to $c(q)(1 + m^\mu)$. We would endogenize here the type and degree of control that the seller wishes to give to the buyer, depending on the quality of his estimates.[20]

Along similar lines, one could investigate a model in which the buyer has a noisy estimate of the producer's cost function, and extend the analysis to the case where several buyers want to influence production by secretly making compensation offers.[21] Equilibrium sharing of costs among principals could be examined, as a function of relative noise or intensity of preferences.

In a different vein, there are many bargaining situations, such as pretrial bargaining, in which rejecting an offer eventually leads to an

---

[17] Offering a quantity q with a margin m means offering this quantity at total price $c(q)(1 + m)$. The margin m_e is equal to $(v(q_e) - c(q_e))/c(q_e)$.

[18] The classic assumption that uncertainty is one-dimensional would introduce a deterministic relationship between $\widehat{q}_e$ and $\widehat{m}_e$. The more general noise structure proposed here captures the fact that there are plausibly many relevant dimensions of uncertainty in this problem.

[19] Alternatively, Q^λ might simply define a lower bound, or an interval $q \in [q^\lambda, q^{1/\lambda}]$ for some $\lambda < 1$.

[20] Note that the classic motive for quantity distortions, and for leaving some limited control to the buyer, is different. In the classic setup where ignorance is modeled as a distribution over types, the seller faces *several kinds* of buyers that he cannot distinguish. Then, the seller may find it optimal to offer a menu of options, where each option in the menu is targeted to a different kind of buyer. In designing this menu, the seller faces the constraint that each kind of buyer choose the offer targeted to him (i.e., the incentive constraint), and the optimal contract embodies distortions: the seller wishes to offer quantities different from efficient ones.

While our suggested model could be cast in similar ways, with two kinds of buyers characterized by (q_e^1, m_e^1) and (q_e^2, m_e^2), and noisy signals received for each type, our basic model does not have multiple types of buyers – just noisy estimates of the characteristics of a *single* kind of buyer. Our model thus suggests another motive for quantity distortions and weaker control by the seller: prudence with respect to one's own estimates (see Caroll (2014) for another perspective on prudence in contracting, in which the seller is prudent with respect to his own beliefs, and in which the maxmin modeling strategy is followed – see Chapter 5).

[21] This is in the spirit of Bernheim and Whinston (1986), but with imperfect information (see also Martimort and Stole (2015)).

outcome on which parties may have different estimates/opinions. One could analyze a model in which the claimant and defendants both have noisy estimates of the merits of the case – merits to be determined by a judge if the defendant's offer is rejected.[22] A nontrivial extension would be that, upon receiving the defendant's offer, or no offer at all, the claimant has three choices: accepting the offer, going to court, or dropping charges to avoid a costly trial.

References

Archibald, C. and Shoram, Y. (2011). Hustling in repeated zero-sum games with imperfect execution. *Proceedings of the Twenty-Second International Joint Conference on Artificial Intelligence.*

Bernheim, B. D. and Whinston, M. D. (1986). Menu auctions, resource allocation, and economic influence. *The Quarterly Journal of Economics*, 101(1), 1–31.

Larkey, P., Kadane, J. B., Austin, R. and Zamir, S. (1997). Skill in games. *Management Science*, 43, 596–609.

Martimort, D. and Stole, L. (2015). Menu auctions and influence games with private information, SSRN working paper 2569703.

Myerson, R. (1981). Optimal auction design. *Mathematics of Operations Research*, 6, 58–73.

Selten, R. (1975). Reexamination of the perfectness concept for equilibrium points in extensive games. *International Journal of Game Theory*, 4, 25–55.

Williams, S. R. (1987). Efficient performance in two agent bargaining. *Journal of Economic Theory*, 41, 154–172.

---

[22] This differs from this chapter in that, in the spirit of the model outlined in Chapter 8, the decision to reject or accept is no longer obvious. A likely outcome is that noiser estimates would make agreement more difficult. This is in contrast with a standard model in which very noisy estimates lead to beliefs converging to priors (see Chapter 10), making an agreement easy to find.

CHAPTER 18

Attrition

1. Most bargaining interactions involve a war of attrition dimension: one party takes and holds a position in the hope that the other will concede to his demand, and delays ensue when both players maintain conflicting positions. For a given player, the main strategic difficulty is that he might be facing a tough player who plans to hold out for a very long time, or a weak player who will soon cave in. In the latter case, it pays to wait, while, in the former it does not. At each instant, a player must thus balance whether to wait (to see if the other caves in) or to concede immediately (fearing that little is to be gained from waiting).

2. Strategic models of attrition are complex dynamic games. Determining the odds that your opponent might only be playing tough is just the beginning. There are arbitrarily many dates at which concession might occur, hence arbitrarily many degrees of toughness. Determining precisely how long one should wait before conceding seems unattainable. Incentives to concede or to continue to hold out must be reexamined at each date. The observation that the other has not yet conceded is evidence of some degree of toughness, but there are many inferences that one can draw about the degree of toughness.

3. We address two issues in this chapter. The first relates to complexity. Traditional models typically start with a joint distribution over value realizations, and then derive behavior that relies on players knowing that distribution precisely. One typically obtains a one-to-one relationship between one's value and the date at which one concedes. Determining that relationship is complex: it relies on sophisticated updating of beliefs as time passes.

Beyond complexity, players' values and their beliefs about the opponent's value play a central role in players' equilibrium behavior. In particular, with identical waiting costs, the player who has the highest value for the object ends up getting it. In practice, delays would seem to be driven at least partially by considerations quite distinct from one's assessments of relative gains or losses, for example, considerations that relate to whether one's claim/position is perceived as legitimate or not. Even if I knew precisely the other's gain if I were to concede, it is questionable that this would allow me to predict with any degree of precision the date at which the other will concede.

We present a simple model of attrition that addresses these issues. It is cognitively less demanding than traditional models, and the perceptions of whether one's claim is legitimate or not play a key role in determining behavior. As one would expect, negative correlation in these perceptions diminishes the severity of the conflict, and translates into less inefficiency or shorter conflicts on average.[1]

4. We consider agents who benefit from getting the object, but who experience a waiting cost c per unit of time while they continue vying for the object. The gain for player i is denoted v_i. Throughout we assume that each agent i controls the rate μ_i at which he concedes, and that this rate is constant over the course of the interaction. This assumption captures the idea that it is difficult for an agent to know how to modify his concession rate.

Formally, a player who employs μ_i has a probability $e^{-\mu_i t}$ of remaining active at date t, that is, denoting by τ_i the random date at which he concedes, we have:

$$\Pr(\tau_i > t) = \exp -\mu_i t.$$

We can then compute player i's expected payoff $g_i(\mu_1, \mu_2)$ when concession rates are μ_1 and μ_2. The expected duration is $1/(\mu_1 + \mu_2)$, and the probability that j concedes first is $\mu_j/(\mu_1 + \mu_2)$. We thus have:

$$g_i(\mu_1, \mu_2) = \frac{\mu_j v_i - c}{\mu_1 + \mu_2}. \tag{18.1}$$

Intuitively, if your opponent is tough and concedes at a low rate, you are better off conceding quickly (large μ_i). If your opponent is weak and concedes at a high rate, you are better off conceding slowly (small μ_i). When $v_i = v_j = v$, one obtains a unique symmetric pure strategy equilibrium, in which each player concedes at rate

$$\mu^* = c/v.$$

In this equilibrium, all the rent is dissipated in delay: each agent's expected gain is 0.

5. *Legitimate claims.* Building on our basic attrition model, we introduce the idea that one may perceive his claim as legitimate and condition his concession rate on this perception.

[1] We don't claim that this type of insight could not be obtained in a standard model. Typically, in a standard model, it would require two-dimensional types, making analysis difficult.

Formally, we assume that each player i receives a signal $z_i > 0$ that captures how strong/legitimate he perceives his claim to be. This strength may bear some relationship to his value v_i, but not necessarily – legitimacy can be orthogonal to value. Any war of attrition involving two agents i and j is thus characterized by a vector $X = (v_i, v_j, z_i, z_j)$, and as analysts, we define a distribution ω over these vectors, which characterizes a typical war of attrition. We assume that the distribution is symmetric with respect to the labeling i, j.

To fix ideas, we provide two examples of values and perceptions.

Case A. Legitimacy as a noisy signal of value. Assume that

$$v_i = v \cdot w_i \text{ and } z_i = y_i \cdot (v_i)^b,$$

where the variables w_i, w_j, y_i and y_j are independent and lognormally distributed (i.e., $\log w_i \sim \mathcal{N}(0, \sigma_w^2)$ and $\log y_i \sim \mathcal{N}(0, \sigma_y^2)$). In the special case where $b = 0$, perceptions of legitimacy are independent of value.

Case B. Legitimacy as a noisy signal of v_i/v_j. Values are distributed as above, but we now assume:

$$z_i = y_i \cdot (v_i/v_j)^b.$$

Thus, one difference with case A is that when $b > 0$, perceptions of legitimacy are now negatively correlated.[2]

6. *Behavioral assumption.* In principle, a player's behavior could depend on v_i and z_i, as well as on time. Our simplifying behavioral assumption is that a player's concession rate μ_i is constant over time, and that it depends on one's perceived strength, according to the following relationship:

$$\mu_i = \lambda_i/z_i,$$

where λ_i is a non-negative parameter. For each $\lambda_i > 0$, high perceived strength z_i translates into a low concession rate. The parameter λ_i is a strategic variable that captures the overall intensity with which player i concedes.

One might allow more degrees of freedom to each player, for example allowing a richer class of functions, say affine rather than linear in z_i. One might also allow even fewer degrees of freedom, by allowing only a limited number of values for λ_i.

7. *Expected values and equilibrium behavior.* Fix a λ played by the opponent (player j). We compute the expected payoff $G(x, \lambda)$ that player i gets when

---

[2] Alternatively, we could consider a case where perceptions of legitimacy are negatively correlated and independent of value. See Footnote 7.

he chooses $x\lambda$. We look for a symmetric equilibrium, that is, a concession intensity λ^* for which player i optimally sets $x = 1$. Using (18.1), we get:

$$G(x,\lambda) = Eg_i\left(x\lambda/z_i, \lambda/z_j\right) = E\left[\frac{v_i z_i/z_j}{x + z_i/z_j} - \frac{c}{\lambda}\frac{z_i}{x + z_i/z_j}\right] \quad (18.2)$$

We will shortly derive the only candidate λ^*. For now, we use (18.2) to write player i's equilibrium value $G^* \equiv G(1,\lambda^*)$ and discuss the various sources of gains and losses:

$$G^* = E\left[\frac{v_i z_i}{z_j + z_i}\right] - \frac{cEz_j}{\lambda^*}E\left[z_j\frac{z_i}{z_i + z_j}\right]/Ez_j.$$

The first term gives the expected gain, net of waiting costs. Ex ante, the probability of getting the object is $1/2$, and when perceptions are not correlated with values, that gain is equal to $Ev_i/2$. When z_i is positively correlated with value, the first term increases because player i is more likely to get it when his value is higher: the outcome is more efficient.

Waiting costs depend on the intensity λ^*, and on the distribution of strength perceptions. With independent strength perceptions, for example, higher dispersion reduces the last term because a higher ratio $z_i/(z_i + z_j)$ signals a lower perception z_j for the other (hence an earlier drop out), and that beneficial effect is stronger when dispersion is higher.[3] We shall come back to this.

To derive λ^* analytically, it will be convenient to define the ratio[4]

$$\rho = z_i/z_j$$

and the functions

$$\phi(y) \equiv E[v_i \mid \rho = y]/Ev_i \text{ and } \eta(y) \equiv E[z_i \mid \rho = y]/Ez_i.$$

Using (18.2), we obtain the following expression:

$$G(x,\lambda) = Ev_i E_\rho\frac{\rho\phi(\rho)}{x + \rho} - \frac{cEz_i}{\lambda}E_\rho\frac{\eta(\rho)}{x + \rho}.$$

---

[3] This is similar to what happens in a second-price auction, where dispersion also benefits the winner. Here, one only pays waiting costs until the point when the other drops out, and in events where one is inclined to wait longer than the other (high z_i/z_j), the drop-out time of the other tends to be smaller than average. Of course, an important difference with second-price is that, as in the all-pay auction, even losers incur waiting costs.

[4] We use this ratio rather than $z_i/(z_j + z_i)$ because given our lognormal distribution assumption for strength perceptions, the ratio ρ is also lognormally distributed.

First-order conditions require that $\frac{\partial G(1,\lambda^*)}{\partial x} = 0$, hence λ^* must satisfy:

$$\frac{cEz_i}{\lambda^*} = Ev_i \frac{E_\rho \rho \phi(\rho)/(1+\rho)^2}{E_\rho \eta(\rho)/(1+\rho)^2}.$$

8. *Discussion: The case of lognormal distributions.* With lognormal distributions, ρ is lognormally distributed as well, with variance denoted σ^2, and the functions ϕ and η take a simple form. This enables us to characterize the equilibrium payoff as a function of only two parameters: the variance of σ^2 and a second parameter (a, see below) that reflects the degree to which the ratio ρ signals a higher value for player i. We have:

Proposition: *Under either case* A *or* B, *there exists a such that*

$$\phi(\rho) = \alpha \rho^a \text{ and } \eta(\rho) = \beta \rho^{1/2}$$

where $\alpha = 1/E\rho^a$ and $\beta = 1/E\rho^{1/2}$.[5] Additionally: (i) when $b = 0$, $a = 0$; (ii) σ increases with b and is larger under case B *than under case* A; *(iii) when b is small relative to σ_w/σ, a increases with b and is larger under case* B *than under case* A.

The proof is in the Appendix. Intuitively, the coefficient $1/2$ in the expression of $\eta(\rho)$ arises from our symmetry assumption, and the coefficient a reflects the degree to which ρ is correlated with player i's value. When $b > 0$ and when z_i is not too noisy (i.e., σ not to large), a higher perception ratio ρ signals a higher value for player i, and the signal is stronger when b is larger. The signal is even stronger in case B, which is why a is larger in that case.

Given these simple expressions, one can fully characterize equilibrium payoffs. Define

$$h_\sigma(d) \equiv E\rho^d/(1+\rho)^2 \text{ and } H_\sigma(d) \equiv E\rho^d/(1+\rho).$$

We have:

$$\frac{cEz_i}{\lambda^*} = Ev_i \frac{\alpha h_\sigma(1+a)}{\beta h_\sigma(1/2)}.$$

The equilibrium payoff G^* can be simply written as a function of a and σ:[6]

$$G^*(a,\sigma) = \alpha(a,\sigma) H_\sigma(1+a) Ev_i \left[1 - \frac{h_\sigma(1+a)}{h_\sigma(1/2)} \frac{H_\sigma(1/2)}{H_\sigma(1+a)} \right].$$

---

[5] Under case A, $\sigma^2 = 2\sigma_y^2 + 2b^2\sigma_w^2$ and $a = b\sigma_w^2/\sigma^2$. Under case B, $\sigma^2 = 2\sigma_y^2 + 2(2b)^2\sigma_w^2$ and $a = 2b\sigma_w^2/\sigma^2$. Expressions for α and β are derived from $E\phi(\rho) = 1$ and $E\eta(\rho) = 1$. We have $\alpha = \exp{-a^2\sigma^2/2}$ and $\beta \exp \sigma^2/8 = \exp \sigma_z^2/2$.

[6] We write $\alpha(a,\sigma)$ as a reminder of the dependence of α on a and σ.

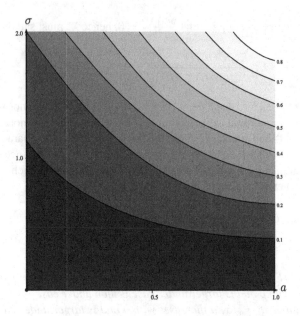

The graph shows how equilibrium values change as a function of a and σ, smaller equilibrium values corresponding to darker regions. It indicates the positive effect of a and σ on equilibrium values.

Intuitively, the parameter a has two effects. The first is on the expected efficiency of the final allocation, through the term $\alpha H(1 + a)$ (increasing in a). Higher a implies that the player who values the object most is more likely to get it. The second effect is on the concession rate. Since h is increasing, an increase in a provides incentives to reduce λ (hence longer delays): the pie is larger (through the effect on efficiency), and this provides incentives to reduce λ. Still, this reduction does not offset the efficiency gain. Overall, an increase in a increases efficiency.

A larger variance σ^2 also has a positive effect, as this makes very asymmetric realizations (high z_i and low z_j, or vice versa) more likely. These asymmetric situations enhance efficiency because they reduce inefficient delays.

Finally, what is the consequence of noisier perceptions of legitimacy (i.e., higher σ_y^2)? The effect may be positive through its effect on σ^2 (and the reduced delay). But noisier perceptions may also diminish a (because z_i/z_j becomes a poorer signal of value), and the overall effect may be negative. When $b = 0$, noisier perceptions are beneficial because z_i/z_j is not informative about value, so the only effect of noise is to reduce expected delay. When b increases and σ_w^2 is large, the marginal effect of noisier perceptions on delays is small; however, it reduces a (hence allocative efficiency is reduced), and the overall effect is negative.[7]

---

[7] We could also consider a variation of case B in which perceptions z_i are anticorrelated, but independent of value – $z_i = \eta_i(y_i/y_j)^b$. In that case, $a = 0$, and σ rises with the degree of anticorrelation b.

9. *Noisy concession rates.* In the basic model, our behavioral assumption is that the agent chooses an optimal concession rate μ, within the set of all concession rates. This is a weaker assumption than that made in traditional models, yet it may appear quite strong. It implies that each player's concession intensity or rate is finely attuned to his opponent's.

To reduce each player's ability to adjust to one another, one might assume that concession rates are noisy: when player i targets a constant concession rate μ_i, he actually implements the (constant) concession rate μ_i/z_i where z_i is lognormally distributed.[8] This noisy concession rate model belongs to the class of legitimate claim models that we have examined (with $\sigma_w = 0$ and $b = 0$). Said differently, one effect of the legitimacy perception z_i is to introduce noise into the "choice" of concession rate, and this noise is a source of rent. Intuitively, rents would be large if players could immediately agree on who concedes. With noise, there is some chance that perceptions are asymmetric, with one player much more inclined to concede quickly than the other, and this is a source of rent for players.

Further Comments

The war of attrition was originally formulated by Maynard Smith (1974), in an environment in which payoffs and costs are symmetric and known. The equilibrium strategy in that game is a mixed strategy. Bishop, Canning and Maynard Smith (1978) subsequently proposed a version of that game where payoffs from winning are randomly (and independently) determined at the start of the game, and where each player knows only his own payoff. Equilibrium behavior in that game determines for each player i a deterministic concession time $\tau_i(v_i)$ as a function of the payoff v_i. As in the auction problem, this concession time is determined as though each player could finely exploit the distribution over values. If values are drawn from an interval $[1,2]$, those getting a value close to 1 should concede immediately, while those getting a value close to 2 should remain tough almost indefinitely. Our modeling strategy allows for some dependence of concession time on v_i, but this dependence is limited: to the extent that higher value increases one's perception of strength, value may affect the propensity to concede through a smaller concession rate.

Our motivation is similar to that in the auction problem. When one desires a given object, it is likely that this interest is shared by others. Disentangling whether one's interest is common or idiosyncratic is difficult, and this is a reason to avoid defining a set of strategies that would (in the model) allow agents to easily surmount that difficulty. Addressing this issue in a standard framework could be done by assuming that values are positively correlated. But this would typically involve complex computations, especially because in that setup, there is no guarantee that a deterministic equilibrium (in which the concession date is a deterministic function of value) exists. Our restriction to

---

[8] We might also limit the number of comparisons that agents can make. For example, we might limit the choice to three strategies – $\mu = 0$, $\mu = c/z$, or $\mu = +\infty$.

a family of stochastic strategies (in which players choose a rate rather than a date) bypasses that difficulty.

> **Suggested research/application**. One obvious avenue would be to extend the models in this chapter to the case of three players. A possible variant would have players observe when there is a drop out, and adjust their concession intensities. This would give rise to a model in which each player's strategy is characterized by two intensities. A second variant would preclude players' observing drop outs until a single player remains. In either variant, one may expect the difficulties mentioned in Chapter 7 to arise. The game has the structure of an all-pay auction (losers pay the waiting cost for the duration that they stay in), and unless players get a reasonably accurate estimate of their relative strength, and use it appropriately, an equilibrium in which players use deterministic intensities is unlikely to arise, or at least, our family of linear strategies is likely to generate incentives to drop out almost immediately even for high valuation players.[9]

Appendix

Proof of Proposition. For two jointly normal distributions $X \sim \mathcal{N}(0,\sigma_x^2)$ and $Y \sim \mathcal{N}(0,\sigma_y^2)$, denote by $\widetilde{X}_y$ the distribution of X conditional on the event $Y = y$. The distribution $\widetilde{X}_y$ is also normal: $\widetilde{X}_y \sim \mathcal{N}(ay,\sigma^2)$ with $a = \frac{EXY}{\sigma_Y^2}$ and $\sigma^2 = \sigma_X^2 - \frac{(EXY)^2}{\sigma_Y^2}$. In addition, $Ee^{\widetilde{X}_y} = e^{ay+\sigma^2/2}$.

To compute $\eta(y) = E[z_i \mid z_i/z_j = y]$, we set $X = \ln z_i$ and $Y = \ln z_i/z_j$ and obtain:

$$\eta(y) \equiv Ee^{\widetilde{X}_{\ln y}} = e^{\sigma^2/2}y^a.$$

Since $EXY = \sigma_z^2 - E\ln z_i \ln z_j$ and

$$\sigma_Y^2 = E(\ln z_i - \ln z_j)^2 = 2\sigma_z^2 - 2E\ln z_i \ln z_j = 2EXY,$$

we get $a = 1/2$ as desired.

To compute $\phi(y) = E[v_i \mid z_i/z_j = y]$, we set $X = \ln v_i$ and $Y = \ln z_i/z_j$ and obtain as above:

$$\phi(y) \equiv Ee^{\widetilde{X}_{\ln y}} = e^{\sigma^2/2}y^a,$$

[9] See Bulow and Klemperer (1999) for an analysis of wars of attrition with many players and many prizes, in a setup (independent private values) that allows for an equilibrium in which exit dates are deterministic functions of value, and that generates perfect sorting of players (highest value player wins). As for the all-pay auction, efficiency properties of that mechanism rely on players finely attuning their exit strategies to the distribution over values.

but the expressions of a now differ. Under case A, we have $EXY = bE(\ln v_i)^2 = b\sigma_w^2$, implying that $a = b\sigma_w^2/\sigma^2$. Under case B, we have $EXY = 2b\sigma_w^2$, implying that $a = 2b\sigma_w^2/\sigma^2$.

References

Bishop, D. T., Cannings, C. and Maynard-Smith, J. (1978). The war of attrition with random rewards. *Journal of Theoretical Biology*, 74(3), 377–388.

Bulow, J. and Klemperer, P. (1999). The generalized war of attrition. *American Economic Review*, 89(1), 175–189.

Maynard-Smith, J. (1974). The theory of games and the evolution of animal conflict. *Journal of Theoretical Biology*, 47, 209–221.

CHAPTER 19

Unraveling

1. Sophistication allows one to precisely tailor behavior to circumstances. In strategic interactions, circumstances may include not only the particular payoff structure an agent faces, but also the behavior of other agents. For some interactions, sophistication improves players *ability to coordinate*, generating multiplicity of possible outcomes.[1] For other interactions, sophistication gives rise to competitive pressures or *unraveling effects*.

The two-person Nash demand game provides a simple illustration of the multiple ways in which players may coordinate in a strategic interaction. There is a pie of given size, S, to be shared, and each makes a demand. If demands are compatible, each gets his demand. If incompatible, the pie is lost. In this game, *any* sharing (x_1, x_2) of the pie (such that $x_1 + x_2 = S$) is an equilibrium outcome.

But players' ability to adjust to one another does not necessarily generate multiple outcomes. The centipede game illustrates the competitive pressures that sophistication creates. In this game, the size of the pie increases over time, and the first to exit gets a larger share of the pie, while the other gets the remainder. Thus there is a joint incentive to wait to enlarge the size of the pie along with a private incentive to exit first, driving both players to exit immediately.

2. In both examples, one may feel that adjustment to the other's behavior is too easily achieved, especially since equilibrium analysis is silent about how equilibrium outcomes come about. A more realistic description of the interaction may thus rely on limiting each player's ability to adjust to others' behavior. This can be done by assuming that agents tremble in making decisions, or by introducing uncertainty on the exact size of the pie or asymmetries in information. As is well known,[2] such imperfections may drastically reduce coordination possibilities in the Nash demand game, and the model then typically generates a single prediction.

In the context of the centipede game, one expects that reducing sophistication will reduce private incentives to exit before the other – smoothing

---

[1] This is the topic of Chapter 20.
[2] See Nash (1953) and Carlson (1991).

competitive pressures, at least to some extent. One purpose of this chapter is to affirm that intuition. Another purpose is to propose a simple model of limited sophistication, based on direct strategy restrictions.

3. *A simple centipede game.* We consider a pie growing linearly over time. The pie stops growing as soon as a player exits, at which point the game terminates and the pie is shared. The player who exits first gets a larger share of the pie.[3]

Formally, the pie at date t has size St, and we denote by a the share of the agent who exits first $(a > 1/2)$.[4] The other player gets the remainder (a share of size $1 - a$). We also denote by $v_i(t_i, t_j)$ player i's payoff when the exit dates chosen are t_i and t_j. To avoid technical difficulties we assume discounting; there is a discount factor, but we take it to be arbitrarily close to 1.[5] Over the range of relevant dates, and letting $\rho = (2a - 1)/a$, we thus have:

$$v_i(t_i, t_j) = aS[\min(t_i, t_j) - \Delta(t_i, t_j)] \text{ with}$$
$$\Delta(t_i, t_j) = 0 \text{ if } t_i < t_j \text{ and}$$
$$= \rho t_j \text{ if } t_j < t_i.$$

The term $\min(t_i, t_j)$ reflects the joint incentive to set high exit dates. The term $\Delta(t_i, t_j)$ reflects the penalty from exiting last. The penalty increases over time, and that penalty is smaller when a is close to $1/2$. When players are allowed to choose exit dates with arbitrary precision, this game has a unique equilibrium in which both exit immediately.[6]

4. *Strategy restrictions and payoffs.* To limit players' ability to adjust to one another, we assume that even when a player *targets* a particular exit date λ_i, his actual exit date t_i is stochastic: t_i is a function $\mathbf{t}(\lambda_i, \tau_i)$ of the target λ_i and a random component τ_i, where each τ_i is drawn independently from a distribution with density h, and cumulative distribution H. In the first part of this chapter, we assume that the noise term is additive:

$$t_i = \mathbf{t}(\lambda_i, \tau_i) = \lambda_i + \tau_i,$$

and in later computations, we assume that each τ_i is exponentially distributed with the same parameter $1/\mu$:

$$H(\tau_i) = 1 - \exp{-\tau_i/\mu} \text{ for } \tau_i \geq 0, H(\tau_i) = 0 \text{ otherwise.}$$

---

[3] This is a continuous time version of the centipede game. The centipede game was originally introduced by Rosenthal (1981). See Brunnermeier and Morgan (2010) for a continuous time version. This game is also called a preemption game: there are two shares available, and when you exit first you preempt the other players and get the larger share.

[4] We assume equal sharing when both exit at the same date, but under the assumptions to be made, this event will have probability 0.

[5] This ensures that payoffs remain bounded, and that for any discount factor δ, there is an upper bound on the termination date.

[6] The form of penalty is not important. We briefly discuss other payoff structures in Section 9.

The parameter μ reflects noise in decision making. A plausible interpretation of this noise is that a player can be in two possible states of mind: one in which he is inclined not to exit (i.e., prior to λ_i) and a second in which he thinks that he should exit (i.e., after λ_i), but doesn't exit with certainty: he exits with probability dt/μ per period of time dt. With this interpretation in mind, the additive noise τ_i seems natural.

For each player i, a target date λ_i generates a distribution over exit dates t_i. We denote by $V_i(x, \lambda)$ the expected payoff obtained by player i when he targets date $\lambda + x$ while the other targets date λ:

$$V_i(x, \lambda) \equiv E_{\tau_i, \tau_j} v_i(\lambda + x + \tau_i, \lambda + \tau_j)$$

5. *Equilibrium.* We are looking for a symmetric equilibrium, that is, a target date λ^* such that neither player wishes to select a different target date, or equivalently such that $V_i(x, \lambda^*)$ is maximized at $x = 0$. Payoffs being proportional to aS, we normalize aS to 1. We have:

$$V_i(x, \lambda) = \lambda + E\min(x + \tau_i, \tau_j) - \rho \int (\lambda + \tau_j) h(\tau_j)(1 - H(\tau_j - x)) d\tau_j.$$

In equilibrium, the target date λ^* satisfies $\frac{\partial V_i(0, \lambda^*)}{\partial x} = 0$, implying that:[7]

$$\rho \left(\lambda^* + E[\tau \mid \tau_1 = \tau_2] \right) = E\left[\frac{1 - H}{h} \,\Big|\, \tau_1 = \tau_2 \right]. \tag{19.1}$$

The right-hand side is the benefit from a marginal increase in the target date, which exploits the fact that the other player's exit date is dispersed, hence possibly higher (when the distribution is concentrated, h is large and this term is small). The left-hand side is the marginal cost of increasing the target date.

For an exponential distribution with parameter $1/\mu$ we get:[8]

$$\lambda^* = \frac{2 - \rho}{2\rho} \mu.$$

The expression reflects the two forces at work. For ρ close to 0, the private incentive to exit before the other player is weak, because there is not much to gain from early exit. When μ is large, these incentives are even weaker, because getting the larger share with meaningful probability requires a substantial (and costly) decrease in the target date.

6. *Noisy instruments and incentives to delay.* As discussed in Chapter 4, one can think of each agent being endowed with a set of instruments that enables

---

[7] Differentiating the above expression yields $\int h(\tau)(1 - H(\tau)) d\tau = \rho \int (\lambda + \tau)(h(\tau))^2 d\tau$, hence the desired conclusion. Note that this is a necessary condition for equilibrium. For the distributions we consider, the local condition is sufficient.

[8] For the exponential distribution, $\frac{1-H}{h} = \mu$ and $E[\tau \mid \tau_1 = \tau_2] = \mu/2$.

234   **Ignorance and Uncertainty**

him to parse the environment and adjust to it. From an ex ante perspective, the pair (λ, μ) defines a mixed strategy $\sigma^{\lambda,\mu}$ over possible exit dates, and we have just examined the consequence of restricting each player's strategy to the family

$$\Sigma^{\mu} = \{\sigma^{\lambda,\mu}\}_{\lambda}.$$

Each strategy $\sigma^{\lambda,\mu}$ can be represented as a cumulative distribution $F^{\lambda,\mu}$ over exit dates. The figure below shows the functions $F^{\lambda,\mu}(t)$ for $\mu = 2$ and for various targets λ.

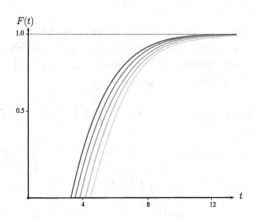

When $\mu = 0$, $\{F^{\lambda,\mu}\}_{\lambda}$ is a family of step functions. When each player has this family available, unraveling is extreme and leads to immediate exit. As μ gets larger, the functions $F^{\lambda,\mu}(.)$ get flatter, and unraveling weakens.

Intuitively, randomness in the *other's action* generates incentives to delay exit, and this effect is sufficient to weaken unraveling. To see why, assume that only player 2's exit date is subject to noise ($\mu_1 = 0$ and $\mu_2 = \mu > 0$). When player 2 targets λ, the optimal exit date t^* for player 1 satisfies:[9]

$$t^* = \frac{1 - H(t^* - \lambda)}{\rho \; h(t^* - \lambda)}.$$

For exponential distributions, $t^* = \mu/\rho$ independently of the target date λ.[10]

Another consequence of noise is randomness in one's *own action*: a player should take this into account in setting his target, as on average, his exit date occurs $E\tau = \mu$ after the target. Anticipating this delay, the target should be

---

[9] A marginal increase of dt yields a gain dt in events where $\lambda + \tau_2 > t$, and a loss $\rho th(\tau)dt$ for τ such that $\lambda + \tau = t$, hence the first-order condition $1 - H(t - \tau) = \rho th(t - \lambda)$.

[10] Similarly, in response to a deterministic exit date t, the optimal target is λ^* such that $\rho t = H(t - \lambda^*)/h(t - \lambda^*)$. Combined with the expression for t^*, we obtain that $H(t^* - \lambda^*) = 1/2$. When the distribution is exponential, we obtain $t^* - \lambda^* = \mu Ln2$, hence $\lambda^* = \mu(1/\rho - Ln2) > 0$.

reduced. Expression (19.1) reflects this component, and shows that in the symmetric equilibrium the target is reduced in equilibrium by $E[\tau \mid \tau_1 = \tau_2] = \mu/2$, hence only half of the expected individual delay μ.

7. *Multiplicative noise.* We provided a motivation for additive noise, but other sources of noise seem equally plausible. The previous analysis suggests that the parameter $\eta \equiv \frac{\mu(2-\rho)}{2\rho}$ should drive the extent of delay, and the agent might wish to adjust his target based on his perception of η. In that case, multiplicative noise about perceptions of η seems plausible, and the relevant model might be

$$t_i = \mathbf{t}(\lambda_i, \eta_i, \tau_i) = \lambda_i \eta_i + \tau_i$$

where the coefficients η_i are drawn independently from a lognormal distribution ($\log \eta_i \sim \mathcal{N}(0, \sigma^2)$). We denote by H^m the cumulative distribution of η_i and by h^m its density.

Multiplicative noise on the exit date may qualitatively alter the outcome. In the additive noise case, the incentive to delay eventually vanishes for large exit dates, because the penalty $\Delta(t_i, t_j)$ becomes large compared to the magnitude of the noise, explaining why target dates have the same order of magnitude as μ.

In contrast, with multiplicative noise, the incentive to delay exit does not vanish for large exit dates, because the randomness in the other's exit date is larger for large exit dates. We illustrate this by ignoring the additive noise (i.e., $\tau_i \equiv 0$), and by computing the expected payoff $V_1^m(x, \lambda)$ for player 1 when his target is $x\lambda$, while the other's target is λ. Player 1 gets $\lambda \min(x\eta_1, \eta_2)$ and he suffers a penalty of $\rho \lambda \eta_2$ when $x\eta_1 > \eta_2$. Thus we have:

$$V_1^m(x, \lambda) = \lambda [E \min(x\eta_1, \eta_2) - \rho \int \eta(1 - H^m(\eta/x))h^m(\eta)d\eta].$$

Consequently, incentives are independent of λ, and it is immediate that when ρ is below some threshold ρ^*,[11] $\frac{\partial V_1^m(1,\lambda)}{\partial x} > 0$ for all λ, demonstrating that players wish to increase their target date indefinitely – competitive pressures completely vanish.[12] The next figure shows the locus of ρ^* for lognormal noise, as a function of the standard deviation σ.[13]

---

[11] Differentiating the above expression, one obtains $\rho^* = \int \eta h(\eta)(1 - H(\eta))d\eta / \int \eta^2(h(\eta))^2 d\eta$.

[12] Of course, with a fixed discount factor, this incentive to set the target date above the other would vanish for sufficiently large targets, and we would find an equilibrium target λ^*. This target would decrease as players become more impatient.

[13] Our analysis ignores the possibility that both choose the target $\lambda_i = 0$. In the absence of additive noise, this target would be implemented without noise, and could constitute an equilibrium. Additive noise, however, would preclude an equilibrium with immediate exit. We omit this issue in the rest of this chapter.

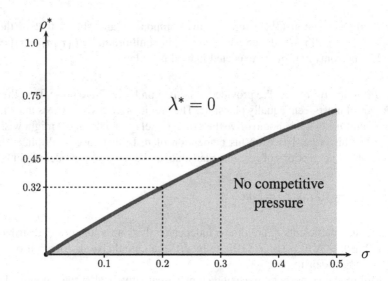

8. *End game effects.* The structure of noise is important and may hinge on how the game is framed. If the game exogenously terminates at date T, and if players are perfectly aware of that termination date, it seems plausible that the noise in exit dates vanishes as players approach the terminal date. An expression for exit dates consistent with this constraint is then:

$$t_i = \mathbf{t}(\lambda_i, \eta_i, T) = \frac{\eta_i \lambda_i T}{1 + \lambda_i \eta_i} \tag{19.2}$$

where η_i is lognormally distributed (i.e., $\log \eta_i \sim \mathcal{N}(0, \sigma^2)$) and $\lambda_i \in (0, \infty)$.
   In the absence of noise ($\eta_i = 1$), the exit date would be a fraction

$$\phi_i \equiv \lambda_i / (1 + \lambda_i)$$

of the total game duration T. The actual exit date is a random fraction of the total duration T, obtained by assuming that λ_i is implemented with noise.
   Proceeding as before, we compute the equilibrium target λ^*, or equivalently, the equilibrium fraction $\phi^* = \lambda^*/(1 + \lambda^*)$. That fraction captures the competitive pressure – when $\phi^* = 0$, these pressures are extreme, and when $\phi^* = 1$, they are completely absent. The figure on the next page shows how ϕ^* varies as a function ρ, for $\sigma = 0.2$ and $\sigma = 0.3$.
   We see from the figure that as ρ decreases, the competitive pressure starts weakening at $\rho^*(\sigma)$ (as defined in the previous section). Because of the presence of an end date, the competitive pressures no longer fully vanish as soon as ρ falls below $\rho^*(\sigma)$, but only do so gradually as ρ decreases below $\rho^*(\sigma)$.

9. *Other payoff structures.* In the centipede game defined in Section 3 above, the loss from late exit (as compared to early exit) grows linearly over time. One might imagine interactions (see below) for which this loss remains constant

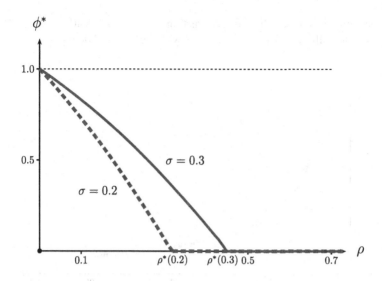

over the course of the interaction: the player who exits first gets a bonus G, while the other suffers a penalty L. Formally, letting $\Delta = G + L$, this yields the following payoff structure:

$$v_1(t_1, t_2) = \begin{cases} G + aS\min(t_1, t_2) & \text{if } t_1 < t_2 \\ G + aS\min(t_1, t_2) - \Delta & \text{if } t_2 < t_1 \end{cases}$$

We consider the noise structure defined above (see (19.2)) with a terminal date T large compared to Δ. For any target fraction φ, we now define the parameter $\gamma = T(1 - \phi)$, which represents the length of the end game.

As the target fraction ϕ decreases from 1, the dispersion in exit dates increases, and for γ large enough, the dispersion is large enough to provide players with incentives to delay exit. In equilibrium, exit dates are thus pushed toward the terminal date T in equilibrium, until some date $T - \gamma^*$, which we calculate next.

To quantify γ^* simply, we use the approximation $1 - \phi \simeq 1/\lambda$ and obtain:

$$t_i \simeq T - \gamma_i/\eta_i.$$

γ_i is a strategic variable for player i that represents the length of the end game, *as targeted by player i*. The term γ_i/η_i corresponds to a noisy implementation of that target. As before, we define player 1's expected gain $V_1(x, \gamma)$ when he targets $x\gamma$ and the other targets γ:

$$V_1(x, \gamma) = T - \gamma E\max(x/\eta_1, 1/\eta_2) + \Delta\Pr(x/\eta_1 > 1/\eta_2) - L.$$

This yields a simple expression for the equilibrium length γ^* of the end game. This length γ^* depends only on Δ and the distribution of the noise. It is independent of the length of the interaction, and grows linearly with Δ. The figure below illustrates how γ^*/Δ varies with the standard deviation σ.[14]

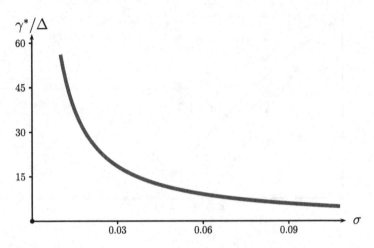

From the figure, we see that even very small noise can seriously suppress unraveling.

10. *Application to finite duration repeated games.* Consider a prisoner's dilemma game played in continuous time until a terminal date T. The payoff structure below describes the flow payoff to the players as a function of the actions currently played (either *C*ooperate or *D*efect):

	C	D
C	$1,1$	$-L,G$
D	$G,-L$	$0,0$

with $G > 1$ and $L > 0$. We assume that when a player defects, his defection is detected with certainty after a lapse of time of d, leading to mutual defection for the rest of the interaction. We are interested in the date t_i at which a player initiates defection. As in the centipede game, both players have a joint interest in choosing late defection dates, but each has a private incentive to defect before the other.

Formally, we look for an equilibrium in which players targets a defection date. The payoff that player 1 obtains as a function of defection dates t_1 and t_2 is:

$$v_1(t_1,t_2) = \begin{cases} \min(t_1,t_2) + G\min(t_2 - t_1, d) & \text{if } t_1 < t_2 \\ \min(t_1,t_2) - L\min(t_1 - t_2, d) & \text{if } t_2 < t_1 \end{cases}$$

[14] We have $\gamma^*/\Delta = \int \eta(h(\eta))^2 d\eta / \int (1/\eta)(h(\eta))(1 - H(\eta)) d\eta$.

The temptation to defect before the other is thus bounded by $(G + L)d$, which makes this game akin to the centipede game examined in the previous section: when the target is implemented with noise, then, even with tiny noise, unraveling is limited. Additionally, the length of the end game (during which players defect) is independent of the duration (T) of the game, and it increases with $(G+L)d$. In other words, that length increases with the stakes (how much one gains from exiting first, how much one loses when the other exits first) and the duration d needed to detect the deviation. The exact characterization is left for future research.

11. *Comparison with a standard Bayesian model.* An alternative modeling strategy might add noise to model parameters, say the share a, with agents observing a noisy signal a_i of a, and assume that each chooses optimally an exit date as a function of the signal a_i received.[15] Our proposed modeling strategy differs in that we do not try to provide a rational justification for each possible exit date that the agent picks. We leave some aspects of decision making unmodeled, arguing only that the exit dates may be subject to shocks. Nevertheless, exit dates are not assumed to be arbitrary. They are driven by realized welfare comparisons on the agent's part, through the optimal choice of the target λ_i.

Said differently, Bayesian models try to endogenize the structure of mistakes that agents make, taking as given the structure of their signals, and assuming that agents can exploit arbitrarily finely these signals, as though they knew precisely the process that generated the signals. In contrast, we make no attempt to endogenize the structure of mistakes, and instead focus on the implications that plausible noise structures have on strategic behavior. We do so for several reasons. We are skeptical of what can fruitfully be endogenized or rationalized as far as mistakes are concerned: the source of mistakes presumably lies in what agents observe or perceive, and we seldom have access to these perceptions. Furthermore, the agents are not likely to have access to the details of the process that generates their perceptions. Also, mistakes need not always be rationalized within the model: one may construct parsimonious models that do not adhere strictly to the Bayesian methodology and, nevertheless, explore strategic consequences of noisy perceptions.

There is another advantage of our approach. One message from this chapter is that the form of the noise may largely shape a model's prediction. One may, of course, rely on perception or psychometric studies to uncover which are the most relevant. But by considering various forms of noise, one may discover which forms lead to predictions that are consistent with our intuitions (or with experimental data). In Section 9, the prediction is that the equilibrium length of the end game is an increasing function of the stake Δ. With additive

---

[15] Brunnermeier and Morgan (2010), for example, examine a similar game, assuming that the date at which the cake starts growing above 0 is random, and that agents observe noisy signals of that starting date.

noise, we would obtain a threshold Δ^* above which the game unravels back to the start of the game, and below which players stay in for most of the game. We find the prediction obtained from the multiplicative noise structure appealing.

Further Comments

The centipede game was originally proposed by Rosenthal (1981). It provides a simple illustration of the strength of backward induction. The finitely repeated prisoner's dilemma and the chain store game (Selten (1978)) are two other examples of games in which backward induction plays a key role in generating somewhat implausible predictions.

In these three games, noise in decision making reduces the strength of backward induction, and generates predictions more in accord with experimental evidence and intuition. For example in the finitely repeated prisoner's dilemma, one expects that subjects do not defect at all dates, and that their propensity to remain cooperative depends on the payoff structure considered (the benefits from mutual cooperation, the gain from defecting, and the loss from being cooperative against an opponent who defects), in the same way that we expect large exit dates when a is close to $1/2$ or ρ close to 0.[16]

Rosenthal (1981) explores the fragility of backward induction arguments to the introduction of noise in decision making. In justifying such departures from "full rationality," he writes:

"Although a player may not consciously intend to randomize [...] it may be that for some reason his intention is not realized [...] If players with preceding moves realize that this may be the case, they would be wise to consider it when making their choices."

Rosenthal thus calls for introducing noisy decisions, but decisions still driven by self-interest. Implementing these two considerations simultaneously is a challenge. How should one model mistakes? How should one model the force toward self-interest? If one sees a move that seems unexpected, should this be viewed as evidence that further unexpected moves are to be expected, or should this be viewed as a one-time mistake, inconsequential to figure the benefits of each alternative available?

These considerations lie at the heart of the reputation literature,[17] which proposed (i) a special structure on mistakes, assuming that with some small probability behavior is determined exogenously (say, an agent never exits) and (ii) a special way of modeling the force toward self-interest: if the agent's behavior is not determined exogenously, then he must be "fully rational" – that is, exploiting to a maximal degree the structure of the model.

Rosenthal follows a different path. He proposed that the decision is subject to a random component, drawn independently at each date, but driven by the

---

[16] See Embrey, Fréchette and Yuksel (2016) for experimental evidence.
[17] See Chapter 13 and Milgrom and Roberts (1982) for example.

utility differences between the alternatives available at that date, where the utility is computed taking into account the mistakes that the agent and others might make in the future.[18]

Our modeling strategy falls in neither category. We do not examine incentives at each date, calculating what each believes based on hypothetical presumptions about what could have led to the other not exiting so far; nor do we presume the existence of various types of players, some of whom are crazy or altruistic, while others are perfectly rational; nor do we tailor the magnitude of mistakes made in each round to the correct value comparisons that would be performed in that round, as proposed by Rosenthal. Our family of noisy decision rules directly embodies the two concerns above, i.e., the need to introduce some randomness in decision making and to introduce self-interest.

Finally, this chapter (as well as the other chapters in which we consider noisy strategies) is related to the literature that introduces noise to capture evolutionary pressure (Foster and Young (1990)), or incomplete learning (Roth and Erev (1995)).[19] *One interpretation of this chapter is that equilibrium in noisy strategies is a shortcut to predict behavior in interactions where learning remains incomplete.*

Further research. One could examine various extensions, varying the number of players involved, and relaxing the assumption that the termination date is known with certainty. One could, for example, define the exit function $\mathbf{t}(\lambda_i, \eta_i, T_i)$ where T_i is a noisy estimate of the terminal date, and analyze the effect of all players missing the true termination date (either the pie is lost, or shared equally). The analysis could provide insight about the effect of the number of players on the duration of the end game in the prisoner's dilemma. It might also provide insight about the Dutch auction and the effect of setting a public reserve price: with several objects sold, this game has the structure of a centipede game,[20] and the reserve price, if public, plays the role of a termination date.[21]

---

[18] McKelvey and Palfrey (1995,1998) elaborate on this idea to define a quantal response equilibrium. In dynamic games, the logic of quantal response applied at each node of the game (rather than ex ante over all dynamic strategies) would be to introduce *independent* noise at each date.

[19] See also Gale et al. (1993).

[20] The Dutch auction is a descending-price auction in which the bidder who exits first gets the object. If there are K objects sold to N bidders, each of whom has the same valuation v for the object, and if, as soon as one bidder exits, others follow immediately, the first mover gets one object with certainty, while the others get it with probability $\rho = (K - 1)/(N - 1)$. This game has the structure of a centipede game (the pie increases linearly once the price reaches v).

[21] If the reserve is not public, players may only have a noisy estimate of that termination date, and, therefore, may risk losing the pie altogether. Other possible extensions include: (i) examining the incentive to exit after the first exit (in the spirit of Bulow and Klemperer (1994)); and (ii) dealing with the case that exit by others is learned with a random delay.

References

Bulow, J. and Klemperer, P. (1994). Rational frenzies and crashes. *Journal of Political Economy*, 102(1), 1–23.

Brunnermeier, M. K. and Morgan, J. (2010). Clock games: theory and experiments. *Games and Economic Behavior*, 68, 532–550.

Carlsson, H. (1991). A bargaining model where parties make errors. *Econometrica*, 59(5), 1487–1496.

Embrey, M., Fréchette, G. and Yuksel, S. (2016). Cooperation in the finitely repeated prisoner's dilemma, working paper.

Foster, D. and Young, H. P. (1990). Stochastic evolutionary game dynamics. *Theoretical Population Biology*, 38(2), 219–232.

Gale, J., Binmore, K. G., and Samuelson, J. (1995). Learning to be imperfect: the ultimatum game. *Games and Economic Behavior*, 8, 56–90.

McKelvey, R. D. and Palfrey, T. R. (1995). Quantal response equilibria in normal form games. *Games and Economic Behavior*, 7, 6–38.

McKelvey, R. D. and Palfrey, T. (1998). Quantal response equilibria for extensive form games. *Experimental Economics*, 1, 9–41.

Milgrom, P. and Roberts, J. (1982). Predation, reputation, and entry deterrence. *Journal of Economic Theory*, 27, 280–312.

Nash, J. (1953). Two person cooperative games. *Econometrica*, 21, 128–140.

Rosenthal, R. (1981). Games of perfect information, predatory pricing, and the chain store paradox. *Journal of Economic Theory*, 25, 92–100.

Roth, A. and Erev, I. (1995). Learning in extensive-form games: experimental data and simple dynamic models in the intermediate term. *Games and Economic Behavior*, 8(1), 164–212.

Selten, R. (1978). The chain-store paradox. *Theory and Decision*, 9, 127–159.

CHAPTER 20

Coordination

1. Sophistication allows one to tailor behavior to circumstances. For some interactions, sophistication improves players' *ability to coordinate*, generating multiplicity in possible outcomes.

The Nash demand game provides a simple illustration of the multiple ways in which players may coordinate in a strategic interaction. There is a pie of given size, S, to be shared, and each makes a demand x_i. If demands are compatible, each gets his demand. If not compatible the pie is lost. In this game, *any* sharing (x_1, x_2) such that $x_1 + x_2 = S$ is an equilibrium. In formal terms, if $B_i(x_j)$ denotes the best response of i when player j chooses x_j, we have, for any $x \in (0, S)$:

$$B_i(x) = S - x, \text{ hence } B_i'(x) = -1$$

2. In this example, one may feel that a player's adjustment to the other's behavior or to the size of the pie S is too easily achieved, especially since equilibrium analysis is silent about how equilibrium outcomes come about. A more realistic description may thus rely on limiting each player's ability to adjust to the other. This can be done by assuming that agents tremble in making decisions, or by introducing uncertainty on the exact size of the pie. As is well known, such imperfections may drastically limit coordination in the Nash demand game, and the model then typically generates a single prediction.[1]

3. Other common examples are coordination games. Consider the following class of games involving two players. Each player i has the option of a safe alternative (L) yielding 0 or a risky alternative (H), yielding either $r - c_i$ or $-c_i$, depending on whether (or not) the other side also takes the risky alternative. The payoffs are summarized in the following matrix.

	H	L
H	$r - c_1, r - c_2$	$-c_1, 0$
L	$0, -c_2$	$0, 0$

---

[1] This chapter is related to the global game literature. This will be discussed in Section 7 and at the end of this chapter.

When $r < c_i$, the risky alternative is thus dominated for player i. We are interested in a class of situations where r is random with density function g and cumulative distribution G. We assume that g remains almost flat over an arbitrarily large support.[2]

A plausible strategy in this game is to play H whenever r is sufficiently large, that is, greater than a threshold x_i.[3] We examine the game where players choose thresholds and denote by $v_i(x_1, x_2)$ player i's expected payoff when (x_1, x_2) is chosen.

When both players choose the same threshold x, player i's expected payoff is

$$v_i(x,x) = \int_{r>x} (r - c_i)g(r)dr,$$

so players have a joint incentive to decrease x down to $\max c_i$.

Despite this joint incentive, *any* pair $(x_1, x_2) = (x, x)$ with $x > \max c_i$ is a Nash equilibrium. In mathematical terms, if we denote by B_i the best response of player i, for any $x > \max c_i$, we have

$$B_i(x) = x \text{ hence } B_i'(x) = 1$$

As in the Nash demand game, the multiplicity hinges on each player's ability to perfectly adjust his strategy to the other's behavior.

To check individual incentives formally, assume that player 2 chooses x. Choosing $x_1 < x$ rather than x is costly because when $r \in (x_1, x)$, player 1 is the only one to play H: he incurs the cost c_i without getting any benefit, hence an expected cost $c_1(G(x) - G(x_1))$. Choosing $x_1 > x$ rather than x is costly as well because when $r \in (x, x_1)$, only player 2 plays H, so player 1 could gain $r - c_1 > x - c_1$ in each of these events. In summary we have:

$$v_1(x_1, x) - v_1(x, x) = \begin{cases} -c_1(G(x) - G(x_1)) & \text{if } x_1 < x \\ -\int_x^{x_1} (r - c_1)g(r)dr & \text{if } x_1 > x \end{cases}$$

4. *Strategy restrictions.* To limit players' ability to precisely adjust behavior to one another, we assume that when a player targets a particular threshold λ_i, his actual threshold x_i is stochastic: x_i is a function $\mathbf{x}(\lambda_i, \eta_i)$ of the target λ_i and a random component η_i. We will focus primarily on the case where noise is additive:

$$x_i = \mathbf{x}(\lambda_i, \eta_i) \equiv \lambda_i + \eta_i,$$

---

[2] Technically, we assume that $\sup |g'|$ is small enough. In the main text, to simplify exposition, we also assume that g is constant over a large interval.

[3] Note that we exclude the strategy where a player chooses L always, hence also the equilibrium where both play L always. Our motivation is that this equilibrium is obviously non-robust: when r is very large, a tiny chance that the other picks H makes H attractive.

where the η_i's are drawn independently from a distribution with bounded support. We denote by f the density and F the cumulative distribution. One may interpret this noise as a tremble, or an inability to target precisely a particular threshold. Alternatively, it may reflect noise in the perception of r.[4]

One can think of other noise structures, and we examine one alternative in the Appendix:

$$x_i = \mathbf{x}(\lambda_i, \eta_i) \equiv c_i(1 + \eta_i \lambda_i),$$

where η_i is a positive and bounded random variable. λ_i is a markup on cost. The noise structure reflects an agent's limited ability to precisely estimate the markup on cost that makes playing H a safe strategy.

5. *Payoffs and best responses.* For each player, the strategic variable is λ_i. Each λ_i generates a distribution over the threshold x_i, and we may compute the expected payoff $V_i(\lambda_i, \lambda_j)$ associated with the targets λ_i and λ_j:

$$V_i(\lambda_i, \lambda_j) \equiv E v_i(x_1, x_2).$$

We look for an equilibrium in targets, that is, a pair $(\lambda_i^*, \lambda_j^*)$ such that, for each player i, the target λ_i^* is a best response to the other's target.

Our main observation is that, in equilibrium, noise eliminates the indeterminacy and flattens best response functions. That is, if we let $B_i(\lambda)$ denote the best response of player i to the target λ, and if we let $B(\lambda) = B_i(B_j(\lambda))$, we have:

Proposition 1: *There is a unique equilibrium, and for any λ such that $B(\lambda) = \lambda$, $0 < B'(\lambda) < 1$.*

The proof is in the Appendix, and we sketch here the intuition under the assumption that g is exactly flat. Given the expression for v_i, the first-order condition is then:

$$c_1 = E(x_1 \mid x_1 > x_2) \Pr(x_1 > x_2).$$

The left-hand side is the marginal saving on costs that a larger target generates. The right-hand side is the marginal cost due to lost coordination opportunities. Letting $\delta = \lambda_1 - \lambda_2$, this may also be written:

$$c_1 = \Phi(\lambda_1, \delta) \equiv \int (\lambda_1 + \eta) f(\eta) F(\delta + \eta) d\eta. \tag{20.1}$$

The main effect of noise is that, for any equilibrium (λ_1, λ_2), the difference δ pin downs a particular target λ_1 (and λ_2).[5] Furthermore, (20.1) implies that a

---

[4] If player i plays H when his perception $r_i = r + \varepsilon_i$ exceeds the threshold λ_i, he actually implements a noisy strategy: he plays H when $r > \lambda_i - \varepsilon_i$, which is formally equivalent to our formulation with $\eta_i \equiv -\varepsilon_i$.

[5] Without noise, at $\delta = 0$, λ_1 is indeterminate.

low λ_1 must be accompanied by a high δ. For player 2, the condition is $c_2 = \Phi(\lambda_2, -\delta) = \Phi(\lambda_1 - \delta, -\delta)$, which implies the opposite relationship between λ_1 and δ, by the same logic – one is ready to take risks (low λ_i) only if he is taking *less* risk than the other (λ_i higher than the other). The consequence is a unique equilibrium.[6]

Proposition 1 should not come as a surprise. Consider player 1 and assume he can target the threshold λ_1 accurately. When player 2's behavior is not noisy, player 1 wishes to set $\lambda_1 = \lambda_2$. If player 2's behavior becomes noisier ($x_2 = \lambda_2 + \eta$), the exact strategic choice λ_2 becomes less important from the perspective of player 1: if the noise term is large, player 1's response must be primarily driven by the characteristics of the noise term. So player 1's best response should be less sensitive to λ_2 as noise increases (even when player 1's behavior is not noisy – see Proposition 3).

6. *Equilibrium.* When $c_1 = c_2 = c$, we may use (20.1) to find the unique equilibrium:[7]

Proposition 2: *When* $c_1 = c_2 = c$, $\lambda_1^* = \lambda_2^* = \lambda^* = 2c - E[\eta_1 \mid \eta_1 > \eta_2]$.

This result is consistent with the global game literature, which typically focuses on the limit when the noise vanishes. In this case, $E[\eta_1 \mid \eta_1 > \eta_2]$ tends to 0, and agents choose the risky alternative when the gain r exceeds twice the cost c. The proposition demonstrates how noise affects decisions: players choose smaller thresholds. Mistakes have asymmetric consequences: the cost is linear in (own) downward mistakes, while it is quadratic in (own) upward mistakes, so, noise depresses targets. Said differently, noise (with respect to own decisions) calls for caution in choosing a target, but caution here means choosing the risky alternative H more often.

To conclude this section, we confirm the insight suggested above that multiplicity disappears with noise even when only one player is subject to noise:

Proposition 3: *Assume* $c_1 = c_2 = c$ *and only player 2's strategy is noisy. Equilibrium thresholds are unique and satisfy* $\lambda_2^* < \lambda_1^* < 2c$.

In line with the intuition above, noise induces player 2 to decrease his target below $2c$. Because player 1 is not subject to noise, the extent to which he decreases his target is less.

7. *Comparison with the global game literature.* This chapter is closely related to the global game literature. This literature prevents players from conditioning

---

[6] $B'(\lambda) < 1$ follows from differentiating totally the identity $c_1 = \Phi(B_1(\lambda_2), B_1(\lambda_2) - \lambda_2)$ and observing that Φ_1' and Φ_2' are positive.

[7] From (20.1) we get $c = \Pr(\eta_1 > \eta_2)(\lambda^* + E[\eta_1 \mid \eta_1 > \eta_2])$, hence the statement since $\Pr(\eta_1 > \eta_2) = 1/2$.

behavior on r by assuming each player observes a noisy signal of r, say $r_i = r + \varepsilon_i$. Thus, in effect, the strategy is a function of r_i, rather than r : players are restricted to random choice rules. There are differences, however: (i) we have focused on a family of strategies parameterized by a single parameter (the threshold), without attempting to endogenize the optimality of threshold strategies; (ii) as in Chapter 19, our analysis is not restricted to the case where noise is small.

Our perspective is that the use of threshold strategies is sufficiently reasonable that one can begin with a restriction to such strategies without endogenizing the restriction through assumptions on the noise structure (which are outside the agent's precise knowledge in any case). Focusing on threshold strategies, and taking the ex ante view, illuminates the primary reason why high multiplicity is nongeneric: noise flattens reaction functions.

8. *Dealing with many parameters or many actions.* One prediction of the global game literature is that players should coordinate on the "risk dominant" equilibrium.[8] Denoting u_i^a the payoff associated with action profile a, HH is the risk dominant equilibrium if:

$$(u_1^{HH} - u_1^{LH})(u_2^{HH} - u_2^{HL}) > (u_1^{LL} - u_1^{HL})(u_2^{LL} - u_2^{LH}).$$

In our setup, this gives the condition $(r - c_1)(r - c_2) > c_1 c_2$, that is:

$$c_1 + c_2 < r.$$

That players could coordinate on the risk dominant equilibrium in *any* 2*2 coordination game seems strong.[9] The mathematical condition is not involved, but it requires that players learn how to play the game as a function of all payoff parameters. Furthermore, generalization to more general classes of games involving more than two actions or more than two players is difficult.

We propose below another method, based on direct strategy restrictions. Our motivation is two-fold; (i) illustrate how players might deal with payoff structures that vary across many dimensions, while still restricting attention

---

[8] Risk dominance has been proposed as a selection criterion among Nash equilibria by Harsanyi and Selten (1988). When $r > \max c_1, c_2$, HH is a Nash equilibrium that payoff dominates LL, but it may not risk dominate LL.

[9] If the game is symmetric, that is, if $u_i^{a_i, a_j} = u_j^{a_j, a_i}$, the condition becomes $u_1^{HH} - u_1^{LH} > u_1^{LL} - u_1^{HL}$, or equivalently: $u_1^{HH} + u_1^{HL} > u_1^{LH} + u_1^{LL}$. This condition has a simple interpretation. It says that one need only maximize expected payoffs as if the other was randomizing with equal probability on each of his actions.

Unfortunately, if each player follows that rule of thumb in the asymmetric game, they won't end up playing the risk dominant equilibrium, nor possibly *any* equilibrium. Playing the risk dominant equilibrium requires that each player select an action according to the criterion above, and it may not be obvious for players that this criterion is the relevant one.

to a limited set of functions, parameterized by a single scalar λ_i for player i; and (ii) show that these strategy restrictions may play the same role as noise, making multiplicity nongeneric.

9. *Illustration.* Assume that costs c_1 and c_2 are drawn uniformly from $[0,1]$ and take r fixed, $r < 1$. Payoffs vary across two dimensions, but we constrain choice to a one-dimensional family of strategies. We assume that players choose L when H is dominated for at least one player (i.e., when either c_1 or c_2 is above r). Otherwise, each player evaluates each alternative $a_i \in \{H, L\}$ via some function $\phi^{\lambda_i}(a_i)$, and chooses the higher value alternative. To illustrate, we choose $\phi^{\lambda_i}(a_i)$ to be a weighted average of the smallest gain player i could receive under a_i and the highest welfare associated with that alternative a_i,[10] that is:

$$\phi_i^{\lambda_i}(H) \equiv (1 - \lambda_i)(-c_i) + \lambda_i(2r - c_1 - c_2)$$
$$\phi_i^{\lambda_i}(L) \equiv 0.$$

The parameter λ_i can be interpreted as the extent to which one weighs social welfare or fears the worst in choosing.

We refer to $A_i^{\lambda_i}$ as the domain where player i plays H,[11] and define the expected payoff $V_i(\lambda_1, \lambda_2)$ associated with the strategies λ_1 and λ_2:

$$V_1(\lambda_1, \lambda_2) = -E[c_1 \mid A_1^{\lambda_1}] \Pr\{A_1^{\lambda_1}\} + r \Pr\{A_1^{\lambda_1} \cap A_2^{\lambda_2}\}.$$

It is easy to check (see the Appendix) that one obtains a unique equilibrium (λ^*, λ^*) and that $\lambda^* \simeq 0.45$.[12] The following figure shows each domain $A_i^{\lambda^*}$ (the grey polygon for player 1 and the hatched for player 2). These domains determine the regions in which coordination (HH, LL) or miscoordination (LH, HL) occur.

10. *Discussion.* Miscoordination is not surprising: given the limited family of rules that each player compares, any interior equilibrium must involve some miscoordination. Had we looked for an optimal parameter λ_i using another

---

[10] Formally, for a general game with payoff structure $u_i(a)$, $\phi_i^{\lambda_i}(a_i) \equiv (1 - \lambda_i)\underline{w}_i(a_i) + \lambda_i \overline{w}_i(a_i)$ where $\underline{w}_i(a_i) = \min_{a_{-i}} u_i(a_i, a_{-i})$ and where, letting $w(a)$ denote the welfare (i.e., the sum of payoffs associated with a), $\overline{w}_i(a_i) \equiv \max_{a_{-i}} w(a_i, a_{-i})$.

[11] $A_i^{\lambda_i} = \{(c_1, c_2) \in [0,1]^2, c_i \leq \min(r, \lambda_i(2r - c_j)), c_j \leq r\}$.

[12] The equilibrium weight λ^* does not depend on r, because the distribution over costs is assumed to be uniform (other cost distributions would generate different equilibrium weights). Also note that both players are assumed to eliminate H when either c_1 or c_2 is above r. One could examine players with less sophistication who eliminate H when their own cost is above r, but not when the other's cost is above r. One can then check that λ^* would be smaller and equal to 0.32 when $2r < \max c_i$.

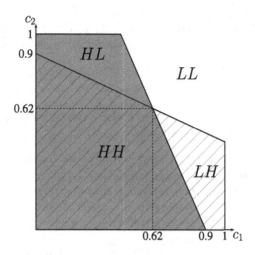

class of strategies, of the form, play H if and only if

$$c_i + \lambda_i c_j < r$$

or, had we looked for a larger class of strategies involving two parameters:

$$c_i + \lambda_i c_j < \lambda_i' r,$$

we might have found an equilibrium that always selects the risk dominant play (i.e., HH if and only if $c_1 + c_2 < g$, LL otherwise), with no miscoordination in equilibrium. But it is not *a priori* obvious that either of these is a reasonable family, nor that it is easy to learn what pair (λ_i, λ_i') is optimal within the larger class. The family of strategies that we consider seems reasonable, focused on a mixture of efficiency considerations and worst-case scenario.

One lesson from the exercise is that direct strategy restrictions may drastically reduce the set of equilibria, exactly as adding noise did: for any strategic choices (λ_i, λ_j) with $\lambda_i < 1$, strategies are misaligned. Misalignment and noise play a similar role: they induce miscoordination, so there cannot be a strategy pair (nor multiple strategy pairs) for which coordination is perfect (and from which deviations necessarily *create* miscoordination).[13] Miscoordination is *always* present and weakens incentives to adjust the stategic variable λ_i, thereby reducing the set of equilibria.

Further Comments

Beliefs and higher-order beliefs. This chapter is closely related to the global game literature. This literature often puts beliefs at the center of the analysis,

---

[13] Interestingly, for the strategy pair $\lambda_1 = \lambda_2 = 1$, strategies are perfectly aligned, and players coordinate on H if and only if HH is more efficient than LL and H is individually rational (i.e., $c_i \leq g$). Without noise, these strategies constitute an equilibrium.

emphasizing the importance of higher-order beliefs even when players get near-perfect information about the environment. For example, Morris and Shin (2003, page 90) write:

"We believe that the noise structures analyzed in global games are interesting because they represent a tractable way of generating a rich structure of higher-order beliefs. The analysis of global games represents a natural vehicle to illustrate the power of higher-order beliefs at work in applications."

Taking an ex ante perspective, and leaving aside questions related to the beliefs that agents might form conditional on their observations, this chapter illuminates the basic selection mechanism at work in these games: if one limits the set of strategies in a way that prevents perfect coordination, either through noisy strategies or direct strategy restrictions, one avoids the multiplicity of possible outcomes otherwise present.

Admittedly, reasoning about beliefs and showing that these games can be solved through iterated dominance arguments nicely illustrates "the power of higher order beliefs." Yet one may question whether this reasoning on beliefs – performed by the analyst to solve the game – is the reason that one expects players to use threshold strategies.

Global games versus isolated games. *One message of the global game approach is that there is value in analyzing an equilibrium rule for an entire class of games, rather than focusing on a single individual game.[14] This distinction between global or isolated games deserves elaboration. Our view is that any game in which some aspects of the environment are ignored is, in essence, a global game, or is modeled as such: the joint distribution over the underlying fundamentals and players' observations is meant to summarize the pool of strategic conditions considered. In modeling an auction, one typically defines a joint distribution over values. As emphasized in Chapter 3, this joint distribution is, in our view, meant to describe a class of auction situations, rather than a single isolated game situation.*

Also, while reasoning at the interim stage may provide an interesting selection argument, we believe that a selection argument based on local considerations alone is somewhat in conflict with the spirit of global games, that is, with the idea of capturing how agents might deal with a class of situations rather than an isolated situation. In our view, a first step in dealing with a class of games consists of identifying plausible rules to determine behavior across games (as we did in Section 9), rather than endogenizing optimal behavior pointwise, observation by observation. Taking a global perspective is useful in that it forces one (both the agent and the analyst) to think of rules that seem reasonable/plausible in a broadly defined environment.

[14] Carlsson and van Damme (1993) write: "The paper's main message is that something can be gained by moving from the conventional local analysis of individual games to a global analysis of classes of games: an equilibrium of a given game need not be consistent with an equilibrium rule for the entire class of games."

Simplicity and coordination. *Despite the above differences in interpretation, we are in agreement with the view in Morris and Shin (2000, 2003) that overly simplified models offer too many (and unrealistic) coordination possibilities to the agents.*[15] *Limiting implausible coordination can be done by enriching the environment or by restricting strategy sets (either through mistakes, through noisy observations of the environment, or through other plausible strategy restrictions).*

Suggested research/applications. We have examined the classic two-person coordination game in which one outcome (*HH*) Pareto dominates another (*LL*). One could examine extensions to cases where more players need to coordinate, or cases in which two coordination possibilities are available ($H^a H^a$) or ($H^b H^b$) and players have conflicting interests over the alternatives a and b.

We have examined in Section 9 a restricted family of strategies. Within that setup, one could examine the effect of less sophistication, either by dropping the assumption that player i removes strategies that are iteratively dominated (hence possibly playing H even though $c_j > r$, as suggested in Footnote 12) or by adding noise to perceptions of the other's cost.

Finally, while our restriction (driven by worst-case and welfare considerations) seems adapted to the class of coordination games we present, it is probably not well adapted to other classes of games such as almost zero-sum games where welfare considerations are probably not a salient driver of behavior. Broad strategic considerations probably shape the responses that players consider, and finding which considerations are relevant for which class of games is, we believe, an interesting challenge.

Appendix

Proof of Proposition 1. Let $\tilde{g}(\lambda_i, \eta) \equiv g(\mathbf{x}(\lambda_i, \eta))/Eg(\mathbf{x}(\lambda_i, \eta))$. Consider an equilibrium (λ_1, λ_2) and let $\lambda_1 - \lambda_2$. The first-order condition for player 1 is

$$c_1 = \Phi(\lambda_1, \delta) \equiv \int (\lambda_1 + \eta)\tilde{g}(\lambda_1, \eta)f(\eta)F(\delta + \eta)d\eta.$$

[15] Morris and Shin (2003, page 57) stated: "the apparent indeterminacy of beliefs in many models with multiple equilibria can be seen as the consequence of two modeling assumptions introduced to simplify the theory. First, the economic fundamentals are assumed to be common knowledge. Second, economic agents are assumed to be certain about others' behavior in equilibrium. Both assumptions are made for the sake of tractability, but they do much more besides. They allow agents' actions and beliefs to be perfectly coordinated in a way that invites multiplicity of equilibria." See also Morris and Shin (2000, page 140).

Let $\phi(\lambda) = \Phi(\lambda, 0)$. Since $\phi(\lambda)$ increases without bound, we can choose $\overline{\lambda}$ such that $\phi(\lambda) > \max_i c_i$ for all $\lambda \geq \overline{\lambda}$. Assume $\lambda_j > \overline{\lambda}$. Then the incentive condition for i requires $\lambda_i \leq \lambda_j$. But then the incentive condition for player j implies $c_j \geq \phi(\lambda_j)$ contradicting $\lambda_j > \overline{\lambda}$. So $\overline{\lambda}$ is an upper bound on λ_1, λ_2. Given this bound, the assumption on g, and the bound on the size of the noise, the argument provided in the main text holds.

For the multiplicative case, define $\widetilde{g}(\lambda_i, \eta) \equiv g(\mathbf{x}(\lambda_i, \eta)) E\eta/E(\eta g(\mathbf{x}(\lambda_i, \eta)))$, $\rho_i = c_i/c_j$ and $z_i = \delta_i/\delta_j$. The first-order condition for player 1 becomes:

$$E\eta = \Phi(\lambda_1, z_1, \rho_1) = \int (1 + \lambda_1 \eta) \eta \widetilde{g}(\lambda_1, \eta) f(\eta) F(\rho_1 - 1 + \rho_1 z_1 \eta) d\eta.$$

A similar argument proves the upper bound and uniqueness. One then easily gets $B_i'(\lambda_j) < z_i$, hence $B_1'(\lambda_2) B_2'(\lambda_2) < z_1 z_2 = 1$.

Proof of Proposition 3. Let $\Delta = \lambda_1 - \lambda_2$. For player 1, the first-order condition gives $c = \lambda_1 F(\Delta)$; while for player 2, the first-order condition gives $c = (1 - F(\Delta))(\lambda_2 + E[\eta_2 \mid \eta_2 > \Delta])$. Taking the difference yields $(\lambda_1 + \lambda_2) F(\Delta) > \lambda_2$, which cannot be satisfied when $\Delta \leq 0$. So $\Delta > 0$, implying $F(\Delta) > 1/2$ and $\lambda_1 = c/F(\Delta) < 2c$. Q.E.D.

Marginal effect of λ_1. When λ_1 increases, costs increase (by an amount equal to the expectation of costs taken over the darker domain), but the domain over which both play H expands.[16]

Let $\underline{x}(\lambda) = \max(0, 1 - 1/(2\lambda))$ and $\overline{x}(\lambda_1, \lambda_2) = \lambda_2(1 - \lambda_1)/(1 - \lambda_1\lambda_2)$. In the figure, $\underline{c}(\lambda_1) = \max(0, 2r\underline{x}(\lambda_1))$ is the cost level c_2 under which the constraint $c_1 \leq r$ binds, and $\overline{c}_i(\lambda_i, \lambda_j) = 2r\overline{x}(\lambda_j, \lambda_i)$ gives the coordinates of the point where the lines $c_i + \lambda_i c_j = 2r\lambda_i$ cross.

Computation of $V_i(\lambda_i, \lambda_j)$ and first-order condition. As suggested by the figure, the first-order condition requires the comparison of only two terms, which we now derive. We first compute the expected cost, denoted $C_1(\lambda_1, \lambda_2)$. Let $\underline{c}(\lambda) = 2r\underline{x}(\lambda)$ with $\underline{x}(\lambda) = \max(0, 1 - 1/(2\lambda))$. If $\underline{c}(\lambda) > 0$, this is the cost for which $c = \lambda(2r - c)$. We have:

$$C_1(\lambda_1, \lambda_2) = \int_0^{\underline{c}(\lambda_1)} \int_0^r c_1 dc_1 dc_2 + \int_{\underline{c}(\lambda_1)}^r \int_0^{\lambda_1(2r - c_2)} c_1 dc_1 dc_2.$$

We now compute the probability $Q(\lambda_1, \lambda_2)$ of coordination on HH. If the lines $c_i = \lambda_i(2g - c_j)$ cross outside the box $[0, r]^2$, then $A_i^{\lambda_i}$ either contains or is included in $A_i^{\lambda_j}$ so at least one player prefers to decrease his target to diminish cost. In equilibrium, the lines must thus cross within the box $[0, r]^2$. This

---

[16] The figure is drawn for $\lambda_1 = \lambda_2 = 0.52$ and $r = 0.9$, and shows an increase of λ_1 to 0.54.

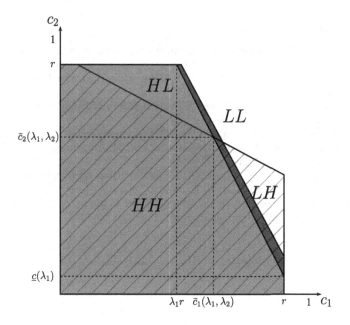

implies $\bar{c}_2(\lambda_1,\lambda_2) \geq \underline{c}(\lambda_1)$ and $Q(\lambda_1,\lambda_2)$ then has the following expression:

$$Q(\lambda_1,\lambda_2) = \int_0^{\underline{c}(\lambda_1)} \int_0^r dc_1 dc_2 + \int_{\underline{c}(\lambda_1)}^{\bar{c}_2(\lambda_1,\lambda_2)} \int_0^{\lambda_1(2r-c_2)} dc_1 dc_2$$
$$+ \int_{\bar{c}_2(\lambda_1,\lambda_2)}^r \int_0^{\max(2r-c_2/\lambda_2,0)} dc_1 dc_2.$$

We have $V_1(\lambda_1,\lambda_2) = -C_1(\lambda_1,\lambda_2) + rQ(\lambda_1,\lambda_2)$. Differentiation of V_1 with respect to λ_1 and the change of variable $x = c/2r$ yields

$$2\lambda_1 \int_{\underline{x}(\lambda_1)}^{\bar{x}} (1-x)^2 dx = \int_{\underline{x}(\lambda_1)}^{\bar{x}(\lambda_1,\lambda_2)} (1-x)dx \qquad (20.2)$$

with $\bar{x} = 1/2$. Simple calculations show that $\lambda^* = 0.45$ solves (20.2).[17] For the case suggested in Footnote 12, the expression of C_1 changes because player 1 may play H even when $c_2 \in (r,1)$. As a result, player 1 incurs costs up to $c_2 = \min(1,2r)$ (rather than r), and in a symmetric equilibrium, (20.2) should hold with $\bar{x} = \min(1,1/(2r)) > 1/2$, explaining why λ^* is smaller in that case, and constant for all $r < 1/2$.

---

[17] At $\lambda \simeq 0.45$, $\underline{x}(\lambda) = 0$ and $\bar{x}(\lambda,\lambda) = \lambda/(1+\lambda)$, and (20.2) becomes $\frac{7}{12} = \frac{2+\lambda}{2(1+\lambda)^2}$.

References

Carlsson, H. (1991). A bargaining model where parties make errors. *Econometrica*, 59, 1487–1496.

Carlsson, H. and van Damme, E. (1993). Global games and equilibrium selection. *Econometrica*, 61, 989–1018.

Harsanyi, J. C. and Selten, R. (1988). *A General Theory of Equilibrium Selection in Games*, Cambridge, MA: MIT Press.

Morris, S. and Shin, H. S. (2000). Rethinking multiple equilibria in macroeconomic modeling. In B. Bernanke and K. Rogoff, eds., *NBER Macroeconomics Annual 2000*, Cambridge, MA: MIT Press, pp. 139–161.

Morris, S. and Shin, H. S. (2003). Global games: theory and applications. In M. Dewatripont, L. Hansen and S. Turnovsky, eds., *Advances in Economics and Econometrics* (Proceedings of the Eighth World Congress of the Econometric Society), Cambridge: Cambridge University Press, pp. 56–114.

CHAPTER 21

Ambiguity and Other Complexity-related Aversions

1. You are on the verge of buying a nice used Mercedes, yet a bit hesitant given the posted price. Now the seller tells you, "you know what? I like you, just give me a $100 and the car is yours." No matter how attractive that proposal may look, you cannot help but feel that this is a strange deal, that there are parts of the deal that escape you, and that you would be better off running away than accepting the deal. It sounds too good to be true.

2. Out of numerous candidates who participated in a contest, you have been selected as the winner, with a cash prize of 1.5 million dollars. Upon receiving your cheque, you are offered the choice of instead getting S million dollars, where $S = \sqrt[4]{8}$. That number might look attractive, but it looks like what you see on insurance contracts that you don't read, and often come with unpleasant surprises. Not seeing an obvious comparison between the two numbers, you opt for the simpler one.

3. These two anecdotes illustrate how perceptions of strangeness or complexity may guide our choices. Whatever impression one gets concerning the value-ranking of two options, other impressions may compete: the inability to make a definitive comparison, the feeling that one option is simpler, the feeling that one option looks stranger.

4. We first illustrate the idea that various impressions/rankings may compete through a very simple model, which we later refine.

Assume that when confronted with a decision problem with two alternatives a and b, one gets two perceptions: a value-related perception $x \in \{a,b,n\}$ suggesting that x is the more valuable alternative when $x \neq n$; and an emotional/cognitive-related perception $y \in \{a,b,n\}$. Across decision problems of this kind, each perception (x or y) defines a ranking over alternatives.

Also, assume that there is a relationship between the actual values of the alternatives involved, denoted $v = (v_a, v_b)$, and the vector of perceptions $z = (x,y)$, with this relationship characterized by a distribution ω over values and perceptions. The distribution reflects the set of choice problems that the agent faces.

In a world where the perception x perfectly reflects preferences over alternatives, that is, $x \in \{a,b\}$ and $x = a$ if and only if $v_a > v_b$, there is no scope for another perception. In a world where the perception x is sometimes inconclusive ($x = n$) or imperfect ($x = a$ even though $v_b > v_a$), other perceptions may play a role.

Our complexity example suggests that complexity-related perceptions may play a role when value-related perceptions are inconclusive. Formally, letting y refer to the alternative perceived as simpler and letting $\bar{y}$ refer to the other alternative, we can express that condition by assuming:

$$E[v_y \mid z = (n,y)] > E[v_{\bar{y}} \mid z = (n,y)] \text{ for } y = a,b. \tag{21.1}$$

Under this condition, when $x = n$, it is better to opt for the simpler alternative.

We may also express formally the condition that complexity perceptions may only matter in events where value-related perceptions are inconclusive:[1]

$$E[v_x \mid z = (x,y)] > E[v_{\bar{x}} \mid z = (x,y)] \text{ for } x = a,b \text{ and all } y. \tag{21.2}$$

In other words, even though perceptions may not perfectly reflect preferences, (conclusive) value-related perceptions are on average sufficiently accurate to overcome other perceptions.

Finally, to illustrate our strangeness example, we may refer to y as the stranger alternative, if any, and assume that for any x:

$$E[v_{\bar{y}} \mid z = (x,y)] > E[v_y \mid z = (x,y)] \text{ for all } x \in X \text{ and } y \in \{a,b\}. \tag{21.3}$$

Under this assumption, the perception of strangeness, if present, is predominant, and outweighs any value-related perception.

5. Despite its coarseness, the model makes clear the channel by which a perception becomes valuable. For a given alternative, complexity in evaluating this alternative is not a characteristic that affects its intrinsic value. The fact that $\sqrt[4]{8}$ is difficult to evaluate does not change the value of $\sqrt[4]{8}$. Complexity is a cue that becomes valuable given the set of problems the decision maker faces, and to the extent that value-related perceptions are not perfect, it helps him reduce the distortions that trusting x would generate. Cues acquire value because, on average over the mix/range of problems for which they are used, they generate choices that better correlate with preferences.

6. For a particular choice problem taken in isolation we might indeed realize that we could have been better off not using the complexity-related cue. In our second story, $\sqrt[4]{8}$ is actually larger than 1.5. The consequence could be that in the future, we will have a reduced incentive to use that cue when similar choice problems come up. But the cue may remain valuable despite the adverse consequence that it has for specific choice problems.

---

[1] For any $x \in \{a,b\}$, $\bar{x}$ refers to the other alternative in $\{a,b\}$.

To illustrate further, imagine an urn filled with red and black balls. You are involved in a bet in which you must predict whether the majority of balls is black or red. You get to pick one ball at random and see its color. The rule of behavior which consists of predicting that the majority is of the same color as the ball you picked seems to be a good rule. Sometimes, the majority and the ball picked will have different colors. In these instances, you would have been better off not following that rule. But on average across problems of this kind, that rule performs well.

Said differently, a cue is like a signal, and you cannot ask that decisions based on signals be perfect every time. A cue/signal generates decisions that are on average better than if you did not use any cue, and made your decision randomly, and instances in which it fails do not warrant ignoring the cue.

7. Why would the conditions above hold? Inequalities (21.1)–(21.3) reflect properties of the distribution ω, and we use these properties to demonstrate that simplicity-related judgments might be used to guide choices. We have not yet offered a compelling reason why and when we expect these properties to hold. In what follows, we endogenize the extent to which complexity-based perceptions might outweigh value-related perceptions by enriching the model with less coarse value-related perceptions (and by endogenizing the categories $x \in \{a,b,n\}$).

Specifically, we assume that any alternative is characterized by a value v and an estimate w of that value. Whether there is a discrepancy between v and w depends on whether the alternative is simple or complex; for simple alternatives, $w = v$; for complex alternatives, $w - v$ may be positive or negative.

The agent faces a family of choice problems in which one alternative is simple and the other is complex. As an omniscient outsider, we label a the simple alternative and b the complex one. For simplicity, we also assume that the agent perfectly recognizes which is the simpler alternative, and he will thus use the same labeling as the outsider.[2]

The family of choice problems is characterized by a joint distribution over $c = (w_a, v_a, w_b, v_b)$. The following distributional assumptions preclude a hidden systematic bias in favor of simple or complex alternative. We assume that for $k \in \{a,b\}$

$$v_k = v_0 + \theta_k,$$

where θ_k are i.i.d. draws, and v_0 is drawn from a uniform distribution with large support. In other words, the difference in value

$$d \equiv v_b - v_a$$

[2] If this were not the case, we would have to label differently each alternative; for example, using $\widehat{a}$ for the alternative which is viewed as simpler by the agent, and introducing discrepancies between a and $\widehat{a}$. This would introduce unnecessary complications, without altering our main point.

between the complex and the simple alternative is distributed symmetrically around 0. We also assume that

$$w_a = v_a \text{ and } w_b = v_b + \varepsilon$$

where ε is a random variable with expectation 0, symmetric around 0. The latter assumption avoids any systematic bias in perception. For simplicity, we may think of θ and ε as normal distributions, so that $\phi(z) \equiv E[\theta_b - \theta_a \mid \theta_b - \theta_a + \varepsilon = z]$ is linear in z (with slope less than 1, i.e., $\phi' < 1$).

8. *From perceptions to partial rankings.* Before making a decision, the agent processes the difference

$$\Delta = w_b - w_a.$$

Δ is a value-related perception that reflects the perceived benefit of the complex alternative, and we denote by f its probability density. The perception Δ can be used to define a (partial) ranking between alternatives. For any given λ, and any given choice problem c, we consider the partial ranking (λ) defined as follows:

$$x = \begin{cases} b & \text{if } \Delta > \lambda \\ a & \text{if } \Delta < \lambda \\ n & \text{otherwise} \end{cases}$$

where, as before, x refers to the alternative, if any, perceived to be more valuable. The various rankings (λ) thus differ in the degree to which the agent perceives a difference between a and b, or finds it difficult to compare the alternatives. We further assume that when $x = n$ the agent chooses the simpler alternative a. Each ranking λ thus defines a decision rule, and we compare below the expected value associated with each ranking.

9. *Optimal ranking.* For each λ, we define $V(\lambda)$ as the additional (expected) gain obtained by the agent when he follows the decision rule λ, rather than always selecting the simpler alternative a. The two rules only differ when $\Delta > \lambda$, so:

$$V(\lambda) = \Pr(\Delta > \lambda)E[d \mid \Delta > \lambda] = \int_{\Delta > \lambda} \phi(\Delta)f(\Delta)\mathbf{d}\Delta.$$

ϕ is increasing, and under our symmetry assumption, $\phi(0) = 0$, so V has a unique maximum at $\lambda^* = 0$. Thus, for the optimal ranking, the simplicity perception plays no role.

10. *Systematic biases.* Given the above assumptions, the agent finds it optimal to take whichever alternative has the higher estimate, irrespective of any complexity considerations. The simplicity perception does not play a role in

decision making because the pool of decisions characterized by ω exhibits no systematic biases: there is no systematic bias in value in favor of the simpler alternative, and there is no systematic bias in perception that would make the more complex alternative look better on average. We illustrate below the consequences of systematic biases.

Biased values. Consider a modified version of the basic model in which

$$v_b = v_0 + \theta_b - e$$

where e is positive. In other words, the pool of complex alternatives is degraded, on average, compared to the pool of simple alternatives. From the perspective of the decision maker, we now have

$$V(\lambda) = \Pr(\Delta > \lambda)E[d \mid \Delta > \lambda] = \int_{\Delta > \lambda} \phi_e(\Delta)f(\Delta)\mathbf{d}\Delta$$

where[3]

$$\phi_e(z) = \phi(z + e) - e.$$

This implies that the optimal λ^* now solves $\phi(\lambda^* + e) = e$, hence $\lambda^* > 0$ (since $\phi' < 1$).

Biased estimates. Consider now an alternative modification to the basic model in which the estimates w_b are biased upward:

$$w_b = v_b + \varepsilon + \eta e$$

where $e > 0$ and where η is a positive random variable. The decision maker's payoff can now be written

$$V(\lambda) = \Pr(\Delta > \lambda)E[d \mid \Delta > \lambda] = \int_{\Delta > \lambda} \varphi_e(\Delta)f(\Delta)\mathbf{d}\Delta$$

where[4]

$$\varphi_e(d) = \int \phi(d - \eta e)g(\eta)\mathbf{d}\eta.$$

This implies that the optimal threshold λ^* satisfies $\varphi_e(\lambda^*) = 0$, or with ϕ linear, $\lambda^* = e\,E[\eta]$.

11. Complexity aversion in our model takes the form of a biased decision rule, or cautious rule, in which the more complex alternative is taken only

---

[3] This is because $\phi_e(z) = E(d \mid \Delta = z) = E[\theta_b - \theta_a - e \mid \theta_b - \theta_a - e + \varepsilon = z]$.
[4] This is because $\varphi_e(z) = E(d \mid \Delta = z) = E[\theta_b - \theta_a \mid \theta_b - \theta_a + \varepsilon + \eta e = z]$.

if its perceived benefit d is larger than some positive threshold (λ^*). Below that threshold, the simpler alternative is preferred. As explained above, the conclusion obtains when there is a systematic bias in value in favor of the simpler alternative, or when there is a systematic bias in perception favoring the complex alternative.

Agents may naturally face such systematic bias, providing a foundation for complexity aversion. Many of the choice problems we face are byproducts of strategic interactions, and we will argue, this affects the pool of decision problems which one faces in ways that may generate the systematic biases portrayed above, hence in ways that are conducive to complexity aversion.

12. *Manipulating perceptions.* In strategic interactions, our opponent has an interest in influencing our value perception. If a seller can successfully raise our perception of the value of the object he sells, he will be able to charge us a higher price for this object. For objects that are simple to evaluate, we can expect that such attempts by the seller will be unsuccessful. In contrast, for objects that are difficult to evaluate, these attempts may be partially successful. Of course some attempts to manipulate our perception will generate a feeling that the deal is strange, and trigger a no-buy response. But, to the extent that some of these attempts go unnoticed, this generates on average a bias in perceptions favoring the complex alternative. The optimal behavioral response is to exert some caution, and opt for the complex alternative only if its perceived benefit is sufficiently large.

The description above hinges on the monitoring technology of the decision maker – his inability to detect perfectly whether he is being influenced/manipulated. To illustrate, we return to the second example above. The seller chooses $e(> 0)$ and we assume that the decision maker detects manipulation if and only if

$$e\eta > A,$$

where η is a lognormally distributed random variable. For completeness, assume also that he avoids the complex alternative in the latter case, and chooses λ^* optimally in the event N where he detects no influence. Under that event, his expected gain is:

$$V(\lambda) = \Pr(\Delta > \lambda \mid N)E[d \mid \Delta > \lambda, N] = \int_{\Delta > \lambda} \phi_{e,N}(\Delta)f(\Delta)d\Delta$$

where

$$\phi_{e,N}(z) \equiv \int \phi(z - \eta e)g(\eta \mid N)d\eta.$$

This implies that the optimal threshold λ^* satisfies $\phi_{e,N}(\lambda^*) = 0$, or equivalently, with ϕ linear

$$\lambda^* = eE[\eta \mid N] = eE[\eta \mid \eta < A/e].$$

Then, even when he detects no influence, it is optimal for the decision maker to distort his decision rule and follow the simplicity heuristic when the decision is a close call.[5]

13. Influencing perceptions is just one channel by which a strategic agent can affect the characteristics of the pool of decisions which our decision maker faces. Another channel is that, through prices, a seller can typically increase or decrease the benefits of the complex alternative (as for buyers, the benefits of buying are generally more complex to evaluate than the consequences of not buying). One consequence is that when a seller has many selling options, his waiting for a profitable selling opportunity tends to reduce the benefits of the complex alternative for potential buyers: one then expects λ^* to rise.

14. *The winner's curse.* The mechanism proposed in this chapter is closely related to the winner's curse. Noise distorts choices: the decision maker has a greater inclination to select alternative b when $\varepsilon > 0$, and a higher inclination to select alternative a when $\varepsilon < 0$. If, ex ante, the alternatives are equally good (and if the noise term is symmetric around 0), these distorted choices do not introduce a bias.

A selection bias arises when the alternatives are not equally attractive ex ante. If alternative b is worse ex ante, then, in events where value estimates are identical (i.e., $w_b = w_a$), the error term is positive on average. Thus, conditional on the event ($w_b = w_a$), selecting b yields strictly less than w_b and one should instead choose the simple alternative (which gives exactly $w_a = w_b$).

In auctions, the alternative b is buying, while alternative a consists of not buying. Competition has the effect of raising the price paid by the winner, hence of decreasing the expected benefit of alternative b. The consequence is that one should be more cautious in bidding when the number of competitors increases. Even in a second-price auction, one should bid below his perceived value to counter the effect of the selection bias.[6]

15. *Other complexity-related aversions.* Although we have emphasized the distinction between simple and complex alternatives, our analysis also applies to other categorizations. Vague or ambiguous[7] alternatives are more difficult to evaluate, hence more prone to estimation errors. Alone, this does not create a motive for aversion: yet, combined with the reasonable assumption that these

---

[5] Regarding the seller's incentive to manipulate (i.e., set $e > 0$), let us observe that when η is lognormal (as assumed), the detection probability is small compared to e^2 near 0, so if the agent gains when the decision maker selects the complex alternative, there is always a first-order gain in setting e positive. In addition, for more complex alternatives, we can expect that A is larger, hence an increased incentive to manipulate.

[6] See Chapter 11 and Compte (2002).

[7] It is common to qualify an alternative as ambiguous when one cannot represent the alternative as a lottery with uniquely defined probabilities over consequences. But, more generally, any alternative with vaguely described consequences can be thought of as being ambiguous.

types of alternatives are more easily subject to manipulation (to the decision maker's disadvantage), we obtain a systematic bias against these alternatives, and derive aversion for these alternatives as an optimal behavioral response, *given the pool of decision problems faced.* While preeminence is often given to the terminology "ambiguous," all these biases have a common basis or root – the difficulty in evaluating an alternative. An objective lottery with many branches and precisely defined probabilities attached to each branch does not usually qualify as being ambiguous. Yet, such a lottery is difficult to evaluate, hence subject to the same evaluation errors as those that we have been discussing.

16. *Perceptions, choices and preferences.* We further emphasize that the optimality is derived *given the pool of decision problems faced,* as this point is crucial to our approach to this question. We view ambiguity, vagueness, or complexity as perceptions, and we think of these perceptions as signals that agents may use to guide their choices. They acquire value across the pool of decision problems that the decision maker faces.

Analysts sometimes view experiments (such as Ellsberg's urn experiments) as illustrating a conflict with rational behavior, as well as a motivation for modifying the way one might represent preferences (ambiguity averse preferences).

Instead, we think of complexity-related aversions as optimal responses to perceptions, where optimality is meant *on average across a relevant pool of problems.* A behavior that exhibits aversion to complexity/ambiguity may be perfectly consistent with standard preferences over alternatives.

Furthermore, and in contrast with much of decision theory, we do not think of choices as necessarily *revealing preferences.* As mentioned earlier, choosing 1.5 over S does not reveal a preference for 1.5, only that the agent has a perception that 1.5 is a better deal. Our view is that choices may only reveal perceptions of what one prefers, and that there may exist a discrepancy between what one prefers and what one perceives as a preferable choice. The number S can be objectively compared to 1.5, and since $S > 1.5$, one can safely assume that for most individuals, S is preferred to 1.5. Despite this preference, choices may point toward selecting 1.5.

The pool of problems matters, and this has other consequences. First, the technology of perceptions available to the agent matters, and changes in aversion may arise simply because of changes in the technology of perceptions. Second, any experimental protocol that attempts to elicit choices in an isolated problem is bound to elicit behavior responsive to perceptions that would also be triggered in a broader class of problems. Judging the rationality or irrationality of choices through the small lens of an isolated problem can lead the experimenter to see mistakes or biases in the subject's behavior, missing the positive role that perceptions may play in a broader context.

17. *Transitivity and money pumps.* In relation to our distinction between preferences and choices, preferences are transitive in our model, yet when perceptions compete, one can easily get nontransitive choices. Consider three alternatives (j, h, k) that can be ranked pairwise according to the simplicity criterion:

$$k \succ_y h \succ_y j.$$

Additionally, assume that according to value estimates, the order is reversed:

$$w_j > w_h > w_k.$$

If $| w_j - w_h | < \lambda$, $| w_h - w_k | < \lambda$ and $| w_j - w_k | > \lambda$, both choice problems (j, h) and (h, k) are close calls, thus subject to the simplicity heuristic,[8] while the choice problem (j, k) is not. Choices are thus intransitive, following a cyclic relationship:[9]

$$k \succ^c h \succ^c j \succ^c k. \tag{21.4}$$

A common objection to intransitive choices is that the individual may then be subject to money pump schemes. If he chooses k over h then presumably, he would be ready to give a small amount of money to get k rather than h. So if there is a cycle in choices as in (21.4) above, one should be able to continually extract small amounts of money. However, finding a cycle does not imply that an agent would fall for this; and even if he falls for one, he will likely stop falling for it in short order. The money pump itself is a rather strange device, and a reasonable conjecture is that we avoid money pumps for the same reason that we avoid other strange proposals.[10]

Further Comments

Following Knight (1921) and Ellsberg (1961), one often terms an alternative "ambiguous" when it involves chance moves for which probabilities are not precisely defined.[11] Our intent in this chapter has been to view aversion

---

[8] An alternative interpretation is that when comparing j and h, or h and k, the agent does not see any "noticeable differences" in values, while he sees a difference in the simplicity dimension. In connection to the idea of "Just Noticeable Difference," the parameter λ endogenizes the degree to which differences in values are noticed.

[9] Fishburn (1986) provides an example in a similar spirit. Consider three alternatives: $A =$ the next 101 flips will give at least 40 heads; $B =$ the next 100 flips will give at least 40 heads; and $C =$ the next 1,000 flips will give at least 460 heads. Fishburn claims that the judgments $A \sim C$, $B \sim C$ and $A \succ B$ do not seem unreasonable. The ease with which some comparisons can or cannot be made is likely driving this claim.

[10] For similar reasons, a ten-page contract might look intimidating, especially if single page contracts are available on the Internet and seem perfectly fine. This observation alone might be a good explanation as to why contracts are often quite incomplete.

[11] A large literature has developed on this topic, both empirical and, following Gilboa and Schmeidler (1989), theoretical.

to ambiguous alternatives as one instance among a number of possible expressions of aversion to alternatives perceived as complex or difficult to evaluate,[12] and relate that aversion to the winner's curse.

Context matters. *Whether a complexity perception arises or not is clearly agent-specific, as agents do not have an identical ability to compare alternatives. It is also context-specific. Going back to the comparison between 1.5 million dollars and S million dollars, evaluating S to a somewhat accurate degree matters, and the perception that S is complex to evaluate comes easily to mind. Now if one compares 1.5 cents to S cents, the exact value of S is no less difficult to evaluate, but the value of determining precisely the value of S is less important, and the perception that S is complex need not surface when the stakes are trivial.[13]*

Primitives. *The terminology "ambiguity averse preferences" suggests that one might take ambiguity aversion as a primitive. The spirit of our exercise is to look for plausible channels by which some aversion to complex or ambiguous alternatives might arise. Even when preferences are standard, one may shy away from alternatives that are difficult to evaluate, not because of some intrinsic aversion to complex alternatives, but because complexity signals a pool of alternatives that is likely to be adversely biased. A plausible explanation is that in strategic environments complex alternatives are more easily manipulated.[14]*

Of course, with further thought, an agent may convince himself that the choice problem is fully nonstrategic, and that the automatic cautious response triggered by complexity may better be suppressed, since in nonstrategic problems, there is no reason to believe that complex alternatives are worse on average. In many instances however, there is no guarantee that such thoughts will come to mind, and even if they do, understanding exactly the

---

[12] Compound lotteries may be precisely defined, and yet difficult to evaluate, explaining why one would want to avoid alternatives that involve them (see Halevy (2007)).

[13] See also Fox and Tversky (1995) for an experiment suggesting that ambiguity perceptions are context specific: the experiment suggests that an urn with unknown composition may only be perceived as ambiguous when one is also confronted with an urn with known composition.

[14] This argument is not novel: several authors have proposed that suspicion of a malevolent experimenter could be responsible for observed ambiguity aversion (Brewer (1963) and Kadane 1992)). Brewer for example writes, "the probability of being 'had' is no doubt the reason why there is a natural tendency in most people to slant down subjective probabilities. It does require some insight to detect that such behavior is irrational [...] The fact that such insight demands time for reflection, before it can be used to make behavior rational, sufficiently explains why most people when confronted with such situations behave instinctively in an irrational fashion."

Our contribution is in casting the decision problem within a broad environment, and in arguing that complexity or vagueness perceptions be perceived "globally." Within that more broadly defined environment, and in contrast with the view expressed in Brewer, the use of vagueness or complexity cues to marginally devalue some alternatives, may not be irrational.

extent of caution embodied in the primary response may be difficult. Said differently, and following Kahneman (2011)'s categorization, there is a basic asymmetry between signals: some, such as complexity perceptions, are likely to belong to the more immediate/intuitive sphere, applying broadly across choice problems, and some signals like "the nonstrategic nature of the choice problem" are likely to require a more sophisticated thought process, and to be more rarely triggered. This may be why even in decision problems where strategic considerations are seemingly nonexistent, behavioral responses may be affected by strategic experience.

Dealing with agents' ignorance. *Lipman (1999) defines a decision problem similar to one of our motivating examples: the agent has to make a choice between $100 and a box that contains X dollars, where $X = 0$ if the $10,000^{th}$ digit of $\sqrt{2}$ is 1, and $X = 200$ otherwise. Lipman then makes an observation that we fully subscribe to: within a standard model, "we are unable to include the uncertainty that seems so obviously present." In Chapter 5, we proposed a way out of that difficulty: introducing noisy perceptions, along with direct strategy restrictions. This chapter has proposed a more classic path: embedding the problem into a family of similar problems. How this is done is, of course, not neutral, as behavior is eventually driven by characteristics of this family. However, it illuminates why and when agents' perceptions of their own limitations may play a role.*

Suggested research/applications. This chapter, as is the case with many works in behavioral economics, may be seen as an attempt to put structure simultaneously on perceptions and on the behavioral responses allowed.[15] What this chapter adds is a simple model in which somewhat coarse perceptions compete, endogenizing the degree to which one perception predominates in triggering the decision, and in particular, highlighting how this may depend on the properties of the pool of problems faced. Along the same lines, one could study other common behavioral responses (the attraction effect,[16] or the small-sample bias)[17] as well as the role of strategic considerations in shaping behavioral responses: first impressions might matter more because after several

---

[15] For example, the work on present bias can be understood along this line: agents have biased perceptions of future outcomes (biased downward), and they have limited instruments (e.g., through memory management) to correct for this bias. Instruments are limited because otherwise agents could simply undo the bias.

[16] The agent has three alternatives to compare a, b and c, and gets value-related signals for pairwise comparisons. In events where two alternatives are difficult to compare, the signal that b obviously dominates c (while a does not) may tilt the decision toward b.

[17] Two types of signals are received: broad statistical information on the occurrence of an event, and occurrence among friends with similar preferences or lifestyles. Small sample bias refers to neglecting the broad statistical information.

encounters, the other understands better how his behavior shapes my impressions.

References

Brewer, K. W. R. (1963). Decisions under uncertainty: comment. *The Quarterly Journal of Economics*, 77(1), 159–161.

Compte, O. (2002). The winner's curse with independent private values, mimeo.

Ellsberg, D, (1961). Risk, ambiguity and the savage axioms. *Quarterly Journal of Economics*, 75, 643–669.

Fishburn, P. (1986). The axioms of subjective probability. *Statistical Science*, 1, 335–358.

Fox, C. R. and Tversky, A. (1995). Ambiguity aversion and comparative ignorance. *Quarterly Journal of Economics*, 110, 585–603.

Gilboa, I. and Schmeidler, D. (1989). Maxmin expected utility with non-unique prior. *Journal of Mathematical Economics*, 18(2), 141–153.

Halevy, Y. (2007). Ellsberg revisited: an experimental study.*Econometrica*, 75, 503–506.

Kadane, J. B. (1992). Healthy scepticism as an expected-utility explanation of the phenomena of Allais and Ellsberg. *Theory and Decision*, 32, 57–64.

Kahneman, D. (2011). *Thinking, Fast and Slow*, New York: Macmillan.

Knight, F. (1921). *Risk, Uncertainty and Profit*, Boston: Houghton Mifflin Company.

Lipman, B. L. (1999). Decision theory without logical omniscience: toward an axiomatic framework for bounded rationality. *The Review of Economic Studies*, 66(2), 339–361.

Miscellanea

Modeling ignorance is at the heart of economic modeling. This chapter attempts to explain how current modeling techniques and interpretations have been shaped by the desire to quantify ignorance, tracing back the various intellectual influences behind these techniques. This book has proposed an alternative way to think of, and model, ignorance that does not require agents to precisely know the contours of their ignorance. We discuss some of the recurrent themes in decision theory and game theory, explaining how our perspective complements or competes with the more traditional views.

1. Making precise what is not known.

To many economists, the Pavlovian response to ignorance consists of *making precise what is not known*. If one is ignorant about the number of balls in an urn, then one should think of the range of possible numbers and put a probability distribution over them. This distribution is a probabilistic belief, meant to be a precise representation and quantification of one's ignorance. Probabilistic beliefs play a central role in modeling ignorance – they are viewed as primitives in many models.

Much of this book is about avoiding probabilistic beliefs in decision making, asking instead that one focus on the perceptions that agents might plausibly get, and on what they can plausibly make of them. This does not mean that we dismiss beliefs altogether. Our view is that beliefs are often more casual than the way most theory portrays them to be, and that by avoiding a fine and detailed representation of what is not known, models may not only be more realistic but also more parsimonious.

2. Risk and uncertainty.

The precise quantification of ignorance is related to the old risk and uncertainty debate. Following Frank Knight,[1] one usually makes a distinction between

---

[1] Knight (1921).

risk, akin to a throw of a die, and *uncertainty*, which cannot be measured. In a literature beginning with Ramsey (1926) and culminating with Savage (1953), it became legitimate to think of any uncertainty as quantifiable. The logic is, essentially, that choices and bets can be made even in situations of ignorance, thus these choices must reflect or reveal some personal measure of likelihoods.

Imagine that you face a magician's hat with an unknown amount of money under it. You are offered a choice between getting $5 or getting the amount under the hat. Choosing the second option might reveal something about your perception of what's hidden (possibly along with the extent to which the contents of a magician's hat piques your curiosity.)

Of course, this single choice cannot reveal anything precise about your perception. The precise quantification comes about when one assumes that you are (most often fictitiously) confronted with other choice situations that are variations of the original one – getting $X = \$5$, or getting whatever amount under the hat that is in excess of $Y = \$50$. Varying X and Y could, in principle, permit one to elicit a precise probabilistic belief that you might hold about the hidden amount. Or at least, if your answers are consistent in a way defined by Savage, your choices can be understood as though you had a precise probability distribution in mind.

This book is not about trying to determine or elicit what is your mind when you see a particular hat. The logic of our exercise is to try to find patterns of behavior or systematic effects that apply *across* choice or strategic situations. For example, many choice problems are akin to the hat experiment: one option is easy to evaluate, while the other has uncertain consequences. When the stakes are high (higher than $5), the perception that there is a qualitative asymmetry between the two options might trigger some systematic cautiousness in behavior that applies across similar problems where that perception is triggered.

3. *Isolated versus representative problems.*

Savage has also shaped the way many theorists think about decision making in situations of ignorance, allowing us to transport consumer theory to such situations. In essence, Savage provided conditions under which analysts may approach decisions under ignorance in the same way they do for decisions with known (and easy to evaluate) consequences. One typically represents decision making as if each alternative was evaluated *in isolation*: that is, *independently of other qualitatively similar problems faced*, with the evaluations then compared.

This book takes a different perspective: decision problems are never considered in isolation. Rather, we emphasize that decisions be viewed as byproducts of a rule of behavior or strategy that applies to a pool of similar decision problems.

Why?

Our view is that many of our choices build on broadly defined perceptions that are neither alternative-specific nor problem-specific.

One sometimes feels that a strange deal is being offered, or that the deal seems too good to be true. We recognize that feeling because we have been confronted with it many times, and we have learned (or been told) to exert greater caution in such situations.

Similarly, we sometimes face choice problems in which one alternative seems easier to evaluate than the other. If one also perceives that the stakes are high and that the decision is not trivial, the perception that one alternative is simpler to evaluate may play a key role, prompting us to opt for the simpler to evaluate alternative.

Perceptions are cues that guide our choices. They acquire relevance (and value) from the numerous instances in which they come to mind, and the benefit that we draw from their use, given the set of instances in which they surface, and our various responses to them.

Said differently, a choice problem offered to us is accompanied by perceptions. But what we make of these perceptions cannot be independent of the various choice problems in which similar perceptions are triggered. Among other things, perceptions create correlations in the way decisions are made across the problems in which given perceptions crop up. What we make of perceptions is unlikely to be problem-specific.

So, whereas standard theory often portrays each decision problem in isolation, independently of other decision problems, our perspective is that perceptions create links across decision problems, common responses, and that one cannot analyze a choice problem without considering: (i) the perceptions that are triggered and (ii) the various choice problems in which similar perceptions would be triggered. This book is an attempt to follow this path, *taking as primitive the class of situations considered*, and modeling it as a (sufficiently rich) joint distribution over problems and perceptions.

Of course, the classic perspective has an advantage. Each perception or signal defines a distinct problem that can be analyzed separately from other problems without questioning how other choice problems might affect the current one. The drawback, however, is that we miss the big picture. We may get buried in second-order details and fail to identify the systematic effect that perceptions have on choices, missing their role in helping us simplify and handle the extraordinarily vast array of problems that we face and that never exactly repeat themselves.

4. *Mistaken or cue-driven behavior.*

Out of numerous candidates who participated in a contest, you have been selected as the winner, with a cash prize of 1.5 million dollars. Upon collecting your check, you are offered the choice of getting instead S million dollars, where $S = \sqrt[4]{8}$. That number might look attractive, yet the second number looks a bit like those that you see on those insurance contracts that you don't read, and that often come with unpleasant surprises. Not seeing an obvious comparison between the two numbers, you opt for the simpler one.

We used this example in Chapter 21 to illustrate how perceptions of complexity may guide our choices. Whatever impression one gets, if any, concerning the value ranking of the two options, other impressions compete and plausibly dominate: the inability to make a definitive comparison, and the feeling that stakes are high and that one option is simpler.

Complexity perception is a cue that one uses to guide choices. For a particular choice problem taken in isolation we might indeed realize that we could have been better off not using the cue – in our story, $\sqrt[4]{8}$ is actually larger than 1.5. Yet a cue may remain valuable in spite of the adverse consequence that it has for one specific choice problem. A cue is like a signal, and you cannot ask that decisions based on signals be perfect every time. A cue/signal generates decisions that are on average better than if you did not use it; and instances in which the cue fails to produce a good outcome do not necessarily constitute a reason to abandon it.

Finding the "right" lens. Analysts often differ in the lens through which they approach problems. Much of decision theory focuses on very precise and detailed examples, in which the consequence of each of the available alternatives can be objectively measured by the analyst. Analysts often presume that since all the characteristics of the choice problem are equally available to both the agent and the analyst, one can assume that the evaluation of each alternative poses no difficulty to the agent. Consequently, choices that are inconsistent with the objectively measurable characteristics of the choice problem are interpreted as mistakes, errors, or biases. In this respect, if the analyst focuses on one particular choice problem (1.5 or S), the choice of 1.5 over S looks like a mistake.

From a broader perspective, however, one can take the position that choices result from perceptions-based strategies which apply *across a broad set of problems*. From this perspective, the choice of 1.5 over S is not an error, despite the fact that, from the analyst's perspective, S is objectively larger than 1.5. It does not reveal a preference for 1.5 million dollars over S million dollars. It might simply reveal that forgoing a large sum for an unknown amount is not worth the risk.

5. *Subjective and objective views.*

To many theorists, beliefs are taken to be a subjective or personal representation of what an agent is ignorant about. If a seller is ignorant about the value of the transaction to a given buyer, one may represent his decision process as though he had in mind a probability distribution over possible values.

A potential problem with this approach is that in general, there is nothing that necessarily ties the agent's beliefs to the real-world consequences of the choices he makes, and possibly little or no discipline on what could be "reasonable" beliefs. The seller's belief about the buyer's valuation could bear no relationship to the actual valuation of the buyer. Trade might be missed, but only because the seller holds implausible beliefs.

In practice, papers often proceed by assuming that:

(i) There is a distribution ω that determines the buyer's valuation v and a signal z received by the seller.
(ii) The seller's belief is then determined for each signal z, as if ω was known and the seller was making an inference from the signal z.

Papers are often ambiguous as to whether one should interpret ω as a "subjective" or an "objective" distribution, as even subjective but "reasonable" distributions may generate interesting insights. For economic problems in which one wishes to quantify real consequences, the "objective" interpretation tends to be favored. In that case, the seller is in the same position as that of a poker player who tries to assess the strength of his opponent's hand (five cards), based on seeing only three of his opponent's cards. Of course, buyers and sellers are not playing a card game, and nobody is distributing cards according to a well-defined process. But we represent the buyer-seller relationship as if there were an objective lottery selecting a valuation v to the buyer, and a signal z to the seller.

The first step, with the definition of an "objective" distribution ω, is a somewhat artificial theoretical construct. Yet we do not fundamentally object to it, as it provides a convenient way to tie perceptions with real consequences. Hunger is correlated with depleting reserves, and fear is correlated with danger. It seems fine to take an omniscient outsider's perspective to define these joint distributions. Our interpretation is that ω represents the typical situation (z, v) that the seller faces.

The second step is more problematic. It presumes that this distribution is known and it allows agents to take full advantage of this knowledge. This book aims to amend that second step, by reducing the agent's ability to take advantage of the structure of the model. He does not know ω, nor can he think about all the consequences of that knowledge. An agent compares strategies given their average performance across the problems that he confronts. His knowledge is limited to these comparisons, and the strategies that he compares are a primitive of the model. His knowledge of ω is implicit, not explicit.

Our perspective is that linking perceptions and real consequences is a useful discipline. We suggest keeping this link as a primitive assumption, without necessarily assuming that agents know precisely this link, or behave as if they knew them precisely. Said differently, this book has been an attempt to separate the question of tying perceptions to real consequences, and the question of what people know of these ties. What agents end up knowing is limited to their experience in using that the perceptions they get – no less and no more.

6. *Subjective and objective views in games.*

Harsanyi made a fundamental contribution to the analysis of games. He provided a relatively parsimonious way to think about beliefs about what others know in a game situation, proposing that we represent the ignorance of each player by a belief derived from a joint distribution over types. For example, to model an auction, we often define a joint distribution over values $f(v_1, \ldots, v_n)$. Each possible value v_i is a possible type for agent i, and to each agent i with type v_i, one may associate the conditional probability distribution $f(\cdot \mid v_i)$. This conditional distribution is a belief that represents the agent's ignorance when his type is v_i. The construction is particularly flexible, as a type can include any thought process that the agent might have. Calling z_i this thought process, one may consider a more elaborate model in which we define a joint distribution $f(z_1, v_1, \ldots, z_n, v_n)$. The pair $t_i = (z_i, v_i)$ is a type, and to each agent i and type t_i, one may associate the conditional probability distribution $f(. \mid t_i)$ (over other agents' types). This distribution represents the agent's ignorance when his type is t_i.

How should one interpret the distribution f? One could hold the subjective view that these distributions and beliefs are only meant to be a representation of the agents' ignorance, and not necessarily tied to any "objective" auction situation. Another view is that the distribution is meant to reflect a typical auction situation, as if values v and perceptions/signals z were drawn from an objective lottery.

This book favors the second interpretation. Essentially, if we want to talk about efficiency in auctions, we should tie what agents perceive or know to real consequences. In contrast to the literature however, we have taken these ties to be a primitive of the model *without necessarily assuming that agents are able to fully exploit them.*

7. Belief hierarchies and common knowledge.

When playing poker, I may try to assess the strength of the other player's hand, But this assessment seems insufficient. The other player's decision to fold or not probably depends on his own assessment of my strength. So my assessment of his assessment of my own strength may thus be relevant.

In the spirit of making precise what is not known, theorists are often tempted to model these assessments as probabilistic beliefs. One thus defines for each player a belief about the other's strength, and a belief over the belief that the other holds over my strength – and so on indefinitely. The collection of these beliefs is a rather abstract object, which can be defined for each player. Such a collection is called a belief hierarchy.

One virtue of Harsanyi's construction mentioned above is that it avoids entering these complex constructions. The analyst defines a set of types for each player (with each type possibly representing one admissible belief hierarchy), and a joint distribution over types. This joint distribution over types is difficult to motivate, especially if one holds the view that a type should be interpreted as a belief hierarchy. In addition, it is assumed that each player knows the distribution, knows that others know, and so on indefinitely. In brief, that this joint distribution is commonly known, or common knowledge.

This common knowledge assumption has been criticized by many. Nevertheless, the general view is that Harsanyi's construction is a useful shortcut to analyze games, and that this shortcut provides a useful and tractable approximation to the "real" problem that a strategic player faces. For example, Morris and Shin write:[2]

"In principle, optimal strategic behavior should[3] be analyzed in the space of all infinite belief hierarchies."

In other words, if we were not constrained by our mathematical abilities, it would seem like a good idea to capture more accurately strategic behavior and understand how each infinite belief hierarchy affects behavior.

We hold a different view. Our perspective is that one should focus on: (i) perceptions that agents can plausibly get; and (ii) perceptions for which players can understand or learn what *use* they can make of them. Belief hierarchy is problematic on both grounds. Thoughts about others may be relevant in some games, but are often too vague to be represented as a precise belief hierarchy. Furthermore, one suspects that these thoughts seldom provide good guidance on how to behave, and may be no more than a recipe for generating random decisions.[4]

8. Vagueness.

Savage himself acknowledged a difficulty with postulates that imply a precise representation of one's ignorance, a difficulty stemming from the vagueness typically associated with judgments:[5]

"The postulates of personal probability imply that I can determine, to any degree of accuracy whatsoever, the probability [for me] that the next president will be a Democrat. Now it is manifest that I cannot determine that number with great accuracy, but only roughly."

Judgments are typically vague, and a theory based on precise probabilistic beliefs seems, at the very least, descriptively inaccurate.

The statement also reveals a common shift in interpretation, reinforced by the terminology used. Through the agent's numerous answers to our hat experiment, an outsider could in principle elicit a probability distribution over the monetary rewards hidden under the hat. Theorists often view this distribution as a *representation* (made by the analyst) of the uncertainty faced by the agent, rather than a personal assessment (made by the agent) of that

---

[2] Morris and Shin (2003, Chapter 3, page 56).
[3] Our emphasis.
[4] This does not mean that we want to exclude sophisticated thinking from models. On the contrary, as suggested in Chapter 4, our view is that strategic thinking potentially shapes the signals that agents pay attention to, as well as the family of behavioral responses that are considered by the agent (see also Chapters 15 and 20).
[5] Savage (1953, page 59).

uncertainty. However, the statement above and the terminology "personal," "belief," "subjective" suggest the latter interpretation, something attached to the agent, rather than the way an outsider might represent the agent's decisions.

A convenient way to circumvent the difficulty has been for theorists to say that agents behave *as if* they held such beliefs, maximizing expected utility given these "as-if beliefs." By and large, however, and despite the cautionary "as-if" qualification, much of the literature treats beliefs as real objects, as if they were actual ingredients of the agent's decision process. An agent's behavior is then often described as a complex mapping between an overly detailed specification of beliefs and a decision, with the hope that this mapping provides intuition – and a foundation, for the behavioral predictions of the model.

This book has been an attempt to avoid endowing agents with detailed representations of uncertainty, unless we have reasons to believe that the representation has relevance in actual decision making. In modeling a repeated interaction, we endowed agents with only two belief states regarding the current state of the relationship (good or bad). Of course, the entire history of play and observations made by the other player influences his current state, hence his current behavior. One player could thus be tempted to calculate more precisely a probability distribution over the other's history, based on his own history of play and observations. We deliberately ignored such elaborate thoughts and focused on comparing simple behavioral rules, each characterized (for example) by one's inclination to spontaneously change belief state from bad to good.

9. *Qualitative insights.*

Modeling vagueness, however, may not be the main challenge, and possibly not even a modeling objective. In the repeated interaction mentioned above, the modeling challenge is to clarify the strategic issue faced by each individual. A theory that results in a complex mathematical object that defines a mapping between the set of possible histories and decisions does not help develop intuition. A theory that focuses on one aspect of behavior, say one's inclination to forgive in a relationship, and that explains the tradeoffs associated with that inclination, is less ambitious, but it opens the door to qualitative statements which may be useful in shaping one's intuition.

In a criticism of quantitative economics, Herbert Simon wrote:[6]

"By 'anticipating the future' I do not mean estimating joint probability distributions, for the most important kind of futurology is to anticipate, qualitatively more than quantitatively, changes in the important dimensions of the space in which the firm will operate."

The claim is that most often, firms do not care about getting the precise details of what may be coming, but rather, the big picture – a broad perspective

---

[6] Herbert Simon (1993, page 135).

on the nature and significant changes to expect. The same applies to many readers of economic models. Readers care for the punch line, the first order effect, the broad statements that capture the essence of a strategic phenomenon.

There is a difficulty with mathematical precision in that it often comes with detailed descriptions, which make it difficult to make qualitative statements and to disentangle the many forces that may affect behavior. What this book has proposed is to cut through the vast array of possible behavioral responses, and attempt to identify the strength of *a priori* selected responses. Our view is that often there is no need to look at large strategy sets to get the punch line; Worse without restriction, we may end up being unable to grasp or appreciate the relevant strategic forces.

We consider this restriction to a few dimensions a useful modeling challenge, a disciplining device that forces one to think *a priori* of the relevant strategic dimensions, before determining whether, indeed, that restriction has the relevance that we anticipate.

10. *Faith in beliefs.*

Another implication of the standard representation exercise is that it portrays agents who behave as if they had complete faith in their beliefs. So long as this remains an "as-if" statement, one is not assuming that agents *do* have faith or confidence in their beliefs. But once one slips into a more literal understanding (in which one would attach actual beliefs to agents), the implication (that agents have faith and confidence in their beliefs) is more questionable. Paraphrasing Savage, I could attach a probability 61 percent that the next president will be a democrat, and a probability 32 percent that he wins by a 3 percent margin at least – but the degree to which I would have confidence in these numbers would seem limited.

As a response to this discomfort, there have been attempts to weaken Savage's postulates, leading to representations of uncertainty that would not have the agent behave as though he had complete faith in a particular distribution. One such attempt leads to the maxmin path, or representations of behavior in which the agent behaves as if he had a set of beliefs in mind.

These more elaborate representations are similarly problematic: (i) they push even further the need to describe in detail what is not known, now relying on the precise description of a *set* of probability distributions (rather than a single probability distribution); (ii) it is still not clear whether the representation is meant to be the analyst's construction (with agents behaving *as if* they had multiple beliefs in mind), or as an actual description of the agent's perception (a description that would attempt to take seriously the idea one cannot be certain of his own belief); (iii) they remain silent on the connection between the agent's perception and the actual situation faced.

11. *The Bayesian route.*

Economic models are mathematical objects that come with precisely defined model parameters. For example, if one wishes to model the relationship between observations and underlying preferences, one defines a joint probability distribution ω over observations and states (see Part I). That distribution ω *is* a model parameter. In solving models, we presume that agents behave as if they knew the model parameters perfectly (including ω). Part II of this book has explained why sometimes we derive insights that hinge (too much, in our view) on the agents' ability to tailor one's behavior to the model parameters.

We have proposed in Part III a way out of this difficulty. We argued that with direct strategy restrictions, one could prevent an overly fine-tuned adjustment to model parameters.

An alternative path consists of taking the classic Bayesian route. If we think that agents are better modeled as being unaware of model parameters, then one should model that ignorance, and make precise, or quantify, the ignorance that agents face regarding model parameters.

For example, in modeling a (common-value) auction, one could assume that the n estimates of the common value v are drawn from a joint distribution f. For example:

$$z_i = v\theta_i$$

where v and θ_i are independent lognormal distributions. In specifying the basic model, we proposed a particular distribution with $\log\theta_i$ distributed according to $\mathcal{N}(0,\sigma^2)$ for some fixed σ.

If one objects, as we did, to the idea that many agents can simultaneously adjust to a particular specification of σ and n, one may assume that σ and n are random variables. This is the route that we took in Chapter 16 on information aggregation. In that problem, fixed σ and n implies that the estimation error of the kth most optimistic estimate is almost entirely determined by k/n. This lack of variability of the kth most optimistic estimate is an artifact of the basic modeling assumption (in which n and σ are fixed), and adding noise to the dispersion of estimates avoids this implausible lack of variability. The Bayesian route can thus sometimes be a useful complement to ours.

Part III of this book, however, suggests that it is often not necessary to introduce artificial randomness in the modeling parameters to prevent players from exploiting the structure of the model. Direct strategy restrictions can do the job in a more parsimonious way.[7]

---

[7] In addition, the Bayesian route is a device that only produces a modification in ω. In the auction example, randomness in the dispersion of values σ only produces a modification of the joint distribution over estimates. This modification may be helpful to check the robustness of initial conclusions (as in information aggregation problems), but it does not modify the basic

12. Wilson's critique and the classic "robustness" route.

The idea that the conclusions of our models hinge on players' assumed ability to exploit the structure of the model is related to Wilson's critique.[8] To address that issue, many advocate the robustness route, which can be portrayed as an enrichment of the original model. In essence, it consists of: (i) allowing the original model parameter to vary (this is the Bayesian route mentioned earlier); and (ii) assuming that players are possibly differentially informed about these variations. In the language of the above auction model, this might mean, for example, that; (i) the dispersion parameter σ becomes a random variable; and (ii) each agent gets a signal σ_i correlated with σ.

There are several difficulties with this route. First, it often leads to intractable models. In the context of the above enriched auction model, this leads to strategies that are two dimensional (bids are functions of value v_i and signal σ_i), with little hope of obtaining a characterization of equilibrium strategies.

Second, the more elaborate model is subject to the same critique as the original, with strategies that potentially exploit finely the structure of the new model. One could obtain an apparent lack of robustness in the original model, simply because one introduces a peculiar signal structure that, when properly exploited, would lead to some unraveling that destroys the original equilibrium. Which setup should one consider as lack robustness? The more complex construction or the original one?[9]

Third, our view is that the main role of the additional signal structure is to introduce artificial randomness in behavior, and we see no reason to endogenize this randomness through such an elaborate mechanism, whereby we simultaneously add an artificial signal structure and request that players behave optimally conditional on each signal realization. There are many plausible sources of randomness and it isn't clear why one should necessarily endogenize them. One can instead circumvent the elaborate construction and directly assume that players inevitably make errors when taking decisions, and evaluate how the general shape or magnitude of these errors affects the conclusions of the original model (see Chapters 19 and 20).

---

assumption that is typically made – namely, that agents are able to tailor their behavior (i.e., the bid function $b_i(v_i)$) to that new joint distribution.

[8] Wilson (1987, page 34) writes, "Game theory has a great advantage in explicitly analyzing the consequences of trading rules that presumably are really common knowledge; it is deficient to the extent it assumes other features to be common knowledge, such as one agent's probability assessment about another's preferences or information. I foresee the progress of game theory as depending on successive reductions in the base of common knowledge required to conduct useful analyses of practical problems."

[9] Many of the constructions inspired by the e-mail game (Rubinstein 1989) rely on a special signal structure. Our view is that, sometimes, it is more the agent's fine ability to exploit that special signal structure that one should question, rather than the initial equilibrium prediction.

13. *Information.*

Economic theory has accustomed us to think of signals as information, with additional signals meaning more information. Throughout this book, we have avoided equating these. Our view is that a signal per se is not helpful. An agent has to determine what use he can make of it, and to be valuable, he must also determine whether he is better off utilizing the signal, rather than ignoring it.

In standard models, this ability comes without cost because one assumes that agents behave as if they can freely exploit the structure of the model. A consequence is that "information/signals" can never hurt in standard decision problems. If an agent is provided with an irrelevant signal, he understands that it is irrelevant, and that he should ignore it. More generally, an agent provided with several signals also understands the relative weight he should attribute to each signal. Information aggregation is never an issue nor an obstacle in these models. Both claims seem at odds with common sense and experiments (Gigerenzer, 2007, page 37).[10]

Our perspective is that one often uses "information" to refer to "raw data," and that raw data seldom comes with a recipe how the data might be used. In real life, richer data comes with questions as to how it might be used or aggregated. Getting richer data is potentially harmful because it creates opportunities to use it in inappropriate ways, hence more opportunities for mistakes. In models, more data cannot hurt because one can always ignore the additional data. But the difficulty is precisely in determining which part of the data should be ignored.

Rather than referring to information as "raw data," we prefer to think of information as the recognition by the agent that some ways of using the data are better than others. Using the language of Gigerenzer (page 60), agents have tools, i.e., a number of plausible behavioral responses to signals or perceptions, each of which can be thought of as an instrument adapted to some (and only some) of the problems he faces.

Information, thus, relates to both with the toolbox (i.e., the set of tools that one is endowed with) and the ability to identify or recognize the most appropriate tool given the environment faced. Our concern is that in many models, the toolbox grows without bound, to a degree that the recognition requirement becomes farfetched. As a consequence, much of the theoretical work in this book involves the analyst being able to: (i) define a plausible toolbox for each broad category of problem; and (ii) highlight interesting connections between properties of the environment faced by individuals and the appropriate tools used within the toolbox.

[10] Gigerenzer for example suggests that having less time to decide forces you to use intuition, while having more time enables you to include more data in your decision process, at the risk of being dragged into decisions driven by irrelevant details.

14. *Rationality.*

How does (or should) a rational agent behave? What does rationality mean? There is little reference to these questions in this book. Our aim has been to describe models that portray the behavior of agents who attempt to behave according to their best interest, and to provide qualitative insights concerning the consequences that this self-interest generates.

For agents, behaving according to one's best interest is a challenge. Situations never exactly repeat themselves. This generates gaps between the situation at hand and the agent's perception of it, and these gaps create discrepancies between the decisions made and the optimal decisions. Whatever behavior that looks attractive beforehand may look less so ex post. We think of rationality as an economic force that tends to reduce these gaps and discrepancies.

For the analyst, the challenge as we see it is to provide a tractable model that seems rich enough to make the optimal decision non-obvious, and yet not so complex that the economic forces that we attempt to characterize cannot be spelled out or captured in a parsimonious way. The goal of modeling is finding the "right" balance between introducing inadequate perceptions (too coarse, too noisy) on one side, and means of countervailing these inadequate perceptions (through the comparison of various instruments or strategies, that is, various ways of handling these perceptions).

In the models we consider, as in standard models, all players are "rational," in the sense that they use the instruments available (i.e., the strategies that they are endowed with) as best as they can. Whether we model a baby getting internal signals correlated to the states of his reserves and "transforming" these signals with more or less delay into a cry for help, or whether we model a chess player getting a reasoned perception about the strength of his position and "transforming" this signal into a safe or a bold move, we think of agents doing the best they can with the tools they have. Across models, players differ only in the degree to which they manage/are allowed to adjust to the specific environment they face.

Throughout the book, our thrust has been:

(i) Sometimes the balance is not right (Part II). We may be giving too many instruments to players, enabling them to undo the mistakes/noise/errors that we introduce in the first place, through strategies that one cannot expect them to play.

(ii) Sometimes the balance is easier to achieve by directly restricting the set of instruments or by adding noise to their instruments (Part III).

Note that this leaves aside the question of how people manage to learn which instrument works best for them. Rather than embedding the analysis into a more complex model, we prefer our shortcut approach. If the analyst believes that learning is unrealistically difficult (either because the set of instrument is too rich, or because the model implies behavior that depends too much on the particular model specification – as in Chapter 12), one can either reduce further the set of instruments or add noise to reduce further the power of these instruments, thereby implicitly limiting further the agent's ability to adjust to the environment.

15. *Focus.*

What do we wish to explain? What do we wish to endogenize? What aspect of behavior do we want to focus on? Focus is at the heart of any modeling enterprise, and any modeling exercise must define what is exogenous, and what is to be endogenized.

In this, the analyst faces two challenges. The first stems from the fact that a simpler environment facilitates focus, yet a simpler environment also facilitates the agent's ability to adjust to the environment and to one another, sometimes implausibly. The consequence is that some models may teach us more about the inner working of our modeling tools than about the economic forces at work. This book (in particular, Chapters 19 and 20) illustrates how one can limit players' ability to exploit the structure of the model, directly introducing noise in behavior that reduces the scope for unraveling and for coordination. It also illustrates that a more complex environment may sometimes be more enlightening (as in Chapter 16 on information aggregation).

Another challenge is to resist the temptation to endogenize many dimensions of behavior simultaneously. This temptation is a natural one, as this seems to be a path to greater generality. What we often get, however, is complex behavior in which first and second-order effects are entangled. What we also often get is an illusion of generality, with players' behavior finely tuned to one another, or to special and artificial features of the model. This book has taken the perspective that limiting the dimensions of strategic behavior under scrutiny is a useful disciplining device.

To illustrate, the standard repeated game framework provides a very flexible tool to analyze social interactions. The framework is an austere world in which any behavioral response to past histories is feasible. In this cold-blooded world, some highly unusual behavior may come to be optimal only because it fares well when played against others' highly unusual behavior. However, the model typically fails to explain how players might come to play these strategies in the first place. In addition, "equilibrium strategies" are abstract mappings that are often difficult to interpret because they lack the *a priori* structure that would facilitate the interpretation in common language. If we wish to endogenize the degree to which one forgives after being upset, we should define *a priori* how we capture that. If we wish to endogenize the extent to which feelings of injustice upset us, we should also translate this into a behavioral rule (and also consider whether the repeated game we analyze is the appropriate vehicle for endogenizing these feelings). Absent an *a priori* structure, we are in the same position as an econometrician who finds a clever but extraordinarily complex rule to describe the process that generates the data, but cannot interpret the process. Meaning arises from pooling histories and testing whether regularities emerge across them.

To summarize, our answer has been that it is useful to propose a class of candidate strategies. It forces one to think beforehand of a class that is plausible within the environment studied, or that reflects how agents plausibly comprehend the environment, even if this implies an ad hoc restriction on the set of histories of the relationship that makes one upset. It forces us to focus on one, or few, behavioral aspects of the interaction, whether one should react harshly to being upset, leaving aside aspects of behavior driven by other considerations (e.g., whether one should feel upset when betrayed).

16. Bounded rationality or limited sophistication?

Our restrictions may be viewed as stemming from bounded rationality considerations. Indeed, the strategy restrictions that we consider can sometimes be motivated by the way the agent thinks *a priori* of the problem he faces, and his way of thinking may not be well adapted to the actual problem faced.

In the repeated game, we modeled the agent as if he had in mind a learning situation, trying to determine from experience and experimentation which of two arms is currently best. This shaped the agent's strategy set in a particular way. In the sender-receiver game, we proposed two models. In the first model, the focus was on the fact that the expert might be biased, with the agent trying to determine the degree to which he should correct the expert's suggestion based on his perception of the expert's bias. In the second, the agent behaves as if the expert was either benevolent or stupid, not considering the possibility that he is biased, trying to determine whether the expert should be trusted. Each of these assumptions shapes the decision maker's strategy set in a particular way. Both aspects of behavior are likely relevant, and, through further endogenization, the degree to which one aspect prevails can be examined. The fact that the two aspects of behavior can be disentangled is, in our view, a plus.

In the end, the proposed strategy restrictions above are just another expression of the necessary gap between perceived and actual situations. One may want to view this gap as stemming from a bound on rationality, or one may think of our models as putting plausible limits on sophistication. Either interpretation is fine with us.

References

Gigerenzer, G. (2007). *Gut Feelings: The Intelligence of the Unconscious*, New York: Viking.

Knight, F. H. (1921). *Risk, Uncertainty, and Profit*, Boston, MA: Hart, Schaffner & Marx; Houghton Mifflin Co.

Morris, S. and Shin, H. S. (2003). Global games: theory and applications. In M. Dewatripont, L. Hansen and S. Turnovsky, eds., *Advances in Economics and*

Econometrics (Proceedings of the Eighth World Congress of the Econometric Society), Cambridge: Cambridge University Press, p 56.

Ramsey, F. P. (1926). Truth and probability. In R. B. Braithwaite, ed., Ramsey, 1931, *The Foundations of Mathematics and other Logical Essays*, pp. 156–198, London: Kegan, Paul, Trench, Trubner & Co., New York: Harcourt, Brace and Company.

Rubinstein, A. (1989). The electronic mail game: strategic behavior under "almost common knowledge." *The American Economic Review*, 79(3), 385–391.

Savage, L. J. (1954). *The Foundations of Statistics*, New York: John Wiley and Sons, 1954.

Simon, H. (1993). Strategy and organizational evolution. *Strategic Management Journal*, 14, 131–142.

Wilson, R. (1987). Game theoretic analysis of trading processes. In T. Bewley, ed., *Advances in Economic Theory*, Cambridge: Cambridge University Press, pp. 33–70.

Author Index

Subject Index

Econometric Society Monograph Series (continued from page iii)

C. Sims (ed.), *Advances in Econometrics, Sixth World Congress, Vols. I & II*, 1994

H. White *Inference, Estimation and Specification Analysis*, 1994

J-J. Laffont (ed.), *Advances in Economic Theory, Sixth World Congress, Vols. I & II*, 1992

W. Härdle *Applied Nonparametric Regression Analysis*, 1990

A. Roth & M. Sotomayor *Two-Sided Matching*, 1990

T. Lancaster, *The Econometric Analysis of Transition Data*, 1990

L. G. Godfrey *Misspecification Tests in Econometrics*, 1989

H. Moulin *Axioms of Cooperative Decision-Making*, 1988

T. Bewley (ed.), *Advances in Economic Theory, Fifth World Congress, Vols. I, II, & III*, 1987

C. Hsiao *Analysis of Panel Data*, 1986

J. Heckman & B. Singer, *Longitudinal Analysis of Labor Market Data*, 1985

A. Mas-Colell, *The Theory of General Economic Equilibrium: A Differentiable Approach*, 1985

R. J. Bowden & D. A. Turkington, *Instrumental Variables*, 1985

B. Peleg, *Game Theoretic Analysis of Voting in Committees*, 1984.

F. M. Fisher, *Disequilibrium Foundations of Equilibrium Economics*, 1983

J.-M. Grandmont *Money and Value*, 1983

G. Debreu, *Mathematical Economics*, 1983

G. S. Maddala *Limited Dependent and Qualitative Variables in Econometrics*, 1983

W. Hildenbrand (ed.), *Advances in Economic Theory*, 1983

W. Hildenbrand (ed.), *Advances in Econometrics*, 1983

Printed in the United States
By Bookmasters